PRICES AND PRODUCTION AND OTHER WORKS:

F.A. HAYEK ON MONEY, THE BUSINESS CYCLE, AND THE GOLD STANDARD

The Ludwig von Mises Institute thanks
Mr. Toby Baxendale
for his magnificent sponsorship
of the publication of this book.

Prices and Production and Other Works:
F.A. Hayek on Money, the Business Cycle, and the Gold Standard

Preface by Danny Quah

Foreword by Toby Baxendale

Edited with an Introduction by Joseph T. Salerno

Ludwig von Mises Institute
Auburn, Alabama

Copyright 2008 Ludwig von Mises Institute

Hayek photograph on back cover courtesy of The Cambridgeshire Collection, Cambridge Central Library.

For information, write the Ludwig von Mises Institute, 518 West Magnolia Avenue, Auburn, Alabama 36832, U.S.A. mises.org.

ISBN: 978-1-933550-22-0

Contents

Preface by Danny Quah vii

Foreword by Toby Baxendale xi

Introduction by Joseph T. Salerno xv

Monetary Theory and the Trade Cycle (1933) 1
   Preface by F.A. Hayek 3
   1. The Problem of the Trade Cycle 9
   2. Non-Monetary Theories of the Trade Cycle 23
   3. Monetary Theories of the Trade Cycle 51
   4. The Fundamental Cause of Cyclical Fluctuations 73
   5. Unsettled Problems of Trade Cycle Theory 105

The "Paradox" of Saving (1929, 1931) 131

Prices and Production (1931, 1935) 189
   Preface to the Second Edition 191
   Lecture 1: Theories of the Influence of Money on Prices 197
   Lecture 2: The Conditions of Equilibrium between the Production
      of Consumers' Goods and the Production of Producers' Goods . . . 223
   Lecture 3: The Working of the Price Mechanism in the Course
      of the Credit Cycle 253
   Appendix to Lecture 3: A Note on the History of the Doctrines
      Developed in the Preceding Lecture 277
   Lecture 4: The Case For and Against an "Elastic" Currency 283
   Appendix to Lecture 4: Some Supplementary Remarks on
      "Neutral Money" 301
   Capital and Industrial Fluctuations: A Reply to a Criticism 305

Monetary Nationalism and International Stability (1937) . . 331
  Preface 333
  Lecture 1: National Monetary Systems 337
  Lecture 2: The Function and Mechanism of International Flows
    of Money 351
  Lecture 3: Independent Currencies 367
  Lecture 4: International Capital Movements 385
  Lecture 5: The Problems of a Really International Standard 403

Reflections on the Pure Theory of Money of
Mr. J.M. Keynes (1931, 1932) 423

The Mythology of Capital (1936) 487
  I. Professor Knight's Argument 489
  II. On Some Current Misconceptions 495
  III. Professor Knight's Criticism Based on a Misunderstanding 501
  IV. His Own Position Prevents Him from Giving Any
    Explanation of How the Limitation of Capital Restricts
    the Increase of Output 505
  V. An Erroneous Assertion Following from His Fundamental
    Position: The Value of Capital Goods When Interest
    Disappears 514
  VI. Problems of Capital and "Perfect Foresight" 517

Investment That Raises the Demand for Capital (1937) . . . 521
  The Relative Significance of the Amount of Investment and
    of the Form That It Takes 524
  "Completing Investments" and the Rate of Interest 526
  Causes of an Urgent Demand for Funds for Completing
    Investments 528

Bibliography 531

Index 547

Preface

Economics never labels anything any more. Well, more accurately, it does; only now it hardly ever uses labels formed from people's names.

In part, this is due to the smorgasbord approach to ideas taken by economics. Like many other academic disciplines, economics ruthlessly mixes and matches, customizes and adapts, rips and mashes the most penetrating insights, the most appropriate models from all different sources, applying them to whichever economic problem is currently being addressed. In those circumstances the message gets through to the practitioner economist that it is more useful to know an idea itself, and how to apply and modify it, than to peer into its provenance or to understand how the originator of that idea thought about three or five other substantively different problems.

In mathematics, this idea is taken even further. The most powerful and insightful practitioners are those whose names become so merged with a discovery that their surnames get lowercased whenever mentioned with the matching idea. The proper name disappears as anything distinctive, and instead becomes just vocabulary.

In economics, perhaps partly at fault as well, those intellectual leaders in the profession now, whose names are most likely to deserve such adjectivization, themselves eschew debates that might lead to such identification. Thus, for instance, the same economists who argued that the money supply is the fundamental cause of inflation also argued for the importance of fiscal balance and discipline in determining, again, inflation. The same economists whose work set the agenda for decades of business cycles research were also the ones who provided calculations showing that such economic fluctuations are fundamentally insignificant for society's well-being overall. Mainstream economics pragmatically emphasizes debate about results, not about methodologies.

So, certainly, individuals' names can be bolted onto specific curves, econometric estimators, statistical tests, probability inequalities, interest-rate rules, and mathematical equations and models—but not onto entire systems or ways of thinking.

The case of Friedrich Hayek, however, provides a rare example of a consistent body of work in the profession where such identification might be justified.

Living the frenetic cultured existence of the mid-1900s—as political events forever changed the global geography of intellectual endeavor—Hayek became one of the twentieth century's most influential economists and political philosophers. In economics he made profound and enduring contributions in areas as diverse as monetary and business cycle theory, the social organization of dispersed knowledge, and the spontaneous emergence of order. But while seemingly varied, all these research questions were attacked by Hayek from a consistent, unified perspective. It is this single perspective then that potentially can be most identified with Hayek.

However, matters are complex from the opposite direction as well.

Hayek viewed business cycles as having their initiating impulse of central bank credit overexpansion and their propagation mechanism of misallocation of capital across short- and long-term investments. This is echoed in many modern technical treatments—both empirical and theoretical—of economic fluctuations.

Hayek saw the price system as the single leading mechanism by which limited local knowledge and actions can be efficiently aggregated into optimal social outcomes—through human action, not human design. This is, in one guise, simply the fundamental theorem of welfare economics. But combining these two Hayek propositions—that on business cycles and that on local knowledge—also recovers critical ingredients of Robert Lucas's rational expectations reconciliation of the short-run Phillips curve with monetary neutrality. Being clear about the distinction between monetary and credit overexpansion brings to the fore modern econometric investigations of the different roles of money and credit over business cycles. Exploring the full implications of whether markets perfectly aggregate imperfect information is precisely the idea underlying a rich seam of technical research in microeconomics.

Hayek's description of order emerging spontaneously, in a self-organized way, from out of seeming chaos—the application of which to economics he coined the term *catallaxy*—turns out to be the defining characteristic of the science of complex adaptive systems. It is an idea that sees profound application not only, again, in the fundamental theorems of welfare economics, but in areas as varied as Alan Turing's explanation for the black and white speckled patterns on cattle, hypotheses on the emergence of peaks and troughs in economic activity across not just time but geographical space, and indeed is embedded deeply in speculations on the origins of life itself, in research on computational and mathematical biology.

While pre-Thatcher, pre-Reagan mainstream politics and social policy worldwide might have grown interventionist with fine-tuning and demand management, and thus distant from Hayek's intellectual position, by contrast, many mainstream economists and social scientists never really left Hayek. Instead, the great majority have absorbed his ideas so implicitly that the name has been not just lowercased but left unmentioned altogether. Hayek's ideas are seamlessly intertwined with so much of modern academic economics that, indeed, practically everyone in the profession has come into contact with or uses Hayekian insights. What this does for intellectual history is likely unfortunate. But, on the other hand, it might be the ultimate accolade for Friedrich Hayek, an intellectual concerned with ideas and knowledge, and their use for good in society.

I congratulate the Ludwig von Mises Institute for bringing back into print Hayek's writings on business cycles. This collection will be a critical touchstone for future thinking in the area.

Danny Quah
London School of Economics
March 2007

Foreword

It is with great pleasure that I fully support the reproduction of these works. I congratulate Lew Rockwell and his team for having the foresight to do this in honor of Hayek, one of the most important economists of the last century.

An old Polish soldier who had settled in London after World War II exposed me to the teachings of Hayek when I was sixteen years old. He had fought the Nazi machine as a member of the Royal Air Force. An equally nasty totalitarian force subsequently occupied his country: the Stalinist Communists. After the war, he settled in my neighborhood, and I got talking to him. He was adamant that I read Hayek as Hayek could show me all that was wrong with totalitarianism. The book offered was *The Road to Serfdom*. I did. I dedicate this reproduction to all those people who have suffered untold hardship under various totalitarian regimes.

Setting my sights on the London School of Economics, where Hayek had taught for twenty-plus years in the 1930s through the 1950s, as a place to study, to my great pleasure, we could study, as part of our political theory course, *The Constitution of Liberty*. Although Hayek had taught at the LSE in the economics department, none of his economic works were taught. Indeed, I was totally ignorant, up until my mid-twenties (i.e., post-university) of his economic works, which needless to say were the works cited in the awarding of his Nobel Prize. Further, it was Hayek who led me to the works of Ludwig von Mises, about whom I am certain that I would have otherwise known nothing.

Just as my Polish friend sparked my social and political interest in Hayek, I hope this volume can do the same for others concerning his economic work. This volume intends to revitalize Hayek's contribution to the study of economic fluctuations (more commonly now called business cycles) and monetary theory. Hayek demonstrated an entrepreneurial and empirical attitude toward his work. Just as his social, political, and legal work is rich with warning about too much well-meaning government interference, so too are his neglected economic works.

After his time at the Institute for Business Cycle Research in Vienna, he funded his own trip to the United States to interview economists and develop his work. Hayek understood the importance of statistical verification but was also committed to getting the theory right rather than counting on empirics to generate their whole result. His legacy should be to complement theoretical quibbles with hard facts, and these essays contain rich avenues to pursue.

One particular area I would like to draw the reader to is his works contained here on the business cycle, which was the work that grew from Mises's initial work on the matter in 1912, which has become known as the Austrian theory of the business cycle. Most contemporary economists have dismissed this work as not being in accordance with the observable facts and thus not worthy of being taught; hence, perhaps why I never saw sight nor sound of his teachings as an undergraduate.

In brief Hayek contends that an artificial manipulation by government of the interest rate creates a subsidy of credit that causes entrepreneurs to bring forth projects that were hitherto marginal. In reality, the consumers do not want the goods of these projects, so there is a misallocation (*malinvestment*) of resources. A careful reading of these early Hayek essays pre-empts the modern debate over rational expectations and shows that the cluster of errors can be avoided by his steadfast commitment to methodological individualism. Entrepreneurs are neither lemmings nor computers because they are heterogeneous.

If we extend the assumption of heterogeneity from capital to entrepreneurs, the question is, which *type* of entrepreneur is creating the cyclical activity of interest? Standard economic theory suggests that it is the *marginal* entrepreneur who moves the market, and Hayek points us in a direction that very few scholars have acted upon. I would find great value in subjecting this point to empirical evidence, to see who these marginal entrepreneurs are (the ones who are exposed when their credit subsidy is removed in a monetary contraction), and the conditions of their entry and exit. Perhaps moral hazard is not the greatest problem created by subsidized credit, and the effects of adverse selection create even larger inefficiencies.

Hayek stressed the role of relative price movements and focused attention on the interest rate. But he also provided a rich and accomplished critique of the use of abstract, aggregate variables. This presents a temptation for theorists to overemphasize interest rate changes, despite the fact that they only affect the risk of highly leveraged firms. In many cases the volume of credit, raw money creation by the Central Bank, seems a more realistic variable than the rate of interest.

Hayek's faculty position at the LSE (1931–1950) not only raised the profile of the Austrian School, but also elevated capital theory to one of the key economic issues, by highlighting (and translating) the key Swedish and Austrian insights for the English-speaking orthodoxy. During this period the LSE was the frontier of the continental tradition, and Hayek, Keynes, Robinson, Sraffa, Shackle, Robbins, et al. were at the peak of their discipline. This volume reminds us of a time when Austrian theory sat at the top of the table of debate, and offers us the way to return there.

Hayek was writing in a tradition where economists were conscious of the practical relevance of their work. To be sure, Hayek utilized grand thought experiments and abstraction, but his theoretical work always sought to understand the real world. Since then a divergence has occurred between self-referential academics and a generation of business consultants who lack the rigor of price theory. I am sure that a reassessment of the likes of Hayek is of fundamental importance to any young economist seeking to bridge these two spheres and return to a science of commerce.

In fact, the critical problem of how individuals coordinate is the thread that runs throughout Hayek's work, and the monetary aspect returns with his late attention to the nationalization of money. In these works we see Hayek as a price theorist, and as a facilitator of economic inquiry. As an entrepreneur I recognize deep insights throughout Hayek's work, but also several points that have to be expanded and verified. This volume should not be seen as an example of preservation, but an engine of discovery.

Toby Baxendale
London
March 2007

Introduction

Friedrich A. Hayek was barely out of his twenties in 1929 when he published the German versions of the first two works in this collection, *Monetary Theory and the Trade Cycle* and "The Paradox of Saving." The latter article was a long essay that was to become the core of his celebrated book and the third work in this volume, *Prices and Production*, the publication of which two years later made him a world-renowned economist by the age of thirty-two. But the young Hayek did not pause to savor his success. He was already hard at work on "Reflections on the Pure Theory of Money of Mr. J.M. Keynes," a lengthy critical review of John Maynard Keynes's two-volume *Treatise on Money*, which had been published in 1930. Hayek's two-part review appeared in late 1931 and 1932. There followed within a few years the other three works collected in this volume. "The Mythology of Capital" appeared in 1936 and was a response to Frank Knight's hostile criticisms of the Austrian theory of capital. A short article on "Investment That Raises the Demand for Capital" and the monograph *Monetary Nationalism and International Stability* were published in 1937.

These seven works taken together represent the first integration and systematic elaboration of the Austrian theories of money, capital, business cycles, and comparative monetary institutions, which constitute the essential core of Austrian macroeconomics.

Indeed these works have profoundly influenced postwar expositions of Austrian or "capital-based" macroeconomics down to the present day.[1] The creation of such an oeuvre is a formidable intellectual feat over an entire lifetime; it is an absolute marvel when we consider that Hayek had completed it in the span of eight years (1929–1937) and still well shy of his fortieth birthday.

Hayek's amazingly precocious intellect and creative genius are on full display in these works. Thus, before the age of thirty, Hayek already had fully mastered and begun to synthesize and build upon the major contributions of his predecessors in the Austrian tradition. These included, in particular: Eugen von Böhm-Bawerk's theory of capital and interest; Knut Wicksell's further elaborations on Böhm-Bawerk's capital theory and his own insights into the "cumulative process" of changes in money, interest rates, and prices; Ludwig von Mises's groundbreaking theories of money and business cycles; and the general analytical approach of the broad Austrian School from Menger onward that focused on both the subjective basis and the dynamic interdependence of all economic phenomena.

There is something else about Hayek that becomes apparent when reading his contributions in this volume. The young Hayek was a *great* economic controversialist, perhaps the greatest of the twentieth century. His entire macroeconomic system was forged within the crucible of the great theoretical controversies of the era. His opponents were some of the great (and not so great) figures in interwar economics: Keynes, W.T. Foster and W. Catchings, Ralph Hawtrey, Irving Fisher, Frank Knight, Josef Schumpeter, Gustav Cassel, Alvin Hansen, A.C. Pigou, and Arthur Spiethoff

---

[1] See, for example, Murray N. Rothbard, *Man, Economy, and State: A Treatise on Economic Principle,* 2 vols., 2nd ed. (Auburn, Ala.: Ludwig von Mises Institute, 1993), pp. 273–559; Roger W. Garrison, *Time and Money: The Macroeconomics of Capital Structure* (New York: Routledge, 2001); Jesús Huerta de Soto, *Money, Bank Credit, and Economic Cycles,* trans. Melinda A. Stroup (Auburn, Ala.: Ludwig von Mises Institute, 2006).

to name a few. Hayek took on all comers without fear or favor and inevitably emerged victorious. As Alan Ebenstein notes, "Hayek came to be seen in Cambridge, as Robbins's and LSE's point man in intellectual combat with Cambridge."[2]

Hayek's prodigious dialectical skills and his relentless drive to root out and correct even the most entrenched economic errors are exhibited throughout this volume. Hayek's review of Keynes's *Treatise on the Pure Theory of Money* is the exemplar of disputation in theoretical economics. Keynes was Hayek's senior by a generation and at the time the leading economist in Great Britain and among the most famous public intellectuals in the Anglophone world. Keynes worked hard and long on his treatise, and clearly intended it to be his *magnum opus*, a dazzling leap forward in the theory of money based on "a novel means of approach to the fundamental problems of monetary theory." But Keynes's reach far exceeded his grasp given his parochial and stunted training in economic theory—one course in economics and the study of Alfred Marshall's clunky and disjointed textbook. Keynes's *Treatise* never stood a chance. For the brilliant and courageous young Hayek was waiting, pen in hand, to show up the *Treatise* as a theoretical dead end rather than the new departure in monetary theory Keynes had hoped for.

Hayek's blistering review essay is a positive thrill to read. He relentlessly scrutinizes and exposes the shaky and patchwork structure of Keynes's theoretical arguments and then dismantles it brick by brick, leaving nothing standing. Keynes's reaction reveals just how deeply Hayek's review cut as well as his own cavalier attitude toward intellectual pursuits. Keynes's reply to the first part of Hayek's essay, which dealt with the first, purely theoretical volume of the *Treatise*, was not properly a reply at all but a critique of Hayek's book *Prices and Production*. Upon publication six months

---

[2] Alan Ebenstein, *Friedrich Hayek: A Biography* (New York: Palgrave, 2001), p. 61.

later of the second part of Hayek's article, which focused on the second, applied volume of the *Treatise* and in which Hayek was a bit more complimentary, Keynes remarked to Hayek, "Oh never mind, I no longer believe all that."[3] Yet Keynes was not done. A month later, Keynes, as chief editor of the *Economic Journal,* published a nasty review of Hayek's *Prices and Production* written by one of Keynes's more uncomprehending and rabid disciples, Piero Sraffa. Keynes's fellow Cambridge economist, Arthur C. Pigou, was aghast at this behavior. Without naming names, Pigou wrote,

> A year or two ago, after the publication of an important book, there appeared an elaborate and careful critique of a number of passages in it. The author's answer was, not to rebut the criticism, but to attack with violence another book, which the critic had himself written several years before. Body-line bowling. The methods of the duello. That kind of thing is surely a mistake.[4]

In the "The Mythology of Capital," Hayek took on the long and bitter crusade against the Austrian theory of capital waged by Frank Knight, fifteen years Hayek's senior, an eminent American economist and the founder and leader of the early Chicago School. Hayek fittingly adopted as the introductory quotation of his article a statement by Eugen von Böhm-Bawerk, not coincidentally the greatest economic disputant of the nineteenth century and Hayek's chief influence in capital theory. Hayek's quotation of Böhm-Bawerk read, "With every respect for the intellectual qualities of my opponent, I must oppose his doctrine with all possible emphasis, in order to defend a solid and natural theory of capital against a mythology of capital." This is actually a concise statement of the early Hayek's general method of

---

[3] As reported in F.A. Hayek, *Hayek on Hayek: An Autobiographical Dialogue,* ed. Stephen Kresge and Leif Wenar (Chicago: University of Chicago Press, 1994), p. 90.

[4] A.C. Pigou quoted in ibid., p. 88.

attaining theoretical breakthroughs: he would carefully develop the correct theoretical position and then use it as a weapon with which to strike down the fallacies of his opponents. In this article he proceeded to demolish Knight's claim that capital, once accumulated, was a permanent fund that perpetually and automatically reproduced itself without regard to human purposes and the prevailing conditions of scarcity. Hayek trenchantly characterized Knight's notion of capital as "a pseudo-concept devoid of content and meaning, which threatens to shroud the whole problem in a mist of words."

"The Paradox of Saving," which was for Hayek "the beginning of a continuous development of thought" that shaped his research agenda throughout the 1930s, was a critique of the underconsumptionist approach to depression. Specifically, Hayek was responding to two American writers, Waddill Catchings and William Trufant Foster who had coauthored a series of essays and tracts on the topic in the 1920s and even offered a $5,000 prize for the best critique of their doctrine in 1925. In the course of his point-by-point refutation of their argument, Hayek integrated Böhm-Bawerk's analysis of the period of production with Mises's theory of the business cycle and provided the latter theory with an explicit basis in capital theory for the first time.

The other works in this volume, although they were not overtly controversial pieces, followed much the same pattern as his critiques of Keynes, Knight, and Foster and Catchings. Hayek wrote *Monetary Theory and the Trade Cycle* as an explication of the monetary causes of the business cycle. However, in order to do so, he believed that he had to "save the sound elements in the monetary theories of the trade cycle" by refuting those naïve quantity theorists who posited a simplistic and mechanical connection between the aggregate money supply and the average price level. Thus he took after the price "stabilizers" like Irving Fisher and Gustav Cassel who were the forerunners of the modern monetarists. He identified "the critique of the program of the 'stabilizers'" as "the central theme of this book."

Nor did Hayek tread lightly in verbalizing his criticisms. He placed the blame for "the exceptional severity and duration of the depression" squarely on central banks', particularly the Fed's, "experiment" in "forced credit expansion," first to stabilize prices in the 1920s, and then to combat the depression in the early 1930s. Hayek defiantly declared:

> We must not forget that, for the last six or eight years [up to 1932] monetary policy all over the world has followed the advice of the stabilizers. It is high time that their influence, which has already done harm enough, should be overthrown.

Prices and Production, often seen as the companion volume to *Monetary Theory and the Trade Cycle,* developed in much greater detail the synthesis of Misesian business-cycle and Böhm-Bawerkian capital theory that Hayek first sketched out in "The Paradox of Saving." Once again, Hayek's positive contribution, i.e., a fully developed statement of Austrian business cycle theory, was at least partially motivated by his intent to engage and refute what he regarded as an economic fallacy, specifically, the Anglo-American version of the quantity theory. After summarizing that theory in three propositions, he referred to them as "delusions" that "make it possible to assume that we can neglect the influence of money [on the real structure of production] so long as the value of money is assumed to be stable." In the short article on "Investment That Raises the Demand for Capital," Hayek drew out the subtle implications of an accepted proposition regarding the sunk costs of already invested capital to show the complete inadequacy of simplistic monetary explanations of the business cycle that treat capital as an abstract homogeneous aggregate and ignore the intricate interrelationships among the concrete goods composing the capital structure. Again, Hayek was not gentle in his rhetoric. He insisted that his positive restatement of the proposition in question rendered it "so obvious as to put its logical correctness beyond dispute," which meant that "much of the purely monetary analysis of the trade cycle now current is built on very insufficient foundations."

In *Monetary Nationalism and International Stability*, Hayek extended Mises's monetary theory to provide a groundbreaking analysis of the international operation of the pure gold standard and the widely misunderstood role of international monetary flows therein. Hayek also identified the systemic flaw in the classical gold standard—a centralization of gold reserves in the hands of national central banks or "the national reserve system"—that led to its destruction by monetary policy. Thus Hayek argued that the demise of the gold standard in 1931 was caused by the influence on monetary policy achieved by the ideas of "Monetary Nationalism" after World War I. Wrote Hayek, "[L]ong before the breakdown of the international gold standard in 1931, monetary policy all over the world was guided by the ideas of monetary nationalism." In critically analyzing the proposals of the monetary nationalists for a regime of fluctuating national fiat currencies, Hayek presented the first comprehensive case against so-called freely fluctuating exchange rates, which has yet to be improved upon. Integrating his argument with Austrian business cycle theory, he demonstrated that fluctuating exchange rates do not prevent the international transmission of macroeconomic fluctuations as long as there exists free trade in all orders of capital goods as well as in consumer goods—even if governments under the influence of monetary nationalism are able to impede international capital flows.

As always, Hayek was not shy about identifying the individuals to whom his critical remarks applied. Thus he characterized Keynes's disciple and later biographer Roy Harrod as "one of the most ardent advocates of monetary nationalism." Hayek also harshly criticized Charles R. Whittlesey for whom "almost the whole argument in favor of monetary nationalism is based on the assumption that different national currencies are different commodities and that consequently there ought to be variable prices of them in terms of each other." Ever the dialectician, Hayek proceeded to point out the naïve fallacy vitiating Whittlesey's argument:

> No attempt is made to explain why or under what conditions and in what sense the different national moneys ought to be regarded as different commodities, and one can hardly avoid the impression that the author has uncritically accepted the difference in denomination as proof of a difference in kind.

This last work, which was a slight volume of fewer than one hundred pages, was basically the reproduction of a series of lectures that Hayek delivered at the Graduate Institute of International Studies in Geneva. We can only speculate what course the Keynesian Revolution and, indeed, the economic history of the Western world would have taken had Hayek abandoned work on his abortive *Pure Theory of Capital* to "undertake the larger investigation" that his friends (viz., LSE economists Lionel Robbins, Frank Paish, and Frederic Benham) advised "the subject deserves." Hayek himself believed that it "would certainly have been a much bigger and much better book" had he incorporated their suggestions. If Hayek, who was at the peak of his academic fame and analytical and rhetorical powers, had revised and expanded the lectures into a proper book, *Monetary Nationalism and International Stability* may have become the Austrian tract for the times that rivaled the *General Theory* and derailed the Keynesian juggernaut right at the outset. *This* was Hayek's great missed opportunity and not, as he often later lamented, the narrowly technical review of the *General Theory* he failed to write.

The present volume thus presents the combative and assertive, yet always polite, Hayek, fully confident in the superiority of the intellectual armamentarium supplied by his great predecessors in the Austrian tradition and in his own ability to wield it. Here we look in vain for the irenic and temporizing Hayek who was later to dedicate a book to "the Socialists of All

Parties."[5] The former Hayek seemed to completely disappear sometime after the publication of the *Pure Theory of Capital* in 1941. It is an open question whether this radical change in attitude was the result of a strategic choice that corresponded to Hayek's shift out of economics into the broader field of social theory. Hayek himself lent credence to this interpretation in later reflections:

> When it proved that ... the *General Theory* ... conquered most of the professional opinion, and when in the end even some of the colleagues I most respected supported the wholly Keynesian Bretton Woods agreement, I largely withdrew from the debate, since to proclaim my dissent from the near unanimous views of the orthodox phalanx would merely have deprived me of a hearing on other matters about which I was more concerned at the time.[6]

Hayek's transformation may also have been a temperamental response to the crushing blow to his reputation as an economist caused by the overwhelming success of the Keynesian Revolution. Hayek also provided some evidence for this view of the matter in another one of his reminiscences:

> I had a period of twenty years in which I bitterly regretted having once mentioned to my wife after Keynes's death that now Keynes was dead, I was probably the best-known economist living. But ten days later it was probably no longer true. At that very moment, Keynes became the great figure, and I was gradually forgotten as an economist.[7]

Many laboring in the thriving cottage industry of Hayek biographers, critics, and interpreters have commented on the transition

---

[5] F.A. Hayek, *The Road to Serfdom* (Chicago: University of Chicago Press, 1976).

[6] F.A. Hayek, *Choice in Currency: A Way to Stop Inflation* (London: Institute for Economic Affairs, 1976), p. 11.

[7] Hayek, *Hayek on Hayek*, p. 143.

from a "Hayek I" to a "Hayek II" that began in the late 1930s, portraying it as almost wholly an intellectual reorientation and change in research interests. Few, if any, have recognized the radical alteration in analytical procedure and rhetorical style that characterized this transformation. This is evident by comparing the works in this volume with later essays penned by Hayek II, e.g., those anthologized in his *Studies in Philosophy, Politics and Economics*.[8] However Hayek I re-emerged almost immediately after receiving the Nobel Prize in 1974 fully armed and with renewed passion for intellectual combat. In a remarkable flurry of articles, pamphlets, booklets, and interviews, he aggressively demolished the intellectual case for postwar Keynesianism and confidently offered new and radical proposals for extricating the Western industrial nations from the stagflationary mire into which they had foundered under the guidance of Keynes's disciples.[9]

The re-publication of these works in a single volume is a magnificent event that fills a yawning gap in the Austrian macroeconomic literature and provides modern Austrians with a model of how to advance economic theory through reasoned debate and criticism.

Joseph T. Salerno
Pace University
April 2007

---

[8] F.A. Hayek, *Studies in Philosophy, Politics and Economics* (New York: Simon and Schuster, 1969).

[9] The most noteworthy of Hayek's post-Nobel works are: *Full Employment at Any Price* (London: Institute of Economic Affairs, 1975); *Choice in Currency: A Discussion with Friedrich von Hayek* (Washington, D.C.: American Enterprise Institute for Public Policy Research, 1975); and *Denationalisation of Money— The Argument Refined: An Analysis of the Theory and Practice of Concurrent Currencies*, 2nd ed. (London: Institute of Economic Affairs, 1978).

MONETARY THEORY AND THE TRADE CYCLE

Translated from the German by N. Kaldor and H.M. Croome (London: Jonathan Cape, 1933). Originally written in German as *Geldtheorie und Konjunkturtheorie* (Vienna: Holder-Pichler-Tempsky, 1929).

Preface

The German essay,[1] of which the following is a translation, represents an expanded version of a paper[2] prepared for the meeting of the *Verein für Sozialpolitik*,[3] held in Zurich in September 1928, and of some remarks contributed to the discussion at that meeting. Although, in revising the translation, I have made numerous minor alterations and additions (mainly confined to the footnotes), the general course of the argument has been left unchanged. The book, therefore, still shows signs of the particular aim with which it was written. In submitting it to a public different from that for which it was originally intended, a few words of explanation are, perhaps, required.

In Germany, somewhat in contrast to the situation in English-speaking countries, monetary explanations of the trade cycle were always, or at least until quite recently, regarded with some mistrust. One of the aims of this study—one on which an English reader may feel that I have wasted unnecessary energy—was to justify the monetary approach to these problems. But I hope that this more explicit

---

[1] *Geldtheorie und Konjunkturtheorie.* Beitrage zur Konjunkturforschung, herausgegeben vom Österreichisches Institut für Konjunkturforschung, no. 1 (Vienna: Holder-Pichler-Tempsky, 1929).

[2] "Einige Bemerkungen über das Verhältnis der Geldtheorie zur Konjunkturtheorie" in *Schriften des Vereins für Sozialpolitik* 173 (1928), part 2.

[3] *Schriften des Vereins für Sozialpolitik* 175 (1929): 369–74.

statement of the role of the monetary factor will not be found quite useless, for it is not only a justification of the monetary approach but also a refutation of some oversimplified monetary explanations that are widely accepted. In order to save the sound elements in the monetary theories of the trade cycle, I had to attempt, in particular, to refute certain theories that have led to the belief that, by stabilizing the general price level, all the disturbing monetary causes would be eliminated. Although, since this book was written, this belief has been somewhat rudely shaken by the crisis of 1929, I hope that a systematic examination of its foundations will still be found useful. The critique of the program of the "stabilizers," which is in many ways the central theme of this book, has now occupied me for many years, and since I deal here only with some special problems that have grown mainly out of these studies, I may perhaps be permitted to refer below to other publications, in which I have partly dealt with certain further theoretical problems and partly attempted to use these considerations for the elucidation of contemporary phenomena.[4] In particular, my *Prices and Production*, originally published in England, should be considered as an essential complement to the present publication. While I have here emphasized the *monetary causes* that *start* the cyclical fluctuations, I have, in that later publication, concentrated on the *successive changes in the real structure of production*, which *constitute* those fluctuations. This essential complement of my theory seems to me to be the more important since, in consequence of actual economic developments, the over simplified

---

[4] "Die Währungspolitik der Vereinigten Staaten seit der Überwindung der Krise von 1920," *Zeitschrift für Volkswirtschaft und Sozialpolitik*, N.F. 5 (1925). "Das intertemporale Gleichgewichtssystem der Preise und die Bewegungen des Geldwertes," *Weltwirtschaftliches Archiv* 28 (1928); "The 'Paradox' of Saving," *Economica* 32 (May 1931), included in this volume; *Prices and Production* (London: Routledge and Sons, 1931), included in this volume; "Reflections on the Pure Theory of Money of Mr. J.M. Keynes," *Economica*, nos. 33–35 (1931–32), included in this volume; "Das Schicksal der Goldwährung," *Der Deutsche Volkswirt* (1932); "Kapitalaufzehrung," *Weltwirtschaftliches Archiv* 36 (1932).

monetary explanations have gained undeserved prominence in recent times. And since, in all my English publications, I have purposely refrained from combining purely theoretical considerations with discussions of current events, it may be useful to add here one or two remarks on the bearing of those considerations on the problems of today.

It is a curious fact that the general disinclination to explain the past boom by monetary factors has been quickly replaced by an even greater readiness to hold the present working of our monetary organization exclusively responsible for our present plight. And the same stabilizers who believed that nothing was wrong with the boom and that it might last indefinitely because prices did not rise, now believe that everything could be set right again if only we would use the weapons of monetary policy to prevent prices from falling. The same superficial view, which sees no other harmful effect of a credit expansion but the rise of the price level, now believes that our only difficulty is a fall in the price level, caused by credit contraction.

There can, of course, be little doubt that, at the present time, a deflationary process is going on and that an indefinite continuation of that deflation would do inestimable harm. But this does not, by any means, necessarily mean that the deflation is the original cause of our difficulties or that we could overcome these difficulties by compensating for the deflationary tendencies, at present operative in our economic system, by forcing more money into circulation. There is no reason to assume that the crisis was started by a deliberate deflationary action on the part of the monetary authorities, or that the deflation itself is anything but a secondary phenomenon, a process induced by the maladjustments of industry left over from the boom. If, however, the deflation is not a cause but an effect of the unprofitableness of industry, then it is surely vain to hope that by reversing the deflationary process, we can regain lasting prosperity. Far from following a deflationary policy, central banks, particularly in the United States, have been making earlier and more far-reaching efforts than have ever been undertaken before to combat the depression by a policy of credit expansion—with the result that the depression has lasted longer and has become more severe than any preceding one. What we need is a readjustment of those elements in the structure of production and of prices that existed before the deflation began and which then made it unprofitable for industry to borrow. But, instead of furthering the inevitable liquidation of the maladjustments brought about by the boom during the last three years, all conceivable means have been used to prevent that readjustment from taking place; and one of these means, which has been repeatedly tried though without success, from the earliest to the most recent stages of depression, has been this deliberate policy of credit expansion.

It is very probable that the much discussed rigidities, which had already grown up in many parts of the modern economic system before 1929, would, in any case, have made the process of readjustment much slower and more painful. It is also probable that these very resistances to readjustment would have set up a severe deflationary process that would finally have overcome those rigidities. To what extent, under the given situation of a relatively rigid price and wage system, this deflationary process is perhaps not only inevitable but is even the quickest way of bringing about the required result, is a very difficult question, about which, on the basis of our present knowledge, I should be afraid to make any definite pronouncement.

It seems certain, however, that we shall merely make matters worse if we aim at curing the deflationary symptoms and, at the same time (by the erection of trade barriers and other forms of state intervention), do our best to increase rather than to decrease the fundamental maladjustments. More than that: while the advantages of such a course are, to say the least, uncertain, the new dangers it creates are great. To combat the depression by a forced credit expansion is to attempt to cure the evil by the very means which brought it about; because we are suffering from a misdirection of production, we want to create further misdirection—a procedure that can only lead to a much more severe crisis as soon as the credit expansion comes to an end. It would not be the first experiment of this kind that has been made. We should merely be repeating, on a much larger scale, the course followed by the Federal Reserve System in 1927, an experiment that Mr. A.C. Miller, the only economist on the Federal Reserve Board and at the same time its oldest member, has rightly characterized as "the greatest and boldest operation ever undertaken by the Federal Reserve System," an operation that "resulted in one of the most costly errors committed by it or any other banking system in the last 75 years." It is probably to this experiment, together with the attempts to prevent liquidation once the crisis had come, that we owe the exceptional severity and duration of the depression. We must not forget that, for the last six or eight years, monetary policy all over the world has followed the advice of the stabilizers. It is high time that their influence, which has already done harm enough, should be overthrown.

We cannot hope for the overthrow of this alluringly simple theory until its theoretical basis is definitely refuted and something better substituted for it. The opponents of the stabilization program still labor—and probably always will labor—under the disadvantage that they have no equally simple and clear-cut rule to propose; perhaps no rule at all that will satisfy the eagerness of those who hope to cure all evils by authoritative action. But whatever may be our hope for the future, the one thing of which we must be painfully aware at the present time—a fact that no writer on these problems should fail to impress upon his readers—is how little we really know of the forces that we are trying to influence by deliberate management; so little indeed that it must remain an open question whether we would try if we knew more.

Friedrich A. Hayek
The London School of Economics
June 1932

CHAPTER 1

The Problem of the Trade Cycle

I

Any attempt either to forecast the trend of economic development, or to influence it by measures based on an examination of existing conditions, must presuppose certain quite definite conceptions as to the necessary course of economic phenomena. Empirical studies, whether they are undertaken with such practical aims in view, or whether they are confined merely to the amplification with the aid of special statistical devices of our knowledge of the course of particular phases of trade fluctuations, can at best afford merely a verification of existing theories; they cannot in themselves provide new insight into the causes or the necessity of the trade cycle.

This view has been stated very forcibly by Professor A. Lowe.[5]

"Our insight into the *theoretical* interconnections of economic cycles, and into the structural laws of circulation," he says, "has not been enriched at all by descriptive work or calculations of correlations." We can entirely agree with him, moreover, when he goes on to say that "to expect an immediate furtherance of *theory* from an increase in *empirical* insight is to misunderstand the logical relationship between theory and empirical research."

---

[5] In his essay, "Wie ist Konjunkturtheorie überhaupt möglich?" *Weltwirtschaftliches Archiv* 24 (1926), part 2, p. 166.

The reason for this is clear. The means of perception employed in statistics are not the same as those employed in economic theory; and it is therefore impossible to fit regularities established by the former into the structure of economic laws prescribed by the latter. We cannot superimpose upon the system of fundamental propositions comprised in the theory of equilibrium, a trade cycle theory resting on unrelated logical foundations. All the phenomena observed in cyclical fluctuations, particularly price formation and its influence on the direction and the volume of production, have already been explained by the theory of equilibrium; they can only be integrated as an explanation of the totality of economic events by means of fundamentally similar constructions. Trade cycle theory itself is only expected to explain how certain prices are determined, and to state their influence on production and consumption; and the determining conditions of these phenomena are already given by elementary theory. Its special task arises from the fact that these phenomena show empirically observed movements for the explanation of which the methods of equilibrium theory are as yet inadequate. One need not go so far as to say that a successful solution could be reached only in conjunction with a positive explanation of elementary phenomena; but no further proof is needed that such a solution can only be achieved in association with, or by means of, a theory that explains how certain prices or certain uses of given goods are determined at all. It is not only that we lack theories that fulfill this condition and that fall outside the category best described as "equilibrium theories"[6]—theories that are characterized by taking the logic of economic action as their starting point; the point is rather that statistical

---

[6] Cf. Löwe: "Der gegenwärtige Stand der Konjunkturtheorie in Deutschland," *Die Wirtschaftswissenschaft nach dem Kriege, Festgabe für Lujo Brentano zum 80. Geburtstag*, ed. M. Bonn and M. Palyi (Munich: Duncker & Humblot, 1925), vol. 2, p. 360.

method is fundamentally unsuited to this purpose. Just as no statistical investigation can prove that a given change in demand must necessarily be followed by a certain change in price, so no statistical method can explain why all economic phenomena present that regular wave-like appearance we observe in cyclical fluctuations. This can be explained only by widening the assumptions on which our deductions are based, so that cyclical fluctuations would follow from these as a necessary consequence, just as the general propositions of the theory of price followed from the narrower assumptions of equilibrium theory.

But even these new assumptions cannot be established by statistical investigation. The statistical approach, unlike deductive inference, leaves the conditions under which established economic relations hold good fundamentally undetermined; and similarly, the objects to which they relate cannot be determined as unequivocally as by theory. Empirically established relations between various economic phenomena continue to present a problem to theory until the necessity for their interconnections can be demonstrated independently of any statistical evidence.[7] The concepts on which such an explanation is based will be quite different from those by which statistical interconnections are demonstrated; they can be reached independently. Moreover, the corroboration of statistical evidence provides, in itself,

---

[7] Cf. the excellent analysis given by E. Altschul in his well-known essay "Konjunkturtheorie und Konjunkturstatistik," *Archiv für Sozialwissenschaft und Sozialpolitik* 55 (Tübingen: Mohr, 1926). Altschul as a statistician deserves especial credit when, recognizing the limitations of statistical methods, he writes (p. 85) "In economics especially, the final decision about the significance of a certain phenomenon can never be left to mathematical and statistical analysis. The main approach to research must necessarily lie through theoretically obtained knowledge." Cf. also A.C. Pigou, *Industrial Fluctuations*, 2nd ed. (London: Macmillan, 1929), p. 37, "The absence of statistical correlation between a given series of changes and industrial fluctuations does not by itself disprove—and its presence does not prove—that these changes are causes of the fluctuations."

no proof of correctness. *A priori* we cannot expect from statistics anything more than the stimulus provided by the indication of new problems.

In thus emphasizing the fact that trade cycle theory, while it may serve as a basis for statistical research, can never itself be established by the latter, it is by no means desired to deprecate the value of the empirical method. On the contrary, there can be no doubt that trade cycle theory can only gain full practical importance through exact measurement of the actual course of the phenomena it describes. But before we can examine the question of the true importance of statistics to theory, it must be clearly recognized that the use of statistics can never consist in a deepening of our theoretical insight.

II

Even as a means of verification, the statistical examination of the cycles has only a very limited value for trade cycle theory. For the latter—as for any other economic theory—there are only two criteria of correctness. First, it must be deduced with unexceptionable logic from the fundamental notions of the theoretical system; and second, it must explain by a purely deductive method those phenomena with all their peculiarities that we observe in the actual cycles.[8] Such a theory could only be "false" either through an inadequacy in its logic or because the phenomena it explains do not correspond with the observed facts. If, however, the theory is logically sound, and if it leads to an explanation of the given phenomena as a necessary consequence of these general conditions of economic activity, then the best that statistical investigation can do is to show that there still remains

---

[8] Professor A. Löwe, in his report "Über den Einfluss monetärer Faktoren auf den Konjunkturzyklus," *Schriften des Vereins für Sozialpolitik* 173 (1928), part 2, p. 357, expresses his views in almost the same words. The above sentences first appeared in another article in the same volume.

an unexplained residue of processes. It could never prove that the determining relationships are of a different character from those maintained by the theory.⁹

It might be shown, for instance, by statistical investigation that a general rise in prices is followed by an expansion of production, and a general fall in prices by a diminution of production; but this would not necessarily mean that theory should regard the movement of price as an independent cause of movements of production. So long as a theory could explain the regular occurrence of this parallelism in any other way, it could not be disproved by statistics, even if it maintained that the connection between the two phenomena was of a precisely opposite nature.¹⁰ It is therefore only in a negative sense that it is possible to verify theory by statistics. Either statistics can demonstrate that there are phenomena the theory does not sufficiently explain, or it is unable to discover such phenomena. It cannot be expected to confirm the theory in a positive sense. The possibility is completely ruled out by what has been said above, since it would presuppose an assertion of *necessary* interconnections, such as statistics cannot make. There is no reason to be surprised,

---

⁹ Cf. the analysis concerning "Argument der Wirklichkeitswidrigkeit" in the recent book by E. Carell, *Sozialökonomische Theorie und Konjunkturproblem* (Munich and Leipzig: Duncker & Humblot, 1929), for a very acute methodological argument. He opposes the thesis of Löwe (which remains, however, despite his analysis, the basis of my own work) that the incorporation of cyclical phenomena into the system of economic equilibrium theory, with which they are in apparent contradiction, remains the crucial problem of trade cycle theory.

¹⁰ A well-known instance of such an apparent contradiction between a correct theoretical assertion and experience is the connection between the level of interest rates and the movement of prices. Cf. Wicksell, *Vorlesungen*, vol. 2, *Geld und Kredit* (Jena: Gustav Fischer, 1922). See also my essay, "Das intertemporale Gleichgevichts-system der Preise und die Bewegungen des Geldweries" (*Weltwirtschaftiches Archiv* 28 [1928], p. 63 *et seq.*).

therefore, that although nearly all modern trade cycle theories use statistical material as corroboration, it is only where a given theory fails to explain all the observed phenomena that this statistical evidence can be used to judge its merits.

III

Thus it is not by enriching or by checking theoretical analysis that economic statistics gain their real importance. This lies elsewhere. The proper task of statistics is to give us accurate information about the events that fall within the province of theory, and so to enable us not only to connect two consecutive events as cause and effect, *a posteriori,* but to grasp existing conditions completely enough for forecasts of the future and, eventually, appropriate action, to become possible. It is only through this possibility of forecasts of systematic action that theory gains practical importance.[11] A theory might, for instance, enable us to infer from

---

[11] It should be noted that the idea of forecasting is by no means a new one, although it is often regarded as such. Every economic theory, and indeed all theory of whatever sort, aims exclusively at foretelling the necessary consequences of a given situation, event, or measure. The subject matter of trade cycle theory being what it is, it follows that ideally it should result in a collective forecast showing the total development resulting from a given situation under given conditions. In practice, such forecasts are attempted in too unconditional a form, and on an inadmissibly oversimplified basis; and, consequently, the very possibility of scientific judgments about future economic trends today appears problematical, and cautious thinkers are apt to disparage any attempt at such forecasting. In contrast to this view, we have to emphasize very strongly that statistical research in this field is meaningless except insofar as it leads to a forecast, however much that forecast may have to be hedged about with qualifications. In particular any measures aimed at alleviating the trade cycle (and necessarily based on statistical research) must be conceived in the light of certain assumptions as to the future trend to be expected in the absence of such measures. Statistical research, therefore, serves only to furnish the bases for the utilization of existing theoretical principles.

Dr. O. Morgenstern's recent categorical denial (*Wirtschaftsprognose: Eine Untersuchung ikrer Voraussetzungen und Möglichkeiten* [Vienna: Springer,

the comparative movements of certain prices and quantities an imminent change in the direction of those movements: but we should have little use for such a theory if we were unable to ascertain the *actual* movements of the phenomena in question. With regard to certain phenomena having an important bearing on the trade cycle, our position is a peculiar one. We can deduce from general insight how the majority of people will behave under certain conditions; but the actual behavior of these masses at a given moment, and therefore the conditions to which our theoretical conclusions must be applied, can only be ascertained by the use of complicated statistical methods. This is especially true when a phenomenon is influenced by a number of partly known circumstances, such as, e.g., seasonal changes. Here very complicated statistical investigations are needed to ascertain whether these circumstances whose presence indicates the applicability of theoretical conclusions were in fact operative. Often statistical analysis may detect phenomena that have, as yet, no theoretical explanation, and which therefore necessitate either an extension of theoretical speculation or a search for new determining conditions. But the explanation of the phenomena thus detected, if it is to serve as a basis for forecasts of the future, must in every case utilize other methods than statistically observed regularities; and the observed phenomena will have to be deduced from the theoretical system, independently of empirical detection.

The dependence of statistical research on preexisting theoretical explanation hardly needs further emphasis. This holds good not only as regards the practical utilization of its results, but also in the course of its working, in which it must look to theory for guidance in selecting and delimiting the phenomena

---

1928]) of the possibility of forecasting seems to be due only to the fact that he demands more from forecasting than is justifiable. Even the ability to forecast a hailstorm would not be useless—but, on the contrary, very valuable—if the latter could thereupon be averted by firing rockets at the clouds!

to be investigated. The oft-repeated assertion that statistical examination of the trade cycle should be undertaken without any theoretical prejudice is therefore always based on self-deception.[12]

---

[12] Professor Bullock, the Principal of the Harvard Economic Service (now the Harvard Economic Society), constantly emphasizes the complete absence of theoretical prepossession with which the work of the Institute is carried out. Sincere as this belief unquestionably is, however, one may doubt its validity when one reads, for instance, the following account given by Professor Bullock's chief collaborator, Mr. W.M. Persons, the inventor of the famous Harvard Barometer. Here he attempts the following popular explanation of the latter:

> This account of the business cycle, based upon our statistical analysis, revolves about the fluctuation of short-time interest rates, speculation, and business. We may think of interest rates as varying inversely with the amount of the bank reserves in the credit reservoir. The flow in the supply pipe to this reservoir depends upon the volume of gold imports, gold production, and the volume of paper currency. There are two outlets from this reservoir of credit: one pipe furnishes credit for speculation in securities; the other pipe is for the flow of credit into business. When the level
>
> of credit in the reservoir is high, and perhaps the outlet to business is partially clogged, the flow of funds into speculation begins. After this flow goes on for some time, however, and the flow into business increases, the level of credit in the reservoir falls. Obstruction is offered to the flow into speculative markets by the devices of higher interest rates and direct discrimination against speculation and in favor of business. The outlet into speculation therefore becomes clogged but the flow into business goes on. The level in the reservoir becomes still lower until the time is reached when bankers consider it dangerous to allow the outflow to continue. We then have a halt in further credit expansion, or to use our illustration, both outlets are clogged for a time and bank reserves are brought back to normal by allowing the supply to again fill the tank. ("A non-technical explanation of the index of general business conditions," *The Review of Economic Statistics* 2 [1920]: 47)

On the whole, one can say without exaggeration that the practical value of statistical research depends primarily upon the soundness of the theoretical conceptions on which it is based. To decide upon the most important problems of the trade cycle remains the task of theory; and whether the money and labor so freely expended on statistical research in late years will be repaid by the expected success depends primarily on whether the development of theoretical understanding keeps pace with the exploration of the facts. For we must not deceive ourselves: not only do we now lack a theory that is generally accepted by economists, but we do not even possess one that could be formulated in such an unexceptionable way, and worked out in such detail, as eventually to command such acceptance. A series of important interconnections have been established and some principles of the greatest significance expounded; but no one has yet undertaken the decisive step that creates a complete theory by using one of these principles to incorporate all the known phenomena into the existing system in a satisfactory way. To realize this, of course, does not hinder us from pursuing either economic research or economic policy; but then we must always remember that we are acting on certain theoretical assumptions whose correctness has not yet been satisfactorily established. The "practical man" habitually acts on theories that he does not consciously realize; and in most cases this means that his theories are fallacious. Using a theory consciously, on the other hand, always results in some new attempt to clear up the interrelations that it assumes, and to bring it into harmony with which theoretical assumptions; that is, it results in the pursuit of theory for its own sake.

IV

The value of business forecasting depends upon correct theoretical concepts; hence there can, at the present time, be no more important task in this field than the bridging of the gulf that divides monetary from non-monetary theories.¹³ This gulf leads to differences of opinion in the front rank of economists; and is also the characteristic line of division between trade cycle theory in Germany and in America—where business forecasting originated. Such an analysis of the relation between these two main trends seems to me especially important because of the peculiar position of the monetary theories. Largely through the fault of some of their best-known advocates in Germany, monetary explanations became discredited, and their essentials have, moreover, been much misunderstood; while, on the other hand, the reaction against them forms the main reason for the prevailing skepticism as to the possibility of any economic theory of the trade cycle—a skepticism which may seriously retard the development of theoretical research.¹⁴

There is a fundamental difficulty inherent in all trade cycle theories that take as their starting point an empirically ascertained disturbance of the equilibrium of the various branches of production. This difficulty arises because, in stating the effects of that disturbance, they have to make use of the logic of equilibrium

---

[13] Since the publication of the German edition of this book, I have become less convinced that the difference between monetary and non-monetary explanations is *the most important* point of disagreement between the various trade cycle theories. On the one hand, it seems to me that within the monetary group of explanations the difference between those theorists who regard the superficial phenomena of changes in the value of money as decisive factors in determining cyclical fluctuations, and those who lay emphasis on the real changes in the structure of production brought about by monetary causes, is much greater than the difference between the latter group and such so-called non-monetary theorists as Professor Spiethoff and Professor Cassel. On the other hand, it seems to me that the difference between these explanations, which seek the cause of the crisis in the scarcity of capital, and the so-called "underconsumption" theories, is theoretically as well as practically of much more far-reaching importance than the difference between monetary and non-monetary theories.

[14] Cf. the above-mentioned essay of A. Löwe in the *Weltwirtschaftliches Archiv*.

theory.[15] Yet this logic, properly followed through, can do no more than demonstrate that such disturbances of equilibrium can come only from outside—i.e., that they represent a change in the economic data—and that the economic system always reacts to such changes by its well-known methods of adaptation, i.e., by the formation of a new equilibrium. No tendency toward the special expansion of certain branches of production, however plausibly adduced, no chance shift in demand, in distribution or in productivity, could adequately explain, within the framework of this theoretical system, why a general "disproportionality" between supply and demand should arise. For the essential means of explanation in static theory—which is, at the same time, the indispensable assumption for the explanation of particular price variations—is the assumption that prices supply an automatic mechanism for equilibrating supply and demand.

The next section will deal with these difficulties in more detail: a mere hint should therefore be sufficient at this point. At the moment we have only to draw attention to the fact that the problem before us cannot be solved by examining the effect of a certain cause within the framework, and by the methods, of equilibrium theory. Any theory that limits itself to the explanation of empirically observed interconnections by the methods of elementary theory necessarily contains a self-contradiction. For trade cycle theory cannot aim at the adaptation of the adjusting mechanism of static theory to a special case; this scheme of explanation must itself be extended so as to explain how such discrepancies between supply and demand can ever arise. The obvious, and (to my mind) the only possible way out of this dilemma, is to explain

---

[15] By "equilibrium theory" we here primarily understand the modern theory of the general interdependence of all economic quantities, which has been most perfectly expressed by the Lausanne School of theoretical economics. The significant basic concept of this theory was contained in James Mill's and J.B. Say's *Théorie des Débouchés*. Cf. L. Miksch, *Gibt es eine allgemeine Uberproduktion?* (Jena: Gustav Fischer, 1929).

the difference between the course of events described by static theory (which only permits movements toward an equilibrium, and which is deduced by directly contrasting the supply of and the demand for goods) and the actual course of events, by the fact that, with the introduction of money (or strictly speaking with the introduction of indirect exchange), a new determining cause is introduced. Money being a commodity that, unlike all others, is incapable of finally satisfying demand, its introduction does away with the rigid interdependence and self-sufficiency of the "closed" system of equilibrium, and makes possible movements that would be excluded from the latter. Here we have a starting point that fulfils the essential conditions for any satisfactory theory of the trade cycle. It shows, in a purely deductive way, the possibility and the necessity of movements that *do not* at any given moment tend toward a situation which, in the absence of changes in the economic "data," could continue indefinitely. It shows that, on the contrary, these movements lead to such a "disproportionality" between certain parts of the system that the given situation cannot continue.

But while it seems that it was a sound instinct that led economists to begin by looking on the monetary side for an explanation of cyclical fluctuations, it also seems probable that the one-sided development of the theory of money has, as yet, prevented any satisfactory solution to the problem being found. Monetary theories of the trade cycle succeeded in giving prominence to the right questions and, in many cases, made important contributions toward their solution; but the reason why an unassailable solution has not yet been put forward seems to reside in the fact that all the adherents of the monetary theory of the trade cycle have sought an explanation either exclusively or predominantly in the superficial phenomena of changes in the value of money, while failing to pursue the far more profound and fundamental effects of the process by which money is introduced into the economic system, as distinct from its effect on prices in general. Nor did they follow up the consequences of the fundamental diversity between a money economy and the pure barter economy that is assumed in static theory.[16]

V

Naturally it cannot be the business of this essay to remove all defects and deficiencies from the monetary theories of the trade cycle, or to develop a complete and unassailable theory. In these pages I shall only attempt to show the general significance for this theory of the monetary starting point, and to refute the most important objections raised against the monetary explanation by proving that certain rightly exposed deficiencies of some monetary theories do not necessarily follow from the monetary approach. All that is wanted, therefore, is, first, a proof, using as our examples some of the best-known non-monetary theories, that the "real" explanations adduced by them do not, in themselves, suffice to build up a complete and consistent theory; second, a demonstration that the existing monetary theories contain the germ of a true explanation, although all suffer, more or less, from that oversimplification of the problem which results from reducing all cyclical fluctuations to fluctuations in the value of money; finally that the monetary starting point makes it possible, in fact, to show deductively the inevitability of fluctuation under the existing monetary system and, indeed, under almost any other that can be imagined. It will be shown, in particular, that the Wicksell-Mises theory of the effects of a divergence between the "natural" and the money rate of interest already contains the most important elements of an explanation, and has only to be freed from any direct reference to a purely imaginary "general money value" (as has already been partly done by Professor Mises) in order to form the basis of a trade cycle theory sufficing for a deductive explanation of all the elements in the trade cycle.

---

[16] Similar views are expressed by W. Röpke, "Kredit und Konjunktur," *Jahrbücher für Nationalökonomie und Statistik*, 3rd series, vol. 69 (1926), p. 264 et seq.

CHAPTER 2

Non-Monetary Theories of the Trade Cycle

I

Any attempt at a general proof, within the compass of a short essay, of the assertion that non-monetary theories of the trade cycle inevitably suffer from a fundamental deficiency, appears to be confronted with an insuperable obstacle by reason of the very multiplicity of such theories. If it were necessary for our purpose to show that every one of the numerous disequilibrating forces which have been made starting points for trade cycle theories was, in fact, nonexistent, then the conditions of our success would, indeed, be impossible of fulfillment; for not only would it be almost impossible to deal with all extant theories but no conclusive answer could result, seeing that we should still have to reckon with a new and hitherto unrefuted crop of such theories in the future. Moreover the existence of most of the interconnections elaborated by the various trade cycle theories can hardly be denied, and our task is rather their coordination in a unified logical structure than the development of entirely new and different trains of thought. In fact, it is by no means necessary to question the material correctness of the individual interconnections emphasized in the various non-monetary theories in order to show that they do not afford a sufficient explanation. As has already been indicated in the first chapter, none of them is able to overcome the contradiction between the course of economic events as described by them and the fundamental ideas of the theoretical system which they have to utilize in order to explain that course. It will, therefore, be sufficient to show, by examination of some of the best-known theories, that they do not answer this fundamental question; nor can they ever do so by their present methods and by reference to the circumstances they now regard as relevant to trade cycle theory. When, however, the question is answered on different lines, viz., by reference to *monetary* circumstances, it can be shown that the elements of explanation adduced by different theories lose their independent importance and fall into a subordinate position as necessary consequences of the monetary cause.

It is rather difficult to select the main types of trade cycle theory for this purpose, since we have no theoretically satisfactory classification. The latest attempts at such classifications, by Mr. W.M. Persons,[17] Professor W.C. Mitchell,[18] and Mr. A.H. Hansen,[19] show that the usual division, which relies on external features and hardly touches the solution of fundamental problems, gives far too wide a scope for arbitrary decisions. As Professor Löwe[20] has correctly emphasized (and as should be obvious from what has been said above), the only classification that could be really unobjectionable would be one that proceeded according to the manner in which such theories explain the absence of the "normal course" of economic events, as presented

---

[17] "Theories of Business Fluctuations," *Quarterly Journal of Economics* 41 (1926): 923.

[18] *Business Cycles: The Problem and Its Setting* (New York: National Bureau of Economic Research, 1927).

[19] *Business Cycle Theory: Its Development and Present Status* (Boston: Ginn, 1927).

[20] See *Der Gegenwärtige Stand der Konjunkturforschung,* p. 359 *et seq.*

by static theory. In fact, the various theories—as we shall hope to show later—make no attempt whatever to do this. As there is, therefore, no classification that would serve our purpose, our choice must be more or less arbitrary; but by choosing some of the best-known theories and exemplifying the train of thought to which our objection particularly applies, we should be able to make the general validity of the latter sufficiently clear. The task is made rather easier by the fact that there does exist today, on at least one point, a far-reaching agreement among the different theories. They all regard the emergence of a *disproportionality* among the various productive groups, and in particular the excessive production of capital goods, as the first and main thing to be explained. The development of theory owes a real debt to statistical research in that, today, there is at least no substantial disagreement as to the thing to be explained.

There is, however, a point to be emphasized here. The modern habit of going beyond the actual crisis and seeking to explain the entire cycle, suffers inherently from the danger of paying less and less attention to the crucial problem. In particular, the attempt to give the object of the theory as neutral a name as possible (such as "industrial fluctuations" or "cyclical movements of industry") threatens to drive the real theoretical problem more into the background than was the case in the old theory of crisis. The simple fact that economic development does not go on quite uniformly, but that periods of relatively rapid change alternate with periods of relative stagnation, does not in itself constitute a problem. It is sufficiently explained by the adjustment of the economic system to irregular changes in the data—changes whose occurrence we always have to assume and which cannot be further explained by economic science. The real problem presented to economic theory is: Why doesn't this adjustment come about smoothly and continuously, just as a new equilibrium is formed after every change in the data? Why is there this temporary possibility of developments leading away from equilibrium and finally, without any changes in data, necessitating a change in the economic trend? The phenomena of the upward trend of the cycle and of the culminating boom constitute a problem only because they inevitably bring about a slump in sales—i.e., a falling-off of economic activity—which is *not* occasioned by any corresponding change in the original economic data.

II

The prevailing disproportionality theories are in agreement in one respect. They all see the cause of the slump in the fact that, during the boom, for various reasons, the productive apparatus is expanded more than is warranted by the corresponding flow of consumption; there finally appears a scarcity of finished consumption goods, thus causing a rise in the price of such goods relatively to the price of production goods (which amounts to the same thing as a rise in the rate of interest) so that it becomes unprofitable to employ the enlarged productive apparatus or, in many cases, even to complete it. At present there is hardly a recognized theory that does not give this idea, which we only sketch for the moment,[21] a decisive place in its argument, and we should therefore be well advised to begin by seeing how the various theories try to deal with the phenomenon in question. Apart from the monetary theories, which, as will be shown later, *can only be considered satisfactory if they explain that phenomenon,* there are two groups of explanations that can be entirely disregarded. In the first place there is nothing to be gained from an examination of those theories that seek to explain cyclical fluctuations by corresponding cyclical changes in certain external circumstances, while merely using the unquestionable methods of equilibrium theory to explain the economic phenomena that follow from these changes. To decide on the correctness of these theories is beyond the competence of economics. In the second place, it is best, for the moment, to exclude from consideration those theories whose

---

[21] Cf. below, p. 115 *et seq.* esp. p. 117.

argument depends so entirely on the assumption of monetary changes that when the latter are excluded no systematic explanation is left. This category includes Professor J. Schumpeter,[22] Professor E. Lederer,[23] and Professor G. Cassel,[24] and to a certain extent Professor W.C. Mitchell and Professor J. Lescure.[25] We shall have to consider later, with regard to this category, how far it is theoretically permissible to treat these monetary interconnections as determining conditions on the same footing as the other phenomena used in explanation.

It is, of course, impossible at this point to go into the peculiarities of all types of theory, as worked out by their respective authors. We must leave out of account the forms in which the various explanations are presented, and confine ourselves to certain underlying types of theory that recur in a number of different guises. Inevitably, this treatment of contemporary theories must fail to do full justice to the intellectual merits exemplified in each; but for the purposes of this chapter—that is, to show the fundamental objections to which all non-monetary theories of the trade cycle are open—this somewhat cursory and imperfect treatment may be enough.

We may begin our demonstration by pointing out that all those forms of disproportionality theory with which we have to deal here rest on the existence of quite irregular fluctuations of "economic data" (that is, the external determining circumstances of the economic system, including human needs and abilities).

---

[22] *Theorie der wirtschaftlichen Entwicklung*, 2nd ed. (Munich and Leipzig: Duncker & Humblot, 1936).

[23] "Konjunktur und Krisen," *Grundriss der Sozialökonomik* 4, no. 1 (1926); also "Zur Morphologie der Krisen," in *Die Wirtschaftstheorie der Gegenwart*, ed. by H. Mayer (Vienna: Springer, 1928), vol. 4.

[24] *Theory of Social Economy* (New York: Harcourt, Brace, 1932).

[25] *Des Crises générales et périodiques de surproduction* (Paris: Domat, 1913); and "Krisenlehre," in *Die Wirtschaftstheorie der Gegenwart*, ed. Mayer, vol. 4.

From this assumption, they try to explain in one way or another that the fluctuations in consumption or some other element in the economic system occasioned by these changes are followed by relatively greater changes in the production of production goods.[26] These wide fluctuations in the industries making production goods bring about a disproportionality between them and the consumption industries to such an extent that a reversal of the movement becomes necessary. *It is not, therefore, the simple fact of fluctuation in the production of capital goods (which is certainly inevitable in the course of economic growth) which has to be explained.* The real problem is the growth of excessive fluctuations in the capital goods industries out of the inevitable and irregular fluctuations of the rest of the economic system, and the disproportional development, arising from these, of the two main branches of production. We can distinguish three main types of non-monetary theories explaining the exaggerated effect of given fluctuations on capital goods industries. The most common, at the moment, are those explanations that try to show that, on account of the *technique of production,* an increase in the demand for consumption goods, whether expected or actual, tends to bring about a relatively larger increase in the production of goods of a higher

---

[26] It should be noted here that the assumption of initial changes in the economic data, which no theory of the trade cycle can dispense with, in itself throws no light on the proper way of explaining cyclical fluctuations. It is not the occurrence of disturbances of equilibrium, necessitating readjustment, which presents a problem to trade cycle theory; it is the fact that this adjustment is brought about only after a series of movements have taken place which cannot be considered "adjustments" in the sense used by the theory of economic equilibrium. "The phenomenon is never made clear until it is explained why its cause, whatever it may be, does not call forth a continuous equilibrating process" (Professor J. Schumpeter, *Theorie der wirtschaftlichen Entwicklung,* 2nd ed. [Munich and Leipzig: Duncker & Humblot, 1926]). These changes of data could serve as a complete explanation only if it could be shown that the successive phases of the trade cycle are conditioned by a series of such changes, following each other in a certain order.

order, either generally or in a certain group of these goods. Hardly less common, and differing only in appearance, are explanations that seek to derive these augmented fluctuations from special circumstances (non-monetary in character) arising in the field of *savings and investment*. Finally, as a third group, we must mention certain *psychological* theories, which, for the most part, have however no pretension to rank as independent explanations and which merely reinforce other arguments, and are open to the same objections as the two other main types.

III

We shall mention only the most important of our objections to the first type, which is the easiest to discuss from this point of view. It is common to so many economists that it is hardly necessary to mention particular representatives. The simplest way of deductively explaining excessive fluctuations in the production of capital goods is by reference to the *long period of time* that is necessary, under modern conditions, for preparing the fixed capital goods which enable the expansion of the productive process to take place.[27] According to a widely held view, this circumstance alone is enough to make every increase in the sales of consumption goods, whether brought about by an intensification of demand or by a fall in the costs of production, capable of bringing about a more-than-proportional increase in the production of intermediary goods. This is explained either by the individual producer's ignorance of what his competitors are doing, or—as is common in American writings—by the "cumulative effect" of each change in the sale of consumption goods on the higher stages of production. Owing to circumstances that will be explained later, the leading idea in all these types of explanation is that the long period which, with the present technique of production, elapses between the

---

[27] Cf. A. Aftalion, *Les crises périodiques de surproduction* (Paris: Marcel Rivière, 1913), bks. 2–6, chaps. 3 to 8; and D.H. Robertson, *Industrial Fluctuations* (London: P.S. King, 1915), p. 14.

beginning of a productive process and the arrival of its final product at the market, prevents the gradual adjustment of production to changes in demand through the agency of prices and makes it possible, from time to time, for an excessively large supply to be thrown on the market. This idea is supported by another, which however, can be independently and more widely applied; that is, that *every change in demand,* from the moment of its appearance, *propagates itself cumulatively* through all the grades of production, from the lowest to the highest. This cumulative effect arises because at each stage, besides the change that would be appropriate to the actual shift in demand, another change arises from the adjustment of stocks and of productive apparatus to the alteration in market conditions.[28] An increase in the demand for consumption goods will not merely call forth a proportional increase in the demand for goods of a higher order: the latter will also be increased by the amount needed to raise current stocks to a proportional level, and, finally, by the further amount by which the requirements for producing new means of production exceed those for keeping the existing means of production intact. (For instance, an extension of 10 percent, in one particular year, in the machinery of a factory that normally renews 10 percent of its machinery annually, causes an increase of 100 percent in the production of machinery—i.e., a given increase in the demand for consumption goods occasions a tenfold increase in the production of production goods.) This idea is offered as an adequate reason not only for the relatively greater fluctuations in production-goods industries but also for their *excessive* expansion in periods of boom. Similarly, the extensive use of *durable capital equipment* in the modern economy is often singled out for responsibility.[29] Industries using heavy equipment

---

[28] Cf. T.N. Carver, *Quarterly Journal of Economics* (1903–04): 492; A. Aftalion, *Journal d'Economie Politique* (1909): 215 *ff.*; Mitchell, *Business Cycles;* and Robertson, *Industrial Fluctuations,* p. 122 *ff.*

[29] Cf. Robertson, *Industrial Fluctuations,* p. 31 *et seq.*

are prone to excessive expansion in boom periods because small increments in this equipment are impossible; expansion must necessarily take place by sudden jerks. Once the new equipment is available, on the other hand, the volume of production has little influence on total costs, which go on even if no production takes place at all. New inventions and new needs, however, although they are often adduced as explaining the accelerated and excessive growth of capital goods industries, cannot be dealt with on the same footing. They only represent a special group of the many possible causes from which the cumulative processes described above may originate.

IV

There is virtually no doubt that all these interconnections, and many others that are given prominence in various trade cycle theories and which similarly tend to disturb economic equilibrium, do actually exist; and any trade cycle theory that claims to be comprehensively worked out must take them into consideration. But none of them get over the real difficulty—namely: why do the forces tending to restore equilibrium become temporarily ineffective and why do they only come into action again when it is too late? They all try to explain this phenomenon by a further, usually tacit, assumption, which one of the advocates of these theories, Mr. C.O. Hardy,[30] has himself put forward as their common idea, by which, in my opinion, he brings out with the utmost clarity their fundamental weakness. He states that all those theories that are based on the length of the production period under modern technical conditions agree in regarding these conditions as a source of difficulty to producers in adjusting production to the state of the market; producing,

---

[30] *Risk and Risk Bearing* (Chicago: University of Chicago Press, 1923), p. 72. See also Mr. Hardy's reply to the above criticism in the revised 2nd edition (1931), of the same book (p. 94), which, however, does not seem to solve the fundamental difficulty.

as they must, for a future period, the market possibilities of which are necessarily unknown to them. He then emphasizes that in general it is the task of the price mechanism to adjust supply to demand; he thinks, however, that this mechanism is imperfect, if a long period has to lapse between production and the arrival of the product at the market, because

> prices and orders give information concerning the prospective state of demand compared with the known facts of the present and future supply, but they give no clue to the changes in supply which they themselves are likely to cause.[31]

He tries to show how periodic over- and underproduction may result from an increase in demand acting as an incentive to increased production. He here states explicitly what others assume tacitly, and thus his exposition completely gives away the question-begging nature of all such arguments. For he holds that under free competition, in the case considered, more and more people try to profit by the favorable situation, all ignoring one another's preparations, and *"no force intervenes to check the continual increase in production until it reflects itself in declining orders and falling prices."*[32] In this statement (according to which the price mechanism comes into action only when the products come on to the market, while, until then, producers can regulate the extent of their production solely according to the estimated *total volume of demand*) the fundamental error that can be shown to recur in all these theories is plainly revealed. It arises from a misconception of the deliberations that regulate the entrepreneur's actions and of the significance of the price mechanism.

If the entrepreneur really had to guide his decisions exclusively by his knowledge of the quantitative increase in the total demand for his product, and if the success of economic activity were really

---

[31] Hardy, *Risk and Risk Bearing*, p. 73.
[32] Ibid. my emphasis.

always dependent on that knowledge, no very complicated circumstances would be needed to produce constant disturbances in the relation between supply and demand. But the entrepreneur in a capitalist economy is not—as many economists seem to assume—in the same situation as the dictator of a socialist economy. The protagonists of this view seem to overlook the fact that production is generally guided not by any knowledge of the actual size of the total demand, but by the price to be obtained in the market. In the modern exchange economy, the entrepreneur does not produce with a view to satisfying a certain demand—even if that phrase is sometimes used—but on the basis of a calculation of profitability; and it is just that calculation that will equilibrate supply and demand. He is not in the least concerned with the amount by which, in a given case, the total amount demanded will alter; he only looks at the price he can expect to get after the change in question has taken place. None of the theories under discussion explains why these expectations should generally prove incorrect. (To deduce their incorrectness from the fact that overproduction, arising from false expectations, causes prices to fall, would be mere argument in a circle.) Nor can this generalization be theoretically established by any other method. For so long, at least, as disturbing monetary influences are not operating, we have to assume that the price that entrepreneurs expect to result from a change in demand or from a change in the conditions of production will more or less coincide with the equilibrium price. For the entrepreneur, from his knowledge of the conditions of production and the market, will generally be in a position to estimate the price that will rule after the changes have taken place, as distinct from the quantitative changes in the total volume of demand. One can only say, as to this prospective price of the product concerned, that it is just as likely to be lower than the equilibrium price as to be higher and that, on the average, it should more or less coincide, since there is no reason to assume that deviations will take place only in one direction. But this prospective price only represents one factor determining the extent of production. The other factor, no less important but all too often overlooked, is the price the producer has to pay for raw materials, labor power, tools and borrowed capital—i.e., his costs. These prices, taken together, determine the extent of production for all producers operating under conditions of competition; and the producer's decisions as to his production must be guided not only by changes in expectations as to the price of his product, but also by changes in his costs. To show how the interplay of these prices keeps supply and demand, production and consumption, in equilibrium, is the main object of pure economics, and the analysis cannot be repeated here in detail. It is, however, the task of trade cycle theory to show under what conditions a break may occur in that tendency toward equilibrium which is described in pure analysis—i.e., why prices, in contradiction to the conclusions of static theory, do not bring about such changes in the quantities produced as would correspond to an equilibrium situation. In order to show that the theories under discussion do not solve this problem, and only as far as is necessary for this purpose, we shall now study the most important of the interconnections which bring about equilibrium under the assumptions of static theory.

V

We may attempt this task by asking what kind of reactions will be brought about by the original change in the economic data that is supposed to cause the excessive extension of the production of capital goods, and how, in such cases, a new equilibrium can result. Whether the original impetus comes from the demand side or the supply side, the assumption from which we have to start is always a price—or rather an expected price—that renders it profitable under the new conditions to extend production. As stated above, we can assume—since none of the theories in question give any reason to the contrary—that this expected price will approximate the new equilibrium price. We can assume, that is, that if the impetus is a fall in unit costs, the producer will consider the effects of an increased supply; if the impetus is an increase in demand, he will consider the increase in the cost per unit following the increase in the quantity produced. The existence of a general misconception in this respect would require a special explanation, and unless this is to rest on a circular argument, it can only be accounted for by a monetary explanation, which we cannot consider at this point.

Now the length of time required to produce modern means of production cannot induce a tendency to an excessive extension of the productive apparatus; or, more accurately, any such tendency is bound to be effectively eliminated by the increase in price of the factors of production. Thus we cannot give a sufficient explanation for the occurrence of the disproportionality in these terms. This becomes obvious as soon as we drop the assumption that the price mechanism begins to function only from the moment at which the increased supply comes on the market, and consider that whenever the price obtainable for the finished product is correctly estimated, the adjustment of the prices of factors of production must ensure that the amount produced is limited to what can be sold at remunerative prices. The mere existence of a lengthy production period cannot be held to impair the working of the price mechanism, so long, at any rate, as no additional reason can be given for the occurrence of a general miscalculation in the same direction concerning the effect of the original change in data on the prices of the products.

We must next inquire what truth there is in the alleged tendency toward a cumulative propagation of the effect of every increase (or decrease) of demand from the lower to the higher stages of production. The arguments given below against this frequently adduced theory must serve at the same time to refute all other theories based on similar technical considerations, for space will not permit us to go into every one of these, and the reader can be trusted to apply the same reasoning as is employed in this demonstration to all similar explanations—such as those based on the necessary discontinuity of the extension of productive apparatus. Does the cumulative effect of every increase in demand represent a new price-determining factor, as a result of which prices, and therefore quantities produced, will be different from those needed to achieve equilibrium? Is the regulating effect of prices on the extent of production really suspended by the fact that when turnover increases merchants try to increase stocks, and manufacturers to extend production? If the increase in the prices of production goods were the only counterbalancing factor to set against the increase in the demand for these goods, it would still be possible for more investments to be undertaken than would prove permanently profitable. According to the view we are considering, there will be an increase in the quantity of factors of production demanded at any price, as compared with the equilibrium situation, and therefore it would appear possible that at every price at which producers still think they can profitably make use of this quantity, investments will be undertaken to an unwarrantable extent.

This way of stating the position, however, entirely overlooks the fact that every attempt to extend the productive apparatus must necessarily bring about, besides the rise in factor prices, a further checking force: viz., a rise in the rate of interest. This greatly strengthens the effect of the rise in factor prices. It makes a greater margin between factor prices and product prices necessary just when this margin threatens to diminish. The maintenance of equilibrium is thus further secured.

For we must not forget that not only the volume of current production, but also the size at any given moment of the productive apparatus (including stocks, which cannot be omitted) is regulated through prices, and especially—apart from the above-mentioned prices for goods and services—by the price paid for the use of capital, that is, interest. Whatever particular explanation of interest we may accept, all contemporary theories agree in regarding the function of interest as one of equalizing the supply of capital and the demand arising in various branches of production. Until some special reason can be adduced why it should not fulfill this function in any given case, we have to assume, in accordance with the fundamental thesis of static theory, that it always keeps the supply of capital goods in equilibrium with that of consumption goods. This assumption is just as indispensable, and just as inevitable, as a starting point, as the main assumption that the supply of and demand for any kind of goods will be equilibrated by movements in the prices of those goods. In our case, when we are considering a tendency to enlarge the productive apparatus and the size of stocks, this function must be performed in such a way as to increase the rate of interest, and hence the necessary margin of profit between the price of the products and that of the means of production. This, however, automatically excludes that part of the increase in the demand for productive goods, which would have been satisfied despite the increase in their prices if the rise in the rate of interest had not taken place. None of the various trade cycle theories based on some alleged peculiarity of the technique of production can even begin to explain why the equilibrium position, determined by the various above-mentioned processes of price formation, should be reached at a different point from where it would be without these peculiarities.

Now as regards the prices of goods and services used for productive purposes, there seems to be no reason why they should not fulfill their function of equilibrating supply and demand. For supply and demand are here in direct relation with one another, so that any discrepancy which may arise between them, at a given price must, directly and immediately, lead to a change in that price. Only when we come to consider the second group of prices (those paid for borrowed capital or, in other words, interest) is it conceivable that disturbances might creep in, since, in this case, price formation does not act directly, by equalizing the marginal demand for and supply of capital goods, but indirectly, through its effect on money capital, whose supply need not correspond to that of real capital. But the process by which divergences can arise between these two is left unexplained by all the theories with which we have hitherto dealt. Yet before going on to see how far interest may present such a breach in the strict system of equilibrium as may serve to explain cyclical disturbances, we must briefly examine the explanation offered by the second important group of non-monetary theories, which attempt to explain the origin of periodical disturbances of equilibrium purely through the phenomena arising out of the accumulation and investment of saving.[33]

VI

The earlier versions of these theories start from the groundless and inadmissible assumption that unused savings are accumulated for a time and then suddenly invested, thus causing the productive apparatus to be extended in jerks. Such versions can be passed over without further analysis. For one thing, it is impossible to give any plausible explanation why unused savings should accumulate for a time;[34] for another thing, even if such an explanation were forthcoming, it would provide no clue to the disproportional development in the production of capital goods. The fact that the mere existence of fluctuations in saving activity does not in itself explain this problem is realized (in contrast to many other economists) by the most distinguished exponent of these theories, Professor A. Spiethoff. This is plain from his negative answer to the analogous question, whether in a barter economy an increase in saving can create the necessary conditions for depression.[35] Indeed, it is difficult to see how spontaneous variations in the volume of saving

---

[33] In revising the above paragraphs my notice has been called to the fact that they are in many respects in accordance with the reasoning of S. Budge in his *Grundzüge der theoretischen Nationalökonomie* (Jena: Gustav Fischer, 1925), p. 201 *et seq.*) to which I should therefore like to call attention.

[34] Cf. the very effective remarks of W. Eucken in his interesting viva-voce report to the Zurich Assembly of the Verein für Sozialpolitik (*Schriften des Vereins für Sozialpolitik* 175 [1928], p. 295 *et seq.*).

[35] "Krisen," in *Handwörterbuch der Staatswissenschaften*, 4th ed., vol. 6 (1925), p. 81.

(which are not themselves open to further economic explanation, and must therefore be regarded as changes of data) within the limits in which they are actually observed can possibly create the typical disturbances with which trade cycle theory is concerned.[36]

Where, then, according to these theories, may we find the reason for this genesis of disequilibrating disturbances in the processes of saving and investment? We will keep to the basis of Spiethoff's theory, which is certainly the most complete of its kind. We may disregard his simple reference to the "complexity of capital relations," for it does not in itself provide an explanation. The main basis of his explanation is to be found in the following sentence: "If capitalists and producers of immediate consumption goods want to keep their production in step with the supply of acquisitive loan capital, these processes should be *consciously adjusted to one another*."[37] But the creation of acquisitive loan capital ensues independently of the production of intermediate goods and durable capital goods; and conversely, the latter can be produced without the entrepreneur knowing the extent to which acquisitive capital (i.e., savings) exists and is available for investment; and thus there is always a danger that one of these processes may lag behind while the other hastens forward. This reference to the entrepreneur's ignorance of the situation belongs, however, to that category of explanation that we had to reject earlier. Instead of showing why prices—and in this case, particularly, the price of capital, which is interest—do not fulfill, or fail to

---

[36] It is, however, not inconceivable, theoretically, that sudden and violent fluctuations in the volume of saving might give rise to the phenomena of a crisis during their downward swings. On this point, see below chap. 5, p. 111.

[37] Spiethoff, "Krisen," p. 76. My italics. The same general view, though in a somewhat different connection, has since been expressed by Mr. J.M. Keynes in several passages of his *Treatise on Money* (2 vols.; London: Macmillan, 1930). Cf., for example, vol. 1, p. 175 and esp. p. 279: "There is, indeed, no possibility of intelligent foresight designed to equate savings and investment unless it is exercised by the banking system."

fulfill adequately, their normal function of regulating the volume of production, it unexpectedly overlooks the fact that the extent of production is regulated on the basis not of a knowledge of demand but through price determination. Assuming that the rate of interest always determines the point to which the available volume of savings enables productive plant to be extended—and it is only by this assumption that we can explain what determines the rate of interest at all—any allegations of a discrepancy between savings and investments must be backed up by a demonstration why, in the given case, interest does not fulfill this function.[38] Professor Spiethoff, like most of the theorists of this group, evades this necessary issue—as we shall see later—by introducing another assumption of crucial importance. It is only by means of this assumption that the causes that he particularly enumerates in his analysis gain significance as an explanation; and therefore it should not have been treated as a self-evident condition, to be casually mentioned, but as the starting point of the whole theoretical analysis.

VII

Before going into this question, however, we must turn our attention to the importance in trade cycle theory of *errors of forecast,* and, in connection with these, to a third group of theories that have not been considered up to now: the *psychological theories*. Here, as elsewhere in our investigations, we shall only be concerned with those theories that are *endogenous*—i.e., which explain the origin of general under- and overestimation from the economic situation itself, and not from some external circumstance such as weather changes, etc. As we said earlier, fluctuations of economic activity that merely represent an adjustment to

---

[38] Elements of the same reasoning can also be found in G. Cassel, *Theory of Social Economy,* 4th German ed. (1927), p. 575; when he derives high conjuncture from an overestimate of the supply of capital (i.e., savings) which is available to take over the supply of real capital produced.

corresponding changes in external circumstances present no problem to economic theory. The various psychological factors cited are only relevant to our analysis insofar as they can cast light on its central problem: that is, how an overestimate of future demand can occasion a development of the productive apparatus so excessive as automatically to lead to a reaction, unprecipitated by other psychological changes. Those who are familiar with the most distinguished of these theories, that of Professor A.C. Pigou (which, owing to lack of space, cannot be reproduced here)[39] will see at once that the endogenous psychological theories are open to the same objections as the two groups of theories we have already examined. Professor Pigou does not explain why errors should arise in estimating the effect, on the price of the final product, of an increase in demand or a fall in cost; or, if the estimate is correct, why the readjustment of the prices of means of production should not check the expansion of production at the right point. No one would deny, of course, that errors can arise as regards the future movements of particular prices. But it is not permissible to assume without further proof that the equilibrating mechanism of the economic system will begin its work only when the excessively increased product due to these mistaken forecasts actually comes on the market, the disproportional development continuing undisturbed up to that time. At one point or another, all theories that start to explain cyclical fluctuations by miscalculations or ignorance as regards the economic situation fall into the same error as those naïve explanations that base themselves on the "planlessness" of the economic system. They overlook the fact that, in the exchange economy, production is governed by prices, independently of any knowledge of the whole process on the part of individual producers, so that it is only when the pricing process is itself disturbed

---

[39] Cf. A.C. Pigou, *Industrial Fluctuations* (London: Macmillan, 1927; 2nd ed. 1929), and also O. Morgenstern, "Qualitative und Quantitative Konjunkturforschung," *Zeitschrift für die gesamte Staatswissenschaft* 84 (1928).

that a misdirection of production can occur. The "wrong" prices, on the other hand, which lead to "wrong" dispositions, cannot in turn be explained by a mistake. Within the framework of a system of explanations in which, as in all modern economic theory, prices are merely expressions of a necessary tendency toward a state of equilibrium, it is not permissible to reintroduce the old Sismondian idea of the misleading effect of prices on production without first bringing it into line with the fundamental system of explanation.

VIII

It is perhaps scarcely necessary to point out that all the objections raised against the non-monetary theories, already cited in our investigations, are justified by one particular assumption that we had to make in order to examine the independent validity of the so-called "real" explanations. In order to see whether the "real" causes (whose effect is always emphasized as a proof that monetary changes are not the cause of cyclical fluctuations) can provide a sufficient explanation of the cycle, it has been necessary to study their operation under conditions of pure barter. And even if it were impossible to prove fully that, under these conditions, no non-monetary explanation is sufficient, enough has been said, I think, to indicate the general trend of thought which would refute all theories based exclusively on productive, market, financial, or psychological phenomena. None of these phenomena can help us to dissolve the fundamental equilibrium relationships that form the basis of all economic explanation. And this dissolution is indispensable if we are to protect ourselves against objections such as those outlined above.

If the various theories comprised in these groups are still able to offer a plausible explanation of cyclical fluctuations, and if their authors do not realize the contradictions involved, this is due to the unconscious importation of an assumption incompatible with a purely "real" explanation. This assumption is adequate to dissolve the rigid reaction mechanisms of barter economy, and thus makes possible the processes described; but for this very reason it should not be treated as a self-evident condition, but as the basis of the explanation itself. The condition thus tacitly assumed—and one can easily prove that it is in fact assumed in all the theories examined above—is *the existence of credit* which, within reasonable limits, is always at the entrepreneur's disposal at an unchanged price. This, however, assumes the absence of the most important controls that, in the barter economy, keep the extension of the productive apparatus within economically permissible limits. *Once we assume that, even at a single point, the pricing process fails to equilibrate supply and demand, so that over a more or less long period, demand may be satisfied at prices at which the available supply is inadequate to meet total demand, then the march of economic events loses its determinateness and a range of indeterminateness appears, within which movements can originate leading away from equilibrium.* And it is rightly assumed, as we shall see later on, that it is precisely the behavior of interest, the price of credit, which makes possible these disturbances in price formation. We must not, however, overlook the fact that the range of indeterminateness thus created is "indeterminate" only in relation to the absolute determinateness of barter economy. The new price formation, together with the new structure of production determined by it, must in turn conform to certain laws, and the apparent indeterminateness does not imply unfettered mobility of prices and production. On the contrary, *every departure from the original equilibrium position is definitely determined by the new conditioning factor.* But if it is the existence of credit that makes these various disturbances possible, and if the volume and direction of new credit determine the extent of deviations from the equilibrium position, it is clearly not permissible to regard credit as a kind of passive element, and its presence as a self-evident condition. One must regard it rather as the new determining factor whose appearance causes these deviations and whose effects must form our starting point when deducing all those phenomena that can be observed in cyclical fluctuations. Only when we have succeeded in doing this can we claim to have explained the phenomena described.

The neglect to derive the appearance of disproportionality from this condition, which must be assumed in order to keep the argument within the framework of equilibrium theory, leads to certain consequences that are best exemplified in the work of Professor Spiethoff. For, in his theory, all-important interconnections are worked out in the fullest detail and none of the observed phenomena remains unaccounted for. But he is not able to deduce the various phenomena described from the single factor which, by virtue of its role in disturbing the interrelationships of general equilibrium, should form the basis of his explanation. At each stage of his exposition he calls in experience to back him up and to show what deviations from the equilibrium position actually occur within the given range of indeterminateness. Consequently it never becomes clear why these phenomena *must* always occur as they are described; and there always remains a possibility that, on some other occasion, they may occur in a different way, or in a different order, without his being able to account for this difference on the basis of his exposition. In other words, the latter, however accurately and pertinently it describes the observed phenomena, does not qualify as a theory in the rigid sense of the word, for it does not set out those conditions in whose presence events *must* follow a scientifically determined course.

IX

Although there is no doubt that all non-monetary trade cycle theories tacitly assume that the production of capital goods has been made possible by the creation of new credit, and although this condition is often emphasized in the course of the exposition,[40] no one has yet proved that this circumstance should form the exclusive basis of the explanation. As far as strict logic is

---

[40] Cf. Spiethoff, "Krisen," pp. 77–78 and 81.

concerned, it would not be impossible for such theories to make use of some other assumption that is capable of dissolving the rigid interrelationships of equilibrium and, therefore, of forming the basis of an exact theoretical analysis. But once we assume the existence of credit in our explanation, we can attack the problem by seeing how far the objections raised earlier against the validity of the various theories under a barter economy are invalidated when the new assumption is made. Then we shall also be able to determine whether this assumption has necessarily to be made in the usual form, or whether it only represents a special instance of a far more widely significant extension of the assumptions of elementary theory.

The question we have to ask ourselves is: what new price-determining factor is introduced by the assumption of a credit supply that can be enlarged while other conditions remain unchanged—a factor capable of deflecting the tendency toward the establishment of equilibrium between supply and demand? Whether we necessarily accept the answer that, to my mind, is the only possible one depends on whether we agree with a certain basic proposition, which could only be briefly outlined here and whose full proof could only be given within the framework of a complete system of pure economics; namely, the proposition that, in a barter economy, interest forms a sufficient regulator for the proportional development of the production of capital goods and consumption goods, respectively. If it is admitted that, in the absence of money, interest would effectively prevent any excessive extension of the production of production goods, by keeping it within the limits of the available supply of savings, and that an extension of the stock of capital goods that is based on a voluntary postponement of consumers' demand into the future can never lead to disproportionate extensions, then it must also necessarily be admitted that disproportional developments in the production of capital goods can arise only through the independence of the supply of free money capital from the accumulation of savings, which in turn arises from the elasticity of the volume of money.[41] Every change in the volume of means of circulation is, in fact, an event to be distinguished from all other real causes, for the purpose of theoretical reasoning; for, unlike all others, it implies a loosening of the interrelationships of equilibrium. No change in "real" factors, whether in the amount of available means of production, in consumers' preferences, or elsewhere, can do away with that final identity of total demand and total supply on which every conception of economic equilibrium is based. A change in the volume of money, on the other hand, represents, as it were, a one-sided change in demand, which is not counterbalanced by an equivalent change in supply. Money, being a pure means of exchange, not being wanted by anyone for purposes of consumption, must by its nature always be re-exchanged without ever having entirely fulfilled its purpose; thus when it is present it loosens that finality and "closedness" of the system which is the fundamental assumption of static theory, and leads to phenomena that the closed system of static equilibrium renders inconceivable.[42]

Together with the "closedness" of the system there necessarily disappears the interdependence of all its parts, and thus prices

---

[41] "Volume of money," in this connection, does not mean merely the quantity of money in circulation but the volume of the money stream or the effective circulation (in the usual terminology—quantity *times* velocity of circulation). Even so, certain changes in the effective circulation may have no disturbing effect because of certain compensating changes in business organization. On this point see my *Prices and Production*, Lecture 4.

[42] This dissolution of the "closedness" of the system, arising because a change in the volume of money is a one-sided change in demand unaccompanied by an equivalent change in supply, does not mean of course that Lowe's plea for an "open" system ("Wie ist Konjunkturtheorie überhaupt möglich") has been granted. (Lowe thinks of a system when one or several "independent variables" are drawn in for explanation.) This plea, which one is tempted to believe has been dictated by a desire to free theory from the trammels of exact deduction, has been justly and strongly criticized by E. Carell (*Sozialökonomische Theorie und Konjunkturproblem*, pp. 2 *et seq.* and 115).

become possible which do not operate according to the self-regulating principles of the economic system described by static theory. On the contrary, these prices may elicit movements that not only do not lead to a new equilibrium position but actually create new disturbances of equilibrium. In this way, through the inclusion of money among the basic assumptions of exposition, it becomes possible to deduce *a priori* phenomena such as those observed in cyclical fluctuations. One instance of these disturbances in the price mechanism, brought about by monetary influences—and the one which is most important from the point of view of trade cycle theory—is that putting out of action of the "interest brake" which is taken for granted by the trade cycle theories examined above. How far this circumstance forms a sufficient basis for a theory of the trade cycle is a problem of the concrete elaboration of monetary explanation, and will therefore be dealt with in the next chapter, where we shall examine how far existing monetary theories have already tackled those problems that are relevant to a theory of the trade cycle.

X

The purpose of the foregoing chapter was to show that only the assumption of primary monetary changes can fulfill the fundamentally necessary condition of any theoretical explanation of cyclical fluctuations—a condition not fulfilled by any theory based exclusively on "real" processes. If this is true then at the outset of theoretical exposition, those monetary processes must be recognized as decisive causes. *For we can gain a theoretically unexceptionable explanation of complex phenomena only by first assuming the full activity of the elementary economic interconnections as shown by the equilibrium theory, and then introducing, consciously and successively, just those elements that are capable of relaxing these rigid interrelationships.* All the phenomena that become possible only as a result of this relaxation must then be explained—as consequences of the particular elements, through whose inclusion among the elementary assumptions they become explicable within the framework of general theory. In place of such a theoretical deduction, we often find an assertion, unfounded on any system, of a far-reaching indeterminacy in the economy. Paradoxically stated as it is, this thesis is bound to have a devastating effect on theory; for it involves the sacrifice of any exact theoretical deduction, and the very possibility of a theoretical explanation of economic phenomena is rendered problematic.

Similar objections of a general nature must be leveled against another large group of theories that we have not yet mentioned. This group pays close attention to the monetary interconnections and expressly emphasizes them as a necessary condition for the occurrence of the processes described. But they fail to pass from this realization to the necessary conclusion; to make it a starting point for their theoretical elaboration, from which all other particular phenomena have to be deduced. To this group belongs the theory of Professor J. Schumpeter, and certain "underconsumption theories"[43] notably that of Professor E. Lederer; and, similarly, the various "realistic" theories: that is, those that renounce any unified theoretical deduction, such as those of Professors G. Cassel, J. Lescure, and Wesley Mitchell. With regard to all these semi-monetary explanations, we must ask whether—once we have been compelled to introduce new assumptions foreign to the static system—it is not the first task of a theoretical investigation to examine all the consequences that must necessarily ensue from this new assumption, and, insofar as any phenomena are thus proved to be logically derivable from the latter, to regard them in the course of the exposition as effects of the new condition introduced. Only in this way is it possible to incorporate trade cycle theory into the static system that is the basis of all theoretical economics; and, for this very reason, the monetary elements must be regarded as decisive factors in the

---

[43] For a detailed criticism of a representative specimen of modern underconsumption theories, that of Messrs. W.T. Foster and W. Catchings, see my article on "The 'Paradox' of Saving," *Economica* 32 (May 1931).

explanation of cyclical fluctuations. The contrast therefore can be reduced to a question of theoretical presentation, and it may even seem, when comparing these theories, that the matter of the express recognition of the monetary starting point is one of purely methodological or even terminological importance, having no bearing on the essential solution of the problem. But the same procedure that in one case may only lead to a lapse from theoretical elegance, breaking the unity of the theoretical structure, may in another case lead to the introduction of thoroughly faulty reasoning, against which only a rigid systematical procedure provides an effective security.

CHAPTER 3

Monetary Theories of the Trade Cycle

I

The argument of the foregoing chapters has demonstrated the main reason for the necessity of the monetary approach to trade cycle theory. It arises from the circumstance that the automatic adjustment of supply and demand can only be disturbed when money is introduced into the economic system. This adjustment must be considered, according to the reasoning that it most clearly expressed in Say's *Théorie des Débouchés,* as being always present in a state of natural economy. Every explanation of the trade cycle that uses the methods of economic theory—which of course is only possible through systematic coordination of the former with the fundamental propositions of the latter—must, therefore, start by considering the influences that emanate from the use of money. By following up their results it should be possible to demonstrate the total effect on the economic system, and formulate the result into a coordinated whole. This must be the aim of all theories that set out to explain disturbances in equilibrium, which by their very nature cannot be regarded as immediate consequences of changes in data, but only as arising out of the development of the economic system itself. For that typical form of disturbance that experience shows to be regularly recurrent, and which can properly be called the trade cycle, the influence of money should be sought in the fact that when the volume of money is elastic, there may exist a lack of rigidity in the relationship between saving and the creation of real capital. This is a fact that nearly all the theories of the disproportional production of capital goods are agreed in emphasizing. It is, therefore, the first task of monetary trade cycle theory to show why and how monetary influences directly bring about regular disturbances in just this part of the economic system.

II

Naturally no attempt will be made at this stage to present such a theory systematically. This chapter is concerned with one particular task: it attempts to show how far existing monetary theories have already gone toward a satisfactory solution of the problem of the trade cycle, and what corrections are needed in order to invalidate certain objections that, up to the present, have appeared well founded.

It should already be clear that what we expect from a monetary trade cycle theory differs considerably from what most of the monetary trade cycle theories regard as the essential aim of their explanation. We are in no way concerned to explain the effect of the monetary factor on trade fluctuations through changes in the value of money and variations in the price level—subjects that form the main basis of current monetary theories. We expect such an explanation to emerge rather from a study of all the changes originating in the monetary field—more especially, variations in its quantity—changes that are bound to disturb the equilibrium interrelationships existing in the natural economy, *whether the disturbance shows itself in a change in the so-called "general value of money" or not.* Our plea for a monetary approach to all trade cycle theory does not, therefore, imply that henceforward such theories should be exclusively, or even principally, based on those arguments that usually predominate in writings on money, and that set out to explain the general level of prices and alterations in the "value of money." On the contrary, monetary theory should not merely be concerned with money for its own sake, but should also study those phenomena that distinguish the money economy from the equilibrium interrelationships of barter economy that must always be assumed by "pure economies."

It must of course be admitted that many trade cycle theorists regard the importance of monetary theory as residing precisely in its ability to explain the cause of fluctuations by reference to changes in the general price level. Hence, it is not difficult to understand why certain economists believe that, once they have rejected this view, they have settled once and for all with the monetary explanations of the trade cycle. It is not surprising that monetary theories of the trade cycle should be rejected by those who, like Professor A. Spiethoff in his well-known work on the quantity theory as *"Haussetheorie,"*[44] identify them with the naïve quantity theory explanations that derive fluctuations from changes in the price level.[45] Against such a conception it can rightly be urged that there are a number of phenomena tending to bring about fluctuations, which certainly do not depend on changes in the value of money, and which can, in fact, exert a disturbing effect on the economic equilibrium without these changes occurring at all. Again, in spite of many assertions to the

---

[44] "Die Quantitätstheorie, insbesondere in ihrer Verwertbarkeit als Haussetheorie," *Festgaben für A. Wagner zur 70 Wiederkehr seines Geburtstages* (Leipzig: Hinrich, 1905), pp. 299 *et seq.*

[45] F. Burchardt, A. Lowe, and other more recent critics of monetary trade cycle theory, also fall within this category. They recognize no other kind of monetary influence than that which manifests itself through changes in the price level; and as a result of this undoubtedly false conception they quite definitely conclude that there can be no such thing as pure monetary trade cycle theory. In their view the theories that are usually so called nearly always depend, in fact, on what they regard as non-monetary factors.

contrary, fluctuations in the general price level need not always be ascribed to monetary causes.[46]

III

But theories that explain the trade cycle in terms of fluctuations in the general price level must be rejected not only because they fail to show why the monetary factor disturbs the general equilibrium, but also because their fundamental hypothesis is, from a theoretical standpoint, every bit as naïve as that of those theories which entirely neglect the influence of money. They start off with a "normal position" which, however, has nothing to do with the normal position obtaining in the static state; and they are based on a postulate, the postulate of a constant price level, which, if fulfilled, suffices in itself to break down the interrelationships of equilibrium. All these theories, indeed, are based on the idea—quite groundless but hitherto virtually unchallenged—that if only the value of money does not change, it ceases to exert a direct and independent influence on the economic system. But this assumption (which is present, more or less, in the work of all monetary theorists), so far from being the necessary starting point for all trade cycle theory, is perhaps the greatest existing hindrance to a successful examination of the course of cyclical fluctuations. It forces us to assume variations in the effective quantity of money as given. Such variations, however, always dissolve the equilibrium interrelationships

---

[46] The assertion that changes in the *general* level of prices must always originate on the monetary side, as is argued for example by Professors G. Cassel and Irving Fisher, obviously depends on circular reasoning. It starts from the postulate that the amount of money must be adjusted to changes in the volume of trade in such a way that the price level shall remain unchanged. *If it is not, and the volume of money remains unaltered, then,* according to this remarkable argument, *the latter becomes the cause* (!) of changes in the price level. This statement is made quite baldly by Professor G. Cassel in his book *Money and Foreign Exchange After 1914* (London: Constable, 1922).

described by static theory; but they must necessarily be assumed if the value of money is to remain constant despite changes in data; and therefore they cannot be used to explain deviations from the course of events which static theory lays down. The only proper starting point for any explanation based on equilibrium theory must be the effect of a change in the volume of money; for this, in itself, constitutes a new state of affairs, entirely different from that generally treated within the framework of static theory.

In complete contrast to those economic changes conditioned by "real" forces, influencing simultaneously total supply and total demand, changes in the volume of money have, so to speak, a one-sided influence that elicits no reciprocal adjustment in the economic activity of different individuals. By deflecting a single factor, without simultaneously eliciting corresponding changes in other parts of the system, it dissolves its "closedness," makes a breach in the rigid reaction mechanism of the system (which rests on the ultimate identity of supply and demand) and opens a way for tendencies leading away from the equilibrium position. As a theory of these one-sided influences, the theory of monetary economy should, therefore, be able to explain the occurrence of phenomena that would be inconceivable in the barter economy, and notably the disproportional developments that give rise to crises.[47] A starting point for such explanations should be found in the possibility of alterations in the quantity of money occurring automatically and in the normal course of events, under the present organization of money and credit, without the need for violent or artificial action by any external agency.

---

[47] F. Wieser in "Der Geldwert und seine geschichtlichen Veränderungen," *Zeitschrift für Volkswirtschaft Sozialpolitik und Verwaltung* 13 (1904): 57, reprinted in F. Wieser, *Abhandlungen* (Tubingen: Mohr, 1929), p. 178, has dealt with the special effects of a "one-sided money supply."

IV

Even if a systematic treatment of the trade cycle problem has not yet been forthcoming, it should be noted that, throughout the different attempts at monetary explanation, there runs a secondary idea that is closely allied to that of the direct dependence of fluctuations on changes in the value of money. It is true that this idea is used merely as a subordinate device or technique to assist in the explanation of fluctuations in the value of money. But its development included the analysis of the most important elements in the monetary factors chiefly connected with the trade cycle. This was done in the teaching that began with H. Thornton[48] and D. Ricardo[49] and was taken up again by H.D. Macleod,[50] H. Sidgwick, R. Giffen, and J.S. Nicholson,[51] and finally developed by A. Marshall,[52]

---

[48] *An Enquiry into the Nature and Effects of the Paper Credit of Great Britain* (London: J. Hatchard, 1802), esp. pp. 287 *et seq*. This is one of the most remarkable accomplishments in monetary theory, and still commands great attention; cf. the references to it by K. Wicksell in the preface to the second volume of his *Vorlesungen über Nationalökonomie auf Grundlage des Marginalprinzipes* (Jena: Gustav Fischer, 1922), p. xii; and Burchardt, *op. cit*. For a fuller discussion of these earlier theories, see my *Prices and Production*, p. 11 f; p. 205 in this volume.

[49] Cf. "The high price of bullion" (*Economic Essays*, ed. E.K.C. Gonner [London: G. Bell and Sons, 1923], p. 35), where Ricardo says that "interest would, during that interval be *under its natural level*," and also chap. 27 of his *Principles* (included in *The Works of David Ricardo*, ed. J.R. McCulloch [London" John Murray, 1846], p. 220), which for a long time have passed almost unnoticed but which already contained much of what is set out in later theories.

[50] *Theory and Practice of Banking* (London: Longmans, Green, Reader and Dyer, 1855) and later editions. See particularly vol. 2, pp. 278 *et seq*.

[51] For H. Sidgwick, R. Giffen, and J.S. Nicholson, cf. J.W. Angell's *Theory of International Prices: History, Criticism and Restatement* (Cambridge, Mass.: Harvard University Press, 1926), pp. 117–22.

[52] Cf. his evidence before the various Parliamentary Commissions, which is collected in the volume *Official Papers by Alfred Marshall* (London: Macmillan,

K. Wicksell,[53] and L. v. Mises,[54] whose works trace the development of the effects on the structure of production of a rate of interest that alters relatively to the equilibrium rate, as a result of monetary influences. For the purpose of this review it is unnecessary to go back to the earlier representatives of this group; it is enough to consider the conceptions of Wicksell and Mises, since both the recent improvements that have been effected and the errors that still subsist can be best examined on the basis of these studies.[55]

It must be taken for granted that the reader is acquainted with the works of both Wicksell and Mises. Wicksell, from the outset,[56] regards the problem as concerning explicitly the *average* change in the price of goods, which from the theoretical standpoint is quite irrelevant. He starts from the hypothesis

---

1926), esp. pp. 38–41, 45, 46 *et seq.*, 273 *et seq.*, as well as the later account in *Money, Credit, and Commerce* (London: Macmillan, 1926), pp. 255–56.

[53] Especially in *Geldzins und Güterpreise* (Jena: Gustav Fischer, 1898), as well as in the second volume of his later *Vorlesungen,* already quoted, which has not had the influence it deserved, mainly on account of the exceedingly bad German translation in which it appeared. I had unfortunately no means of access to the other Swedish works connected with that of Wicksell, which should certainly not be overlooked if one is to achieve a complete survey of the development of this theory.

[54] *Theorie des Geldes und der Umlaufsmittel,* 1st ed. (Munich: Duncker & Humblot, 1912; 2nd ed., 1924); also the more recent *Geldwertstabilisierung und Konjunkturpolitik* (Jena: Gustav Fischer, 1928).

[55] Professor A. Hahn, whose views regarding trade cycle theory (put forward in *Volkswirtschaftlichen Theorie des Bankkredits* [Tübingen: Mohr, 1920]) are in some respects similar to those of Professor Mises, cannot be considered here, since we are unable to follow him in all those points in which he differs from the latter. Similar theories have also been put forward quite recently by Professors W. Röpke and S. Budge.

[56] See, e.g., *Geldzins und Güterpreise,* p. 125.

that, in the absence of disturbing monetary influences, the average price level must remain unchanged. This assumption is based on another, only incidentally expressed,[57] which is not worked out and which, from the point of view of most of the problems dealt with, is not even permissible; the assumption of a stationary state of the economy. His fundamental thesis is that when the money rate of interest coincides with the natural rate (i.e., that rate which exactly balances the demand for loan capital and the supply of savings)[58] then money bears a completely *neutral* relationship to the price of goods, and tends neither to raise nor to lower it. But, owing to the nature of his basic assumptions, this thesis enables him to show deductively only that every lag of the money rate behind the natural rate must lead to a rise in the general price level, and every increase of the money rate above the natural rate to a fall in general price level. It is only incidentally, in the course of his analysis of the effects on the price level of a money rate of interest differing from the natural rate, that Wicksell touches on the consequences of such a distortion of the natural price formation (made possible by elasticity in the volume of currency) on the development of particular branches of production; and it is this question that is of the most decisive importance to trade cycle theory. If one were to make a systematic attempt to coordinate these ideas into an explanation of the trade cycle (dropping, as is essential, the assumption of the stationary state), a curious contradiction would arise. On the one hand, we are told that *the price level remains unaltered when the money rate of interest is the same as the natural rate;* and, on the other, that *the production of capital goods is, at the same time, kept within the limits imposed by the supply of real savings.* One need say no more in order to show that there are cases—certainly all cases of an expanding

---

[57] Ibid., p. 126.

[58] Ibid., p. 93 and also *Vorlesungen*, vol. 2, p. 220.

economy, which are those most relevant to trade cycle theory—in which the rate of interest that equilibrates the supply of real savings and the demand for capital cannot be the rate of interest that also prevents changes in the price level.[59] In this case, stability of the price level presupposes changes in the volume of money; but these changes must always lead to a discrepancy between the amount of real savings and the volume of investment. *The rate of interest at which, in an expanding economy, the amount of new money entering circulation is just sufficient to keep the price level stable, is always lower than the rate that would keep the amount of available loan capital equal to the amount simultaneously saved by the public;* and thus, despite the stability of the price level, it makes possible a development leading away from the equilibrium position. But Wicksell does not recognize here a monetary influence tending, independently of changes in the price level, to break down the equilibrium system of barter economics; so long as the stability of the price level is undisturbed, everything appears to him to be in order.[60] Obsessed by the notion that the only aim of monetary theory is to explain those phenomena that cause the value of money to alter, he thinks himself justified in neglecting all deviations of the processes of money economy from those of barter economy, so long as they throw no direct light on the determination of the value of money; and thus he shuts the door on the possibility of a general theory covering all the consequences of the phenomena he indicates.[61] But although his thesis of a direct relationship between

---

[59] Similarly also W. Eucken, *Schriften des Vereins für Sozialpolitik* 175, pp. 300 et seq.

[60] Wicksell's justification of this view in *Geldzins und Güterpreise* (see p. 97) is incomprehensible to me.

[61] R. Stucken in his *Theorie der Konjunkturschwankungen* (Jena: Gustav Fisher, 1926), p. 26, was one of the first to draw attention to the fact that the relation, indicated by Wicksell, between a money rate of interest diverging from

movements in the price level and deviations of the money rate of interest from its natural level, holds good only in a stationary state, and is therefore inadequate for an explanation of cyclical fluctuations, his account of the effects of this deviation on the price structure and the development of the various branches of production constitutes the most important basis for any future monetary trade cycle theory. But this future theory, unlike that of Wicksell, will have to examine not movements in the general price level but rather those deviations of particular prices from their equilibrium position that were caused by the monetary factor.

V

The investigations of Professor Mises represent a big step forward in this direction, although he still regards the fluctuations in the value of money as the main object of his explanation, and deals with the phenomena of disproportionality only insofar as they can be regarded as consequences—in the widest sense of the term—of these fluctuations. But Professor Mises's conception of

---

the natural rate, and movements in the price level only exists in a stationary economy; while, if the flow of goods is increasing, only an addition to purchasing power can secure stability in the price level. He remains, however, entirely steeped in the prevalent opinion that a stable price level is indispensable to undisturbed economic development, and therefore holds that the additional money necessary to secure that condition cannot be regarded as an element of disturbance in the economic process. Similarly Mr. D.H. Robertson pointed out at about the same time (*Banking Policy and the Price Level* [London: P.S. King, 1926], p. 99) that the rate of interest that keeps the price level stable need not coincide with that which equates the supply of savings with the demand for capital. I am now informed that, even before the war, this objection formed the basis of a criticism directed by Professor David Davidson of Upsala against Wicksell's theory. Professor Davidson's article and the subsequent discussion with Wicksell in the Swedish *Economisk Tidskrift* are, however, inaccessible to me.

the intrinsic value of money extends the notion of "fluctuations in money value" far beyond the limits of what this term is commonly understood to mean; and so he is in a position to describe within the framework, or rather under the name, of a theory of fluctuations in the value of money, all monetary influences on price formation.[62] His exposition already contains an account of practically all those effects of a rate of interest altered through monetary influences, which are important for an explanation of

---

[62] If one follows C. Menger and now Professor Mises in disregarding ordinary usage and including in the theory of the value of money *all* influences of money on prices, instead of restricting it to an explanation of the general purchasing power of money (by which is understood the absolute level of money prices as distinct from the relative prices of particular goods) then it is correct to say that any economic theory of money must be a theory of the value of money. But this use of the phrase is hardly opportune, for "value of money" is usually taken to mean "general purchasing power," while *monetary theory has by no means finished its work when it has explained the absolute level of prices (or, as Wicksell would call it, the "concrete" level); its far more important task is to explain those changes in the relative height of particular prices which are conditioned by the introduction of money.* On the other hand, to avoid any possible misunderstanding we must particularly insist at this point that in the sense of the famous contrast between such nominalistic theories as the "state theory" of Knapp, and the catallactic theories in general, the monetary theory we are seeking will also have to be exclusively a "theory of money values." In justice to Menger and Mises, it should be pointed out that what they mean when they speak of the stability of the "inner" value of money, has nothing to do with any measurable value, in the sense of some price level; but is only another and, as it seems to me, misleading, expression for what I now prefer to call neutrality of money. (Cf. my *Prices and Production*, pp. 27–28; and pp. 217–19 in this volume, and *passim*.) This expression, first used by Wicksell in the passage quoted earlier in the text, has of late become fairly common in German and Dutch writings on money. Cf. L. v. Bortkiewicz, *Die Frage der Reform unserer Währung* 6 (1919): 57–59; W.G. Behrens, *Das Geldschöpfungsproblem* (Jena: Gustav Fischer, 1928), pp. 228 *et seq.*, 286 and 312; G.M. Verrijin Stuart and J.G. Koopmans in the reports and discussions of the 1929 meeting of the "Vereinigung voor de Staathuishoudkunde en de Statistik."

the course of the trade cycle. Thus he describes the disproportionate development of various branches of production and the resulting changes in the income structure. And yet this presentation of his theory under the guise of a theory of fluctuation in the value of money remains dangerous, partly because it always gives rise to misunderstandings, but mainly because it seems to bring into the foreground a secondary effect of cyclical fluctuations, an effect that generally accompanies the latter but need not necessarily do so.

This is no place to examine the extent to which Professor Mises escapes from this difficulty by using the concept of the inner objective value of money. For us, the only point of importance is that the effects of an artificially lowered rate of interest, pointed out by Wicksell and Mises, exist whether this same circumstance does or does not eventually react on the general value of money, in the sense of its purchasing power. Therefore they must be dealt with independently if they are to be properly understood.[63] Increases in the volume of circulation, which in an expanding economy serve to prevent a drop in the price level, present a typical instance of a change in the monetary factor calculated to cause a discrepancy between the money and natural rate of interest without affecting the price level. These changes are consequently neglected, as a rule, in dealing with phenomena of disproportionality; but they are bound to lead to a distribution of productive resources between capital goods and consumption goods that differs from the equilibrium distribution, just as those changes in the monetary factor that do manifest themselves in changes in the price level. This case is particularly important, because under contemporary currency systems, the automatic

---

[63] Professor Mises recently admitted this, in principle, when he explicitly emphasized the fact that *every* new issue of circulating media brings about a lowering of the money rate of interest in relation to the natural rate (*Geldwertstabilisierung und Konjunkturpolitik*, p. 57).

adjustment of the value of money in the form of a flow of precious metals will regularly make available new supplies of purchasing power that will depress the money rate of interest below its natural level.[64]

Since a stable price level has been regarded as normal hitherto, far too little investigation has been made into the effects of these changes in the volume of money, which necessarily cause a development different from that which would be expected on the basis of static theory and which lead to the establishment of a structure of production incapable of perpetuating itself once the change in the monetary factor has ceased to operate. Economists have overlooked the fact that the changes in the volume of money, which, in an expanding economy, are necessary to maintain price stability, lead to a new state of affairs foreign to static analysis, so that the development that occurs under a stable price level cannot be regarded as consonant with static laws. Thus the disturbances described as resulting from changes in the *value* of money form only a small part of the much wider category of deviations from the static course of events brought about by changes in the volume of money—which may often exist without changes in the *value* of money, while they may also fail to accompany changes in value of money when the latter occur.

VI

As has been briefly indicated above, most of the objections raised against monetary theories of cyclical fluctuations rest on the mistaken idea that their significant contribution consists in deducing changes in the volume of production from the movement of prices *en bloc*. In particular, the very extensive criticism recently leveled by Dr. Burchardt and Professor Lowe against

---

[64] Cf. also my article, "Das intertemporale Gleichgewichtssystem der Preise und die Bewegungen des Geldwertes."

monetary trade cycle theory is based throughout on the idea that this theory must start from the wave-like fluctuations of the price level, which are conditioned mainly by monetary causes; the rise, as well as the fall, of the price level being brought about by particular new forces originating on the side of money. It is only through this special assumption, which is also stated explicitly, that Professor Lowe's systematic presentation of his objections in his latest work[65] becomes comprehensible; he is completely misleading when he asserts that, if it is to raise the monetary factor to the rank of a *conditio sine qua non* of the trade cycle, monetary theory ought to prove that the effectiveness of all non-monetary factors depends on a previous price boom.[66] We have already shown that it is not even necessary, in order to ascribe the cause of cyclical fluctuations to monetary changes, to assume that these monetary causes act through changes in the general price level. It is therefore impossible to maintain that the importance of monetary theories lies solely in an explanation of price cycles.[67]

But even the essential point in the criticism of Lowe and Burchardt—the assertion that all monetary theories explain the transition from boom to depression not in terms of monetary causes but in terms of other causes super-added to the monetary explanation—rests exclusively on the idea that only general price changes can be recognized as monetary effects. But general price changes are no essential feature of a monetary theory of the trade cycle; *they are not only unessential, but they would be completely irrelevant if only they were completely "general"—that is, if they affected all prices at the same time and in the same proportion.* The point of real interest to trade cycle theory is the existence of certain deviations in individual price relations occurring because

---

[65] "Über den Einfluss monetärer Faktoren auf den Konjunkturzyklus," pp. 361–68.

[66] Ibid., p. 366.

[67] As is maintained by Professor Lowe ("Wie ist Konjunkturtheorie überhaupt möglich," p. 364).

changes in the volume of money appear at certain individual points; deviations, that is, away from the position that is necessary to maintain the whole system in equilibrium. Every disturbance of the equilibrium of prices leads *necessarily* to shifts in the structure of production, which must therefore be regarded as consequences of monetary change, never as additional separate assumptions. The nature of the changes in the composition of the existing stock of goods, which are effected through such monetary changes, depends of course on the point at which the money is injected into the economic system.

There is no doubt that the emphasis placed on this phenomenon marks the most important advance made by monetary science beyond the elementary truths of the quantity theory. Monetary theory no longer rests content with determining the final reaction of a given monetary cause on the purchasing power of money, but attempts instead to trace the successive alterations in particular prices, which eventually bring about a change in the whole price system.[68] The assumption of a "time lag" between the successive changes in various prices has not been spun out of thin air solely for the purposes of trade cycle theory; it is a correction, based on systematic reasoning, of the mistaken conceptions of older monetary theories.[69] Of course, the expression "time lag," borrowed from Anglo-American writers and denoting a temporary lagging behind of the changes in the price of some goods relatively to the changes in the price of other goods, is a very unsuitable expression when the shifts in relative prices are due to

---

[68] On the development of this point of view, see chap. 1 of my *Prices and Production*.

[69] We cannot, therefore, regard Mises's pronouncement at the Zurich debate of the Verein für Sozialpolitik as a surrender of the monetary standpoint. On this occasion, he not only admitted but indeed emphasized the fact that monetary causes can only act by producing a "lag" between various prices, wages, and interest rates. (Cf. "Verhandlungen des Vereins für Sozialpolitik in Zurich," *Schriften des Vereins für Sozialpolitik* 175 [1929].)

changes in demand that are themselves conditioned by monetary changes. For such shifts are bound to continue so long as the change in demand persists. They disappear only with the disappearance of the disturbing monetary factor. They cease when money ceases to increase or diminish further; *not*, however, when the increase or diminution has itself been wiped out. But, whatever expression we may use to denote these changes in relative prices and the changes in the structure of production conditioned by them, there can be no doubt that they are, in turn, conditioned by monetary causes, which alone make them possible.

The only plausible objection to this argument would be that the shifts in price relationships occurring at any point in the economic system could not possibly cause those typical, regularly recurring, shifts in the structure of production that we observe in cyclical fluctuations. In opposition to this view, as we shall show in more detail later, it can be urged that those changes that are constantly taking place in our money and credit organization cause a certain price—the rate of interest—to deviate from the equilibrium position, and that deviations of this kind *necessarily* lead to such changes in the relative position of the various branches of production as are bound later to precipitate the crisis.[70] There is one important point, however, that must be emphasized against the above-named critics; namely, that it is not only when the crisis is directly occasioned by a new monetary factor, separate from that which originally brought about the boom, that it is to be regarded as conditioned by monetary causes. Once the monetary causes have brought about that development in the

---

[70] It is not essential, as Burchardt maintains (*op. cit.*, p. 124) to base this analysis on any particular theory of interest, such as that of Böhm-Bawerk; it is equally consonant with all modern interest theories. The reason why, under the circumstances assumed, interest fails to equilibrate production for the future and production for the present, is bound up not with the special form in which interest in general is explained, but with the deviations, due to monetary causes, of the current rate of interest from the equilibrium rate.

whole economic system, which is known as a boom, sufficient forces have already been set in motion to ensure that, sooner or later, when the monetary influence has ceased to operate, a crisis must occur. The "cause" of the crisis is, then, the disequilibrium of the whole economy occasioned by monetary changes and maintained through a longer period, possibly, by a succession of further monetary changes—a disequilibrium the origin of which can only be explained by monetary disturbances.

Professor Lowe's most important argument against the monetary theory of the trade cycle—an argument that, so far as most existing monetary theories are concerned, is unquestionably valid—will be discussed in more detail later. The sole purpose of the next chapter of this book is to show that the cycle is not only due to "mistaken measures by monopolistic bodies" (as Professor Lowe assumes),[71] but that the reason for its continuous recurrence lies in an "immanent necessity of the monetary and credit mechanism."

VII

Among the phenomena that are fundamentally independent of changes in the value of money, we must include, first of all, the effects of a rate of interest lowered by monetary influences, which must necessarily lead to the excessive production of capital goods. Wicksell and Mises both rightly emphasize the decisive importance of this factor in the explanation of cyclical phenomena, as its effect will occur even when the increase in circulation is only just sufficient to prevent a fall in the price level. Besides this, there exist a number of other phenomena, by virtue of which a money economy (in the sense of an economy with a variable money supply) differs from a static economy, which for this reason are important for a true understanding of the course of the trade cycle. They have been partly described already by Mises, but they can only be clearly

---

[71] "Wie ist Konjunkturtheorie überhaupt möglich," p. 365 *et seq*.

observed by taking as the central subject of investigation not changes in general prices but the divergences of the relation of particular prices as compared with the price system of static equilibrium. Phenomena of this sort include the changes in the relation of costs and selling prices and the consequent fluctuations in profits, which Professors Mitchell and Lescure in particular have made the starting point of their exposition; and the shifts in the distribution of incomes that Professor Lederer investigates—both of these phenomena depending for their explanation on monetary factors,[72] while neither of them can be immediately connected with changes in the general value of money. It is, perhaps, for this very reason that their authors, although perfectly realizing the monetary origin of the phenomena they described, did not present their views as monetary theories. While we cannot attempt here to show the position these phenomena would occupy in a systematically developed trade cycle theory (a task that really involves the development of a new theory, and is unnecessary for the purposes of our present argument) it is not difficult to see that all of them can be logically deduced from an initiating monetary disturbance,[73] which, in any case, we are compelled to assume in studying them. The special advantages of the monetary approach consist precisely in the fact that, by starting from a monetary disturbance, we are able to explain deductively all the different peculiarities observed in the course of the trade cycle, and so to protect ourselves against objections such as were raised in an earlier chapter against non-monetary theories. It makes it possible to look upon empirically recognized interconnections, which would otherwise rival one another as independent clues to an explanation, as necessary consequences of one common cause.

---

[72] That Professor Lederer himself sees this clearly is evident from his analysis, mentioned earlier, contained in the *Grundriss der Sozialökonomik*, pp. 390–91.

[73] Cf. Mises's presentation of the social effects of changes in the value of money, *Theorie des Geldes und der Umlaufsmittel*, pp. 178–200.

Much theoretical work will have to be done before such a theoretical system can be worked out in such detail that all the empirically observed characteristics of the trade cycle can find their explanation within its framework. Up to now, the monetary theories have unduly narrowed the field of phenomena to be explained, by limiting research to those monetary changes that find their expression in changes in the general value of money. Thus they are prevented from showing the deviations of a money economy from a static economy in all their multiplicity. The problem of cyclical fluctuations can only be solved satisfactorily when a theory of the money economy itself—still almost entirely lacking at present—has been evolved, comprising a detailed discussion of all those points in which it differs from the equilibrium analysis worked out on the assumption of a pure barter economy. The full elaboration of this intermediate step of theoretical exposition is indispensable before we can achieve a trade cycle theory, which—as Böhm-Bawerk has expressed it in a phrase, often quoted but hardly ever taken to heart—must constitute the last chapter of the complete theory of social economy.[74] In my opinion, the most important step toward such a theory, which would embrace all new phenomena arising from the addition of money to the conditions assumed in elementary equilibrium theory, would be the emancipation of the theory of money from the restrictions that limit its scope to a discussion of the *value* of money.

VIII

Once, however, we have accomplished this urgently necessary displacement of the problem of monetary value from its present central position in monetary theory, we find ourselves in a position to come to an understanding with the most important

---

[74] This expression occurs in connection with a review of E. v. Bergmann's "Geschichte der Nationalökonomischen Krisentheorien," in *Zeitschrift für Volkswirtschaft, Sozialpolitik und Verwaltung* 7 (1898): 112.

non-monetary theorists of the trade cycle; for the effect of money on the "real" economic processes will automatically be brought more to the surface, while monetary theory will no longer appear to be insisting on the immediate dependence of trade cycle phenomena on changes in the value of money—a claim which is certainly unjustified. On the other hand, a number of non-monetary theories do not question in the least the dependence of the processes they describe on certain monetary assumptions; and in their case, the only conflict now arising concerns the systematic presentation of these. It should be the task of our analysis to show that the placing of the monetary factor in the center of the exposition is necessary in the interest of the unity of the system, and that the various "real" interconnections, which, in certain theories, form the main basis of the explanation, can only find a place in a closed system as consequences of the original monetary influences. There can hardly be any question, in the present state of research, as to what should be the basic idea of a completely developed theory of money. One can abandon those parts of the Wicksell-Mises theory that aim at explaining the movements in the general value of money, and develop to the full the effects of all discrepancies between the natural and money rates of interest on the relative development of the production of capital goods and consumption goods—a theory that has already been largely elaborated by Professor Mises. In this way, one can achieve, by purely deductive methods, the same picture of the process of cyclical fluctuations that the more realistic theories of Spiethoff and Cassel have already deduced from experience. Wicksell himself[75] drew attention to the way in which the processes

---

[75] *Vorlesungen*, vol. 2, p. 238; Wickell's review of Cassel's textbook, which has since appeared in a German translation (Schmollers *Jahrbuch für Volkswirtschaft, Gesetzbebung und Verwaltung* 53 [1928]), shows that, although he rights opposes Cassel's general system, he agrees to a large extent with his theory of the trade cycle.

deduced from his own theory harmonize with the exposition of Spiethoff; and conversely, Spiethoff, in a statement already quoted, has emphasized the fact that the phenomena he describes are all conditioned by a change in monetary factors. But it is only by placing monetary factors first that such expositions as those of Spiethoff and Cassel can be incorporated into the general system of theoretical economics. A final point of decisive importance is that the choice of the monetary starting point enables us to deduce simultaneously all the other phenomena—such as shifts in relative prices and incomes—that are more empirically determined and utilized as independent factors, and thus the relations existing between them can be classified and their relative position and importance determined within the framework of the theory.

Even when these phenomena are, as yet, much further from a satisfactory explanation than are the disproportionalities in the development of production, which are cleared up in a greater degree, there can be no doubt that it will become possible to incorporate them also into a self-sufficient theory of the effects of monetary disturbances. These effects, however, although ultimately caused by monetary factors, do not fall within the narrower field of monetary theory. A well-developed theory of the trade cycle ought to deal thoroughly with them; but as this book is exclusively concerned with the monetary theories themselves, we shall, in the following chapters, only study the reasons why these monetary causes of the trade cycle inevitably recur under the existing system of money and credit organization, and what are the main problems with which future research is faced by reason of the realization of the determining role played by money.

CHAPTER 4

The Fundamental Cause of Cyclical Fluctuations

I

So far we have not answered, or have only hinted at an answer to the question why, under the existing organization of the economic system, we constantly find those deviations of the money rate of interest from the equilibrium rate[76] which, as we have seen, must be regarded as the cause of the periodically recurring disproportionalities in the structure of production. The problem is, then, to discover the gap in the reaction mechanism of the modern economic system that is responsible for the fact that certain changes of data, so far from being followed by a prompt readjustment (i.e., the formation of a new equilibrium) are, actually, the cause of recurrent shifts in economic activity that subsequently have to be reversed before a new equilibrium can be established.

---

[76] The term "equilibrium rate of interest" which, I believe, was introduced into Germany in this connection, by K. Schlesinger in his *Theorie der Geld und Kreditwirtschaft* (Munich and Leipzig: Duncker & Humblot [1914], p. 128) seems to me preferable in this case to the usual expression of "natural rate" or "real rate." Alfred Marshall used the term "equilibrium level" as early as 1887 (cf. *Official Papers of Alfred Marshall,* p. 130). Cf. also the next chapter here.

The analysis of the foregoing chapters has shown that when it is possible to detect, in the organization of our economy, a dislocation in the reaction mechanism described by equilibrium theory, it should be possible (and should, indeed, be the object of a fully developed trade cycle theory) to describe deductively, as a necessary effect of the disturbance—quite apart from their observed occurrence—all the deviations in the course of economic events conditioned by this dislocation. It has been shown, in addition, that the primary cause of cyclical fluctuations must be sought in changes in the volume of money, which are undoubtedly always recurring and which, by their occurrence, always bring about a falsification of the pricing process, and thus a misdirection of production. The new element we are seeking is, therefore, to be found in the "elasticity" of the volume of money at the disposal of the economic system. It is this element whose presence forms the "necessary and sufficient" condition for the emergence of the trade cycle.[77]

The question we now have to examine is whether this elasticity in the volume of money is an immanent characteristic of our present money and credit system; whether, given certain conditions, changes in the volume of money and the resulting differences between the natural and the monetary rate of interest must necessarily occur, or whether they represent, so to speak, casual

---

[77] Mr. R.G. Hawtrey regards the following theses as important for monetary trade cycle theories: (1) That certain monetary and credit movements are necessary and sufficient conditions of the observed phenomena of the trade cycle; and (2) that the periodicity of those phenomena can be explained by purely monetary tendencies which cause the movements to take place successively and to be spread over a considerable period of years ("The Monetary Theory of the Trade Cycle and its Statistical Test," *Quarterly Journal of Economics* 41, no. 3 [May 1927]: 472). This entirely correct definition of Mr. Hawtrey's should have prevented Dr. Burchardt and Professor Lowe, who expressly fasten on this point in their criticism of monetary trade cycle theories, from looking from monetary influences to changes in the general value of money, while disregarding the changes in the distributive process which are conditioned by monetary causes.

phenomena arising from arbitrary interferences by the authorities responsible for the regulation of the volume of currency media. Is it an inherent necessity of the existing monetary and credit system that its reaction to certain changes in data is different from what we should expect on the basis of economic equilibrium theory; or are these discrepancies to be explained by special assumptions regarding the nature of the monetary administration, i.e., by a series of what might be called "political" assumptions? The question whether the recurrence of credit cycles is, or is not, due to an unavoidable characteristic of the existing economic organization, depends on whether the existing monetary and credit organization in itself necessitates changes in the currency media, or whether these are brought about only by the special interference of external agencies. The answer to this question will also decide into which of the most commonly accepted categories a given trade cycle theory is to be placed. We must deal briefly with this point because a false classification, which is largely the fault of the exponents of the monetary theories, has contributed much to make them misunderstood.

II

If we are to understand the present status of monetary theories of the trade cycle, we must pay special attention to the assumptions upon which they are based. At the present day, monetary theories are generally regarded as falling within the class of so-called "exogenous" theories, i.e., theories that look for the cause of the cycle not in the interconnections of economic phenomena themselves but in external interferences. Now it is, no doubt, often a waste of time to discuss the merits of classifying a theory in a given category. But the question of classification becomes important when the inclusion of a theory in one class or another implies, at the same time, a judgment as to the sphere of validity of the theory in question. This is undoubtedly the case with the distinction, very general today, between *endogenous* and *exogenous* theories—a distinction introduced into economic literature some twenty years ago by Bouniatian.[78] Endogenous theories, in the course of their proof, avoid making use of assumptions that cannot either be decided by purely economic considerations, or regarded as general characteristics of our economic system—and hence capable of general proof. Exogenous theories, on the other hand, are based on concrete assertions whose correctness has to be proved separately in each individual case. As compared with an endogenous theory, which, if logically sound, can in a sense lay claim to general validity, an exogenous theory is at some disadvantage, inasmuch as it has, in each case, to justify the assumptions on which its conclusions are based.

Now as far as most contemporary monetary theories of the cycle are concerned, their opponents are undoubtedly right in classifying them, as does Professor Lowe[79] in his discussion of the theories of Professors Mises and Hahn, among the exogenous theories; for they begin with arbitrary interferences on the part of the banks. This is, perhaps, one of the main reasons for the prevailing skepticism concerning the value of such theories. A theory that has to call upon the *deus ex machina*[80] of a false step by bankers, in order to reach its conclusions is, perhaps, inevitably suspect. Yet Professor Mises himself—who is certainly to be regarded as the most respected and consistent exponent of the monetary theory of the trade cycle in Germany—has, in his latest work, afforded ample justification for this view of his theory by attributing the periodic recurrence of the trade cycle to the general tendency of central banks to depress the money rate of interest below the natural rate.[81]

---

[78] *Studien zur Theorie und Geschichte der Wirtschaftskrisen* (Munich, 1908), p. 3.

[79] *Der gegenwärtige Stand der Konjunkturforschung in Deutschland*, p. 349.

[80] Cf. Neisser, *Der Tauschwert des Geldes* (Jena: Gustav Fischer, 1928), p. 161.

[81] While it seems to me that in the analysis of the effects of a money rate of interest diverging from the natural rate, Professor Mises has made considerable progress as compared with the position adopted by Wicksell, the latter succeeded better than Mises did in explaining the origin of this divergence. We shall go into Wicksell's explanation in somewhat more detail below.

Both the protagonists and the opponents of the monetary theory of the trade cycle thus agree in regarding these explanations as falling ultimately within the exogenous and not the endogenous group. The fact that this is not an inherent necessity of the monetary starting point is, however, shown by the undoubtedly endogenous nature of the various older trade cycle theories, such as that of Wicksell. But since this suffers from other deficiencies, which have already been indicated, the question of whether the exogenous character of modern theories is or is not an inherent necessity of their nature remains an open one.[82] It seems to me that this classification of monetary trade cycle theory depends exclusively on the fact that a single especially striking case is treated as the normal, while in fact it is quite unnecessary to adduce interference on the part of the banks in order to bring about a situation of alternating boom and crisis. By disregarding those divergencies between the natural and money rate of interest that arise automatically in the course of economic development, and by emphasizing those caused by an artificial lowering of the money rate, the monetary theory of the trade cycle deprives itself of one of its strongest arguments; namely, the fact that the process it describes *must* always recur under the existing credit organization, and that it thus represents a tendency inherent in the economic system, and is in the fullest sense of the word an *endogenous* theory.

It is an apparently unimportant difference in exposition that leads one to this view that the monetary theory can lay claim to an endogenous position. The situation in which the money rate of interest is below the natural rate need not, by any means, originate in a *deliberate lowering* of the rate of interest by the banks. The same effect can be obviously produced by an improvement in the expectations of profit or by a diminution in the rate of saving,

---

[82] Part of the two following paragraphs repeats word for word my contribution to the discussion on "Credit and the Trade Cycle" at the Zurich Assembly of the Verein für Sozialpolitik (cf. *Schriften des Vereins für Sozialpolitik*, vol. 175, pp. 370–71).

which may drive the "natural rate" (at which the demand for, and the supply of, savings are equal) above its previous level; while the banks refrain from raising their rate of interest to a proportionate extent, but continue to lend at the previous rate, and thus enable a greater demand for loans to be satisfied than would be possible by the exclusive use of the available supply of savings. The decisive significance of the case quoted is not, in my view, due to the fact that it is probably the commonest in practice, but to the fact that it *must inevitably recur* under the existing credit organization.

III

The notion that the increase in circulation is due to arbitrary interference by the banks owes its origin to the widespread view that banks of issue are the exclusive or predominant agencies that can change the volume of the circulation; and that they do so of their own free will. But the central banks are by no means the only factor capable of bringing about a change in the volume of circulating media;[83] they are, in their turn, largely dependent upon other factors, although they can influence or compensate for these to a great extent. Altogether, there are three elements that regulate the volume of circulating media within a country—changes in the volume of cash, caused by inflows and outflows of gold; changes in the note circulation of the central banks: and last, and in many ways most important, the often-disputed "creation" of deposits by other banks. The interrelations of these are, naturally, complicated.

As regards original changes in the first two factors—that is, changes that are not set in motion by changes in one of the other factors—there is comparatively little to say. It has already been

---

[83] This fact has already been pointed out by the representatives of the Banking School, and later by C. Juglar, *Du change et de la liberté d'émission* (Paris: Guillaumin, 1868), chap. 3, *passim;* and *Des crises commerciales et leur retour périodique,* 2nd ed. (Paris: Guillaumin, 1889), p. 57. Wicksell, *Geldzins und Güterpreise,* p. 101, also points, first of all, to the deposit business of the banks as the cause of the "elasticity" of the volume of currency media.

pointed out that, in principle, an increase in the volume of cash, occasioned by an increase in the volume of trade, also implies a lowering of the money rate of interest—which gives rise to shifts in the structure of production that seem, though only temporarily, to be advantageous. It must certainly appear very problematical whether the deviations in the money rate of interest thus occasioned would, as a rule, be large enough to cause fluctuations of an empirically ascertainable magnitude. Central banks, on the other hand, are by law or custom bound to preserve such a close connection between note issues and cash holdings that we have no reason to assume that they, and they alone, provide the original impetus. Of course, it is possible to assume, with Professor Mises, that the central banks, under the pressure of an inflationist ideology, are always trying to expand credit and thus provide the impetus for a new upward swing of the trade cycle; and this assumption may be correct in many cases. The credit expansion is then conditioned by special circumstances, which need not always be present; and the cyclical fluctuations caused by it are, therefore, not the necessary consequence of an inherent tendency of our credit system, for the removal of the special circumstances would eliminate them. But before deciding in favor of this special assumption—which requires a proof of its own, to be given separately in the case of each cycle—we have to ask whether, in some other part of our credit system, such extensions may not take place automatically under certain conditions—without the necessity for any special assumption of the inadequate functioning of any part of the system. To me this certainly appears to be true as regards the third factor of money expansion—the "credit creation" of the commercial banks.

There are few questions upon which scientific literature, especially in Germany, is so lacking in clarity as on the possibility and importance of an increase in circulating media due to the granting of additional credit by the banks of deposit. To give an answer to the question of whether credit creation is a regular consequence of the existing organization of banking, we shall have to attempt to clear up our conception of the methods and extent of such credit creation by deposit banks. Besides dealing with the fundamental question of the possibility of credit creation and the limits to which it can extend, we shall have to discuss two special questions that are important for our further investigations: namely, whether the practical importance of credit creation depends upon certain practices of banking technique, as is often assumed; and second, whether it is, in fact, possible to determine whether a given issue of credit represents credit freshly created or not.

If in the course of our investigation, it is possible to prove that the rate of interest charged by the banks to their borrowers is not promptly adjusted to all changes in the economic data (as it would be if the volume of money in circulation were constant)—either because the supply of bank credit is, within certain limits, fundamentally independent of changes in the supply of savings, or because the banks have no particular interest in keeping the supply of bank credit in equilibrium with the supply of savings and because it is, in any case, impossible for them to do so—then we shall have proved that, under the existing credit organization, monetary fluctuations must inevitably occur and must represent an immanent feature of our economic system—a feature deserving of the closest examination.

IV

The main reason for the existing confusion with regard to the creation of deposits is to be found in the lack of any distinction between the possibilities open to a single bank and those open to the banking system as a whole.[84] This is connected with the fact

---

[84] As it is impossible to deal exhaustively with this problem, it must be sufficient to draw attention to the main literature of the subject. The first author known to me who definitely stated that "the balances in the bank are to be considered in very much the same light with the paper circulation," was Henry Thornton (see his evidence before the Committee on the Bank Restriction, 1797). The development of a more definite theory of credit creation by the banks began, however, with the criticisms leveled by the Banking School against the Currency School, and represent the former's only

that, in Germany, the whole theory has been taken over bodily from England, where, owing to differences in banking technique, the limits imposed on any individual bank are, perhaps, somewhat less narrow, so that the general possibilities open to the banking system as a whole have not been indicated with the degree of emphasis that their importance deserves. In Germany, following the popular exposition of Mr. Hartley Withers, the

---

correct contribution to the science of economics. As Professor T.E. Gregory has recently shown (introduction to Tooke and Newmarch's *History of Prices* [London: P.S. King, 1928], pp. 11 *et seq.*) it was James Pennington who originally developed this thesis, first in an appendix to T. Tooke's *Letter to Lord Grenville on the Effects ascribed to the Resumption of Cash Payments* (London: Murray, 1829), then in further contributions to R. Torrens's *Letter to the Rt. Hon. Viscount Melbourne* (London, 1837) and finally in an appendix to the third volume of Tooke's *History of Prices, and the State of Circulation, in 1838 and 1839* (London: Longman, Brown, Green, and Longmans, 1840). If one wanted to trace the further progress of this theory during the nineteenth century, one would have to draw particular attention to the writings of H.D. Macleod (cf., in particular, his *Dictionary of Political Economy* [London: Octavo edition, 1863], article on *Credit*), C.F. Dunbar and F. Ferrara.

Modern developments follow the exposition of H.J. Davenport, *The Economics of Enterprise* (New York: Macmillan, 1915), pp. 250 *et seq.*; and mention should, in particular, be made of C.A. Phillips's, *Bank Credit* (New York: Macmillan, 1920), esp. chap. 3, "The Philosophy of Bank Credit"; W.F. Crick, "The Genesis of Bank Deposits," *Economica* 7, no. 20 (June 1927); and R.G. Rodkey, *The Banking Process* (New York: Macmillan, 1928). Apart from these, we must include in our list the well-known works of Hartley Withers, Irving Fisher, and R.G. Hawtrey and, in German literature, K. Wicksell, *Geldzins und Güterpreise*, p. 101; A. Weber, *Depositenbanken und Spekulationsbanken*, 2nd ed. (Munich: Duncker & Humblot, 1922); the works which we have already mentioned by Mises and Hahn, G. Haberler's essay on the latter "Hahns Volkswirtschaftliche Theorie des Bankkredits," *Archiv für Sozialwissenschaften* 57 (1927); and, finally, H. Neisser, *Der Tauschwert des Geldes* (Jena: Gustav Fischer, 1928).

The theory has been severely criticized especially by Professor Cannan, W. Leaf, and more recently by R. Reisch, "Die 'Deposit'-Legende in der Banktheorie," *Zeitschrift für Nationalökonomie* 1 (1930).

most generally accepted view starts from English banking practice, which (except in the case of "overdrafts") credits the account of the customer with the amount borrowed before the latter is actually utilized. Granted this assumption, the process leading to an increase of circulating media is comparatively easy to survey and therefore hardly ever disputed. So long and insofar as the credit a bank is able to grant, considering its cash position, remains on current account—and in the United States, for example, it is a regular condition for the granting of a loan that the current account of the borrower shall never fall below a certain relatively high percentage of the sum borrowed[85]—every new grant of credit must, of course, bring about an equivalent increase of deposits and a proportionately smaller diminution of cash reserves. Against these "deduced deposits" (Phillips), which regularly occur in the normal course of business, the banks naturally have to keep only a certain percentage of cash reserve; and thus it is clear that every bank can, on the basis of a given increase of deposits resulting from public payments, grant new credit to an amount exceeding this increase in deposits.

Against this method of proof it can rightly be objected that, while banking practices of this kind may well lead to the possibility of credit creation, the conditions this argument assumes are not present on the Continent. It has been justifiably and repeatedly emphasized that there is no reason why the borrower, so long as he is not forced to do so, should borrow money at a higher rate of interest merely to leave that money on deposit at a lower rate.[86]

If the possibility of creating credit depended only on the fact that borrowers leave part of their loans on current account for a

---

[85] Cf. Phillips, *Bank Credit*, p. 50.
[86] R. Reisch in "Die Wirtschaftliche Bedeutung des Kredites im Lichte von Theorie und Praxis," *Mitteilungen des Verbandes Österreichischen Banken und Bankiers*, 10th year, nos. 2–3 (1928), p. 38 and A. Jöhr in his verbal report on Credit and the Cycle, in the Zurich Assembly of the Verein für Sozialpolitik, *Schriften*, vol. 175, p. 311.

time, then credit creation would be practically impossible on the Continent;[87] while even in England and the United States it would have only a very secondary importance. It should be noted that this applies to the case in which the borrower pays the sum borrowed into another account in the *same* bank, so that it is transferred from one to the other without diminishing the total volume of deposits in the bank concerned. We need not, therefore, go separately into this case.

But, in adopting this line of argument, by far the most important process by which deposits are created in the course of current banking business, even in Anglo-Saxon countries, is neglected, and the sole way in which they are created on the Continent is left entirely out of consideration. The latter could easily be overlooked, since the ability of individual banks to make an increase in their deposits the basis of a far greater amount of new credit can only be accounted for by means of the assumptions used above, while in the banking system as a whole the same process occurs independently. In the following pages, therefore, we shall examine how an increase in deposits, paid in in cash, influences the lending capacity of the whole banking system; starting from the assumption, more appropriate to Continental conditions, that the sums granted will be credited to the account of the borrower only at the time when, and to the extent that, he makes use of them.

V

We may start as before by examining the procedure of a single bank. At this bank a certain amount of cash is newly deposited; a sum, let us say, equal to 5 percent of its previous total deposits. If the policy of the bank was to keep a reserve of 10 percent against deposits, that ratio has now been increased, by the new deposit, to 14.3 percent, and the bank is therefore in a position, in accordance

---

[87] As Bouniatian, evidently for this reason, actually assumes (cf. his essay, "Industrielle Schwankungen, Bankkredit und Warenpreise," *Archiv für Sozialwissenschaften und Sozialpolitik* 58 [1927]: 463).

with its policy, to grant new credit. If we assume further that it re-lends 90 percent of the newly deposited money and that the whole of this is immediately utilized by the borrower (in order, let us say, to increase his purchases of raw materials), then the ratio of cash to deposits has again sunk to 10 percent. Insofar as the bank does not change its policy, its individual lending capacity is exhausted, in these circumstances, before it has even re-lent the whole of the amount newly deposited.

The effect of the sums newly deposited at one bank on the lending capacity of the whole banking system is, however, not exhausted by this transaction. If the borrower does not use the credit in a way that leads quickly to the market for consumers' goods, such as wage payments, but devotes it instead to the purchase of raw materials or half-finished products, then it is to be assumed that payment will be made by check and that the seller will hand over the sum received to his own bank for encashment, the amount being credited to his own account. The next consequence must be that the clearinghouse position of this bank improves by exactly the amount transferred, and it therefore obtains an equivalent amount of cash from the bank that originally granted the credit.

For the second bank, therefore, the sum originating in the granting of credit and paid into its accounts (representing, as we remember, 90 percent of the original deposit) is just as much an original deposit, based on cash payments, as it was to the bank we originally considered. It will, therefore, be regarded as a basis for additional lending and used in just the same way as any other new deposit. If the second bank also keeps 10 percent of its deposits as cash reserves, it too will be in a position to lend 90 percent of the new deposit, and the same process will be continued as long as the amounts are merely transferred from bank to bank and are not taken out in cash. As every bank re-lends 90 percent of the amount paid into it and thus causes an equivalent increase in deposits for some other bank, the original deposit will give rise to credit representing $0.9 + 0.9^2 + 0.9^3 + 0.9^4 \ldots$ times the original amount. As the sum of this converging infinite series is 9, the banks will be enabled, in an extreme case, to create, against an amount of cash flowing in from an outside source, credit equal to nine times that amount. This becomes clear when we consider that the process can only stop when the last part of this cash is required for the 10 percent reserve of the deposits.

For simplicity's sake we have made use of an assumption that is undoubtedly incorrect, but which affects our conclusion only insofar as it reduces the actual amount of new credit the banks can create with a reserve ratio of 10 percent. Its omission leaves our fundamental conclusion intact; i.e., that they can grant credit to an amount several times greater than the sum originally deposited. In fact some part of the credit at least, if not on the first, then on subsequent occasions, will always be withdrawn in cash and not deposited with other banks. For example, if 70 percent is always re-deposited instead of the full 90 percent, this amount being re-lent by every bank and the remainder being used in cash transactions, then the increase in deposits will give rise to additional credit equal to only $0.7 + 0.7^2 + 0.7^3$ ... times (i.e., two and one-third times) the original. So long as any part of the credit granted is not withdrawn in cash but re-deposited with the banks, the latter will be able to create additional credit, of a larger or smaller amount, as a consequence of every increase in their cash holdings.[88] The lifetime of

---

[88] The maximum amount of credit, to the creation of which the increase in the cash holdings of the banks may give rise under such an assumption, is easily found by inserting the factor representing the proportion of the original deposit which is re-lent and redeposited with another bank into the mathematical formula expressing the limit which a convergent geometrical series approaches, viz., $\frac{1}{x-1}$. The result gives the total of credits that originate in the series of transactions, including the original deposit; and, in order to arrive at the amount of additional credits, 1 has to be subtracted from the result. It is thus easily seen that even if, for example, only 1/9th of the 90 percent re-lent by the first bank, or 10 percent of the original deposit, is re-deposited with another bank—and this process is repeated, *additional* credits amounting to 0.111 times the original deposit will be created.

this pyramid of credit is limited to that of the first credit granted, save in the case (which can be assumed as long as there are no withdrawals from deposits) where it is immediately replaced by a fresh credit. If, however, deposits unexpectedly diminish at any part of the banking system, the process will be reversed, and the original diminution of deposits will occasion a contraction of credit correspondingly exceeding the amount withdrawn.[89]

In this connection we must note for further emphasis later the fact that the proportion in which the credit granted is transferred to other accounts—and not paid out in cash—must be regarded as subject to very wide fluctuations as between different individuals at a given moment, as well as between various periods of time for the economic system as a whole. We return later to the significance of this fact.

What has been said above should be sufficient to show that the possibility of creating credit over and above the sums deposited—which, under Continental banking conditions, is not open to any individual bank—is, however, open to the whole banking system of the country to a considerable extent. The fact that a single bank cannot do what is automatically done by the banking system as a whole also explains another circumstance, which might otherwise easily be cited as a proof of the impossibility of additional credit creation. If every bank could re-lend several times the amount deposited, there would be no reason against its offering a much higher rate of interest on deposits than it actually does, or, in particular, under the existing discount rates of the central banks, against its procuring cash in unlimited quantities by way of rediscount; for it would only have to charge its customers a small part of the rate of interest charged by the

---

[89] On this question, and on the interesting effects of a transference of deposits from one bank to another, cf. the more elaborate treatment of Phillips, *Bank Credit*, p. 64 *et seq.*; also the remarks of Crick, "The Genesis of Bank Deposits," p. 196.

banks in order to make the business pay. This apparent contradiction between theory and practice is cleared up as soon as one realizes that an increase of deposits by a single bank only offers possibilities for credit creation to the banking system as a whole. But the importance of this circumstance transcends the mere clearing up of this difficulty.

VI

As credit created on the basis of additional deposits does not normally appear in the accounts of the same bank that granted the credit, it is fundamentally impossible to distinguish, in individual cases, between "those deposits which arose through cash payment and those which find their origin in credit."[90] But this consideration rules out, *a priori*, the possibility of bankers limiting the amount of credit granted by them to the amount of "real" accumulated deposits—that is, those arising from the accommodation of temporarily unused money. The same fact enables us to understand why it is generally just those economic writers who are also practical bankers who are most unwilling to admit in any circumstances that they are in a position to create credit.[91] "The banker simply does not notice that through this process there is

---

[90] Neisser (*Der Tauschwert des Geldes*, p. 53) deserves credit for clearing up an untenable conception, which was quite recently held by no less an authority than Professor J. Schumpeter (*Theorie der wirtschaftlichen Entwicklung*, 2nd ed. [Munich and Leipzig: Duncker & Humblot, 1926], p. 144).

[91] Cf., for example, Walter Leaf, the late chairman of the Westminster Bank, in his book *Banking* (London: Williams & Norgate, 1926), or the contributions of A. Jöhr and B. Dernburg to the Zurich Debate on the Trade Cycle (*Schriften des Vereines für Sozialpolitik* 175 [1929]: 311 and 329). These arguments were perfectly correctly answered by another "practical" banker, K. Schlesinger (ibid., p. 355). Professor A. Hahn, on the other hand, falls into the opposite error. The standpoint of Professor R. Reisch will be discussed later.

an increase in the amount of money in circulation."[92] Once the impetus has been given to any part of the banking system, mere adherence to the routine of banking technique will lead to the creation of additional deposits without the possibility arising, at any point, of determining whether any particular credit should properly be regarded as "additional." Every time money that has been deposited is re-lent—provided that the depositor is not prevented from using his deposits for making payments—this process is to be regarded as the creation of additional purchasing power; and it is merely this comparatively simple operation that is at the root of the banks' ability to create purchasing power—although the process appears so mysterious to many people. It is thus by no means necessary that the banks should grant this credit, as Dr. Dernburg seems to assume, in an "improper or wanton" way.

It is of course quite another question whether bankers can or do create additional credit of their own free will. The objections to this theory of additional credit, which are leveled against the statement that the banks create credit "as they please," although holding good at a given rate of interest, do not in the least affect that part of the theory we need for our analysis. If Professor Reisch, for example, emphasizes that bank deposits generally increase only "according to the needs of business,"[93] or if Professor Bouniatian objects that "it does not depend on the banks, but on the demands made by commerce and industry, how far banks expand credit,"[94] then these assertions, coming as they do from opponents of the theory of bank credit, already contain all that is

---

[92] Neisser, *Der Tauschwert des Geldes,* p. 54. He goes on to say, quite correctly, that "the mere fact that cheque-deposits represent money, without being covered by cash up to 100 percent, already explains the money-creating nature of bank credit."

[93] "Die Wirtschaftliche Bedeutung des Kredites im Lichte von Theorie und Praxis," p. 39.

[94] "Industrielle Schwankungen, Bankkredit und Warenpreise," p. 465.

needed for a deductive proof of the necessity for the recurrence of credit cycles. What interests us is precisely the question of whether the banks are able to satisfy the increased demands of businessmen for credit without being obliged immediately to raise their interest charges—as would be the case if the supply of savings and the demand for credit were to be in direct contact, without the agency of the banks (as, for example, in the hypothetical "savings market" of theory); or whether it is even possible for the banks to raise their interest charges immediately the demand for credit increases. Even the bitterest opponents of this theory of bank credit are forced to admit that "there can be no doubt that, with the upward swing of the trade cycle, a certain expansion of bank credit takes place."[95]

We must not, however, be satisfied with registering the general agreement of opinion on this point. Before passing on to analyze the consequences of this phenomenon, we must ask whether the causes which bring it about—that banks increase their deposits through additional credit in periods of boom and thus postpone, at any rate temporarily, the rise in the rate of interest that would otherwise necessarily take place—are inherent in the nature of the system or not.

VII

So far, the starting point of our argument concerning the origin of additional credit has been the assumption that the banks receive an increased inflow of cash, which they then use as a basis for new credit on a much larger scale. We must now inquire how banks behave when an increased demand for credit makes itself felt.

Assuming, as is preferable, that this increased demand was not caused by a lowering of their own interest rates, this additional demand is always a sign that the natural rate of interest has

---

[95] Dernburg, *Schriften des Vereines für Sozialpolitik* 175, p. 329. He merely adds to this statement the remark that the banks and the central bank should see to it that this expansion is "kept in order"!

risen—that is, that a given amount of money can now find more profitable employment than hitherto. The reasons for this can be of very different kinds:[96] new inventions or discoveries, the opening up of new markets, or even bad harvests,[97] the appearance of entrepreneurs of genius who originate "new combinations" (Schumpeter), a fall in wage rates due to heavy immigration, the destruction of great blocks of capital by a natural catastrophe, or many others. We have already seen that none of these reasons is in itself sufficient to account for an *excessive* increase of investing activity, which necessarily engenders a subsequent crisis; but that they can lead to this result only through the increase in the means of credit they inaugurate.

But how is it possible for the banks to extend credit, as they undoubtedly do, following an increase in demand, when no additional cash is flowing into their vaults? There is no reason to assume that the same cause that has led to an increased demand for credit will also influence another factor, the cash position of the banks—which as we know is the only factor determining the extent to which credit can be granted.[98] So long as the banks maintain a constant proportion between their cash reserves and their deposits it would be impossible to satisfy the new demand

---

[96] "A great variety of causes," observes R.G. Hawtrey, very correctly in *Trade and Credit* (London: Longmans, 1928), p. 175.

[97] Regarding the influence of harvests on the trade cycle, cf. the useful compilation of various contradictory theories by V.P. Timoshenko, "The Role of Agricultural Fluctuations in The Business Cycle," *Michigan Business Studies* 2, no. 9 (1930).

[98] It is of course possible that an improvement in the conditions of production and profit-making will also indirectly cause an increased flow of cash to the banks, for a flow of funds for investment, as well as an increased flow of payments for goods, can be expected from abroad. But, in the first place, this increased flow of cash can only be expected in a comparatively late stage of the boom, so that it can hardly explain the latter's origin; and in the second place, such an explanation could only be adduced in the case of a single country, and not for the world economy as a whole, or in a closed system.

for credit. The fact that in reality deposits always do expand relatively to cash reserves, in the course of the boom, so that the liquidity of the banks is always impaired in such periods, does not of course constitute a sufficient starting point for an argument in which the increase in credit is regarded as *the* decisive factor determining the course and extent of the cyclical movement. We must attempt to understand fully the causes and nature of this credit expansion and in particular its limits.

The key to this problem can only be found in the fact that the ratio of reserves to deposits does not represent a constant magnitude, but, as experience shows, is itself variable. But we shall achieve a satisfactory solution only by showing that the reason for this variability in the reserve is not based on the arbitrary decisions of the bankers, but is itself conditioned by the general economic situation. Such an examination of the causes determining the size of the reserve ratio desired by the banks is all the more important since we had no theoretical warrant for our previous assumption that it always tends to be constant.

It is best to begin our investigation by considering once again the situation of a single bank, and asking how the manager will react when the credit requirements of the customers increase in consequence of an all-around improvement in the business situation.[99] For reasons that will shortly become clear, we must assume that the bank under consideration is the first to feel the new credit requirements of industry, because, let us say, its customers are drawn from just those industries that first feel the effects of the new recovery. Among the factors that determine the volume of loans granted by the bank, only one has changed; whereas previously, at the same rate of interest and with the same security, no new borrowers came forward, now, under the same conditions of borrowing, more loans can be placed. On the other

---

[99] The problems with which the manager of a single bank is confronted in deciding the bank's credit policy are very neatly analysed by Mr. W.F. Crick, "The Genesis of Bank Deposits," p. 197, *et seq.*

hand, the cash holdings of the bank remain unchanged. This does not mean, however, that the considerations of liquidity that dictate the amount of loans to be granted will lead to the same result now as when fresh loans could only have been placed at a lower rate of interest or with inferior security than was the case with loans already granted. In this connection, finally, we must mention that the sums we have, for simplicity's sake, hitherto called cash balances, which form the bank's liquid reserve, are by no means exclusively composed of cash—and are not even of a constant magnitude, unrelated to the size of the profits they make possible. The danger that, in case of need, the reserves may have to be replenished by rediscounting bills through the central bank,[100] or that, in order to correct an unfavorable clearing-house balance, day-money may have to be borrowed at a given rate of interest, is far less abhorrent when it is possible to extend credit at an undiminished rate of interest than when such an extension would involve a lowering of that rate. But even disregarding this possibility and assuming that the bank recognizes that it can satisfy its eventual need for cash only at correspondingly higher rates, we can see that the greater loss of profit entailed by keeping the cash reserve intact will, as a rule, lead the bank to a policy that involves diminishing the size of this non-earning asset. Besides this, we have the consideration that, in the upward phase of the cycle, the risks of borrowing are less; and therefore a smaller cash reserve may suffice to provide the same degree of security. But it is above all for reasons of competition that the bank that first feels the effect of an increased demand for credit cannot afford to reply by putting up its interest charges; for it would risk losing its best customers to other banks that had not

---

[100] On this point see J.S. Lawrence, "Borrowed Reserves and Bank Expansion," *Quarterly Journal of Economics* 42 (1928), where Mr. Phillips's exposition, mentioned above, is extensively criticized; also the rejoinder of Mr. F.A. Bradford, published under the same title in the next volume (43) of the same journal.

yet experienced a similarly increased demand for credit. There can be little doubt, therefore, that the bank or banks that are the first to feel the effects of new credit requirements will be forced to satisfy these even at the cost of reducing their liquidity.

VIII

But once one bank or group of banks has started the expansion, then all the other banks receive, as already described, a flow of cash that at first enables them to expand credit on their own account without impairing their liquidity. They make use of this possibility the more readily since they, in turn, soon feel the increased demand for credit. Once the process of expansion has become general, however, the banks soon realize that, for the moment at any rate, they can safely modify their ideas of liquidity. While expansion by a single bank will soon confront it with a clearinghouse deficit of practically the same magnitude as the original new credit, a general expansion carried on at about the same rate by all banks will give rise to clearinghouse claims which, although larger, mainly compensate one another and so induce only a relatively unimportant cash drain. If a bank does not at first keep pace with the expansion it will, sooner or later, be induced to do so, since it will continue to receive cash at the clearinghouse as long as it does not adjust itself to the new standard of liquidity.

So long as this process goes on, it is practically impossible for any single bank, acting alone, to apply the only control by which the demand for credit can, in the long run, be successfully kept within bounds; that is, an increase in its interest charges. Concerted action in this direction, which for competitive reasons is the only action possible, will ensue only when the increased cash requirements of business compel the banks to protect their cash balances by checking further credit expansion, or when the central bank has preceded them by raising its discount rate. This, again, will only happen, as a rule, when the banks have been induced by the growing drain on their cash to increase their rediscount. Experience shows, moreover, that the relation between check payments and cash payments alters in favor of the latter as the boom proceeds, so that an increased proportion of the cash is finally withdrawn from the banks.[101]

This phenomenon is easily explained in theory by the fact that a low rate of interest first raises the prices of capital goods and only subsequently those of consumption goods, so that the first increases occur in the kind of payments that are effected in large blocks.[102] It may lead to the consequence that banks are not only prevented from granting new credit, but even forced to diminish credit already granted. This fact may well aggravate the crisis, but it is by no means necessary in order to bring it about. For this *it is quite enough that the banks should cease to extend the volume of credit;* and sooner or later this must happen. Only so long as the volume of circulating media is increasing can the money rate of interest be kept below the equilibrium rate; once it has ceased to increase, the money rate must, despite the increased total volume in circulation, rise again to its natural level and thus render unprofitable (temporarily, at least) those investments which were created with the aid of additional credit.[103]

---

[101] Cf. the statements contained in the well-known tenth yearly Report of the Federal Reserve Board, for 1923 (Washington, D.C.: Government Printing Office, 1924), p. 25:

> This is the usual sequence—an increase of deposits being followed by an increase of the currency. Ordinarily the first effect of an increase in business activity upon the banking position is a growth in loans and deposits. ... There comes a time when the increase of business activity and the fuller employment of labor and increased pay rolls call for an increase of actual pocket money to support the increased wage disbursements and the increased volume of purchases at retail.

[102] Neisser (*Der Tauschwert des Geldes*, p. 162) doubts this, but his criticism results from an inadequate grasp of the effects of an unduly low money rate of interest. But even if he were right on this point, the arguments of monetary trade cycle theory would remain unaffected, since the latter, as is shown in the text, does not depend on this assumption for its proof.

[103] We need not stay to examine the case of a continuous increase in circulating media, which can only occur under a free paper standard.

IX

The assertion that forms the starting point of the "Additional Credit Theory of the Trade Cycle," and whose proof has been attempted in the preceding pages, has never in fact been seriously questioned; but hardly any attempts have been made to follow up all the unpleasant consequences of the state of affairs it indicates. Yet what is implied when the beneficial effects of bank credit are praised but, thanks to the activities of banks, an increased demand for credit is followed by a greater increase in its supply than would be warranted by the supply of contemporary saving? Wherein lie the often-praised effects of credit, if not in the fact that it provides means for enterprises for which no provision could be found if the choices of the different economic subjects were strictly followed? By creating additional credit in response to an increased demand, and thus opening up new possibilities of improving and extending production, the banks ensure that impulses toward expansion of the productive apparatus shall not be so immediately and insuperably balked by a rise of interest rates as they would be if progress were limited by the slow increase in the flow of savings. But this same policy stultifies the automatic mechanism of adjustment that keeps the various parts of the system in equilibrium and makes possible disproportionate developments that must, sooner or later, bring about a reaction.

Elasticity in the credit supply of an economic system is not only universally demanded but also—as the result of an organization of the credit system which has adapted itself to this requirement—an undeniable fact, whose necessity or advantages are not discussed here.[104] But we must be quite clear on one point. *An economic system with an elastic currency must, in many instances, react to external influences quite differently from an economy in which economic forces*

---

[104] Cf. K. Wicksell, *Geldzins und Güterpreise*, p. 101, "The more elastic is the currency system the longer can a more or less constant difference persist between the two interest rates and the greater, therefore, will be the influence of this discrepancy on prices."

impinge on goods in their full force—without any intermediary; and we must, a priori, *expect any process started by an outside impulse to run an entirely different course in such an economy from that described by a theory that only takes into account changes originating on the side of goods.* Once, owing to the disturbing influence of money, even a single price has been fixed at a different level from that which it would have formed in a barter economy, a shift in the whole structure of production is inevitable; and this shift, so long as we make use of static theory and the methods proper to it, can only be explained as an exclusive consequence of the peculiar influence of money. The immediate consequence of an adjustment of the volume of money to the "requirements" of industry is the failure of the "interest brake" to operate as promptly as it would in an economy operating without credit. This means, however, that new adjustments are undertaken on a larger scale than can be completed; a boom is thus made possible, with the inevitably recurring "crisis." *The determining cause of the cyclical fluctuation is, therefore, the fact that on account of the elasticity of the volume of currency media the rate of interest demanded by the banks is not necessarily always equal to the equilibrium rate, but is, in the short run, determined by considerations of banking liquidity.*[105]

---

[105] In a previous work (*Die Währungspolitik der Vereinigten Staaten,* p. 260), I have already dealt with the elasticity of bank credit as *the* cause of cyclical fluctuations. This view of its determining importance is now also put forward by Professor F.A. Fetter in a very interesting essay, "Interest Theories and Price Movements," *American Economic Review* 17 (March 1927), supplement, see esp. pp. 95 *et seq*. Professor Fetter, of course, is also under the influence of the prevailing dogma, which holds that the existence of a stable price level is sufficient proof of the absence of all monetary influences. The crucial part of his argument, not having received the attention it deserves in recent monetary literature, is reprinted here:

> The foregoing presents the extreme case of the expansion and contraction of bank loans in relation to prices, *but in principle quite small changes in the loan policies of banks affecting the volume of commercial loans,* discount rates, and percentages of reserves, *are of*

The main question set by this inquiry is thus answered. A deductive explanation embracing all the phenomena of the trade cycle would require far-reaching logical investigations entirely

---

the same nature. They cause and constitute inflation and deflation of the exchange medium and of commercial purchasing power, not originating in the amount of standard money but in the elasticity of banking loan funds. *This word "elasticity" has long been used in discussions of banking policy to designate a quality assumed to be wholly desirable in bank note issues and customers' credits,* but with only vague suggestions as to what is the need, standard, or means, with reference to which bank loans should expand and contract.

Rather, it may be more exact to say, the tacit assumption has been that the bank loan funds should be elastic in response to the "needs of business." *But "the needs of business" appears to be nothing but another name for changes in customers' eagerness for loans;* and this eagerness increases when prices are beginning, or are expected, to rise and often continues to gather momentum while prices rise and until, because of vanishing reserve percentages (and other factors), the limit of this elasticity and also the limit of price increase are in sight. In this situation the most conservative business operations become intermixed with elements of investment speculation, motivated by the rise of prices and the hope of profit that will be *made possible by a further rise. Throughout this process the much-esteemed elasticity of bank funds is the very condition causing, or making possible, the rising prices which stimulate the so-called "needs of business." Truly a vicious circle, to be broken only by crisis and collapse when bank loans reach a limit and prices fall.* (My italics)

Further, we should point out the connection between our theory and a famous thesis of Mr. R.G. Hawtrey. The phrase "so long as credit is regulated with reference to reserve proportions, the trade cycle is bound to recur" (*Monetary Reconstruction*, 2nd ed. [London: Longmans, Green, 1926], p. 135) is undoubtedly correct, though perhaps in a sense somewhat different from that intended by the author; for a regulation of this volume of loans exclusively from the point of view of liquidity can never effect a prompt adjustment of the rates charged on loans to the changes in the equilibrium rate, and thus cannot help providing opportunities for the temporary creation of additional credits as

transcending the scope of this work, which aims merely at an exposition of the monetary basis of trade cycle theory. For the present, we must content ourselves with a reference to existing literature on the subject.[106] In the present work we shall only draw a few conclusions that follow from our previous arguments, some with regard to practical policy, some with regard to further scientific research. Before going on to this, however, we shall venture a few remarks on the question of whether the result of our investigations unequivocally settles the controversy between the protagonists and opponents of the monetary trade cycle theory in favor of the former.

X

It must be emphasized first and foremost that there is no necessary reason why the initiating change, the original disturbance eliciting a cyclical fluctuation in a stationary economy, should be of monetary origin. Nor, in practice, is this even generally the case. The initial change need have no specific character at all; it may be any one among a thousand different factors that may at any time increase the profitability of any group of enterprises. For it is not the occurrence of a "change of data" that is significant, but the fact that the economic system, instead of reacting to this change with an immediate "adjustment" (Schumpeter)— i.e., the formation of a new equilibrium—begins a particular movement of "boom" that contains within itself the seeds of an

---

soon as (at a given rate of interest) the demand for credit surpasses the accumulation of savings; that is, when the natural rate of interest has risen. See, finally, the remarks of Professor W. Röpke, *Kredit und Konjunktur*, p. 274.

[106] Besides Professor Mises's *Theorie des Geldes und der Umlaufsmittel* we must mention the last chapter of S. Budge's *Gründzuge der Theoretischen Nationalökonomie* (Jena: Gustav Fischer, 1925) and Professor Strigl's paper on "Die Produktion unter dem Einfluss einer Kreditexpansion" in *Schriften des Vereins für Sozialpolitik* 173, no. 2 (1928), concerning trade cycle theory and business research, a volume that has been repeatedly quoted above. Since the above was written, I have tried to carry the analysis of these phenomena a step further in *Prices and Production*.

inevitable reaction. This phenomenon, as we have seen, should undoubtedly be ascribed to monetary factors, and in particular to "additional credit" that also necessarily determine the extent and duration of the cyclical fluctuation. Once this point is agreed upon, it naturally becomes quite irrelevant whether we label this explanation of the trade cycle as a monetary theory or not. What is important is to recognize that it is to monetary causes that we must ascribe the divergences of the pricing process, during the trade cycle, from the course deduced in static theory.

From the particular point of view from which we started, our theory must be regarded most decisively as a monetary one. As to the incorporation of trade cycle theory into the general framework of static equilibrium theory (for the clear formulation of which we are indebted to Professor A. Lowe, one of the strongest opponents of monetary trade cycle theory), we must maintain, in opposition to his view, not only that our own theory is undoubtedly a monetary one but that a theory other than monetary is hardly conceivable.[107] It must be conceded that the monetary theory as we have presented it—whether one prefers to call it a monetary theory or not, and whether or not one finds it a sufficient explanation of the empirically determined fluctuations—has this definite advantage: *it deals with problems that must, in any case, be dealt with, for they are necessarily given when the central apparatus of economic analysis is applied to the explanation of the existing organization of exchange. Even if we had never noticed cyclical fluctuations, even if all the actual fluctuations of history were accepted as the consequences of natural events, a consequential analysis of the effects that follow from the peculiar workings of our existing credit organization would be bound to demonstrate that fluctuations caused by monetary factors are unavoidable.*

It is, of course, an entirely different question whether these monetary fluctuations would, if not reinforced by other factors, attain the extent and duration we observe in the historical cycles, or whether

---

[107] Cf. my report, "Über den Einfluss monetärer Faktoren auf den Konjunkturzyklus," *Schriften des Vereins für Sozialpolitik* 173, no. 2 (1928): 362 *et seq.*

in the absence of these supplementary factors they would not be much weaker and less acute than they actually are. Perhaps the empirically observed strength of the cyclical fluctuations is really only due to periodic changes in external circumstances, such as short-period variations of climate, or changes in subjective data (as, e.g., the sudden appearance of entrepreneurs of genius), or perhaps the interval between individual cyclical waves may be due to some natural law.[108] Whatever further hypothetical causes are adduced to explain the empirically observed course of the fluctuations, there can be no doubt (and this is the important and indispensable contribution of monetary trade cycle theory) that the modern economic system cannot be conceived without fluctuations ascribable to monetary influences; and therefore any other factors that may be found necessary to explain the empirically observed phenomena will have to be regarded as causes *additional* to the monetary cause. In other words, any non-monetary trade cycle theory must superimpose its system of explanation on that of the monetarily determined fluctuations; it cannot start simply from the static system as presented by pure equilibrium theory.

Once this is admitted, however, the question of whether the monetary theory of the trade cycle is correct or not must, at any rate, be presented in a different form. For if the correctness of the interconnections described by monetary theory is unquestioned, there still remains the problem of whether it is also sufficient to explain all those phenomena that are observed empirically in the course of the trade cycle; it may perhaps need supplementing in order to make it an instrument suitable to explain the working of the modern economic system. It seems to me, however, that before we can successfully tackle this problem we ought to know exactly how much of the empirically observed fluctuations are due to the monetary factor, which is actually always at work; and therefore we shall have to work

---

[108] From now to the end of the section the exposition follows, in part word for word, my contribution to the Zurich discussion of the Verein für Sozialpolitik. Ibid., p. 372 *et seq.*

out in the fullest detail the theory of monetary fluctuations. It is hardly permissible, methodologically speaking, to go in search of other causes whose existence we may conjecture, before ascertaining exactly how far and to what extent the monetary factors are operative. It is our duty to work out in detail the necessary consequences of those causes of disturbance that we know, and to make this train of thought a definite part of our logical system, before attempting to incorporate any other factors that may come into play.

XI

The fact, simple and indisputable as it is, that the "elasticity" of the supply of currency media, resulting from the existing monetary organization, offers a sufficient reason for the genesis and recurrence of fluctuations in the whole economy is of the utmost importance—for it implies that no measure that can be conceived in practice would be able entirely to suppress these fluctuations.

It follows particularly from the point of view of the monetary theory of the trade cycle that it is by no means justifiable to expect the total disappearance of cyclical fluctuations to accompany a stable price level—a belief Professor Lowe[109] seems to regard as the necessary consequence of the monetary theory of the trade cycle. Professor Röpke is undoubtedly right when he emphasizes the fact that "even if a stable price level could be successfully imposed on the capitalist economy the causes making for cyclical fluctuations would not be removed."[110] But to realize this, as the preceding argument shows, is by no means "equivalent to a rejection of a 100 percent monetary Trade Cycle theory."[111] On the contrary, on this view, we must regard Professor Röpke's theory, which coincides in the more important points with our own,[112] as itself constituting such a 100 percent monetary trade cycle theory.

---

[109] Ibid., p. 369.

[110] *Kredit und Konjunktur*, p. 265.

[111] Ibid., p. 278

[112] Ibid., cf. esp. pp. 274 *et seq.* of the work mentioned.

Once this is realized, we can also see how nonsensical it is to formulate the question of the causation of cyclical fluctuations in terms of "guilt," and to single out, e.g., the banks as those "guilty" of causing fluctuations in economic development.[113] Nobody has ever asked them to pursue a policy other than that which, as we have seen, gives rise to cyclical fluctuations; and it is not within their power to do away with such fluctuations, seeing that the latter originate not from their policy but from the very nature of the modern organization of credit. So long as we make use of bank credit as a means of furthering economic development we shall have to put up with the resulting trade cycles. They are, in a sense, the price we pay for a speed of development exceeding that which people would voluntarily make possible through their savings, and which therefore has to be extorted from them. And even if it is a mistake—as the recurrence of crises would demonstrate—to suppose that we can, in this way, overcome all obstacles standing in the way of progress, it is at least conceivable that the non-economic factors of progress, such as technical and commercial knowledge, are thereby benefited in a way we should be reluctant to forgo.

If it were possible, as has been repeatedly asserted in recent English literature,[114] to keep the total amount of bank deposits entirely stable, that would constitute the only means of getting rid of cyclical fluctuations. This seems to us purely utopian. It would necessitate the complete abolition of all bank money—i.e., notes and checks—and the reduction of the banks to the role of brokers, trading in savings. But even if we assume the fundamental possibility of this state of things, it remains very questionable whether many would wish to put it into effect if they

---

[113] As Professor S. Budge seems inclined to do (*Gründzuge der Theoretischen Nationalökonomie*, p. 216). His exposition in other respects largely coincides with ours.

[114] Certain statements of Mr. R.G. Hawtrey seem to point to this, esp. *Monetary Reconstruction*, p. 121.

were clear about its consequences. The stability of the economic system would be obtained at the price of curbing economic progress. The rate of interest would be constantly above the level maintained under the existing system (for, generally speaking, even in times of depression some extension of credit takes place).[115] The utilization of new inventions and the "realization of new combinations" would be made more difficult, and thus there would disappear a psychological incentive toward progress, whose importance cannot be judged on purely economic grounds. It is no exaggeration to say that not only would it be impossible to put such a scheme into practice in the present state of economic enlightenment of the public, but even its theoretical justification would be doubtful.

As regards the practical bearing of our analysis on the trade-cycle policy of the banks, all that can be deduced from it is that bankers will have to weigh carefully the relative advantages and disadvantages of granting credit on an increasing scale, and to take into account the demand, now fairly widespread, for the early application of a check to credit expansion. But the utmost that can be achieved on these lines is only a mitigation, never the abolition, of the trade cycle. Apart from this, the only way of minimizing damage is through a far-reaching adjustment of the economic system to the recognized existence of cyclical movements; and for this purpose the most important condition is an increased insight into the nature of the trade cycle and a knowledge of its actual phase at any particular moment.[116]

---

[115] Cf. Professor A.C. Pigou *Industrial Fluctuations,* 2nd ed., p. 145: "Banks do not in bad times reduce the amount of new real capital flowing to business men below what it would have been had there been no banks, but merely increase it to a smaller extent than they do in good times."

[116] In this connection, apart from empirical research, the greatest consideration should be given to the plea made by O. Morgenstern ("Qualitative und Quantitative Konjunkturforschung," p. 123 *et seq.*) for giving increased publicity to company developments.

CHAPTER 5

Unsettled Problems of Trade Cycle Theory

I

So much has already been said (in chapter 3, sections 4 and 6) about the most important of the outstanding problems of monetary influences on economic phenomena, that only a brief supplement is needed at this point. With regard to the problems of monetary theory in the narrower sense I may restrict myself chiefly to what has been said above, as I hope to publish the results of a separate investigation concerning this problem elsewhere.[117] A few remarks may, however, be ventured merely as a summing-up of what has already been said, and in doing this we shall touch on a number of other important problems. The most significant result of our investigation must be the grasp of the elementary fact that *we have no right to assume that an economic system with an "elastic" currency will ever exhibit those movements that can be immediately deduced from the propositions of static theory.* On the contrary, it is to be expected that movements will arise which would not be possible

---

[117] Cf. "Das intertemporale Gleichgewichtssystem der Preise und die Bewegungen des Geldwertes," *Weltwirtschaftliches Archiv* (1928); and more specifically *Prices and Production*, where I have attempted to develop some of the points touched upon in this chapter.

under the conditions usually assumed by that theory. It is particularly important to realize that this proposition is true whether the changes in the volume of money also effect changes in the so-called "general value of money" or not. With the disappearance of the idea that money can only exert an active influence on economic movement when the value of money (as measured by one kind of price level) is changing, the theory that the general value of money is the sole object of explanation for monetary theory must fall to the ground. Its place must, henceforth, be taken by an analysis of *all* the effects of money on the course of economic development. All changes in the *volume* of effective monetary circulation, and only such changes, will therefore rank for consideration as changes in economic data capable of originating "monetary influences."

The next task of monetary theory is, therefore, a systematic investigation of the effects of changes in the volume of money. In the course of this approach, relationships will inevitably be contemplated that do not have the permanence of the equilibrium relationships. All these results, however (and this must be emphasized to prevent misunderstanding), will be reached by the aid of the methods of static analysis, for these are the only instruments available to economic theory. The only difference is that these methods will be applied to an entirely new set of circumstances that have never, up till now, received the attention they deserve. It is vitally necessary that such an investigation should keep clear of the notion that the adjustment of the supply of money to changes in "money requirements" is an essential condition for the smooth working of the equilibrating process of the system, as presented in equilibrium theory.[118] It must always start

---

[118] This notion rests on a confusion between the demand for money and the demand for cash, i.e., that portion of the total amount of money which at any given moment is utilized in cash, and which undergoes sharp seasonal fluctuations. This phenomenon, however, is itself a consequence of the use of bank credit. For a somewhat more detailed discussion of these problems, cf. Lecture 4, of *Prices and Production*.

from the assumption that the natural determining factors will exert their full effect only when the effective volume of money remains unchanged, whatever may be the actual changes in the extent of economic activity.

Precise propositions as to the effects of changes in the volume of money can be laid down only when accurate information is available both as to the genesis of the change and the part of the economic system where it took place. For this reason little can be said about changes resulting from the decumulation of hoarded treasure or the discovery of new gold deposits. The way in which an individual will elect to spend money coming to him as a gift or as a result of other non-economic motives cannot be determined from deductive considerations. Similarly, little can be said *a priori* about bank credit granted to the state, so long as we have no information as to how they are to be used. The situation is different, however, when we are dealing with productive credit granted by the banks to industry—which constitute the most frequent form of increase in the volume of circulating media. This credit is only given when and where its utilization is profitable, or at least appears to be so. Profitability is determined, however, by the ratio of the interest paid on this credit to the profits earned by their use. So long as the amount of credit obtainable at any given rate of interest is limited, competition will ensure that only the most profitable employments are financed out of a given amount of credit. The uses to which the additional money can be put are thus determined by the rate of interest, and the amount that can be said about those uses will therefore depend, in turn, on how much is known about the importance and the effects of interest. Whatever may have been written or thought on this old problem of theoretical economics, it is undeniable that those particular aspects of interest theory that are important for our analysis have so far received less attention and even less recognition than is their due. It is not practicable to work out, within the limits of this essay, the supplementary analysis that seems to me to be necessary in this field; but I should like, at least, to indicate, before I conclude, some angles of approach that appear to have been unduly neglected hitherto. Needless to say, the sections that follow have even less claim than their predecessors to be regarded as comprehensive.

II

In the economic system of today, interest does not exist in the form in which it is presented by pure economic theory. Not only do we find, instead of one uniform rate, a great number of differing rates, but, beyond this, none of the various rates of interest existing is entitled to rank as *the* rate of interest described by static theory, on which all other rates depend, differing only to the extent to which they are affected by special circumstances. The process of interest fixation, which is at the basis of pure theory, never in fact follows the same course in a modern credit economy; for in such an economy the supply of, and the demand for, savings never directly confront each other.

All existing theories of interest, with a few not very successful exceptions, restrict themselves to the explanation of that *imaginary* rate of interest that would result from such an immediate confronting of supply and demand. The fact that the rate of interest that these theories explain is one never found in practice does not mean that they are of no importance, or even that any explanation of the actual rates can afford to ignore them. On the contrary, an adequate explanation of that "natural rate" is the indispensable starting point for any realization of the conditions necessary to the achievement of equilibrium, and for an understanding of the effects that every rate of interest actually in force exerts on the economic system. It is true that it does not suffice to explain all empirically observed rates since it takes into consideration only one of the factors determining those rates (though that factor is, of course, the one that is always operative); but any consideration of ruling interest rates that did not relate its analysis to that of the imaginary interest rate of static theory would hang entirely in the air. For the most part, however, no solution has been found to the wider problem of building up on the basis of the theory of an equilibrium rate of interest, which can be deduced from the creditless economy, the structure of different rates that can be simultaneously observed in a modern economy. The solution of this particular problem should provide a most valuable contribution to a deeper insight into cyclical fluctuations.

But before we set out to explore on the one hand the difference between the natural rate of interest and the actual rate, and on the other hand that between the various kinds of the latter, we must say something about the importance of changes in the equilibrium rate itself, since some very confused ideas prevail as to the function of the equilibrium rate of interest in a dynamic economy. This is not very surprising since, as we have seen above, an insufficient appreciation of the role of interest is the cause of most misunderstanding in trade cycle theory. Perhaps it is not too much to say that the importance an economist attaches to interest as a regulator of economic development is the best criterion of his theoretical insight. It is therefore all the more regrettable that recent economic literature has been quite fruitless so far as the theory of interest is concerned.[119] This too is perhaps due in part to the fact that the earlier economists, to whom we owe our present knowledge of interest theory, stopped short in their investigations and never came to the point of explaining the actual rates.

III

Under the rubric of *pure interest theory* (by which we understand the explanation of that rate of interest which is not modified

---

[119] The best confirmation of this view is given by Mr. G. Heinze, who, in his recent study, *Static or Dynamic Interest Theory* (Leipzig: H. Beyer, 1928), comes to the correct conclusion that "In spite of all the partly justified criticism that was leveled against the interest theory of Böhm-Bawerk, the latter still represents the most logically perfect economic explanation of the phenomenon of interest, and is, moreover the one which comes nearest to the observed facts" (p. 165).

by monetary influences, although paid, of course, on capital reckoned in money terms) we shall have to deal briefly with the question of the effect of transitory fluctuations in the natural rate of interest, conditioned by "real" factors. This question is of great importance, taking as it does a decisive place in some of the best-known trade cycle theories of our day. In particular Professor Cassel's view (mentioned above, p. 39) that the real cause of cyclical fluctuations lies in an overestimate of the supply of new capital, is based on the assumption that a temporary fall in the rate of interest conditioned by real causes can bring about overinvestment in the same way as a rate of interest artificially lowered by monetary factors. This view, which seems to be supported by a considerable body of experts, has to be judged quite differently according to the changes that elicit fluctuations in the rate of interest originate on the demand or the supply side. Fluctuations caused by changes on the demand side, which Professor Cassel uses as an explanation in his trade cycle theory, certainly cannot be regarded as an adequate explanation of the cycle; for, as Professor Amonn has already pointed out,[120] this is no reason why entrepreneurs should (assuming an unchanged rate of interest) expect to obtain more credit in the future than they can now. However there can be no doubt that violent fluctuations in savings and the consequent temporary changes in the equilibrium rate of interest act similarly to an artificial lowering of the money rate of interest in causing an extension of capital investments that cannot be maintained later owing

---

[120] Cassel's "System der Theoretischen Nationalökonomie," *Archiv für Sozialwissenschaften und Sozialpolitik* 51 (1924): 348 *et seq*. In order to remain within the scope of our work, we have to forgo the very alluring task of criticizing Professor Cassel's argument. Such a criticism would also have to deal with the very ingenious theoretical interpretation of this argument by Dr. G. Halm ("Das Zinsproblem am Geld- und Kapitalmarkt," *Jahrbücher far Nationalökonomie und Statistik*, 3rd series, 70 [1926]: 16 *et seq*.) Here we may only point out that in this study, Halm is driven to make use of the old hypothesis that savings accumulate for a time and are then suddenly utilized "at the moment when the real boom begins" (p. 21).

to the diminished supply of savings.[121] In this case, therefore, it is permissible to speak of non-monetary cyclical fluctuations. This differs, however, from the conception of cyclical fluctuations employed hitherto, in that the passage from boom into depression is not a necessary consequence of the boom itself, but is conditioned by "external circumstances." A downward turn of this sort can occur just as well in a hitherto stationary economy or during a depression as at the end of a boom; and it should therefore be regarded less as an example of a cyclical movement than as a particularly complicated case of the direct process of adjustment to changes in data. In any case, for reasons given above, such an explanation, as compared with an endogenous theory, would only come into play when the latter had proved insufficient to explain a given concrete phenomenon.

But there can be no doubt that such fluctuations in the natural rate, conditioned by changes in the rate of saving activity, present some very important problems in interest theory, the solution of which would be an important aid in estimating the effect of fluctuations conditioned by monetary changes. We have entirely disregarded the circumstances determining the supply of savings and the fluctuations in this supply; and the examination of these is a promising field for future research. It might even be possible to show that fluctuations in saving activity are a necessary concomitant of economic progress, and thus to give a firm basis to the theories we have mentioned. This is, perhaps, not very probable.

In direct relation to the above problem stands the question of the effects of alterations in the rate of interest on the price system as a whole. An examination of this subject should throw light on the point of view, emphasized by Professor Fetter,[122] that

---

[121] Cf. Dr. A. Lampe, *Zur Theorie des Sparprozesses und der Kreditschöpfung* (Jena: Gustav Fischer, 1926), p. 67 *et seq.*

[122] "Interest Theories and Price Movements," esp. p. 78. Cf. also Lecture 3 of *Prices and Production*.

the height of interest rate at any given moment expresses itself in the whole structure of price relationships, while every change in that rate must *pari passu* bring about changes in the relation between particular prices and thus in the quantitative relationships of the whole economy.

But here we must content ourselves with drawing attention to the problems arising out of the changes in the natural rate of interest, without contributing further to their solution. We shall only venture a further remark on a question concerning not the consequences but the causes of these changes, since this is important in what follows. This is the question of whether the rate of interest at any moment depends on the total amount of capital existing at that moment or only on *the amount of free capital available for new investment*.[123] We mention this here only in order to emphasize the untenability of the widespread view that the determining factor, on the supply side, is the whole existing stock of capital. If that were so it would hardly be possible to explain any large fluctuations of the rate of interest, since the *relative* changes that the existing capital stock undergoes within brief periods and under normal circumstances is insignificant. A thorough investigation of the interconnections in this field must show that the actual rate of interest depends (apart from the demand for loan capital) only on the supply of newly produced or reproduced capital. The existing stock of fixed capital affects only the demand side, by determining the yields to be expected from new investments. This explains how, in a country that is well equipped with fixed capital, the rate of interest can temporarily rise higher than that obtainable in a country that is poorly equipped, provided that there is relatively more free capital available for *new* investment in the latter than in the former.

---

[123] "Capital disposable for investment" was the phrase usually employed by the classical writers to distinguish this free capital from the stock of real capital. Cf., e.g., J.S. Mill, *Essays on Some Unsettled Questions of Political Economy* (London: Parker, 1844), pp. 113 ff.

This fact has some significance in connection with the phenomenon of enforced saving with which we shall deal later.

IV

As regards the relationship of the natural or equilibrium rate of interest to the actual rate, it should be noted, in the first place, that even the existence of this distinction is questioned. The objections, however, mainly arise from a misunderstanding that occurred because K. Wicksell, who originated the distinction, made use in his later works of the term "real rate" (which to my mind is less suitable than "natural rate") and this expression became more widespread than that which we have used.[124] The expression "real rate of interest" is also unsuitable, since it coincides with Professor Fisher's "real interest,"[125] which, as is well known, denotes the actual rate plus the rate of appreciation or minus the rate of depreciation of money, and is thus in accordance with common usage, which employs the term "real wages" or "real income" in the same sense. Unfortunately Wicksell's change in terminology is also linked up with a certain ambiguity in his definition of the "natural rate." Having correctly defined it once as "that rate at which the demand for loan capital just equals the supply of savings,"[126] he redefines it, on another occasion, as that rate which would rule "if there were no money transactions and real capital were lent *in natura*."[127] If this last definition were correct, Dr. G. Halm[128] would be right in raising, against the conception of a "natural rate," the

---

[124] Cf. the works of Professor Röpke and Dr. Burchardt, mentioned above; also E. Egner, *Zur Lehre vom Zwangsparen* (1928), p. 537. Occasionally Wicksell (*Geldzins und Güterpreise*, p. 111) also uses the expression "normal rate."

[125] Cf. esp. *Appreciation and Interest*. Publications of the American Economic Association, 3rd series, 11, no. 4 (1896).

[126] *Vorlesungen*, vol. 2, p. 220.

[127] *Geldzins und Güterpreise*, p. 93.

[128] *Das Zinsproblem am Geld- und Kapitalmarkt, Jahrbücher far Nationalökonomie und Statistik*, p. 7, footnote.

objection that a uniform rate of interest could develop only in a money economy, so that the whole analysis is irrelevant. If Dr. Halm, instead of clinging to this unfortunate formula, had based his reasoning on the correct definition, which is also to be found in Wicksell, he would have reached the same conclusion as Professor Adolf Weber—the distinguished head of the school of which he is a member: that is, that the natural rate is a conception "which is evolved automatically from any clear study of economic interconnections."[129] In accordance with this view, Wicksell's conception must be credited with fundamental significance in the study of monetary influences on the economic system; especially if one realizes the practical importance of a money rate of interest depressed below the natural rate by a constantly increasing volume of circulating media. Unfortunately, although Wicksell's solution cannot be regarded as adequate at all points, the attention it has received since he propounded it has borne no relation to its importance. Apart from the works of Professor Mises, mentioned above, the theory has made no progress at all, although many questions concerning it still await solution.[130] This may be due to the fact (on which we have touched already) that the problem had become entangled with that of fluctuations in the general price level. We have already stated our views on this point (pp. 105–06), and indicated what is necessary for the further development of the theory. Here we shall try to restate the problem in its correct form, freed from any reference to movements in the price level.

---

[129] *Depositenbanken und Spekulationsbanken*, 3rd ed. (1922), p. 171.

[130] Another attempt to develop Wicksell's theory—of which I have learned only since the above was written—was made, at roughly the time when Mises's work was published, by Professor M. Fanno of Padua in a work entitled *Le banche e il mercato monetario* (Rome: Athenaeum, 1913). An abridged restatement of Professor Fanno's theory will shortly appear, in German, in a volume of essays on monetary theory by a number of Dutch, Italian, and Swedish authors, edited by the author of the present essay.

V

Every given structure of production—i.e., every given allocation of goods as between different branches and stages of production—requires a certain definite relationship between the prices of the finished products and those of the means of production. In a state of equilibrium, the difference necessarily existing between these two sets of prices must correspond to the rate of interest, and at this rate, just as much must be saved from current consumption and made available for investment as is necessary for the maintenance of that structure of production. The latter condition necessarily follows from the fulfillment of the former, since the prices paid for the means of production, plus interest, can only correspond to the prices of the resulting products when, at the given prices and rate of interest, the supply of producers' goods is exactly adequate to maintain production on the existing scale. The price margins between means of production and products, therefore, can only remain constant and in correspondence with the rate of interest so long as the proportion of current income, which at the given rate of interest is not consumed but reinvested in production, remains exactly equal to the necessary capital required to carry on production. Every change in this proportion must begin by impairing the correspondence of price margins and the interest rate; for it influences both in opposite directions, and so leads to further shifts in the whole structure of production, representing an adjustment to altered price relationships. These resulting changes in the structure of production will not always be the same; they will vary according to whether the change in the proportions of the social income going respectively to consumption goods and investment goods corresponds to real changes in the decisions of individuals as to spending and saving, or whether it was brought about artificially, without any corresponding changes in individual saving activity.

Apart from individual saving activity (which includes, of course the savings of corporations, of the state, and of other bodies entitled to raise compulsory contributions) the proportions between consumption and capital creation can only change as a result of alterations in the effective quantity of money.[131] When changes in the division of the total social dividend, in favor of capital creation, result from changes in the saving activity of individuals, they are self-perpetuating. This is not true of such variations between "consumption and accumulation" (if we may use for once the terminology of Marxian literature) as are due to additional credit granted to the entrepreneurs; these can be assumed to persist only so long as the proportion is kept artificially high by a progressively increasing rate of credit creation. Such an injection of money into circulation acts only temporarily—*until the additional money becomes income. At that moment, the proportion of capital creation must relapse to the level of voluntary saving activity,* unless *new* credit is granted bearing the same relation to the new total of money incomes as the first injection bore to the former total.[132]

It is clear that such a process of progressive increase in the supply of money cannot be maintained under our existing credit system, especially since, as it proceeds, more extensive use will be

---

[131] Very instructive investigations of the problems considered here were carried out by A. Lampe, *Zur Theorie des Sparprozesses und der Kreditschöpfung.*

[132] The argument presented in the text (and put in this form for brevity's sake) is imperfect in two respects. First, the flow of voluntary saving can itself vary as a result of a single change in the proportion of capital formation. This factor, however, is unlikely to become important enough for its omission to affect the exposition given in the text. Second, the way in which the additional money, which was given in the first instance to entrepreneurs and used by them to lengthen the period of production, will always swell incomes in the long run, needs further elaboration. As a general proposition, however, it is obvious that whoever uses the additional credits to make additional investment goods can do so only by employing additional factors of production; and therefore, since there is in our case no compensating decrease in the demand for factors elsewhere, the total incomes of the factors must increase.

made of cash. On the other hand, a mere cessation of further increases—not, therefore, a reversal of credit policy, toward deflation—is sufficient to bring back the proportion of total income available for capital formation to the extent of voluntary savings.

The differences in the effects of these two kinds of variation between consumption and capital formation manifest themselves first of all on the price system, and thus on the natural or equilibrium rate of interest. The first effect of *a diminution of the rate on loans arising from increased saving activity*—so long as the structure of production remains unchanged—is to bring that rate below the margin between the prices of means of production and of products. The increased saving activity, however, must soon cause on the one hand a falling off in the demand for consumption goods, and hence a tendency for their prices to fall (a tendency that may merely find expression in decreasing sales at existing prices) and, on the other hand, an increase in the demand for investment goods and thus a rise in their prices. The extension of production will have a further depressing effect on the prices of consumption goods, as the new products come on the market, until, finally, the difference between the respective prices has shrunk to a magnitude corresponding to the new, lower, interest rate. If, however, the fall in the rate of interest is due to an *increase in the circulating media,* it can never lead to a corresponding diminution in the price margin, or to a readjustment of the two sets of prices to the level of an equilibrium rate of interest that will endure. In this case, moreover, the increased demand for investment goods will bring about a net increase in the demand for consumption goods; and therefore the price margin cannot be narrowed more than is permitted by the time lag in the rise of consumption goods prices—a lag existing only as long as the process of inflation continues. As soon as the cessation of credit inflation puts a stop to the rise in the prices of investment goods, the difference between these and the prices of consumption goods will increase again, not only to its previous level but beyond, since, in the course of inflation, the structure of production has been so shifted that in comparison with the division of the social income between expenditure and saving the supply of consumption goods will be relatively less, and that of production goods relatively greater, than before the inflation began.[133]

VI

There have recently been increasingly frequent objections to this account of the effects of an increased volume of currency, and the artificial lowering of interest rates conditioned by it, on the grounds that it disregards certain supposedly beneficial effects that are closely connected with this phenomenon. What the objectors have in mind is the phenomenon of so-called "forced saving," which has received great attention in recent literature.[134] This phenomenon, we are to understand, consists in an increase in capital creation at the cost of consumption, through the granting of additional credit, *without* voluntary action on the part of the individuals who forgo consumption, and without their deriving any immediate benefit. According to the usual presentation of the theory of forced saving, this occurs through a fall in the general value of money, which diminishes the consumers' purchasing power; the volume of goods thus freed can be used by the producers who obtained additional credit. We must, however, raise the same objection to this theory that we raised against the usual

---

[133] Cf. my article on "The 'Paradox' of Saving," p. 160; p. 133 and *passim* in this volume.

[134] Besides Léon Walras—the originator of this theory (Cf. his *Etudes d'économie politique appliquée* [Lausanne and Paris, 1898, pp. 348–56], Wicksell and the well-known works of Professors Mises and Schumpeter, one must mention the recent works of Professor Röpke, Dr. Egner, and Dr. Neisser; and in Anglo-Saxon literature, Mr. D.H. Robertson's *Banking Policy and the Price Level*. As I have pointed out, however, in Lecture 1 of *Prices and Production* and—at somewhat greater length—in "A Note on the Development of the Theory of Forced Saving," *Quarterly Journal of Economics* (November 1932), the concept of "forced saving" was already known to J. Bentham, H. Thornton, T.R. Malthus and a number of other writers in the early nineteenth century, down to J.S. Mill.

account of the effects of an artificial lowering of the money rate of interest, i.e., that in principle, forced saving takes place whenever the volume of money is increased, and does not need to manifest itself in changes in the value of money.[135]

The "depreciation" of money in the hands of the consumer can be, and frequently will be, only relative, in the sense that those diminutions in price that would otherwise have occurred are prevented from occurring. Even this causes a part of the social dividend to be distributed to individuals who have not acquired legitimate claim to it through previous services, nor taken them over from others legitimately entitled to them. It is thus taken away from this part of the community against its will. After what has been said above, this process needs no further illumination.

Nor do we need to adduce further proof that every grant of additional credit induces "forced saving"—even if we have avoided using this rather unfortunate expression in the course of our argument. There is only one further point—the effect of this artificially induced capital accumulation—on which a few remarks should be added. It has often been argued that the forced saving arising from an artificially lowered interest rate would improve the capital supply of the economy to such an extent that the natural rate of interest would have to fall finally to the level of the money rate of interest, and thus a new state of equilibrium would be created—that is, the crisis could be avoided altogether. This view is closely connected with the thesis, which we have already rejected, that the level of the natural rate of interest depends directly upon the whole existing stock of real capital. Forced saving increases only the existing stock of real capital goods, but not necessarily the current supply of free capital disposable for investment—that portion of total income that

---

[135] Cf. D.H. Robertson, *Money*, 2nd ed. (London: Macmillan, 1929), p. 99 and A.C. Pigou, *Industrial Fluctuations*, 2nd ed. (London: Macmillan, 1929), pp. 251–57.

is not consumed but used as a provision for the upkeep and depreciation of fixed plant. But any addition to the supply of free capital available for new investment or reinvestment must come from those of the investments induced by forced savings which already yield a return—a return large enough to leave over, after providing for supplementary costs connected with the new means of production, a surplus for depreciation and for interest payments on the capital. If the capital supply from this source is to lower the natural rate of interest, it must not, of course, be offset by a diminution elsewhere—resulting from the decline of other undertakings confronted with the reinforced competition of those newly supplied with capital.

The assumption that an artificial increase of fixed capital (i.e., one caused by additional credit) tends to diminish the natural rate of interest in the same way as one effected through voluntary savings activity presupposes, therefore, that the new capital must be incorporated into the economic system in such a way that the prices of the products imputed to it shall cover interest and depreciation. Now a given stock of capital goods is not a factor that will maintain and renew itself automatically, irrespective of whether it is in accordance with the current supply of savings or not. The fact that investments have been undertaken that cannot be "undone" offers no guarantee whatever that this is the case. Whether capital can be created beyond the limits set by voluntary saving depends—and this is just as true for its renewal as for the creation of new plant—on whether the process of credit creation continues in a steadily increasing ratio. If the new processes of production are to be completed, and if those already in existence are to continue in employment, it is essential that additional credit should be continually injected at a rate that increases fast enough to keep ahead, by a constant proportion, of the expanding purchasing power of the consumer. If a new process of roundabout production can be completed while these conditions still hold good, it can contribute temporarily to a lowering of the natural rate of interest; but this provides no final solution of the difficulty.

For "eventually" a moment must inevitably arrive when the banks are unable any longer to keep up the rate of inflation required, and at that moment there must always be some processes of production, newly undertaken and not yet completed,[136] that were only ventured because the rate of interest was kept artificially low. It does not follow, of course, that these processes in particular will be left unfinished because of the subsequent rise in that rate; on the other hand, their existence does cause the rate of interest to be higher than it would be in their absence, when capital would be required only by processes made possible by voluntary saving without any competing demand arising from processes which were only enabled to start by "forced saving." The capital invested in new and not yet completed processes of production will thus merely intensify the demand for further supplies by calling for the capital necessary to complete them—an effect that will be the more pronounced the greater the ratio of capital invested to capital still required. It may therefore quite easily come about that, in order to complete these newly initiated processes, capital may be diverted from the maintenance of complete and old-established

---

[136] The existence of new long processes that have not yet been completed is not a necessary condition in order that the relative increase in the demand for consumers' goods may lead to the abandonment of such processes and, therefore, to the destruction of part of the capital employed there; but it is the case that will always be given in practice and where this effect is most easily seen. In this connection it should, however, be noted that the introduction of a longer roundabout process of production will, in almost all cases, affect not only a single enterprise but a series of enterprises representing successive stages of production. Even a completed plant may, in this sense, represent part of an incomplete process—if the capital is lacking which would have to be invested in the machines or other capital goods to be produced by this plant. A plant equipped to satisfy a demand for machinery that cannot be permanently maintained is, in this sense, part of a roundabout process that cannot be continued. For a fuller description, see *Prices and Production*, Lecture 3, and especially my article "Kapitalaufzehrung" in the *Weltwirtschaftliches Archiv* 36 (July 1932).

undertakings, so that a new plant is put into operation and an old plant closed down, although the latter would have been kept up, and the former never put in hand, if it had been a question of building up the whole capital equipment of the economy from the start. This does not merely mean that the total return comes to less than it otherwise would; it also means, primarily, that production is forced into channels to which it will only keep for as long as the new and spuriously produced stock of fixed capital can remain in use. The value of capital invested in processes that can be continued, and, still more that in processes where continuance is impracticable, will shrink rapidly in value—this shrinkage being accompanied by the phenomena of a crisis. Thus on purely technical grounds it will become uneconomic to maintain them. It should be particularly remarked that, from the point of view of the fate of individual enterprises, capital invested in a fixed plant, but raised by borrowing, is of precisely the same importance as working capital, i.e., the loss of value does not merely necessitate writing down; it generally makes it impossible to carry on at all.

The cause of this development is, evidently, that an unwarranted accumulation of capital has been taking place; though people may regard it (under the alluring name of "forced saving") as a thoroughly desirable phenomenon. After what has been said above *it is probably more proper to regard forced saving as the cause of economic crises than to expect it to restore a balanced structure of production.*

VII

There remains one problem of interest theory, in the wider sense of the word, that we need to examine more closely than we have yet done—in order to exhibit a problem of first-class importance to the progress of trade cycle theory. This is the problem of the varying height and independent movements of rates of interest ruling at the same place and at the same time. We are not thinking, of course, of differences conditioned either by the unequal standing of borrowers or by the fact that, under the name of interest, payments are also made for the services or costs connected with the granting of credit. We are interested only in the problem of variations arising *within* the pure or net rate of interest, as they can be observed between varying durations of credit—the problem usually known in economic literature as the problem of interest rates, in the *money*, and in the *capital* (investment) market, respectively.

In this respect we may repeat what we have already said at the beginning of this chapter—that the theoretical investigations of interest have been broken off at far too early a stage to afford much understanding of the rates actually ruling at any given moment. It is very remarkable that none of the great theorists to whom we owe our insight into the fundamental factors determining the equilibrium rate of interest made the slightest attempt to explain these differences between interest rates. Systematic investigation of this problem came much later and then characteristically the investigation related chiefly to the question of the "external order of the capital or money market"; and it is only recently that Dr. G. Halm[137]

---

[137] "Das Zinsproblem am Geld und Kapitalmarkt." Of the comprehensive bibliography given by Halm, the following, together with some more recent additions, are worth mention: A. Spiethoff: (1) "Die äussere Ordnung des Kapital und Geldmarktes," (2) "Das Verhältnis von Kapital, Geld und Güterwelt," (3) "Der Kapitalmangel in seinem Verhältnis zur Güterwelt," all in Schmoller's *Jahrbuch* 33 (Munich, 1909), and "Der Begriff des Kapital und Geldmarktes," Schmoller's *Jahrbuch* 44 (1920). H. von Beckerath *Kapital und Geldmarkt* (Jena: Gustav Fischer, 1916).

Professor Schumpeter's, Dr. Neisser's, and Professor Fetter's works already mentioned; A. Hahn, "Zur Theorie des Geldmarktes," *Archiv für Sozialwissenschaften und Sozialpolitik* 51 (1924). Karin Kock, "A Study of Interest Rates," *Stockholm Economic Studies* no. 1 (London: P.S. King, 1929).

W.W. Riefler, *Money Rates and Markets in the United States* (New York and London: Harper and Brothers, 1930).

The problems arising out of empirical research are well summarized by O. Donner and A. Hanau, "Untersuchung zur Frage der Marktzusammenhänge," *Vierteljahrshefte zur Konjunkturforschung*, 3rd year, no. 3 A (Institut für Konjunkturforschung, Berlin 1928), an investigation which is a model of its kind.

has treated the simultaneous existence of varying interest rates "as a problem of interest theory." Although Dr. Halm deserves full credit for the undeniable service he has rendered in putting the problem in the proper form for discussion, his attempt at solution can hardly be regarded as fully successful. Thus we still stand at the beginning of a crucially important development of a special theory of money rates of interest.

The clearing up of these interconnections is of primary importance to trade cycle theory, since the discrepancies between the expected yields of existing means of production and the actual yield obtainable from the available liquid capital must necessarily arise in the course of the cycle. Given a sufficient insight into the influences determining the yields of both types of investment, the simultaneous changes in the height of both kinds of interest rates should afford extraordinarily valuable material for the diagnosis of any actual situation, and thus the growth of this part of interest theory would provide an important basis for the development of empirical research and forecasting. A particularly promising approach might consist of an examination of the question from the point of view of an equalization of the time differences between the rates of interest that would prevail if the whole supply of capital at any time had to be invested for a longer period. Such an equalization would be brought about by a kind of *arbitrage* for which, naturally, only money lent at call or at short notice could be considered.

In this field, too, the extension of equilibrium analysis to successively occurring phenomena, which I have attempted in another work,[138] may prove fruitful. At any rate, an explanation of this arbitrage could also explain why the rates on short-term credit can be temporarily lower, or on the other hand higher, than the long-term rate, since both borrower and lender would

---

[138] Cf. "Das intertemporale Gleichgewichtssystem der Preise und die Bewegungen des Geldwertes."

find such an arbitrage to their advantage. This view cannot be refuted by the objection that the rates on short-term credit not only change earlier but also change to a greater degree than those in the capital market; for it may be economically entirely justifiable to pay higher rates or obtain lower ones, for a short term, than one expects for a long term, since the expectation of getting better terms at a later period, under more favorable conditions, may compensate for the relative disadvantages suffered in the short run.

VIII

Finally, we should like to point out quite briefly certain tasks in the field of statistical research that according to our theoretical analysis seem likely to be particularly fruitful. In connection with the last question dealt with, we should draw attention to the statistics of the money market, which are still, unfortunately, in a very elementary stage, partly for technical reasons but mainly because of difficulties of interpretation. These latter arise largely from the fact that the statistical determination of the absolute height of the interest rate, or even of its movements, discloses almost nothing as to its bearing on the economic system.[139] The same rate of interest that at one moment may be too low in relation to the whole economic situation may be too high at the next, or *vice versa*. Misunderstandings on this point may be responsible for certain erroneous views, concerning the alleged insignificance of the height of interest rates, that are often held by statistical economists. The innumerable attempts to minimize the significance of interest rates by means

---

[139] The statistical determination of nominal changes in the interest rate is also rendered very difficult by the fact that changes can take place in the form of changes in stipulations as to the quality of the bills discounted at a given rate, and so on. The same rate may be merely applied to a better class of borrowers, or the same borrowers may be required to pay a higher rate.

of statistical investigations, which abound in the United States[140] (where they do not even shrink from such absurdities as an attempt to find an explanation [!] of interest by way of statistical investigation) would be impossible but for the complete confusion persisting as to the limits of statistical research. Here again we have to repeat what was asserted at the beginning of this book: statistics can never prove or disprove a theoretical explanation; they can only present problems or offer fields for theoretical research.

For precisely this reason—viz., that the absolute height of interest rates tells us nothing of their significance—an examination of the extent and regularity of *shifts* between various interest rates offers a promising field for statistical technique. An interesting first attempt in this direction is the famous "Three Market Barometer" of the Harvard Economic Service, which uses the trend of the long-term interest rate as a baseline in plotting the curve of the money market rates. Such an empirical consideration of the differences between interest rates does not, of course, exhaust the lines of approach that a complete theoretical explanation of these rates might indicate as suitable for empirical research. The fact that theoretical research itself can be stimulated and awakened to new problems to an important degree from the application of our sketchy knowledge to statistical investigations is amply demonstrated by the investigations of Donner and Hanau, which we have already mentioned.

It is in the statistics of private banking, however, that the heaviest task presents itself. In Europe we are still worse supplied with these than with those of the money market proper. In the United States, on the other hand, some pioneer work has been

---

[140] Cf., e.g., Snyder, "The Influence of the Interest Rate on the Business Cycle," *American Economic Review* 15 (December 1925); reprinted in *Business Cycles and Business Measurements* (New York: Macmillan, 1927).

done in this field,[141] since the ample statistical material available there provided is itself a sufficient incentive for such investigations. In Europe, the lack of any kind of material makes even a first step in this direction impossible.

In many respects the most remarkable of these enquiries are those of Mr. Holbrook Working. Using the data concerning the state of deposits in the "National Banks," which are available for many years past and at intervals of only a few months, he succeeds in establishing a far-reaching parallelism between the movements of deposits and the fluctuations of the wholesale price level. Like most theoretical investigations in the same field, however, his results are distorted by the superficial assumption that monetary influences can only manifest themselves in movements of the price level, while those changes in the volume of bank credit that are just sufficient to prevent changes in the price level are supposed, on this assumption, to exercise no active influence on the trade cycle. It should be mentioned—as having particular bearing upon the views developed in this essay—that, according to Mr. Working's calculations, before the war a yearly increase in deposits of more than 5 percent would have been necessary in order to keep the price level

---

[141] Cf. first of all A.A. Young, "An Analysis of Bank Statistics for the United States," reprinted from *The Review of Economic Statistics* (October 1924; January; and April 1925; and July 1927; Cambridge, Mass.: Harvard University Press, 1928); H. Working, "Prices and the Quantity of the Circulating Medium, 1890–1921," *The Quarterly Journal of Economics* 37 (1923), and "Bank Deposits as a Forecaster of the General Wholesale Price Level," *The Review of Economic Statistics* (1926), of the same author; C. Snyder, "Deposits Activity as a Measure of Business Activity," *Review of Economic Statistics* (1924), reprinted in *Business Cycles and Business Measurements* (New York: Macmillan, 1927); W.M. Persons, "Cyclical Fluctuations of the Ratio of Bank Loans to Deposits," *The Review of Economic Statistics* (1924); L.A. Hahn, "Zur Frage des volkswirtschaftlichen Erkenntnisinhaltes der Bankbilanzziffern," *Vierteljahrshefte zur Konjunkturforschung* 1, no. 4 (1927).

steady; that is to say, additional credit would have had to be created to an extent that must have caused considerable changes in the structure of production.

If the results of our theoretical analysis were to be subjected to statistical investigation, it is not the connection between changes in the volume of bank credit and movements in the price level that would have to be explored. Investigation would have to start on the one hand from alterations in the rate of increase and decrease in the volume and turnover of bank deposits and, on the other, from the extent of production in those industries that as a rule expand excessively as a result of credit injection.[142] Every increase in the circulating media brings about the same effect, so long as each *stands in the same proportion* to the existing volume; and only an increase in this proportion makes possible a further increase in investment activity. On the other hand, every diminution of the *rate of increase* in itself causes some portion of existing investment, made possible through credit creation, to become unprofitable. It follows that a curve exhibiting the monetary influences on the course of the cycle ought to show, not the movements in the total volume of circulating media, but the alteration in the rate of change of this volume.[143] Every upturn of this curve would show that an artificial lowering of the money rate of interest or, if the curve was already rising, a further lowering of the money rates, was making possible additional investments for which voluntary savings would not suffice; and every downturn would show that current credit creation was no longer sufficient to ensure the continuance of all the enterprises it

---

[142] Cf. the instructive graphs given by Harold L. Reed in his *Federal Reserve Policy 1921–1930* (New York: McGraw-Hill, 1930), pp. 181 *et seq.*

[143] Mathematically speaking, the question is one of the graphical presentation, in place of the curve showing the original movements at any moment, of the first differential of this function. On the subject of this method, which has been frequently used of late, cf. I. Fisher, "The Business Cycle Largely a 'Dance of the Dollar'," *Journal of the American Statistical Association* (December 1923).

originally called into existence. It would be of great interest to correlate this presentation of the influence causing an excessive production of capital goods with actual changes in the production of these goods, on the basis of available data.

The possible contributions of banking statistics to trade cycle research are by no means exhausted by the chance they offer of observing the immediate connection between the granting of credit and the movements of production, though these may some day constitute the most important basis of business forecasting. No less important would be an investigation into the volume, at any given moment, of those factors that determine credit expansion, under the other headings of bank balance sheets, and in particular an examination of the relation between the total amount of earning assets and the current accounts, the relation between these and the cash circulation, and so on. Such an investigation, if it were not merely to exhibit their movements in time but also to analyze the deeper connections between them—and most especially if it were to clear up the relationship between interest rates, profits, and the liquidity of the banks—would further our insight into the factors determining credit expansion as well as our knowledge of their limits, and thus make it possible to forecast movements in the factors determining the total development of the economic situation.

It is very unfortunate that such inquiries, especially on the continent of Europe, are almost impossible owing to the lack of necessary data in the form of returns showing the state of the banks, and published at short intervals; insofar as they are possible at all it is only in a few countries and for a very short period. As soon as it is realized that, owing to the existence of banks, the equilibrating forces of the economic system cannot bring about that automatic adjustment of all its branches to the actual situation, which is described by classical economic theory, it is justifiable even from a liberal point of view that the banks should be subjected to degrees of publicity as to the state of their business which is not necessary in the case of other undertakings; and this would by no means imply a violation of the principle of business secrecy, since it would be quite sufficient for this purpose if the authorities were to adopt the United States's plan of publishing summary returns for all banks at frequent intervals. Our reflections thus yield the conclusion that an alleviation of cyclical fluctuations should be expected preeminently from a greater publicity among business enterprises, and particularly among the banks. The example of the United States, which is far ahead in this respect in all the branches of its economic system, will not only silence in time the objections raised against such publicity, but sooner or later will force us to follow in their path.

The "Paradox" of Saving

The "Paradox" of Saving

I

The assertion that saving renders the purchasing power of the consumer insufficient to take up the volume of current production, although made more often by members of the lay public than by professional economists, is almost as old as the science of political economy itself. The question of the utility of "unproductive" expenditure was first raised by the mercantilists, who were thinking chiefly of luxury expenditure.

The idea recurs in those writings of Lauderdale and Malthus that gave rise to the celebrated *Théorie des Débouchés* of James Mill and J.B. Say, and, in spite of many attempts to refute it, it permeates the main doctrines of socialist economics right up to T. Veblen, and Mr. J.A. Hobson.

But while in this way the idea has found a greater popularity in quasi-scientific and propagandist literature than perhaps any other economic doctrine hitherto, fortunately it has not succeeded as yet in depriving saving of its general respectability, and we have yet to

---

This essay originally appeared in the *Zeitschrift für Nationalökonomie* 1, no. 3 (1929), under the title "Gibt es einen Widersinn des Sparens?" The translation is the work of Mr. Nicholas Kaldor and Dr. Georg Tugendhat and was published in *Economica* (May 1931).

learn that any of the numerous monetary measures intended to counteract its supposedly harmful effects have been put into practice. On the contrary, we have recently witnessed the edifying spectacle of a "World Saving Day," on which central bank governors and ministers of finance vied with each other in attempting to disseminate the virtue of saving as widely as possible throughout their respective nations. And even though there are those who demand an increase in the currency on the grounds that there is an increased tendency to save, it is hard to believe that the presidents of central banks at any rate will prove very ready listeners.

This state of affairs, however, may yet be endangered by a new theory of underconsumption now current in the United States and in England. Its authors are people who spare neither money nor time in the propagation of their ideas. Their doctrine is no less fallacious than all the previous theories of underconsumption, but it is not impossible that with able exposition and extensive financial backing it may exert a certain influence on policy in Anglo-Saxon countries. For this reason it seems worthwhile subjecting this theory to detailed and exhaustive criticism.

II

The teachings of Messrs. Foster and Catchings, with which I am primarily concerned in this study, attained their widest circulation in the United States where they have achieved considerable repute not only among members of the public, but also among professional economists. To understand this success it is necessary to know something of the background of the theory and the very able means by which it has been and still is being propagated. Quite apart from its analytical significance, for European observers at any rate, the story has a certain spectacular interest. I propose, therefore, to deal with it at some length.

Let us start with the two authors. The history of their joint careers provides certain points that give a clue to the origin of their teaching. Waddill Catchings was born in the South; he had a successful career as a lawyer and banker, finally reaching a high position in the iron and steel industry. In 1920 he, and a number of fellow-students from Harvard, decided to commemorate a deceased friend. For this purpose they founded the "Pollak Foundation for Economic Research." They appointed as director another Harvard friend, William Trufant Foster, a pedagogue, at one time a college president. The Foundation had an annual income of $25,000 and it soon began to be responsible for the publication of important books on economic subjects, some of them by well-known economists, such as Irving Fisher's *Making of Index Numbers* (1922), others by members of the Foundation, such as A.B. Hasting's *Costs and Profits* (1923), and, above all, *Money* by Messrs. Foster and Catchings themselves. In this latter work, although it is primarily a very able and instructive exposition of the theory of money, the authors laid the basis of their theory of trade depression later to be fully expounded in their work on *Profits*. In *Money,* they emphasize especially those parts dealing with the circulation of money and the effects on markets of changes in the rate of flow of money. After describing how circulation starts from the market for consumption goods, from which it passes into the market for production goods, and finally returns to its original source, they discuss the conditions under which this process creates a steady demand for the goods offered for sale, and the factors which influence the circulation of money either by accelerating or retarding it. While, in a barter economy, supply and demand are necessarily identical, the appearance of money is shown to be capable of disturbing this equilibrium, since it is only possible to maintain production at the existing level if the producers spend money at the same rate as that at which they receive it. Thus the circulation of money between the various stages of the economic process becomes the central problem of all investigation, not only of changes in the value of money, but also of the influences affecting cyclical fluctuations.

Indeed they even go so far as to lay it down that:

> Money spent in the consumption of commodities is the force that moves all the wheels of industry. When this force

remains in the right relation to the volume of commodities offered for sale, business proceeds steadily. When money is spent faster than the commodities reach the retail markets, business booms forward. When commodities continue to reach the retail markets faster than money is spent, business slackens. To move commodities year after year without disturbing business, enough money must be spent by consumers, and no more than enough, to match all the commodities, dollar for dollar.[1]

It is this theory which forms the basis of the trade cycle theory, which is set forth in great detail in *Profits*,[2] published three years later. In this voluminous work, with which we shall be concerned in the next sections, Messrs. Foster and Catchings give the most elaborate and careful exposition of their theory. But, despite the clear and entertaining exposition, it failed to secure for the theory the wide circulation desired by its authors. They proceeded, therefore, to restate the main principles in popular language, first in their *Business without a Buyer*,[3] and later in abridged form in an essay in the *Atlantic Monthly*, which was distributed freely as a reprint in hundreds of thousands of copies.[4] Most effective, however, in advertising their ideas was the peculiar competition held in connection with the publication of *Profits*. By offering a prize of

---

[1] W.T. Foster and W. Catchings, *Money*. Publications of the Pollak Foundation for Economic Research, No. 2 (Boston and New York: Houghton Mifflin, 1923), p. 277. A third edition was published in 1928.

[2] W.T. Foster and W. Catchings, *Profits*. Publications of the Pollak Foundation, No. 8 (Boston and New York: Houghton Mifflin, 1925).

[3] W.T. Foster and W. Catchings, *Business without a Buyer*. Publications of the Pollak Foundation for Economic Research, No. 10 (Boston and New York, Houghton Mifflin, 1927); 2nd rev. ed. (1928).

[4] W.T. Foster and W. Catchings, *The Dilemma of Thrift* (Newton, Mass.: Pollak Foundation, 1926), reprinted from an article in the *Atlantic Monthly* under the title: "Progress and Plenty, a Way out of the Dilemma of Thrift;" together with another article published in *Century Magazine*. The pamphlet was published by the Pollak Foundation.

$5,000 for the best adverse criticism of the theory contained in this work, the promoters invited the whole world to refute them. But before dealing with the results of this competition it is necessary to consider the general principles of their work.

III

The theory of crises advanced by Messrs. Foster and Catchings in *Profits* is preceded by a detailed explanation of the organization of the present economic structure. This justification of the existing "Money and Profit System," as it is called by the authors, fills about one-half of the volume of four hundred pages. For our purpose, it is sufficient to mention that in this part the function of entrepreneur's profit as a factor determining the direction and extent of production is investigated; but it is worth remarking even at this juncture that the authors succeed in completing this investigation without at any point making clear the real function of capital as a factor of production. Our main concern in this article, however, is confined to the fifth and last part of *Profits* which deals with "Money and Profits in Relation to Consumption," and which, according to the authors themselves, represents a more or less independent object for critical study.[5] It will be necessary in this connection also to refer in some detail to the short essay entitled *The Dilemma of Thrift*.

The main thesis of the book is stated as follows: "The one thing that is needed above all others to sustain a forward movement of business is enough money in the hands of consumers."[6] Now in the present state of affairs a situation arises from time to time when the buying power in the hands of the consumers is insufficient to purchase the whole industrial output at prices that cover costs. The consequent diminution in sales in the market for consumption goods results in unemployment of factories and

---

[5] Cf. *Pollak Prize Essays: Criticisms of "Profits,"* a book by W.T. Foster and W. Catchings (Newton, Mass., 1927).

[6] *Profits,* p. 11.

plant, that is to say, in crises and trade depressions. The question is: where does the deficit in the consumers' income originate? The earlier exposition in *Money* and *Profits* affords no explanation of this phenomenon, since it does not take into account the three principle factors upon which the velocity of circulation, and therefore the "annual production-consumption equation" depend, i.e., the influence of saving, of profits, and of changes in the volume of currency. The most important of these factors is saving, both individual and corporate. To elucidate this point the authors proceed to examine a series of numerical examples and, in the course of this examination, they introduce a number of fictitious assumptions, which, as we shall see later, have an important bearing upon their conclusions. They assume, that by a process of vertical and horizontal integration, the whole industry of the isolated country considered has been united into one single enterprise, payments from which in the form of wages, dividends and salaries form the only source of the community's income. (There are no taxes or government expenditure of any kind.) It is assumed further that the price level, the volume of currency, and the velocity of circulation remain constant, and that wages are received and spent during the same economic period in which the goods are manufactured, while these goods are only sold in the following period, and the profits earned on them are also distributed and spent by the recipients during this same period.[7]

With the aid of numerical examples of this sort, the authors demonstrate that, under these conditions, there can be no difficulty in selling the goods manufactured, either in the case of a constant volume of production or of a rising volume per wage unit, so long as "industry continues to return to consumers in some way all the money that it took from consumers in the sales price of its product, and as long as consumers spend all that they

---
[7] *Money*, p. 268.

receive."⁸ But as soon as the company retains part of the profits in the business, not for the purpose of carrying larger stocks, financing the sale of an increased product, or in *unsuccessful* attempts to improve equipment—for these things are comparatively harmless—but in order to improve "capital facilities," which puts it in the position to increase the volume of production, this happy state of affairs changes. As soon as the increased volume of products reaches the market, it is inevitable that the means of payment in the hands of the consumer should prove insufficient to take up the product at remunerative prices. So long as the process of investment is going on no difficulty arises, since the rise in the total wage bill resulting from the increased number of workmen necessary to carry out the extension equals the loss in the shareholders' income resulting from the reduction in dividends, and thus the relation between the volume of production and the money spent on it remains unaltered. The crisis sets in with the appearance on the market of the surplus output. The money in the hands of the consumer does not increase any further (the sums necessary for the extension of production having already been spent by the wage earners in the previous period to take up the smaller volume) and, since it is assumed that there is no fall in prices, a proportion of the enlarged product must therefore remain unsold.

In *The Dilemma of Thrift*, Messrs. Foster and Catchings provide the following description of the events leading up to this crisis:[9]

> Suppose, however, it [the corporation] uses the remaining one million dollars of profits to build additional cars, in such a way that all this money goes directly or indirectly to consumers. The company has now disbursed exactly enough money to cover the full sales-price of the cars it has already marketed; but where are the consumers

---

[8] Ibid., p. 273.
[9] *Dilemma of Thrift*, p. 15.

to obtain enough money to buy the additional cars? The corporation has given them nothing with which to buy these cars.

The new cars, therefore, must remain unsold, "unless the deficiency (in consumers' income) is made up from outside sources."[10]

According to Messrs. Foster and Catchings the significant difference between the money spent upon consumption goods and money invested rests upon the fact that money of the former kind is "used *first* to take away consumers' goods, whereas in many cases money invested is used *first* to produce more consumers' goods."[11]

> Money that is once used to bring about the production of goods is again used to bring about the production of goods, before it is used to bring about the consumption of goods. In other words, it is used twice in succession to create supply; whereas if the $100,000 in question, instead of having been *invested* in the production of additional goods, had been paid out as dividends and *spent* by the recipients, the $100,000 would have been used alternately to bring goods to the markets and to take goods off the markets.[12]

Statements of this sort, which are repeatedly used by the authors, have led so acute a thinker as Mr. D.H. Robertson to remark that he could not attach any sense to them whatever.[13] It therefore seems worthwhile attempting to restate this part of the

---

[10] *Profits*, p. 281, where the following remark is appended to that qualification: "We here make that qualification, once and for all, with respect to every case in this and the following chapters," which later gave the authors' critics an opportunity to accuse them (*Prize Essays*, p. 12) of a misunderstanding of the main point of their argument.

[11] *Profits*, p. 284.

[12] Ibid., p. 279.

[13] D.H. Robertson: "The Monetary Doctrines of Messrs. Foster and Catchings," *Quarterly Journal of Economics* 43 (May 1929): 483.

theory in more familiar language. Granting the initial presuppositions of the authors, it is, I think, unassailable. So long as the total disbursements during the course of production are spent on consumption goods, the expenses of production are necessarily equal to the proceeds of the sale of the goods purchased. If, however, certain amounts, such as interest earned on capital, or profit, which could be spent on consumption goods without reducing the existing capital stock, are applied to purchasing additional means of production, the sum total spent on production rises without being accompanied by an equivalent increase in the sums available to buy the final product. It is in this "short circuit" in the circulation of money, as Mr. P.W. Martin,[14] whose ideas are closely related to those of Messrs. Foster and Catchings, describes it, that we find the alleged cause of the deficiency in the buying power of the consumer.

Now since the results of corporate saving and of individual saving must be alike, since individuals as well as corporations must save if they are to progress, but since, if this theory is correct, they cannot save at present without frustrating to a certain extent the social purpose of saving, the *Dilemma of Thrift* is inescapable.

> From the standpoint of society, therefore, it is impossible to save intelligently without first solving the problem of adequate consumer income. As it is to-day, certain individuals can save at the expense of other individuals; certain corporations can save at the expense of other corporations; and, from the standpoint of the individual and of the corporation, these savings are real. But society as a whole cannot save anything worth saving at the expense of consumers as a whole, for the capacity of consumers to benefit by what is saved is the sole test of its worth.[15]

---

[14] P.W. Martin, *The Flaw in the Price System* (London: P.S. King, 1924), *The Limited Market* (London: P.S. King, 1926), and *Unemployment and Purchasing Power* (London: P.S. King, 1929).

[15] *Profits*, p. 294.

After the main thesis of the theory has thus been expounded, the authors drop a number of artificial assumptions and attempt to bring the theory nearer to reality. The first assumption to be abandoned is that of a stable price level (this assumption, by the way, was never consistent with their other assumptions). They then examine the effects of falling prices, which alone make it possible to sell the whole of the enlarged product. But falling prices, they argue, make it impossible for industry to maintain production at the new level. The fall of prices causes profits to disappear, and with profits every incentive to the continuation of production.[16] Moreover, it is argued, it is a matter of experience that falling prices render an extension of production impossible. "If there is any fact concerning which our statistical evidence fully supports our reasoning, it is the fact that falling prices put a damper on productive activity."[17] Only on paper is it possible, in spite of falling prices, to carry out productive extensions by means of falling costs, because only on paper can you regulate the diminution of cost so that even the enlarged product can be sold with sufficient profits. In the existing economic system, with the many independent units composing it, such a development is not to be expected. On the contrary, we should rather expect price movements in the wrong direction. A fall in the price of consumption goods, therefore, must always bring about a diminution of production.[18]

Having thus attempted to show that a general fall in prices can never bring about a solution of the problem, the authors next proceed to consider *changes in the volume of money*. After all that has been said, it is argued, it should be clear that even changes in the volume of money can only solve the problem insofar as they influence the "production-consumption equation."

---

[16] Ibid., p. 299.

[17] Ibid., p. 302.

[18] Ibid., pp. 302–13.

> It is not sufficient for this purpose that the total volume of money be increased. The money must go into circulation in such a way that the flow of new money into the hands of the consumers is equal in value, at the current retail price-level, to the flow of new goods into consumers' markets. The question is not, then, whether currency or bank-credit, or both, should be increased year after year, but in what way the new money should be introduced into the circuit flow.[19]

Now unhappily, under the existing system of money and credit, additional money gets into circulation, not on the side of the consumers but on the side of the producers, and thus only aggravates the evil of the discrepancy between producers' disbursements and consumers' money expenditure. Moreover, this system of increasing the money supply through productive credits has the further effect that additions to the money supply take place when they are least necessary. The extension of production that they finance is a response to a lively demand. But when a falling off of consumers' demand is noticeable then credit is restricted and the trouble is aggravated. Thus the modern claim to restrict credit at the first sign of increasing warehouse stocks, and *vice versa,* is thoroughly pernicious.

> In this way ... every advance toward higher standards of living would promptly be checked; for whenever it appeared that consumer income was too small, it would be made smaller still through wage reductions, and under-production would follow promptly.[20]

Nevertheless, it would be easy to arrange an increase in consumers' credits, and it is only in this way that the deficiency in the purchasing power of the consumer, and thus the cause of the depression, can be removed.

---

[19] Ibid., p. 307.
[20] Ibid., p. 324.

Theoretically, then, it is always possible to add to the money circulation in such a way as to benefit the community.... In any conceivable situation ... an all-wise despot could make a net gain to the community by increasing the volume of money in circulation.... If any safe and practicable means could be devised, in connection with increased public works and decreased taxes, or in any other connection, of issuing just enough money to consumers to provide for individual savings and to enable them to buy an enlarged output, and business men were confident that issues to consumers would continue at this rate and at no other rate, there would be no drop in the price-level and no reason for curtailing production, but, on the contrary, the most powerful incentive for increasing production.[21]

In *Profits*, the authors do not go further than to hint at these proposals. After a not very successful attempt at statistical verification they conclude that, under the present order of things, every attempt at increasing production must be checked by the fact that the demand of the consumer cannot keep pace with the supply. To remove the causes of this underconsumption is one of the most promising and most urgent problems for the present generation. "Indeed, it is doubtful whether any other way of helping humanity holds out such large immediate possibilities."[22]

But before such reforms can be achieved, professional economists will have to admit the inadequacy of their present theories. "If the main contentions of *Money* and *Profits* are sound, much of our traditional economic teaching is unsound, and overlooks some of the fundamentals which must be better understood before it will be possible to solve the economic problem."[23] Conversion of professional economists was therefore the main purpose of the

---

[21] Ibid., pp. 330–31.
[22] Ibid., p. 417.
[23] Ibid., p. 416.

campaign that was launched by offering a prize for the best adverse criticism of *Profits*.

IV

The result of this competition for the best adverse criticism of their theory was the most remarkable success achieved by Messrs. Foster and Catchings. The three members of the jury, Professor Wesley C. Mitchell, the late Allyn A. Young, and Mr. Owen D. Young, the President of the General Electric Company, of "Young Plan" fame, had no fewer than four hundred and thirty-five essays to examine. In the Introduction to the little volume in which the prize essay and others were published,[24] Messrs. Foster and Catchings relate, with some pride, that at least fifty universities, forty-two American States, and twenty-five foreign countries were represented. Among the authors were at least forty authors of books on economics, fifty professors of political economy, sixty accounting experts, bankers, editors, statisticians, directors of large companies, etc.—among them "some of the ablest men in the Federal Reserve System," a functionary of the American Economic Association, a former President of that Society, and "several of the most highly-reputed economists in the British Empire."

But despite this highly respectable mass attack of adverse criticism, Messrs. Foster and Catchings remained convinced that their theory still held its own. Moreover, they were able to quote the opinion of one of the umpires,[25] that notwithstanding all that had been said against it, the substance of the theory remained untouched. This sounds extraordinary. But what is more extraordinary is that a candid perusal of the various criticisms that have been published forces one to admit that it is

---

[24] Essays by R.W. Souter, Frederick Law Olmsted, C.F. Bickerdike, and Victor Valentinovitch Novogilov, and others. Cf. also the Introduction to *Business without a Buyer*.

[25] Ibid., p. 6. See also the Introduction to *Business without a Buyer*.

true. So far, the main theory, and what in my opinion is the fundamental misconception of Messrs. Foster and Catchings, has remained unanswered. The meritorious and readable works that were published in the *Prize Essays*, equally with criticisms published elsewhere,[26] direct their criticism only against details. They accept the main thesis of Messrs. Foster and Catchings. Only the two essays of Novogilov and Adams, which we shall have occasion to mention later on, touch upon the critical points, and even here they do not make their respective objections the basic part of their criticism, or develop them into an independent refutation.

In the case of Novogilov's work, it is possible that this is an injustice. In the *Prize Essays* it was only published in abridged form, and just the part dealing with the influence of varying quantities of product at the various stages of production on the level of profits was entirely left out.[27] It is to be hoped that one day it will be published in its entirety. Mr. A.B. Adams's essay, on the other hand, whose criticism on many points coincides with that developed in this essay, and which in an incidental remark foreshadows one of its main theses,[28] suffers from the fact that the author himself does not realize the full importance of his objections, and therefore only criticizes the application of Messrs. Foster and Catchings's theory to the case of investment in fixed capital, while admitting its correctness in the case of investment in circulating capital. But even Mr. Adams seems insufficiently to appreciate the function of capital and the conditions determining

---

[26] To be mentioned especially are: A.B. Adams, *Profits, Progress and Prosperity* (New York: McGraw-Hill, 1927); A.H. Hansen, *Business Cycle Theory: Its Development and Present Status* (Boston: Ginn, 1927); a prize essay published separately); H. Neisser, "Theorie des wirtschaftlichen Gleichgewichtes," *Kölner sozialpolitische Vierteljahrschrift* 6 (1927): esp. 124–35; Robertson, "The Monetary Doctrines of Messrs. Foster and Catchings."

[27] Cf. *Prize Essays*, pp. 118–24.

[28] See section IX beginning on p. 163 below.

its utilization—a deficiency that is common both to the authors of the theory and to all their critics.

As for the rest, they all endeavor to prove that the existing currency organization suffices to increase the supply of money in the course of an extension of production so as to avoid a fall in the price level. Some of them also point out that the extension of production can also bring about a diminution in costs per unit, so that falling prices need not always put a damper on production. But the alleged necessity to ease the sale of the enlarged product by an increase in the money supply is, in general, allowed to pass unquestioned. In doing this, however, the critics place themselves in a difficult position. For the contention of Messrs. Foster and Catchings that productive credits aggravate still more the deficiency in the purchasing power of the consumer is clearly a corollary of the fundamental concept on which the claim for increasing the volume of money by productive extensions is based. To meet this difficulty the critics resort to various expedients. Some make very ingenious investigations into the order of succession of various money movements. Some attempt to refute the rather shaky assumptions in regard to the formation of profits in the course of productive extensions. Correct as these objections may be, they miss the point. The main thesis remains untouched.

V

It is clear that this is the opinion of Messrs. Foster and Catchings, for in their *Business without a Buyer*, published after the close of the prize competition, they do not make any significant alterations in the exposition of their theory. Fortified by the result of the competition, they then proceeded to develop the practical consequences of their theory. In *The Road to Plenty*,[29]

---

[29] W.T. Foster and W. Catchings, *The Road to Plenty*. Publications of Pollak Foundation for Economic Research, No. 11 (New York, Houghton Mifflin, 1928). A popular edition of 50,000 copies of the *Road to Plenty* was published and sold (230 pages in full cloth binding) for 25 cents!

which embodies the results of these further reflections, they make no attempt to appeal to economists. Despite the extremely favorable reception of their former books, it appears they are far from satisfied with professional economists. Both in the introduction to the *Prize Essays* and in *Business without a Buyer* they dwelt with some sprightliness on the lack of enlightenment in such circles. Next they turned to the general public and cast their theory in the form of a novel. The book records a conversation in the smoking compartment of a train where the complaints of a warm-hearted friend of humanity cause a genial business man to explain the causes of crises and unemployment according to the theory of the authors, and then to defend the latter against the objections of a solicitor and a professor of economics (who, of course, comes out worst). Finally, all those present (including a member of the House of Representatives) are roused to a great pitch of enthusiasm about the concrete proposals based upon it.

These proposals are formulated still more clearly in a further essay, *Progress and Plenty*,[30] and before proceeding to examine the theory it is worthwhile setting them forth explicitly. The first demand of the authors, and the condition for the execution of their further proposals, is an extension of business statistics in the direction of a more exact knowledge of the sales of consumption goods—in the first place, a complete and reliable index of retail prices; second, statistics of all factors influencing these prices (i.e., all possible economic data). These should be collected by public authorities and published promptly, in order to give information and orientation to the business world. On the basis of such statistics, all public works and all financial operations of the government should be directed in such a way as to

---

[30] W.T. Foster and W. Catchings, *Progress and Plenty: A Way out of the Dilemma of Thrift* reprinted from the *Century Magazine* (July 1928). Reprinted also together with *The Dilemma of Thrift*. The second edition of *The Road to Plenty*, which I received after writing this article, takes over almost word for word the statements quoted here from *Progress and Plenty*.

even out fluctuations in the demand for consumption goods. In *Progress and Plenty*,[31] Messrs. Foster and Catchings recommend the delegation of the business of collecting data, and their application to the distribution of public works to a separate body, the "Federal Budget Board." Just as the Federal Reserve Board directs a system for the financing of production, the Federal Budget Board should direct the financing of consumption and prevent disturbances of the economic system arising from consumption lagging behind production.

So far, apart from the demand for a new board, the proposal contains nothing beyond the much-discussed plan for distributing public works in time in such a way as to concentrate all those capable of being postponed to times of depression. But Messrs. Foster and Catchings are not satisfied with this. They realize that such a plan would have undesirable effects if the necessary sums were collected and locked up in the public treasury in times of prosperity and spent in case of need. On the other hand, to raise the money by taxation at the time when it is needed for public works would be still less likely to achieve the desired end. Only an increase in the volume of money for the purpose of consumption can solve the problem:

> Progress requires a constant flow of new money to consumers. If, therefore, business indexes show the need for a reinforced consumer demand which cannot be met without additional Government expenditure, the Board should bring about such expenditure, not only out of funds previously accumulated for that purpose, but at times out of loans which involve an expansion of bank credit. *This feature of the plan is essential.*[32] It follows that the Government should borrow and spend the money

---

[31] Page 16 of the independent reprint, p. 37 of the reprint together with *The Dilemma of Thrift* (the reference to the latter will always be given in parenthesis). Cf. also *The Road to Plenty*, 2nd ed., p. 188.

[32] My italics.

whenever the indexes show that the needed flow of money will not come from other sources.[33]

As might be expected, the authors protest[34] that all this is not to be regarded as inflationary. Before its publication they had promised that it should contain "nothing dangerous or even distasteful," and that it would not involve "unlimited issues of fiat money."[35] We shall deal critically, with these proposals in the last section of this article. At present, it need only be remarked that even critics who sympathize with Messrs. Foster and Catchings's theory have been unable to conceal their scruples on this point. Mr. D.H. Robertson[36] remarks very correctly that he has no doubts that

> they were born with a double dose of the inflation bacillus in their composition; and though they have done their best to exorcise it with prayer and fasting, so that they are able to look down with detached pity on more gravely affected sufferers, such as Major Douglas, yet at critical moments the bacillus is always apt to take charge of the argument.

It is, therefore, all the more astounding that they are able to quote in the advertisements to *The Road to Plenty* (it is true without mentioning the source) the opinion of no less an authority than the late Professor A.A. Young, that "on economic grounds, the plan for prosperity" proposed in *The Road to Plenty* "is soundly conceived," and that (according to the same source) Mr. W.M. Persons should have thought the plan "practicable and important."

In wider circles, the proposals of Messrs. Foster and Catchings seem to have had an extraordinary effect. President Hoover's pledge to carry out, within practical limits, such a regulation of public works as would alleviate unemployment, has

---

[33] *Progress and Plenty*, p. 22 (42), and almost in the same words in *The Road to Plenty*, 2nd ed., p. 193.

[34] *The Road to Plenty*, 2nd ed., p. 209.

[35] *Prize Essays*, p. 5.

[36] "The Monetary Doctrines of Messrs. Foster and Catchings," p. 498.

been a powerful lever to their argument. In a recent pamphlet[37] they announce that Senator Wagner from New York has already brought a bill before Congress for creating a "Federal Unemployment Stabilization Board" with very similar functions to their "Federal Budget Board." So far it has not been proposed that this board should finance public works with additional bank money, and even Messrs. Foster and Catchings have guarded themselves from demanding the execution of this part of their proposals—even in connection with the Hoover Plans. Instead they have concentrated on a criticism of the policy of the Federal Reserve Board in raising its discount rate at a time of falling prices and falling employment.[38] It is pressure of this sort that constitutes a danger both in America and elsewhere if such theories gain further popularity. At this point, therefore, we may pass to a criticism of their validity.

VI

It is constantly assumed by Messrs. Foster and Catchings that the investment of savings for the extension of production necessarily increases the total costs of production by the full amount of the invested savings. This follows clearly from their continual emphasis on the "fact" that the value of the increased product is raised by the amount invested, and that therefore it can only be sold profitably for a proportionately higher sum. It is implied by the examples, in which it is always assumed that the increase in the current outlay in wages, etc., exactly corresponds with the sums invested. Now there is a certain initial obscurity in this assumption, since it is obvious that the costs of the product produced during an economic period cannot rise by the whole of the

---

[37] W.T. Foster and W. Catchings, "Better Jobs and More of Them: The Government's Part in Preventing Unemployment." Reprinted from the *Century Magazine* (July 1929).

[38] Ibid., p. 17.

newly invested sum if this is invested in durable instruments, but only in proportion to the depreciation of the new durable capital goods; a fact that is not made clear in their exposition. My main objection, however, is not concerned with this circumstance—which it is impossible to believe that the authors could entirely overlook—but rather with their assumption that generally, over *any* length of time, the costs of production can increase by the whole of the newly invested amount. This view, which is based on a complete misunderstanding of the function of capital as a "carrying" agent, assumes that the increased volume of production brought about by the new investments must be undertaken with the same methods as the smaller volume produced before the new movement took place. Such an assumption may be true for a single enterprise, but never for industry as a whole. For in industry as a whole an increase in the available supply of capital always necessitates a *change* in the methods of production in the sense of a transition to more capitalistic, more "roundabout," processes.

For in order that there may be an increase in the volume of production without a change in the methods of production, not only the available supply of capital, but also the supply of all other factors of production must be increased in similar proportion. In regard to land, at any rate, this is practically impossible. It is just as inadmissible to assume that the complementary factors that are necessary for the extension of production are previously unemployed and find employment only with the appearance of the new savings.[39]

---

[39] Messrs. Foster and Catchings seem to avail themselves of the assumption of an "industrial reserve army"—a notion much favored in trade cycle theory—from which the labor power necessary for a proportional extension of production can always be obtained at will. Quite apart from the incompatibility of this assumption with the known facts, it is theoretically inadmissible as a starting point for a theory that attempts, like Messrs. Foster and Catchings, to show the causes of crises, and thus of unemployment, on the basis of the modern "equilibrium theory" of price determination. Only on the basis of an

A correct view of the reactions on production as a whole of the investment of new savings must be envisaged in this way: At first the new savings will serve the purpose of *transferring a portion of the original means of production previously employed in producing consumers' goods to the production of new producers' goods.* The supply of consumers' goods must, therefore, temporarily fall off as an immediate consequence of the investment of new savings (a circumstance constantly overlooked by Messrs. Foster and Catchings).[40] No unfavorable effects on the sales of consumption goods follow from this, for the demand for consumption goods and the amount of original means of production employed in producing them decrease in similar proportions. And indeed even Messrs. Foster and Catchings do not make any such assertion. Their difficulties begin only at the moment when the increased volume of consumption goods, brought about by the new investment, comes on to the market.

Now this increase in the volume of consumption goods can only be effected through an increase in the volume of capital employed in production. Such capital, once it has been brought into existence, does not maintain itself automatically. This increase makes it necessary that, henceforward, a greater proportion of the existing means of production should be permanently devoted to the production of capital goods, and a smaller part to finishing consumption goods; and this shift in the immediate utilization of means of production must, under the conditions prevailing in the modern economic system, conform with a change in

---

economic theory that, like the Marxian, tries to explain the existence of permanent unemployment of considerable proportions independently of crises would such an assumption be theoretically permissible.

[40] Novogilov, who—as far as I can see—is the only critic who emphasizes this circumstance (*Prize Essays*, p. 120), puts a favorable interpretation on the exposition in *Profits*, namely that the authors assume that "the population as a whole must increase its expenditure of labor, but consume not more than in the first years" (p. 108). But how should savings occasion an increased expenditure of labor?

the relative amount of money expended in the various stages of production. But this question of the relation between the sums of money expended in any period on consumption goods on the one hand and on production goods on the other, brings us to the fundamental flaw in Messrs. Foster and Catchings's theory.

VII

Messrs. Foster and Catchings base the whole of their exposition on an hypothesis of what may be called single-stage production, in which, in a state of equilibrium the money received in every period from the sale of consumption goods must equal the amount of money expended on all kinds of production goods in the same period.[41] Hence they are incapable of conceiving an extension of production save, so to speak, in the "width"—an extension involving the expenditure of the new savings side by side with the sums which were already being spent on the ultimate factors of production, this is to say, the recipients of net income. It is easy to see how they arrive at this position. They assume a single enterprise in which all goods are produced from beginning to end (there will be much to say about this later), and because of this they entirely overlook the phenomenon of changes to more or less capitalistic methods of production.

Let us for the time being avoid this assumption, and instead, consider an economy in which the different stages and branches of production are divided into different independent enterprises.

---

[41] This conception, which is completely erroneous at any rate as far as it applies to a modern economic system, is very often met in economic literature, and may be traced back as far as Adam Smith, who wrote (*Wealth of Nations*, ed. Cannan [London: Methuen, 1904], vol. 1, p. 305): "The value of the goods circulated between the different dealers never can exceed the value of those circulated between dealers and consumers; whatever is bought by the dealer being ultimately destined to be sold to the consumer." It is interesting to note that this statement of Smith is quoted by T.H. Tooke in support of the doctrines of the Banking School. Cf. *An Inquiry into the Currency Principle* (London: Smith, Elder, 1844), p. 11.

We can return later to the special case of single-enterprise production considered by Messrs. Foster and Catchings. But we will adhere throughout to another assumption that they make: the assumption that the amount of money in circulation remains unchanged. It is especially important to do this because most of the criticisms of the theory that have been made up to the present have sought the solution of the alleged dilemma chiefly in a proportional adjustment of the supply of money to the enlarged volume of production.[42] To me, at any rate, the fundamental error of the theory seems to arise rather in the presentation of the origin of the dilemma, the supply of money remaining unchanged. I shall return to the question of the effects of a change in the supply of money in the last section, in which I deal with Messrs. Foster and Catchings's proposals for positive reform.

What happens, then, under the conditions assumed, when somebody saves a part of his income hitherto devoted to consumption, or when a company does not distribute its profits, and the sums thus saved are reinvested in production? At first, clearly the demand that is directed to means of production increases, and that directed to consumption goods correspondingly decreases. Does that mean that the expenditure on production will now be greater than is justified by the sums of money that will be available for the purchase of consumption goods?

That this need not be the case is surely clear from the most superficial consideration of the modern capitalistic economy. For at every moment of time raw materials, semi-finished products,

---

[42] Cf. the criticism of F.L. Olmsted (*Prize Essays,* p. 68), where it is expressly stated:

> This brings us back to the "Dilemma," and also brings us back to *the obvious and only escape from the Dilemma;* namely, the progressive increase, in relation to the price-level of goods, of the scale of money compensation to individuals for their productive effort if that productive effort is progressively increasing in efficiency. (Italics mine)

and other means of production are coming into the market, the value of which is several times greater than the value of the consumption goods that are simultaneously offered in the market for consumption goods.[43] It follows that the sum spent on the purchase of means of production of all kinds at any period is several times greater than the sum spent on the purchase of consumption goods at the same time. The fact that the total costs of production are, nevertheless, not greater than the value of the consumption goods produced is explained by the circumstance that every good on its way from raw material to finished product is exchanged against money as many times, on the average, as the amount of money expended on the purchase of means of production at every period exceeds the amount spent on consumption goods. And it is just a lengthening of this average process of production (which, *on our assumption*, shows itself in an increase of the number of independent stages of production) that makes it possible, when new savings are available, to produce a greater amount of consumption goods from the same amount of original means of production.

The proposition that savings can only bring about an increase in the volume of production by permitting a greater and more productive "roundaboutness" in the methods of production has been demonstrated so fully by the classical analysis of Böhm-Bawerk that it does not require further examination. It is necessary here only to go further into certain monetary aspects of the phenomenon.

The questions that interest us are as follows: how does the increase in the money stream *available for productive purposes* following the investment of new savings distribute the additional

---

[43] M.W. Holtrop computes on the basis of statistical data taken from publications of I. Fisher and the National Bureau of Economic Research that in the United States in the year 1912 the sum of all money payments was more than twelve times larger than the sum of all money incomes (*De Omloopssnelheid van het Geld* [Amsterdam: H.J. Paris, 1928], p. 181). Cf. also his further exposition that gives interesting figures in regard to the variations of this proportion in the course of the trade cycle.

The "Paradox" of Saving

demand for means of production through the economic system, and under what conditions is this distribution effected in such a way as to achieve the purpose of saving with the smallest possible disturbance. After what has been said already in this connection it will be of fundamental importance to distinguish between changes in the demand for original means of production, i.e., labor and land, and changes in the demand for means of production which are themselves products (intermediate products or capital goods) such as semi-finished goods, machinery, implements, etc. On the other hand it is not important for our present purpose to distinguish between durable and non-durable means of production because it is irrelevant, for instance, that a loom has only to be renewed after eight periods of time, since, in a continuous process of production, this amounts to the same thing as if every eighth loom has to be renewed in every period.

For the sake of simplicity, we may assume that the path from the original means of production to the final product is of equal length for all parts of the total money stream, although, in fact, this differs according to the moment when the particular original means of production are employed in the different stages of production; so that the assumed uniform length of the roundabout ways of production only corresponds to the *average* length of the various processes which lead to the production of a consumption good. The only case in real life strictly corresponding to this assumption would be the production of a good requiring expenditure of labor only at the beginning of the production process, the rest being left to nature; as, for example, in the case of the planting of a tree. But even this would only completely conform to our assumption if the saplings changed hands every year, i.e., if one man held one-year saplings, another two-year saplings, and so on. This difficulty only arises because, for purposes of exposition, it is easier to treat the average length of production as if it were uniform for all processes. In the real world, of course, it is the very fact that the period between the expenditure of the original means of production and the completion of the consumers' goods is different for every original means of production used, which makes it necessary that the goods should pass through several hands before they are ready for consumption. We assume, therefore, that, for example, the value of all means of production coming to the market during one period is eight times as great as the value of the consumption goods produced during the same period, and the latter is sold for 1,000 units of money, say pounds sterling. We disregard the differences in value conditioned by interest, that is to say, we make the assumption that interest on capital employed, together with the remuneration of the original means of production, is paid out only in the highest stage of production. The whole process of production and the circulation of money connected with it can then be represented schematically in the following way:

SCHEME A

		£
Demand for consumption goods (= products of stage of production No. 1)		1,000
	No. 2	1,000
	No. 3	1,000
	No. 4	1,000
Demand for the products of the stages of production	No. 5	1,000
	No. 6	1,000
	No. 7	1,000
	No. 8	1,000
	No. 9	1,000
Total demand for produced means of production—8 × 1,000 =	....	8,000

Relation of the demand for consumption goods to the demand for produced means of production—1:8.[44]

---

[44] If it were desired, in order to bring the scheme closer to reality to demonstrate, instead of the average length of the production process, the various lengths of its particular branches, it should be represented somewhat as follows:

Such a table represents at once both the products of the various stages of production coming on to the market *simultaneously* with the consumption goods and the *successive* intermediary products from which the actual product finally emerges, since, in a stationary economy, these are the same. We exhibit, that is to say, the total supply of goods originating in one branch of production (or, if the scheme is applied to the whole economy, all branches of production), and coming on to the market in one period of time. The sums paid at the ninth stage of production for the original means of production correspond necessarily with

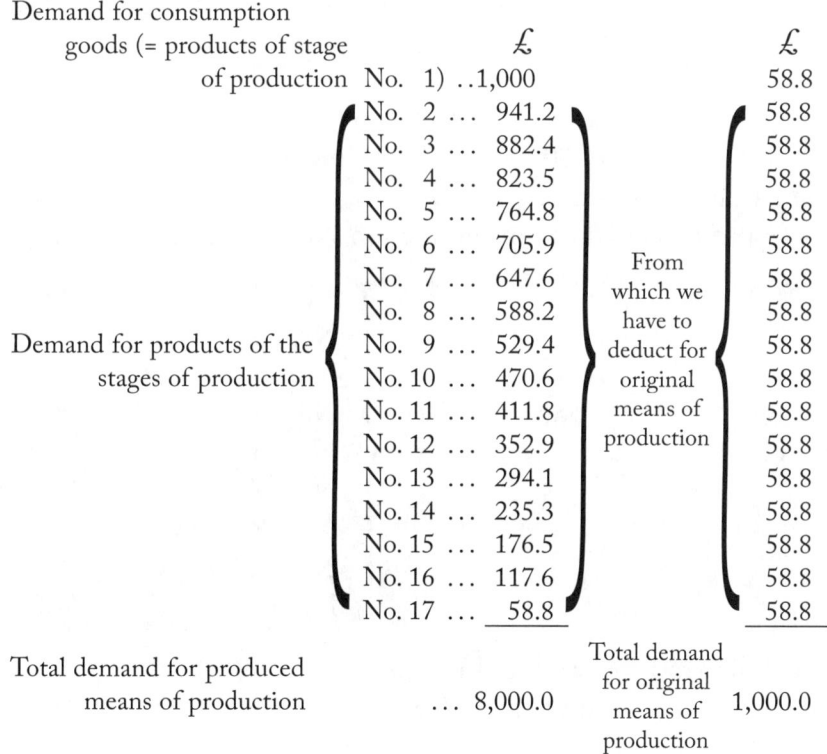

	£		£
Demand for consumption goods (= products of stage of production No. 1) ..1,000			58.8
No. 2 ... 941.2			58.8
No. 3 ... 882.4			58.8
No. 4 ... 823.5			58.8
No. 5 ... 764.8			58.8
No. 6 ... 705.9		From which we have to deduct for original means of production	58.8
No. 7 ... 647.6			58.8
No. 8 ... 588.2			58.8
Demand for products of the stages of production — No. 9 ... 529.4			58.8
No. 10 ... 470.6			58.8
No. 11 ... 411.8			58.8
No. 12 ... 352.9			58.8
No. 13 ... 294.1			58.8
No. 14 ... 235.3			58.8
No. 15 ... 176.5			58.8
No. 16 ... 117.6			58.8
No. 17 ... 58.8			58.8
Total demand for produced means of production	... 8,000.0	Total demand for original means of production	1,000.0

Relation of the demand for consumption goods to the demand for produced means of production—1:8.

Such an exposition, more complete than the former, alters nothing of its results, but complicates considerably the clarity of the presentation.

the value of the consumption goods, and form the origin of the funds for which the consumption goods are sold.

Let us assume, then, that the owners of the original means of production spend from their total income of £1,000 only £900, and invest in production the remaining £100 thus saved. There is, therefore, £8,100 now available for the purchase of production goods, and the relation between the demand for consumption goods and the demand for production goods changes from 1:8 to 1:9.

In order that the increased sum of money now available for the purchase of means of production should be profitably utilized, the average number of stages of production must increase from eight to nine; the situation, represented in Scheme A, has therefore to be altered in the following way:

Scheme B
(£100 is saved and invested)

		£
Demand for consumption goods (= products of stage of production No. 1)		900
Demand for the products of the stages of production {	No. 2	900
	No. 3	900
	No. 4	900
	No. 5	900
	No. 6	900
	No. 7	900
	No. 8	900
	No. 9	900
	No. 10	900
Total demand for produced means of production—9 × 900 =	. . . .	8,100

Relation of the demand for consumption goods to the demand for produced means of production—1:9.

In this case also, the total sum that is spent in the last stage for the original means of production, and which is therefore available as income for the purchase of the product, coincides with the value of the product after the necessary adjustments have taken place. The allocation of the additional means of production has been effected by maintaining the equilibrium between costs of production and the prices of consumption goods in such a way that the money stream has been lengthened and narrowed down correspondingly, i.e., the average number of the successive turnovers during the productive process has risen in the same ratio as the demand for means of production in relation to the demand for consumption goods has increased. If the supply of money remains unaltered this is necessarily connected with a fall in the prices of the factors of production, the unchanged amount of which (disregarding the increase of capital) has to be exchanged for £900; and a *still greater fall* in the prices of consumption goods, the volume of which has increased on account of the utilization of more roundabout methods of production while their total money value has diminished from £1,000 to £900.

This demonstrates at any rate the *possibility* that, by an increase in the money stream going to production and a diminution of that going to consumption, production *can* still be organized in such a way that the products can be sold at remunerative prices. It remains to show (1) that with an unchanged amount of money, production will be governed by prices so that such an adjustment does take place, (2) that by such an adjustment of production the purpose of saving is achieved in the most favorable way, and (3) that on the other hand every change in the volume of currency, especially every monetary policy aiming at the stability of the prices of consumption goods (or any other prices) renders the adaptation of production to the new supply of saving more difficult and indeed frustrates more or less the end of saving itself.

VIII

In order to remain as faithful as possible to the example which Messrs. Foster and Catchings have put in the foreground, let us consider the case of a joint stock company reinvesting a portion of its profits that was hitherto distributed. In what way will it utilize the additional capital? This utilization may be different in different individual cases, yet important conclusions may be drawn from a consideration of the general possibilities of additional investments.

In principle it is possible for a single enterprise—in contrast to the whole industry—to utilize the available amount of capital for extending production by retaining existing methods but employing larger quantities of *all* factors.[45] We can leave the possibility of this out of consideration for the moment, as our undertaking could only get additional labor and other original means of production by drawing them away from other undertakings, by outbidding them. And this process will change the relative proportion of capital to the other factors in the other enterprise, and thus a transition of production to new methods will become necessary. This is clearly the general economic effect of the increase of capital, and it is this in which we are interested. For the sake of simplicity let us assume, then, that the transition has already taken place in the first enterprise that undertook the savings.

---

[45] In practice, such a *linear* extension of production will be of importance insofar as, by an increase in the supply of capital, not only will the share of capital in every branch of production increase, but there will be an increase in the relative size of more capitalistic branches of production as compared with less capitalistic ones, i.e., the former will employ *more* labor, and this extension of the whole undertaking can so far overshadow the increase in the relative share of capital as to create the impression of a linear (proportional) extension of the more capitalistic undertakings. Even if the proportion between capital and the original means of production employed remains absolutely constant in the individual industries, but the more capitalistic undertakings were extended at the expense of the less capitalistic ones (as may be the case with undertakings of average roundaboutness), this implies, from the point of view of the whole industry, a transition to more capitalistic methods. (It may perhaps be mentioned here that the original German terms that the translator has rendered as "roundaboutness" and more or less "capitalistic" were *"Kapitalintensität"* and *"kapitalintensiv."*)

But if a "linear" extension of production is ruled out, and the undertaking has to utilize its relative increase in capital supply for a transition to more capitalistic methods, there remain two main types of investment for the additional capital that have to be considered. These are usually distinguished as investment in fixed capital or durable producers' goods, and in circulating capital or non-durable producers' goods respectively. Up to now, in following Messrs. Foster and Catchings, we have only considered investment in circulating capital; in future we shall have to distinguish between these two possibilities.

Whether in any given case investment in fixed capital or in circulating capital is the more profitable, and is therefore undertaken, depends on the technical conditions of the concrete case, and therefore cannot be decided *a priori*. For analytical purposes it is desirable to treat these two cases separately, both as regards the conditions that must be given in order to render more capitalistic methods profitable, and also as regards the effect on prices.

IX

As regards investment in *fixed capital* (i.e., durable means of production), the case is relatively simple. Messrs. Foster and Catchings leave this case entirely out of account (a fact on which, as we have already mentioned, Mr. A.B. Adams bases his criticism) and Mr. P.W. Martin applies a similar theory of his own expressly to the case of investment in circulating capital only.[46] What we shall have to say here, therefore, will hardly meet with much opposition, and for this reason it will be easier in this connection to develop the analysis that is relevant also for the subsequent investigation.

In order that new investment in fixed capital may be profitable, it is necessary that the increase in receipts from the increased product following the investment should be sufficient to cover the

---

[46] Cf. *Unemployment and Purchasing Power*, p. 15.

interest and depreciation of the invested capital. The rate of interest must be somewhat higher where the new investments are made than in the alternative employments that are open to them, but somewhat lower than the rate of interest paid hitherto. It is just the circumstance that the rate of interest has fallen and that the investment in question is the nearest in the scale of profitableness which determines that it, and no other, shall be undertaken. In judging its profitableness, account must be taken of the fact that the enlarged product following the new investment can only be sold in the long run at prices lower relatively to the prices of original means of production than hitherto. This is partly because, owing to the cooperation of new capital, more consumption goods will be produced from a given quantity of original means of production; and also because a greater amount of consumption goods must be sold against the income of the original means of production and of capital, and the increase in the income from the latter (if it occurs at all—if the increase in capital is not more than compensated by the fall in the interest rate) must always be relatively less than the increase of consumption goods.[47]

If the quantity of money remains unchanged, the unavoidable fall in the relative prices of consumption goods will also manifest itself absolutely. It is in this way that the relative fall will establish itself at the moment when the new consumption goods come on to the market. If the supply of money is kept constant, this effect of every extension of production will be well known to producers and they will therefore *only choose such employments for the investment of new savings as remain profitable even if prices are expected to fall.* But these employments—and this, as we shall see presently,

---

[47] The fall in the rate of interest necessitates *ipso facto* such a relative change in the prices of means of production and of products because, in a state of equilibrium, the rate of interest must exactly correspond with the difference between the two. With regard to the relation between changes in the rate of interest and changes in relative prices, cf. the appendix to my essay "Das intertemporale Gleichgewichtsystem der Preise und die Bewegungen des Geldwertes," *Weltwirtschaftliches Archiv* 28 (July 1928).

is the essential point—are the only ones through which the social advantages of saving can be realized without loss.

Even if the volume of money is increased so that the prices of consumption goods do not fall, a new equilibrium must inevitably be established between costs of production and the prices of products. This can come about—if a fall in the prices of consumption goods is excluded—in two ways: either by a rise in the prices of means of production; or by a return to the previous, shorter, less productive method of production; or by both of these ways together. What actually happens depends on where and when the additional money is injected into the economic system. If the increase in the supply of money were only to take place at the time when the additional volume of consumption goods comes on to the market and in such a way as to render it directly available for the purchase of consumption goods,[48] the expectation of unchanged prices for products would result in a portion of the additional amount, rendered available for the purchase of means of production through saving, not being utilized for a lengthening of the production process, i.e., the formation of new capital; it would simply serve to drive up the prices of the means of production. Because of the expectation of stable prices for the products, *more* openings for the new savings will appear profitable than can actually be exploited with their aid. The rate of interest is only sufficient to limit alternatives to those most profitable when price relations are also in equilibrium with it. Competitive selection must therefore take place in the market for the means of production, i.e., the prices of means of production must rise until only so many extensions of the productive process appear profitable at those prices as can actually be carried out by the new savings. That simply means that a portion of the savings will not be utilized for the creation of capital, but merely for the purpose of increasing the prices of available means of production.

---

[48] This is the suggestion made by Messrs. Foster and Catchings; we shall have occasion to go into this case more extensively in the last section, when we come to criticize their proposals for reform.

But the assumption that the supply of money will only be increased when the enlarged volume of consumption goods comes on to the market has little probability. In the first place, the fact that new savings offer possibilities for the extension of production will, as a rule (according to the prevalent opinion, quite justifiably), give rise to an increase in the volume of money in the form of producers' credits. On the other hand, the fact that, in spite of the more capitalistic and more productive methods, the prices of the products do not fall, will provide an incentive to take up additional loans from the banks far beyond the sum voluntarily saved, and will thus increase the demand for means of production much more than would be justified by the new savings. The rise in the prices of these means of production conditioned by it, will gradually cause the excessive price margin between these goods and consumption goods to disappear (and thus take away the incentive for further extensions of credit); at the same time, more means of production than are justified by the new savings will be transferred for use in longer processes (i.e., more lengthy processes will be undertaken than can be carried out). In other words, it will be possible, through an increase in the volume of money, to draw away as many factors from the consumption goods industries, over and above the quota voluntarily saved, as to enable at first the commencement of all enlargements of fixed capital that appear profitable at the lower rate of interest having regard to the unchanged prices.

All these investments, however, can be carried on only so long as the new money used for extensions of production is not utilized by the owners of the factors of production, to whom it is paid, for the purchase of consumption goods or so long as the increase in the demand for consumption goods is offset by a progressive increase in the supply of new productive credits.[49] As soon as the increase in

---

[49] Cf. my *Monetary Theory and the Trade Cycle* (London: Routledge, 1933); also included in this volume.

the volume of credits granted to producers is no longer sufficient to take away as many means of production from the provision of current consumption as would be required for the execution of all the projects that appear profitable under the lower rate of interest and the unchanged price relationship between consumption goods and means of production, then the increasing utilization of means of production for the provision of current needs through less lengthy processes of production will drive up the prices of means of production, both absolutely and relatively to consumption goods, and thus render unprofitable those extensions of production which only became possible through the policy of price stabilization.

As, in the case under consideration, we are dealing with extensions of durable plant, which as a rule must be left in their previous employments even if they become unprofitable (even if their quasi-rents fall to such a level as to drive their value much below the cost of production, and thus prevent their replacement) the adjustments necessary will only proceed very slowly and with great sacrifices of capital. But, apart from this loss of a portion of the savings, the final equilibrium of production will establish itself in that position where it would have been established right from the beginning had no increase in money supply intervened; that is to say, at that point where the diminution in the cost per unit of product brought about by the investment is just great enough to sell the larger quantity of the final product despite the fact that, owing to savings, only a smaller proportion of the total money stream goes to purchase it than hitherto. Although the schematic representation given above is only completely applicable to the case (to which we shall return later) of investment in circulating capital, it is also true in the case of investment in fixed capital that the necessary fall in the price of the final product manifests itself not only in a fall of the price per unit (which must take place even if an unchanged money stream goes to buy a larger product) but also in a diminution in the proportion of the total money stream which is available for the purchase of consumption goods.

The difference between this case and that of investment in circulating capital lies in the fact that in the former case the demand for means of production in relation to the demand for consumption goods does not, in the long run, increase by the whole of the newly invested sum, but only by the amount necessary to keep the additional capital intact. So long as the production of additional capital is going on, the demand for consumption goods diminishes by the whole of the amount newly saved and invested.[50] The transference of factors of production for the production of new means of production which is conditioned by this diminution, is, however, partly temporary. As soon as the new durable means of production are ready, and the production of final products can be correspondingly increased with their aid, the sums available for their purchase in the hands of consumers are not diminished by the value of the newly invested capital, but only by that amount which is necessary for their upkeep and amortization. But an amount of this magnitude will always have to be put aside by the entrepreneur, and thus withdrawn from consumption.

Even if he can only proceed to a renewal of fixed capital (in the absence of new savings) when the old is fully amortized, the sums accumulating for amortization will increase the current demand for means of production in the meantime for the purpose of producing new means of production. The entrepreneur must try to invest these sums to the best advantage until he needs them himself, and thus will increase the supply of capital and exercise a further pressure on interest rates. Without going into the complicated processes that are conditioned by the temporary

---

[50] In order to avoid too much complication in the exposition I disregard the case of an increase in the supply of capital leading to a more than proportional increase in the supply of fixed capital (or *vice versa*) which may occur owing to the fact that a fall in the rate of interest may render it profitable to transform already existing investments in circulating capital into fixed capital.

accommodation of sums accumulated for amortization, it may be said that they signify a temporary transformation of capital (mostly in circulating form), but they also form a current demand for the production of capital goods. As a result, an increase in fixed capital will have the same effects as if every single undertaking continuously renewed the wear and tear of its plant, i.e., spent uniformly a greater proportion of its receipts than before the investment in new capital on the purchase of intermediate products, and a smaller proportion on the purchase of original means of production. As this implies a corresponding diminution in the amounts available for the purchase of consumption goods, investment in fixed capital will therefore also have the effect of "stretching" the money stream, that is to say, it becomes longer and narrower; or, in the terminology of Messrs. Foster and Catchings, the circuit velocity of money diminishes.

X

The same effects manifest themselves still more directly in the case of an investment of new savings in *circulating capital*. And yet, as the examples of Messrs. Foster and Catchings, Mr. P.W. Martin, and Mr. A.B. Adams show, this necessary concomitant phenomenon of *every* increase of capital, is, in just this case, very easily overlooked. The explanation lies in the fact that the case of a single enterprise, which can always utilize its increased circulating capital for a proportional increase of its laborers and other means of production, is applied directly to the economic system as a whole, although it should be clear that an increase in capital, whether fixed or circulating, can only show itself in the economic system as a whole in an increase in intermediate products in relation to original means of production.

One of the most frequent cases of an increase in circulating capital—it is the case which led Messrs. Foster and Catchings and their adherents to overlook completely the capital function of the invested savings—is the case which has already been mentioned[51] of a relative extension of the more capitalistic branches of production at the expense of the less capitalistic ones. In this case, original means of production will be taken away from the latter and utilized in the former, without an increase in their fixed capital, so that at first the original means of production employed there increase relatively to the fixed capital. As has already been emphasized, it is not the increase in the volume of original means of production employed which is significant here, but the fact that they are now employed in a way that causes, on the average, a longer period of time to elapse between their employment and the emergence of their final product, and therefore more intermediary products to exist at any moment than before. It is just because an increase in the supply of capital enables relatively more roundabout processes to be undertaken that the more capitalistic undertakings can now employ more labor (and possibly more land).

At first the increased capital supply will result in the more capitalistic undertakings demanding more original means of production than hitherto, acquiring these by overbidding other undertakings. As more units of factors can only be acquired at a higher cost per unit, the extent to which they are able to do so depends on their expectations of an increase in total receipts from an increase in the volume of the product. In no case, however, will they be able to spend the total amount of new capital on increased employment of original means of production. Even to the extent that capital *is* used for that purpose in a single enterprise, this does not imply that part of the new capital is definitely used to remunerate original means of production. By exactly the same amount by which this enterprise increases its expenditure on original means of production because it expects a corresponding increase of its receipts, other enterprises will have to cut down expenditure on original means of production because their receipts will have

---

[51] See p. 146, note 1.

undergone a corresponding decrease, and will be able to invest that part as capital.

On the assumption, which we still adhere to, that the products of every stage of production come on to the market and are acquired there by the entrepreneur of the next stage, it is evident that only a portion of the newly invested savings can be spent on original means of production, while another—and, in the modern, highly developed economy, much greater—portion must be used to acquire additional quantities of the products of the previous stage of production. This portion will be all the larger, the greater the number of the stages of production (represented by independent enterprises) and, as a rule, several times as large as the portion spent on wages, etc.[52] It serves the purpose of providing all the stages of production (up to the last stage, where the final products of the original means of production now employed in the longer processes emerge) with a correspondingly larger amount of intermediate products; or, which means the same thing, it makes it possible for the additional original means of production to be paid for continuously, period by period, so long as their additional product has not yet reached the final stage.

After what we have seen in the case of investment in fixed capital, we can formulate the problem before us by asking how, when new investment in circulating capital takes place, the price relations between production goods and consumption goods

---

[52] While, in assuming only one stage of production, the value of all products at the end of the production process equals the value of the means of production employed; on the other hand, on the assumption that equal quantities of original means of production are employed at every stage (the case represented in the footnote at p. 146 above), the value of the latter is one and one-half times as great if two, two and one-half times if four, and five and one-half times if ten stages of production are assumed, and so on. (Cf. Böhm-Bawerk, *Positive Theory*, 4th German ed., vol. 1 [Jena: Gustav Fisher, 1921], p. 397.)

must adjust themselves in order that production shall be extended to such and only to such an extent that the new savings just suffice to carry out the enlarged processes?

Again we can start by assuming that, in the long run, the new capital investment must bring about a fall of the price of the products in relation to the prices of the means of production. If entrepreneurs expect—as, if the volume of money were kept constant, they ought to expect from experience—that the prices of the products will fall absolutely, then from the outset they will only extend production in such proportions as to ensure profitability even if the relative prices of products (as opposed to the means of production) fall. This means that the increase in production will be limited, right from the beginning, to that extent which can permanently be maintained. If, however, unchanged prices are expected for the products, it would seem profitable at first to attempt a further extension of production; and that to the extent that would seem profitable at the present prices of the means of production. The latter will not increase at first by as much as will finally be necessary for the establishment of equilibrium; they will rise only gradually as the increased demand for original means of production is passed on from the higher to the lower stages. With the progressive increase in the prices of the means of production, not only that portion of the additional production which would not have been undertaken if falling prices had been expected will become unprofitable; but also—since hitherto too many means of production were used up, a greater scarcity ensues, and their prices will increase more than they otherwise would—some part of the production which would have been profitable but for the dissipation of a part of the supply of means of production. Every attempt to prevent the fall of prices by increasing the volume of money will have the effect of increasing production to an extent that it is impossible to maintain, and thus part of the savings will be wasted.

XI

Let us now consider the case—fundamental to Messrs. Foster and Catchings's analysis—in which production is completely integrated vertically, the case in which all stages of one branch of production are united in one undertaking. In such circumstances there is no necessity to utilize certain parts of the money stream for the purchase of intermediate products; only consumption goods proper on the one hand, and the original means of production on the other are exchanged against money. The examination of this case is essential to prove the validity of our thesis—partly because, in the existing economic order, the various stages of production are not always divided into separate undertakings, and therefore an increase in the number of stages need not necessarily bring about an increase in the number of *independent undertakings*, but chiefly because the lengthening of the production process need not manifest itself in an increase in the number of *distinguishable stages* (as for the sake of clarity of exposition we have assumed up to the present), but simply in the lengthening of a continuous production process.

It is, however, impossible for reasons which are obvious, but which were overlooked by their critics, to follow Messrs. Foster and Catchings in their assumption that all the *various branches* of production are also united in a single enterprise. If that were so, there would be no inducement for that undertaking to save money, or to take up the money savings of private individuals; and there would thus be no opportunity for private individuals to invest their savings. If that undertaking is the only one of its kind, and therefore the only one using original means of production, it can—just as the dictator of a socialist economy can—determine at will what proportion of the original means of production shall go for the satisfaction of current consumption, and what proportion to the making or renewal of means of production. Only if, and insofar as, there is competition between the various branches of production for the supply of means of production, is it necessary, in order to obtain the additional means of production requisite for an enlargement of capital equipment, to have the disposal of additional amounts of money (either saved for that purpose or newly created). Only in such circumstances does there exist, accordingly, any inducement to save.

As it is clearly inadmissible to start from an assumption that renders the phenomenon to be investigated (i.e., the saving of individuals and companies) totally meaningless,[53] we can go no further in our investigations than the case of the complete vertical integration of single branches of production. But here, after what has been demonstrated above, it can be shown without difficulty that, if a transformation of money savings into additional real capital is to come about, the investment must lead to a diminution in the money stream available for the purchase of consumption goods[54] (i.e., to that slowing down of the "circuit velocity of money" of which Messrs. Foster and Catchings are so afraid), and that savings can only be utilized to the best advantage when the supply of money remains unaltered and the price per unit of the enlarged volume of goods diminishes.

Let us assume, therefore, that such an undertaking comprising all stages of production in one branch extends its production by "corporate saving" so that during the extension of capital equipment the sums necessary for this purpose are raised from profits (i.e., interest on capital and earnings of management). In this way it will be able to keep its demand for original means of

---

[53] Messrs. Foster and Catchings, it is true, expressly declare that their assumption about the number of undertakings is insignificant and in no way invalidates their reasoning (*Profits,* p. 270). They do not put forward any proof, however, and the fact that, even in trying to justify it, they do not realize that savings would be entirely meaningless under these circumstances, is the best proof of how completely they misunderstand the real function of saving.

[54] At any rate for so long as the transition of production goes on.

production constant, although, owing to the transformation of production, it can temporarily only bring a smaller volume of ready consumption goods on to the market, and its current receipts must fall. It is a necessary condition of the longer duration of the new production process that either the undertaking cannot for a short period bring any goods on to the market, or if it apportions its sales uniformly through time, it can offer only a smaller amount of the finished product for a longer period. The savings accumulated through individual profits serve just this very purpose of making good the diminution of receipts and enabling it to undertake the more productive, but more lengthy process. It must not, therefore, devote the whole sum to obtain more original means of production than before, for part must be used for bridging over the time during which its receipts will fall below current expenditure. The time during which it will be able to cover the difference between outgoings and receipts by saving forms the limit to the possible lengthening of the production process.

As long as the new investment is going on, a larger sum of money will be expended on means of production than that which is received from the sale of consumption goods at the same time. That occurs, as Messrs. Foster and Catchings repeatedly and correctly emphasize, by "money that is once used to bring about the production of goods being again used to bring about the production of goods before it is used to bring about the consumption of goods," i.e., that sums which represent the remuneration of capital and entrepreneurial services are utilized for the purchase of means of production instead of the purchase of consumption goods. What Messrs. Foster and Catchings misunderstand is the function of and the necessity for this relative increase in the demand for production goods and the corresponding diminution in the sales of consumption goods. It is the natural and necessary corollary of saving, which, in terms of Crusoe-economics, consists in the fact that fewer consumption goods are produced and consumed than could be produced from the means of production employed. The simultaneous increase in the demand for original means of production, i.e., the increase in the sums spent in the last stage of production (from which the original factors are remunerated) during one economic period, does not imply that at a later stage the money demand for consumption goods has to be increased by a similar amount in order to facilitate the sale of the enlarged volume of finished goods. The increase in the demand for means of production originates from the *lengthening* of the production process; so long as this is going on, more means of production are produced at every stage than are consumed at the next; production will serve the double purpose of satisfying current demand with the older (and shorter) process, and future demand with the new (longer) process. The demand for means of production is therefore, so long as new saving is going on, greater in relation to the demand for consumption goods than in the absence of savings because (in contrast to the stationary economy where the product of the means of production used in every period equals the goods consumed in that period) *the product of the means of production applied during the saving period will be consumed during a period which is longer than the saving period itself.*[55]

In order that the means saved should really bring about that extension of productive equipment for which they are just sufficient, the expected prices must make just that extension seem profitable. But that is (as should be clear by now, without a repetition of what has been said before) only the case when the money available for the purchase of the larger product is not greater than the part of the current outlays that served for *its* production. And since longer processes are more productive, in

---

[55] That is correctly recognized by Mr. A.B. Adams in his criticism mentioned above of Messrs. Foster and Catchings in *Profits, Progress and Prosperity,* where it is expressly stated (p. 18): "If the physical volume of current output of consumers' goods should equal the physical volume of all goods produced currently there could be no accumulation of permanent capital—there could be no real savings."

order that this may be the case, the unit prices of the product must now be less. Every expectation of future receipts greater than those necessary to cover the smaller costs per unit will lead to such excessive extensions of production as will become unprofitable as soon as the relative prices are no longer disturbed by the injection of new money.

XII

There is no danger, therefore, that too much money will be spent on production in relation to the sums available for consumption so long as the relative diminution in the demand for consumption goods is of a permanent nature and the latter does not, as *must* be the case with changes in the relative demand brought about by changes in the volume of money, increase again and drive the prices of the original means of production to such a height that the completion of the more capitalistic processes becomes unprofitable. As it is not the absolute level of the prices of the product, but only their relative level in comparison with factor prices which determines the remunerativeness of production, it is, therefore, never the absolute size of the demand for consumption goods, but the relative size of the demands for the means of production to be used for the various methods of producing consumption goods that determines this relative profitableness. *In principle, therefore, any portion, however small, of the total money stream ought to be sufficient to take up the consumption goods produced with the aid of the other portions, as long as, for any reason, the demand for consumption goods does not rise suddenly in relation to the demand for means of production, in which case the disproportionate amount of intermediate products (disproportionate in relation to the new distribution of demand) can no longer be sold at prices that cover costs.*

The problem is therefore not the absolute amount of money spent for consumption goods, but only the question of whether the relative demand for the consumption goods is not *greater* in relation to the money stream utilized for productive purposes than the current flow of consumption goods in relation to the simultaneous output of means of production. In this, and only in this case, will a disproportionate supply of means of production, and thus the impossibility of remunerative employment, arise, *not because the demand for consumption goods is too small, but on the contrary because it is too large and too urgent* to render the execution of lengthy roundabout processes profitable. The idea of a general overproduction in relation to the money *incomes* of the consumers as Messrs. Foster and Catchings conceive it, is as untenable in a money economy as under barter. A crisis occurs only when the available supply of intermediate products in all stages of production in relation to the supply of consumers' goods is greater than the demand for the former in relation to the demand for the latter. Apart from the case of spontaneous consumption of capital, this can only arise when either the *supply* of means of production, or the *demand* for consumption goods has been artificially and temporarily extended by credit policy. In either case a price relation will arise between means of production and finished products that renders production unprofitable.

XIII

That concludes our criticism of the cases in which savings are supposed to involve trade depression if the supply of money is not increased. The whole question is very similar to the old problem of whether, when productivity is increasing, prices should remain stable or fall. As Mr. A.H. Hansen has pointed out, the argument of Messrs. Foster and Catchings is applicable not only to the effect of saving but also to all other cases of increasing productivity.[56] To this extent, both authors became the victims of that uncritical fear of any kind of fall in prices which is so widespread today, and which lends a cloak to all the more refined forms of inflationism—a fashion which is all the more regrettable since

---

[56] *Business Cycle Theory*, p. 44.

many of the best economists, A. Marshall,[57] N.G. Pierson,[58] W. Lexis,[59] F.Y. Edgeworth,[60] Professor Taussig[61] in the past, and more recently Professor Mises,[62] Dr. Haberler,[63] Professor Pigou,[64] and Mr. D.H. Robertson,[65] have repeatedly emphasized the misconception underlying it.

But in the special case which Messrs. Foster and Catchings have made the basis of their proposals for stabilization, their argument is based on a different and less excusable misconception. What they entirely lack is any understanding of the function of capital and interest. The gap in their analytical equipment in this respect goes so far that, in their exposition of the theory of price, while most of the general problems are very thoroughly and adequately treated, any examination of this question is utterly lacking, and in the alphabetical index of *Profits* "capital" is only mentioned as a source of income. I cannot help feeling that, if

---

[57] Cf. his evidence before the Gold and Silver Commission of 1887, now reprinted in *Official Papers by Alfred Marshall* (London: Macmillan, 1926), esp. p. 91.

[58] Cf., e.g., *Gold Scarcity* (translated into German by R. Reisch) in the *Zeitschrift für Volkswirtschaft, Sozialpolitik und Verwaltung* 4, no. 1 (Vienna, 1895), esp. p. 23.

[59] On several occasions in connection with the bimetallist question, e.g., in the *Verhandlungen der deutschen Silberkomission* (Berlin, 1894). Similarly C. Helfferich, E. Nasse, and L. Bamberger.

[60] Cf. "Thoughts on Monetary Reform," *Economic Journal* (1895), reprinted under "Questions connected with Bimetallism" in *Papers Relating to Political Economy* (London: Macmillan, 1925), vol. 1, p. 421.

[61] Cf. *The Silver Situation in the United States* (New York: G.P. Putnam, 1893), pp. 104–12.

[62] Cf. *Geldwertsstabilisierung und Konjunkturpolitik* (Jena: Gustav Fisher, 1928), p. 30.

[63] Cf. *Der Sinn der Indexzahlen* (Tübingen: Mohr, 1927), pp. 112 *et seq.*

[64] Cf. *Industrial Fluctuations*, 2nd ed. (London: Macmillan 1929), pp. 182 *et seq.* and 255 *et seq.*

[65] Cf. *Money*, 2nd ed. (London: Macmillan, 1928).

they had extended their investigations to this field, or even if they had merely thought it worth their while to make themselves familiar with the existing literature of a question so cogent to their problem, they would themselves have realized the untenable nature of their theory. In the literature of monetary theory (with the exception of the works of K. Wicksell and Professor Mises, which are probably inaccessible to them for linguistic reasons) they will, of course, look in vain for the necessary explanation, for so many writers on this subject still labor under the sway of the dogma of the necessity for a stable price level, and this makes recognition of these interconnections extraordinarily difficult. But just as Mr. R.W. Souter, their prize-winning critic, recommended them to read Marshall, so I would recommend them, still more urgently, to make a thorough study of Böhm-Bawerk, whose main work, if only in the first edition, is available in English translation.

XIV

We have repeatedly had occasion while examining the theory of Messrs. Foster and Catchings to point to the effects that would ensue if the proposals based upon it were put into practice. But it may well be that the contrast between the real effects of such proposals and the expectations based upon them may not yet be sufficiently clear. And as similar demands are continually being brought forward everywhere for all kinds of reasons, it seems worthwhile finally attempting a systematic account of the actual consequences to be expected if they were really carried out.

It has already been explained that Messrs. Foster and Catchings's proposals for reform involve increasing the volume of money, either through consumers' credits or the financing of state expenditure, in order to bring about the sale at unchanged prices of a volume of products enlarged by an increase of saving. The effects of such increases of money spent on consumption can best be demonstrated by contrasting them with the effects of additional productive credits. We shall work under the assumption

The "Paradox" of Saving

used in the previous analysis, where the different stages of production are in the hands of different undertakings. The application of this reasoning to that of the completely integrated branch of production should follow more or less of itself.

We may take as a starting point the result of our previous demonstration of the effect of saving, the volume of money remaining unchanged (Scheme B, p. 160). According to this the relation of the demand for consumers' goods to the demand for means of production changed from £1,000:£8,000 to £900:£8,100, or from 1:8 to 1:9, so that the number of stages increased correspondingly from 9 to 10. Now let us assume that, in accordance with the proposal of Messrs. Foster and Catchings, at the moment when the enlarged product comes onto the market, the volume of money is increased by the same sum as the sums spent on production, i.e., by £100[66] and that this additional sum is spent exclusively on consumption goods. Because of this, the demand for consumption goods again increases from £900 to £1,000, while the sums available for means of production remain unchanged, so that the relation between the demand for the two groups of goods changes from £900:£8,100 to £1,000:£8,100, i.e., the relative size of the demand for means of production in comparison with the demand for consumption goods falls from 9 times to 8.1 times the latter. The transformation of production conditioned by this, in the form of a shortening of the productive process, comes about in the manner represented in Scheme C. As the number of stages of production, under our assumption, must then be 8.1, the last stage (No. 10) must be represented by a value that is only one-tenth of the rest.

---

[66] In fact we ought to take an increase of £200, since, as a consequence of saving, the difference between the sums spent on production and on consumption goods increases by that amount. As by taking this larger amount the effect demonstrated will only become more pronounced, it will suffice to regard the more simple case given in the text.

SCHEME C
(£100 is added to the circulation as credit to consumers.)

		£
Demand for consumption goods (= products of stage of production No. 1)		1,000
Demand for the products of the stages of production	No. 2	1,000
	No. 3	1,000
	No. 4	1,000
	No. 5	1,000
	No. 6	1,000
	No. 7	1,000
	No. 8	1,000
	No. 9	1,000
	No. 10	100
Total demand for produced means of production—8.1 × 1,000 =	....	8,100

Demand for consumption goods in relation to the demand for produced means of production—1:8.1.

But this shortening of the production process to the point where it stood before the investment of new savings (cf. Scheme A, p. 158) need not be the final effect, if the increase in money occurs only once and is not repeated again and again. The extension of production became possible because producers consumed, instead of one-ninth (Scheme A), only one-tenth (Scheme B) of their total receipts, and utilized the rest for the purpose of keeping their capital intact. Insofar as they persist in their endeavor to keep their capital intact, in spite of the diminution of the purchasing power of those parts of their receipts which are conditioned by the appearance of new money, the demand for consumption goods in relation to that for means of production will again shift in favor of the latter as soon as the demand for the former is no longer artificially extended through additional spending power. To this extent the shortening of the production process and the devaluation of fixed plant connected with it will only be temporary; but this is contingent upon a cessation of the flow of additional money. What is important, however, is that (even in an expanding economic system) *such an inflationist enlargement of the demand for consumption goods must, in itself, bring about at once similar phenomena of crisis to those that are necessarily brought about in consequence of an increase in productive credits, as soon as the latter cease to increase or their rate of flow diminishes.*[67] This will be best understood if we represent this case schematically also. We again take Scheme B (p. 160) as our starting point, assuming that, in accordance with prevalent opinion, the extension of production is taken as a justification for an extension in money supply. This extension, however, takes the form of productive credits. For simplicity, we assume that the additional money injected in the form of productive credits amounts to £900, and, therefore, the relation between the demand for consumption goods and the demand for production goods alters, as compared with the case represented in Scheme B, from £900:*£8*,100 to £900:£9,000, or from 1:9 to 1:10.

---

[67] It would be a mistake to argue against the representation of the effect of consumptive credits above by saying that the war inflation was also brought about by additional expenditure on consumption, and yet did not lead to crisis, but, on the contrary, to a boom. The war inflation could never have led to such an extension of production as it actually did had the additional credits only been given to undertakings in the form of proceeds for the sale of products, and not—whether in the form of prepayments or directly in productive credits—placed at their disposal in advance for the purpose of extending production. One should visualize what would have happened had the increase in the demand for consumption goods always preceded the increase in the sums available for the purchase of means of production. And one would soon realize that this would only have rendered production of the present extent unprofitable, and would have led to a diminution of the productive apparatus in the form of a consumption of capital. During the war, this phenomenon was also rendered invisible through the appearance of specious profits following currency depreciation, which caused entrepreneurs to overlook that they were, in fact, consuming capital.

The proportional increase in the demand for means of production as compared with the demand for consumption goods permits an extension of the production process as compared with the position in Scheme B, thus:

Scheme D
(In the situation depicted in Scheme B £900 are added as credits to producers, first stage.)

		£
Demand for consumption goods (= products of stage of production No. 1)		900
Demand for the products of the stages of production	No. 2	900
	No. 3	900
	No. 4	900
	No. 5	900
	No. 6	900
	No. 7	900
	No. 8	900
	No. 9	900
	No. 10	900
	No. 11	900
Total demand for produced means of production—10 × 900 =	....	9,000

Demand for consumption goods in relation to the demand for produced means of production—1:10.

This lengthening of the productive process, however, can continue only so long as the demand for means of production is kept at the same relative level through *still further* additions of producers' credits; i.e., so long and so far as the durable production goods produced on account of the temporary increase in the demand for means of production suffice to carry on production of this extent. As soon and insofar as neither of these two assumptions remains true, all consumers whose real income was diminished through the competition of the increased demand for means of production will attempt to bring their consumption up again to the previous level, and to utilize a corresponding portion of their money income for the purchase of consumption goods. But that means that the demand for consumption goods will increase again to more than one-tenth of the total demand for goods of every stage. Accordingly, only a smaller proportion of the total money stream goes to buy produced means of production, and the following changes in the structure of production will occur:

Scheme E
(Same as Scheme D, second stage.)

		£
Demand for consumption goods (= products of stage of production No. 1)		1,000
Demand for the products of the stages of production	No. 2	1,000
	No. 3	1,000
	No. 4	1,000
	No. 5	1,000
	No. 6	1,000
	No. 7	1,000
	No. 8	1,000
	No. 9	1,000
	No. 10	1,000
Total demand for produced means of production—9 × 1,000 =		9,000

Demand for consumption goods in relation to the demand for produced means of production—1:9.

Without any further change in the volume of money, and only because the increase in the form of productive credits has ceased, the whole production process, and thus the length of the circuit velocity of money, tends again to contract to the old level. This contraction, which naturally involves the loss of those means of production which are adapted to the longer processes, and which is directly occasioned by the rise in the price of the means of production brought about by an increase in the demand for consumption goods, which renders the longer processes unprofitable, is a typical phenomenon of any crisis. As is easily seen, it is of the same nature as the effects of a relative increase in the demand for consumption goods brought about by consumers' credits.

It is just because with *every* increase in the volume of money, whether it is made available first for consumption or first for production, the relative size of the demand for those means of production that already exists or which has been directly enlarged by an increase in money must eventually contract in relation to the demand for consumption goods, that a more or less severe reaction will follow. This frantic game of now enlarging, now contracting the productive apparatus through increases in the volume of money injected, now on the production, now on the consumption side, is always going on under the present organization of currency. Both effects follow each other uninterruptedly and thus an extension or contraction of the productive process is brought about, according to whether credit creation for productive purposes is accelerated or retarded. So long as the volume of money in circulation is continually changing, we cannot get rid of industrial fluctuations. In particular, every monetary policy that aims at stabilizing the value of money and involves, therefore, an increase of its supply with every increase of production, must bring about those very fluctuations that it is trying to prevent.

But least of all is it possible to bring about stability by that "financing of consumption" which Messrs. Foster and Catchings recommend, since there would be added to the contraction of the production process which automatically follows from increases of productive credits a still further contraction because of the consumptive credits, and thus crises would be rendered exceptionally severe. Only if administered with extraordinary caution and superhuman ability could it, perhaps, be made to prevent crises: if the artificial increase in the demand for consumption goods brought about by those credits were made exactly to cancel the increase in the demand for means of production brought about by the investment of the current flow of savings, thus preserving constant the proportion between the two, this might happen. *But such a policy would effectively prevent any increase in capital equipment and completely frustrate any saving whatever.*[68] There can be no question, therefore, that in the long run, even a policy of this sort would bring about grave disturbances and the disorganization of the economic system as a whole. So that, we may say, in conclusion, that the execution of Messrs. Foster and Catchings's proposals would not prevent, but considerably aggravate, crises; that is, it would punish every attempt at capital creation by a loss of a portion of the capital. Carried through to its logical conclusion, it would effectively prevent every real capital accumulation.

---

[68] Cf. the remarks of A.B. Adams, quoted above in note 51.

# Prices and Production

First published in London by Routledge and Sons in 1931. The second edition was published by Routledge and Kegan Paul in 1935.

Preface to the Second Edition

This book owes its existence to an invitation by the University of London to deliver during the session 1930–31 four lectures to advanced students in economics, and in the form in which it was first published it literally reproduced these lectures. This invitation offered to me what might easily have been a unique opportunity to lay before an English audience what contribution I thought I had then to make to current discussions of theoretical economics; and it came at a time when I had arrived at a clear view of the outlines of a theory of industrial fluctuations but before I had elaborated it in full detail or even realized all the difficulties which such an elaboration presented. The exposition, moreover, was limited to what I could say in four lectures, which inevitably led to even greater oversimplification than I would probably have been guilty of in any other case. But although I am now conscious of many more defects of this exposition than I was even at the time of its first publication, I can only feel profoundly grateful to the circumstances which were such an irresistible temptation to publish these ideas at an earlier date than I should otherwise have done. From the criticisms and discussions that publication has caused I hope to have profited more for a later more complete exposition than I could possibly have done if I had simply continued to work on these problems for myself. But the time for that more exhaustive treatment of these problems has not yet come.

It is perhaps the main gain which I derived from the early publication that it made it clear to me that, before I could hope to get much further with the elucidation of the main problems discussed in this book, it would be necessary considerably to elaborate the foundations on which I have tried to build. Contact with scientific circles which were less inclined than I was to take for granted the main propositions of the "Austrian" theory of capital on which I have drawn so freely in this book has shown—not that these propositions were wrong or that they were less important than I had thought for the task for which I had used them—but that they would have to be developed in far greater detail and have to be adapted much more closely to the complicated conditions of real life before they could provide a completely satisfactory instrument for the explanation of the particularly complicated phenomena to which I have applied them. This is a task which has to be undertaken before the theses expounded in the present book can be developed further with advantage.

Under these circumstances, when a new edition of this book was called for, I felt neither prepared to rewrite and enlarge it to the extent that a completely adequate treatment of the problems taken up would make necessary, nor to see it reappear in an altogether unchanged form. The compression of the original exposition has given rise to so many unnecessary misunderstandings which a somewhat fuller treatment would have prevented that certain additions seemed urgently necessary. I have accordingly chosen the middle course of inserting into the (on the whole unchanged) original text further elucidations and elaborations where they seemed most necessary. Many of these additions were already included in the German edition which appeared a few months after the first English edition. Others are taken over from a number of articles in which, in the course of the last three years, I have tried to develop or to defend the main thesis of this book. It has, however, been by no means possible to incorporate all the further elaborations attempted in these articles in the present volume, and the reader who may wish to refer to them will find them listed in the footnote below.[1]

By these modifications I hope to have removed at least some of the difficulties which the book seems to have presented in its original form. Others were due to the fact that the book was in some ways a continuation of an argument which I had begun in other publications that at the time of its first appearance were available only in German. In the meantime English translations have, however, been published[2] and in those the reader will find explained some of the assumptions which are implicit rather than explicitly stated in the following discussion.

Some of the real difficulties which I fully realize this book must present to most readers will, however, not be removed by either of these changes because they are inherent in the mode of exposition adopted. All I can do in this respect short of replacing this book by an entirely new one is to draw the attention of the reader in advance to this particular difficulty and to explain why the mode of exposition which causes it had to be adopted. This is all the more necessary since this irremediable defect of the exposition has caused more misunderstandings than any other single problem.

The point in question is briefly this. Considerations of time made it necessary for me in these lectures to treat at one and the

---

[1] "The Pure Theory of Money: A Rejoinder to Mr. Keynes," *Economica* (November 1931); "Money and Capital: A Reply to Mr. Sraffa," *Economic Journal* (June 1932); "Kapitalaufzehrung," *Weltwirtschaftliches Archiv* (July 1932); "A Note on the Development of the Doctrine of 'Forced Saving'," *Quarterly Journal of Economics* (November 1932); "Der Stand und die nächste Zukunft der Konjunkturforschung," *Festschrift für Arthur Spiethoff* (Munich: Duncker & Humblot, 1933); "Über neutrales Geld," *Zeitschrift für Nationalökonomie* 4 (October 1933); "Capital and Industrial Fluctuations," *Econometrica* 2 (April 1934); "On the Relationship between Investment and Output," *Economic Journal* (June 1934).

[2] *Monetary Theory and the Trade Cycle* (London: Routledge, 1933) and "The 'Paradox' of Saving," *Economica* (May 1931); included in this volume.

same time the real changes of the structure of production which accompany changes in the amount of capital and the monetary mechanism which brings this change about. This was possible only under highly simplified assumptions which made any change in the monetary demand for capital goods proportional to the change in the total demand for capital goods which it brought about. Now "demand" for capital goods, in the sense in which it can be said that demand determines their value, of course does not consist exclusively or even primarily in a demand exercised on any market, but to a perhaps even greater degree in a demand or willingness to continue to hold capital goods for a further period of time. On the relationship between this total demand and the monetary demand for capital goods which manifests itself on the markets during any period of time, no general statements can be made; nor is it particularly relevant for my problems what this quantitative relationship actually is. What was, however, of prime importance for my purpose was to emphasize that any change in the monetary demand for capital goods could not be treated as something which made itself felt only on some isolated market for new capital goods, but that it could be only understood as a change affecting the general demand for capital goods which is an essential aspect of the process of maintaining a given structure of production. The simplest assumption of this kind which I could make was to assume a fixed relationship between the monetary and the total demand for capital goods so as to make the amount of money spent on capital goods during a unit period of time equal to the value of the stock of capital goods in existence.

This assumption, which I still think is very useful for my main purpose, proved however to be somewhat misleading in two other, not unimportant, respects. In the first instance it made it impossible to treat adequately the case of durable goods. It is impossible to assume that the potential services, embodied in a durable good and waiting for the moment when they will be utilized, change hands at regular intervals of time. This meant that so far as that particular illustration of the monetary mechanism was concerned I had to leave durable goods simply out of account. I did not feel that this was too serious a defect, particularly as I was under the—I think not unjustified—impression that the role which circulating capital played was rather neglected and accordingly wanted to stress it as compared with that of fixed capital. But I realize now that I should have given proper warning of the exact reason why I introduced this assumption and what function it performed, and I am afraid that the footnote which I inserted in the first edition (page 37, note 2) at the last moment, when my attention was drawn to the difficulty which my argument might present, has served rather to confuse than to clear up the point.

The second effect of this assumption of separate "stages" of production of equal length was that it imposed upon me a somewhat one-sided treatment of the problem of the velocity of circulation of money. It implied more or less that money passed through the successive stages at a constant rate which corresponded to the rate at which the goods advanced through the process of production, and in any case excluded considerations of changes in the velocity of circulation or the cash balances held in the different stages. The impossibility of dealing expressly with changes in the velocity of circulation so long as this assumption was maintained served to strengthen the misleading impression that the phenomena I was discussing would be caused only by actual changes in the quality of money and not by every change in the money stream, which in the real world are probably caused at least as frequently, if not more frequently, by changes in the velocity of circulation than by changes in the actual quantity. It has been put to me that any treatment of monetary problems which neglected in this way the phenomenon of changes in the desire to hold money balances could not possibly say anything worthwhile. While in my opinion this is a somewhat exaggerated view, I should like to emphasize in this connection how small a section of the whole field of monetary theory is actually treated in this book. All that I claim for it is that it deals with an aspect which has been more neglected and misunderstood than perhaps any other and the insufficient understanding of which has led to particularly serious mistakes. To incorporate this argument into the body of monetary theory is a task which has yet to be undertaken and which I could not and did not try to undertake here. But I may perhaps add that so far as the general theory of money (as distinguished from the pure theory of capital) is concerned, it is the work of Professor Mises[3] much more than that of Knut Wicksell which provides the framework inside which I have tried to elaborate a special point.

In addition to this acknowledgment of a great intellectual obligation I should like to repeat from the preface to the first edition not only the acknowledgment of what I owe to the great tradition in the field of the theory of capital which is connected with the names of W.S. Jevons, E. v. Böhm-Bawerk and Knut Wicksell, but also of the more specific debt to those who have helped me in the preparation of these lectures: to Mr. Albert G. Hart, now of the University of Chicago, who gave me the benefit of his advice when I was drafting the original English manuscript of these lectures and particularly to Professor Lionel Robbins, who, when the first edition was published, undertook the considerable labor of putting the manuscript into a form fit for publication and seeing it through the press, and who ever since has most generously given me his help with all my English publications, including the present second edition of this book.

F.A. v. Hayek
The London School of Economics and Political Science
August 1934

---

[3] See particularly his *Theorie des Geldes und der Umlaufsmittel* (Munich: Duncker & Humblot, 1912), first published in 1912 and now fortunately available in an English translation, L. Mises, *The Theory of Money* (London: Jonathan Cape, 1934). Cf. also my *Monetary Theory and the Trade Cycle*, which is concerned more with the monetary factors which *cause* the trade cycle than the present book, which is mainly devoted to the real phenomena which constitute it.

LECTURE 1

Theories of the Influence of Money on Prices

> He realized well that the abundance of money makes everything dear, but he did not analyze how that takes place. The great difficulty of this analysis consists in discovering by what path and in what proportion the increase of money raises the price of things.
> Richard Cantillon (died 1734)
> *Essai sur la nature du commerce en général,* II, 6

(1) That monetary influences play a dominant role in determining both the volume and direction of production is a truth which is probably more familiar to the present generation than to any which have gone before. The experiences of the war- and postwar-inflation, and of the return to the gold standard, particularly where, as in Great Britain, it was accomplished by a contraction of the circulation, have given abundant evidence of the dependence on money of every productive activity. The widespread discussions of recent years concerning the desirability and practicability of stabilizing the value of money are due mainly to a general recognition of this fact. At the present moment many of the best minds believe the cause of the existing worldwide depression to be a scarcity of gold and seek accordingly for monetary means to overcome it.

And yet, if it were asked whether understanding of the connection between money and prices has made great progress during these years, at any rate until very recently, or whether the generally accepted doctrines on this point have progressed far beyond what was generally known a hundred years ago, I should be inclined to answer in the negative. This may seem paradoxical, but I think anyone who has studied the monetary literature of the first half of the nineteenth century will agree that there is hardly any idea in contemporary monetary theory which was not known to one or more writers of that period. Probably the majority of present-day economists would contend that the reason why progress has been so slight is that monetary theory has already reached such a state of perfection that further progress must of necessity be slow. But I confess that to me it still seems that some of the most fundamental problems in this field remain unsolved, that some of the accepted doctrines are of a very doubtful validity, and that we have even failed to develop the suggestions for improvement which can be found in the works of these early writers.

If that be true, and I hope to convince you that it is, it is surely somewhat astonishing that the experiences of the last fifteen years have not proved more fruitful. In the past, periods of monetary disturbance have always been periods of great progress in this branch of economics. The Italy of the sixteenth century has been called the country of the worst money and the best monetary theory. If recently that has not been true to the same extent, the reason seems to me to lie in a certain change of attitude on the part of most economists in regard to the appropriate methodology of economics, a change which in many quarters is hailed as a great progress: I mean the attempt to substitute quantitative for qualitative methods of investigation. In the field of monetary theory, this change has been made even by economists who in general reject the "new" point of view, and indeed several had made it some years before the quantitative method had become fashionable elsewhere.

(2) The best known instance, and the most relevant case in point, is the resuscitation by Irving Fisher some twenty years ago of the more mechanistic forms of the quantity theory of the

value of money in his well-known "equation of exchange." That this theory, with its apparatus of mathematical formulae constructed to admit of statistical verification, is a typical instance of "quantitative" economics, and that it indeed probably contributed a good deal to influence the methodology of the present representatives of this school, are propositions which are not likely to be denied. I do not propose to quarrel with the positive content of this theory: I am even ready to concede that so far as it goes it is true, and that, from a practical point of view, it would be one of the worst things which would befall us if the general public should ever again cease to believe in the elementary propositions of the quantity theory. What I complain of is not only that this theory in its various forms has unduly usurped the central place in monetary theory, but that the point of view from which it springs is a positive hindrance to further progress. Not the least harmful effect of this particular theory is the present isolation of the theory of money from the main body of general economic theory.

For so long as we use different methods for the explanation of values as they are supposed to exist irrespective of any influence of money, and for the explanation of that influence of money on prices, it can never be otherwise. Yet we are doing nothing less than this if we try to establish *direct* causal connections between the *total* quantity of money, the *general level* of all prices and, perhaps, also the *total* amount of production. For none of these magnitudes *as such* ever exerts an influence on the decisions of individuals; yet it is on the assumption of a knowledge of the decisions of individuals that the main propositions of non-monetary economic theory are based. It is to this "individualistic" method that we owe whatever understanding of economic phenomena we possess; that the modern "subjective" theory has advanced beyond the classical school in its consistent use is probably its main advantage over their teaching.

If, therefore, monetary theory still attempts to establish causal relations between aggregates or general averages, this means that monetary theory lags behind the development of economics in general. In fact, neither aggregates nor averages do act upon one another, and it will never be possible to establish necessary connections of cause and effect between them as we can between individual phenomena, individual prices, etc. I would even go so far as to assert that, from the very nature of economic theory, averages can never form a link in its reasoning; but to prove this contention would go far beyond the subject of these lectures. I shall here confine myself to an attempt to show in a special field the differences between explanations which do and explanations which do not have recourse to such concepts.

(3) As I have said already, I do not want to criticize the doctrines of these theories so far as they go; I indicate their characteristics only in order to be able to show later on how much more another type of theory may accomplish. The central preoccupation of these theories is changes in the general price level. Now everybody agrees that a change of prices would be of no consequence whatever if all prices in the widest sense of the term were affected equally and simultaneously. But the main concern of this type of theory is avowedly, with certain suppositions "tendencies, which affect *all* prices equally, or at any rate impartially, at the same time and in the same direction."[4] And it is only after the alleged causal relation between changes in the quantity of money and average prices has thus been established that effects on relative prices are considered. But as the assumption generally is that changes in the quantity of money affect only the general price level, and that changes of relative prices are due to "disturbing factors" or "frictions," changes in relative prices are not part of this explanation of the changes in the price level. They are mere accompanying circumstances which experience has taught

---

[4] This is the formulation of R.G. Hawtrey. Cf. his lecture on "Money and Index Numbers" in the *Journal of the Royal Statistical Society* 93, part 1 (1930): 65.

us to be regularly connected with changes of the price level, not, as might be thought, necessary consequences of the same causes. This is very clear from the form of exposition and the concepts it employs. Certain "lags" are found to exist between the changes of different prices. The prices of different goods are said generally to be affected in a definite sequence, and it is always implied that all this would never take place if the general price level did not change.

When we come to the way in which the influence of prices on production is conceived by this theory, the same general characteristics are to be discovered. It is the price level, the changes of which are supposed to influence production; and the effect considered is not the effect upon particular branches of production, but the effect upon the volume of production in general. In most cases, no attempt is made to show why this must be so; we are referred to statistics which show that in the past a high correlation of general prices and the total volume of production has been present. If an explanation of this correlation is attempted, it is generally simply to the effect that the expectation of selling at higher prices than present costs will induce everybody to expand production, while in the opposite case the fear of being compelled to sell below costs will prove a strong deterrent. That is to say, it is only the general or average movement of prices which counts.

Now this idea that changes of relative prices and changes in the volume of production are consequent upon changes in the price level, and that money affects individual prices only by means of its influence on the general price level, seems to me to be at the root of at least three very erroneous opinions: First, that money acts upon prices and production only if the general price level changes, and, therefore, that prices and production are always unaffected by money—that they are at their "natural" level—if the price level remains stable. Second, that a rising price level tends always to cause an increase of production, and a falling price level always a decrease of production; and third, that "monetary theory might even be described as nothing more than the theory of how the value of money is determined."[5] It is such delusions, as we shall see, which make it possible to assume that we can neglect the influence of money so long as the value of money is assumed to be stable, and apply without further qualification the reasoning of a general economic theory which pays attention to "real causes" only, and that we have only to add to this theory a separate theory of the value of money and of the consequences of its changes in order to get a complete explanation of the modern economic process.

Further details are unnecessary. You are all sufficiently familiar with this type of theory to supply these for yourselves and to correct any exaggerations which I may have committed in my endeavor to make the contrast with the other types of theory as strong as possible. Any further strengthening of the contrast can best be carried out by my proceeding forthwith to the second of the major stages in the development of monetary theory. I wish only to emphasize, before I pass on to that, that henceforward when I speak of stages of development, I do not mean that each of these stages has in turn taken the place of the foregoing as the recognized doctrine. Quite on the contrary, each of these stages is still represented among contemporary monetary theorists and indeed in all probability the first has still the greatest number of adherents.

(4) As might be expected, the second stage arises by way of dissatisfaction with the first. This dissatisfaction makes its appearance quite early. Locke and Montanari, at the end of the seventeenth century, had stated quite clearly the theory I have been discussing. Richard Cantillon, whose criticism of Locke I have taken as the motto of this lecture, realized its inadequacy, and in his famous *Essai sur le Commerce* (published 1755), he provides the first attempt known to me to trace the actual chain

---

[5] Ibid., p. 64.

of cause and effect between the amount of money and prices. In a brilliant chapter, which W.S. Jevons called "one of the most marvelous things in the book," he attempts to show "by what path and in what proportion the increase of money raises the price of things." Starting from the assumption of the discovery of new gold or silver mines, he proceeds to show how this additional supply of the precious metals first increases the incomes of all persons connected with their production, how the increase of the expenditure of these persons next increases the prices of things which they buy in increased quantities, how the rise in the prices of these goods increases the incomes of the sellers of these goods, how they, in their turn, increase their expenditure, and so on. He concludes that only those persons are benefited by the increase of money whose incomes rise early, while to persons whose incomes rise later the increase of the quantity of money is harmful.

Better known is the somewhat shorter exposition of the same idea which David Hume gave a little later in a famous passage of his *Political Discourses*,[6] which so closely resembles the words of Cantillon that it is hard to believe that he had not seen one of those manuscripts of the *Essai* which are known to have been in private circulation at the time when the *Discourses* were written. Hume, however, makes it clear that, in his opinion, "it is only in this interval or intermediate situation, between the acquisition of money and the rise of prices, that the increasing quantity of gold and silver is favourable to industry."

To the Classics, this line of reasoning did not seem susceptible of improvement. While Hume is often quoted, his method of approach was not amplified for more than a century. It was not until the increase of the supply of gold consequent upon the Californian and Australian discoveries that there was any new

---

[6] Published 1752, republished as part of his *Essays Moral, Political and Literary* (part 2, essay 4, "Of Money") which originally appeared in 1742, and therefore are often wrongly quoted with that date.

impetus to this type of analysis. J.E. Cairnes's *Essay on the Australian Gold Discoveries*[7] contains probably the most noteworthy refinement of the argument of Cantillon and Hume before it was finally incorporated into more modern explanations based upon the subjective theories of value.

It was inevitable that modern theory should be sympathetic toward a point of view which traces the effects of an increase of money to its influence on individual decisions. But a generation passed before serious attempts were made to base the explanation of the value of money and the effects of changes in the amount of money upon the fundamental concepts of marginal utility theory. I shall not dwell here at any length on the variety of forms this assumes in the different modern theories which base the explanation of the value of money on the subjective elements determining the demand for money on the part of the individual. In the form this theory has received at the hands of Professor Mises, it belongs already to the third and fourth of our main stages of development, and I shall have occasion to refer to it later. It is worth noticing, however, that, insofar as these theories are confined to an explanation of the manner in which the effects of increase in the amount of money are distributed through the various channels of trade, they still suffer from a not unimportant defect. While they succeed in providing a general scheme for the deduction of the successive effects of an increase or decrease of the amount of money, provided that we know where the additional money enters into

---

[7] "Essays towards a Solution of the Gold Question," in *Essays in Political Economy, Theoretical and Applied* (London: Macmillan, 1873), particularly Essay 2: "The Course of Depreciation." These *Essays* were originally published in 1855–60 in *Frazers Magazine* and the *Edinburgh Review*. It may be of interest to mention here that Carl Menger who has decisively influenced modern development in this field, was well acquainted with Cairnes's exposition. Cf. on this point my Introduction to volume 1 of the *Collected Works of Carl Menger* in the Series of Reprints of Scarce Tracts in Economics (London: London School of Economics, 1934).

circulation, they do not help us to make any *general* statements about the effects which any change in the amount of money must have. For, as I shall show later, everything depends on the point where the additional money is injected into circulation (or where money is withdrawn from circulation), and the effects may be quite opposite depending upon when the additional money comes first into the hands of traders and manufacturers or directly into the hands of salaried people employed by the state.

(5) Very early, and, in the beginning, with only little relation to the problem of the value of money, there had, however, sprung up a doctrine, or rather a number of closely related doctrines, the importance of which was not appreciated at the time, although in the end they were to be combined to fill the gap I have been discussing. I refer to the doctrines of the influence of the quantity of money on the rate of interest, and through it on the relative demand for consumers' goods on the one hand and producers' or capital goods on the other. These form the third stage in the development of monetary theory. These doctrines have had to surmount unusual obstacles and prejudices, and until recently they received very little attention. It almost seems as if economists had for so long a time struggled against the popular confusions between the value of money proper and the price for a money loan that in the end they had become almost incapable of seeing that there was any relation at all between the rate of interest and the value of money. It is therefore worthwhile attempting to trace their development in rather greater detail.

While the existence of some relation between the quantity of money and the rate of interest was clearly recognized very early—traces of an understanding could certainly be found in the writings of Locke and Dutot—the first author known to me to enunciate a clear doctrine on this point was Henry Thornton. In his *Paper Credit of Great Britain*, published in 1802 at the beginning of the discussion on Bank Restriction—a really remarkable performance, the true importance of which is only now beginning to be recognized—he struck for the first time one of the leading notes of the new doctrine. The occasion for his statement was an inquiry into the question whether there existed a natural tendency to keep the circulation of the Bank of England within the limits which would prevent a dangerous depreciation. Thornton denied that such a natural tendency existed and held that, on the contrary, the circulation might expand beyond all assignable limits if the bank would only keep its rate of interest low enough. He based his opinion on considerations so weighty that I cannot resist quoting them at some length:

> In order to ascertain how far the desire of obtaining loans at the Bank may be expected at any time to be carried, we must enquire into the subject of the quantum of profit likely to be derived from borrowing there under the existing circumstances. This is to be judged of by considering two points: the amount, first, of interest to be paid on the sum borrowed; and, secondly, of the mercantile or other gain to be obtained by the employment of the borrowed capital. The gain which can be acquired by the means of commerce is commonly the highest which can be had; and it also regulates, in a great measure, the rate in all other cases. We may, therefore, consider this question as turning principally on a comparison of the rate of interest taken at the bank with the current rate of mercantile profit.[8] (p. 287)

Thornton restated these doctrines in the first of his two speeches on the Bullion Report, which were also published as a booklet[9] and would deserve being recovered from oblivion. In this speech he attempts to call the attention of the House of

---

[8] In order to appreciate the importance of this statement, another passage occurring a little earlier in the same chapter (p. 261) should be consulted. In the course of this passage, Thornton writes: "As soon, however, as the circulating medium *ceases to increase,* the extra profit is at an end." (Italics mine.)

[9] Substance of two speeches by Henry Thornton, Esq., in the debate in the House of Commons on the report of the Bullion Committee on the 7th and 14th May, 1811 (London, 1811). Cf. particularly p. 19 *et seq.*

Commons to the subject of the rate of interest as "a very great and turning point," and, after restating his theory in a shorter form, adds a new and different theory on the relations between prices and interest (which must on no account be confused with his other theory) namely a theory of the influence of an expectation of a rise of prices on the money rate of interest, a theory which later on was to be re-discovered by A. Marshall and Irving Fisher. This theory, however, does not concern us here.[10]

Thornton's theory seems to have been generally accepted among the "bullionists," though it appears to have been forgotten by the time that the doctrine of this school became the target of those attacks of the Banking School to which it would have been a sufficient answer. Within the next two years it had been restated by Lord King[11] and J.L. Foster,[12] and, what is much more important, it was accepted by David Ricardo, in his pamphlet of 1809, who gave it a still more modern ring by speaking of the rate of interest falling below its *natural level* in the interval between the issues of the bank and their effects on prices.[13] He repeated this also in his *Principles*[14] which should have been sufficient to make it generally known. The doctrine makes its appearance in the Bullion Report,[15] and it remained familiar to economists for some time after the restriction period.

---

[10] Cf. T.E. Gregory, Introduction to Tooke and Newmarch's *History of Prices and of the State of the Circulation,* 4 vols. (London: P.S. King, 1928), p. 23. Professor Gregory does not, however, clearly distinguish between the two theories.

[11] *Thoughts on the Effects of the Bank Restriction* (London, 1803), p. 20.

[12] *An Essay on the Principles of Commercial Exchanges* (1804), p. 113.

[13] *The High Price of Bullion a Proof of the Depreciation of Bank Notes,* 3rd ed. (1810), p. 47. *Economic Essays,* ed. E.K.C. Gonner (London: G. Bell and Sons, 1923), p. 35.

[14] "Principles of Political Economy and Taxation," *The Works of David Ricardo,* ed. J.R. McCulloch (London: John Murray, 1846), p. 220.

[15] *Bullion Report,* etc., octavo edition (London, 1810), p. 56; ed. Carman (1894), p. 51.

In 1823, Thomas Joplin, the inventor of the currency doctrine, enunciates the same principle which a few years later he elaborated into a peculiar but very interesting theory of the "pressure and anti-pressure of capital upon currency" and propounds it as a new discovery.[16] Though his theory is interwoven with some quite erroneous opinions, which probably prevented his contemporaries from recognizing the real contributions contained in his writings, yet, nevertheless, he succeeds in providing the clearest explanation of the relations between the rate of interest and the fluctuations of the note circulation which had been given up to that time. The principle which, in Joplin's opinion, neither Thornton nor those who adopted his opinions discovered, and which probably was responsible for "every great fluctuation in prices that has occurred since the first establishment of our banking system," is that when the supply of capital exceeds the demand, it has the effect of compressing the country circulation: when the demand is greater than the supply, it has the effect of expanding it again.[17] He devotes some pages to an exposition of how the rate of interest operates to equalize the demand for and the supply of capital, and how any change of that rate affects productive activity, and then proceeds:

> But, with our currency, or rather the currency of the country banks ... the effects are different. The interest of money, when it is abundant, is not reduced, but the

---

[16] In a work entitled *Outlines of a System of Political Economy* (London: Ridgway and Baldwin, 1823), pp. 62 and 198 *et seq.*; written with a view to prove to the government and the country that the cause of the present agricultural distress is entirely artificial, and to suggest a plan for the management of currency by which it may be remedied now and any recurrence of similar evils be prevented in the future. This work probably contains also the first exposition of the program later advocated and put into practice by the members of the "Currency School" Joplin's second work referred to in the text is *An Analysis and History of the Currency Question* (London: J. Ridway, 1832).

[17] *Analysis and History*, p. 101.

circulation . . . is diminished; and on the contrary, when money is scarce, an enlargement of issues takes place, instead of a rise in the rate of interest. The Country Bankers never vary the interest they charge. . . . He must, of necessity, have one fixed charge, whatever it may be: for he never can know what the true rate is. With a metallic currency, on the contrary, the Banker would always know the state of the market. In the first place, he could not lend money until it had been saved and placed in his hands, and he would have a particular amount to lend. On the other hand, he would have more or fewer persons wanting to borrow, and in proportion as the demand would exceed or fall short of the amount he had to lend, he would raise or lower his terms. . . . But, in consequence of the Country Banks being not only dealers in incipient capital, but issuers of currency, the demand for currency and the demand for capital are so mingled together that all knowledge of either is totally confounded.[18]

For the next seventy-five years there was hardly any progress in this connection. Three years after Joplin, in 1826, Thomas Tooke (who eighteen years later was to enlarge upon the erroneousness of what he then could already call the commonly received doctrine that a low rate of interest is calculated to raise prices and a high rate to depress them)[19] accepted Thornton's doctrine, and developed it in some minor points.[20] In 1832 J. Horsley Palmer reproduced it before the parliamentary committee on the Renewal of

---

[18] Ibid., pp. 108–09. Cf. also pp. 111–13.

[19] T. Tooke, *An Inquiry into the Currency Principle* (London: Smith, Elder, 1844), p. 77.

[20] Tooke, *Considerations on the State of the Currency* (London: John Murray, 1826), p. 22, footnote. As late as 1840 he still reprinted this note in the appendix to the first volume of his *History of Prices* though not without omitting some important sentences. Cf. Gregory, Introduction, p. 25.

the Bank Charter,[21] and as late as 1840 the doctrine that the "demand for loans and discounts at a rate below the usual rate is insatiable" was treated almost as a matter of course by N.W. Senior,[22] and it even entered, though in a somewhat emasculated form, into J.S. Mill's *Principles of Political Economy*.[23]

(6) Before following the more modern development of this theory, I must, however, trace the origins of the second strand of thought which in the end became interwoven with the one just considered to constitute modern doctrine in this matter. While the line of thought we have already considered pays attention only to the relation between the rate of interest, the amount of money in circulation and, as a necessary consequence of the latter, the general price level, the second pays attention to the influence which an increase in the amount of money exercises upon the production of capital, either directly or through the rate of interest. The theory that an increase of money brings about an increase of capital, which has recently become very popular under the name of "forced saving," is even older than the one we have just been considering.

The first author clearly to state this doctrine and the one who elaborated it in greater detail than any of his successors up to very recent times was J. Bentham. In a passage of his *Manual of Political Economy* written in 1804 but not published until 1843, he deals in some detail with the phenomenon which he calls "Forced Frugality." By this he means the increased "addition to the mass

---

[21] *Report on the Committee of Secrecy on the Bank of England Charter* (London, 1833), p. 18. Q. 191–7.

[22] In an anonymous article entitled "Lord King" in the *Edinburgh Review* (October 1846), later reprinted in N.W. Senior's *Biographical Sketches* (London: Longman, Green, 1863). The relevant parts of this article are now all reproduced in Senior's *Industrial Efficiency and Social Economy*, ed. S. Leon Levy (New York: Henry Holt, 1928), vol. 2, pp. 117–18.

[23] Book 3, chap. 23, para. 4, ed. William James Ashley (London: Longmans Green, 1848), p. 646 *et seq*.

of future wealth" which a government can bring about by applying funds raised by taxation or the creation of paper money to the production of capital goods. But interesting and important as this discussion by Bentham is, and although it is more than probable that it was known to some of the economists of this circle, the fact that it appeared in print only so many years later reduces its importance for the development of the doctrine very much.[24]

The honor of first having discussed the problem in some detail in print is apparently due to T.R. Malthus, who, in 1811, in an unsigned review[25] of Ricardo's first pamphlet, introduces his remarks with the complaint that no writer he is acquainted with "has ever seemed sufficiently aware of the influence which a different distribution of the circulating medium of the country must have on those accumulations which are destined to facilitate future production." He then demonstrates on an assumed "strong case" that a change of the proportion between capital and revenue to the advantage of capital so "as to throw the produce of the country chiefly in the hands of the productive classes" would have the effect that "in a short time, the produce of the country would be greatly augmented." The next paragraph must be quoted in full. He writes:

> Whenever, in the actual state of things, a fresh issue of notes comes into the hands of those who mean to employ them in the prosecution and extension of profitable business, a difference in the distribution of the circulating

---

[24] Bentham's contribution to this problem is discussed in somewhat greater detail in a note by the present author on "The Development of the Doctrine of Forced Saving," *Quarterly Journal of Economics* (November 1932) where also an even earlier reference to the problem by H. Thornton and a number of later contributions to the discussion on it are mentioned, which are omitted in the present sketch.

[25] *Edinburgh Review* 17, no. 34 (February 1811): 363 *et seq*. Cf. also the reply of Ricardo in appendix to the fourth edition of his pamphlet on the *High Price of Bullion* (1811).

> medium takes place, similar in kind to that which has been last supposed; and produces similar, though of course comparatively inconsiderable effects, in altering the proportion between capital and revenue in favour of the former. The new notes go into the market as so much additional capital, to purchase what is necessary for the conduct of the concern. But, before the produce of the country has been increased, it is impossible for one person to have more of it, without diminishing the shares of some others. This diminution is affected by the rise of prices, occasioned by the competition of the new notes, which puts it out of the power of those who are only buyers, and not sellers, to purchase as much of the annual produce as before: While all the industrious classes—all those who sell as well as buy—are, during the progressive rise of prices, making unusual profits; and, even when this progression stops, are left with the command of a greater portion of the annual produce than they possessed previous to the new issues.

The recognition of this tendency of an increased issue of notes to increase the national capital does not blind Malthus to the dangers and manifest injustice connected with it. He simply offers it, he says, as a rational explanation of the fact that a rise of prices is generally found conjoined with public prosperity.

With a single exception this suggestion of Malthus does not seem to have been appreciated at the time—though the mere fact that Ricardo replied to it at length should have made it familiar to economists. The exception is a series of memoranda on the Bullion Report which Dugald Stewart prepared in 1811 for Lord Lauderdale and which were later reprinted as an appendix to his lectures on political economy.[26] Objecting to the oversimplified

---

[26] Cf. *The Collected Works of Dugald Stewart*, ed. Sir William Hamilton (London: Longman, Brown, Green, 1855), vol. 8, pp. 440–49. A fuller discussion of D. Stewart's views on the subject will be found in the note on "The Development of the Doctrine of Forced Saving," quoted before.

version of the quantity theory employed in the reasoning of the Bullion Report, he attempts to explain the more "indirect connection between the high prices and an increased circulating medium." In the course of this discussion he comes very near to the argument employed by Malthus and in one of the later memoranda actually refers to the article which in the meantime had come to his notice, and reproduces the paragraph quoted above.

There are further allusions to the problem by other authors of the early nineteenth century, notably by T. Joplin and R. Torrens, and John Stuart Mill in the fourth of his *Essays on Some Unsettled Questions of Political Economy*—"On Profits and Interest"—(written in 1829 or 1830) goes at least so far as to mention that, as the result of the activity of bankers, "revenue" may be "converted into capital; and thus, strange as it may appear, the depreciation of the currency, when effected in this way, operates to a certain extent as a forced accumulation."[27]

But he believed then that this phenomenon belonged to the "further anomalies of the rate of interest which have not, so far as we are aware, been hitherto brought within the pale of exact science." The first edition of his *Principles* seems to contain nothing on this point. But in 1865, in the sixth edition, he added to his chapter on "Credit as a Substitute for Money" a footnote which so closely resembles the statement by Malthus that it seems very probable that something—perhaps the publications of D. Stewart's *Collected Works*—had directed his attention to the earlier discussion of the point.[28]

(7) In the period after the publication of J.S. Mill's *Principles* for a long time attention was paid only to the first of the two related ideas we have been analyzing. For many years there was very little progress at all. Occasional restatements of the views of

---

[27] *Essays on Some Unsettled Questions of Political Economy* (London: Parker, 1844), p. 118.

[28] Mill, *Principles of Political Economy*, ed. Ashley, p. 512.

the earlier authors occurred, but added nothing and received little attention.[29] The doctrine of the "indirect chain of effects connecting money and prices," as developed by Sidgwick, Giffen, Nicholson, and even Marshall,[30] adds hardly anything to what had been evolved from Thornton to Tooke. More significant is the further development and perhaps independent rediscovery of the forced saving doctrine by Léon Walras in 1879.[31] Although his contribution had been practically forgotten and has only recently been recovered from oblivion by Professor Marget, it is of special interest because it is probably through Walras that this doctrine reached Knut Wicksell. And it was only this great Swedish economist who at the end of the century finally succeeded in definitely welding the two, up to then, separate strands of thoughts into one. His success in this regard is explained by the fact that his attempt was based on a modern and highly developed theory of interest: that of Böhm-Bawerk. But by a curious irony of fate, Wicksell[32] has become famous, not for his real improvements on the old doctrine, but for the one point in his exposition in which he definitely erred: namely, for his attempt to establish a rigid connection between the rate of interest and the changes in the general price level.

---

[29] An instance of such restatement of earlier doctrine which is somewhat surprising in view of the later opinions of this author, occurs in Adolf Wagner's early *Beiträge zur Lehre von den Banken* (Leipzig: Voss, 1857), pp. 236–39.

[30] Cf. J.W. Angell, *The Theory of International Prices* (Cambridge, Mass.: Harvard University Press, 1926), p. 117 *et seq.*

[31] Léon Walras, *Théorie Mathématique du Billet de Banque* (1879); reprinted in *Études d'Économie Politique Appliqué* (Lausanne and Paris, 1898).

[32] Wicksell's first and most important exposition of this doctrine is in his *Geldzins und Güterpreise* (German edition; Jena: Gustav Fischer, 1898), which should be consulted together with Wicksell's later restatement in the second volume of his *Vorlesungen über Nationalökonomie* (Jena: Gustav Fischer, 1922).

Put concisely, Wicksell's theory is as follows: If it were not for monetary disturbances, the rate of interest would be determined so as to equalize the demand for and the supply of savings. This equilibrium rate, as I prefer to call it, he christens the natural[33] rate of interest. In a money economy, the actual or money rate of interest ("Geldzins") may differ from the equilibrium or natural rate, because the demand for and the supply of capital do not meet in their natural form but in the form of money, the quantity of which available for capital purposes may be arbitrarily changed by the banks.

Now, so long as the money rate of interest coincides with the equilibrium rate, the rate of interest remains "neutral" in its effects on the prices of goods, tending neither to raise nor to lower them. When the banks, however, lower the money rate of interest below the equilibrium rate, which they can do by lending more than has been entrusted to them, i.e., by adding to the circulation, this must tend to raise prices; if they raise the money rate above the equilibrium rate—a case of less practical importance—they exert a depressing influence on prices. From this correct statement, however, which does not imply that the price level would remain unchanged if the money rate corresponds to the equilibrium rate, but only that, in such conditions, there are no *monetary* causes tending to produce a change in the price level, Wicksell jumps to the conclusion that, so long as the two rates agree, the price level must always remain steady. There will be more to say about this later. For the moment, it is worth observing a further development of the theory. The rise of the price level, which is supposed to be the necessary effect of the money rate remaining below the equilibrium rate, is in the first

---

[33] Sometimes also the "normal" (p. 111) or "real" rate of interest. This latter form of expression has given rise to a confusion with a different theory concerning the influence of an expectation of price changes on the rate, which is commonly associated with the name of Fisher, but which, as mentioned before, was already known to Thornton, Ricardo, and Marshall.

instance brought about by the entrepreneurs spending on production the increased amount of money loaned by the banks. This process, as Malthus had already shown, involves what Wicksell now called enforced or compulsory saving.[34]

That is all I need to say here in explanation of the Wicksellian theory. Nor shall I here discuss the important development of this theory added by the Austrian economist, Professor Mises.[35] An exposition of the present form of this theory will

---

[34] *Geldzins und Güterpreise,* pp. 102, 143.

[35] *Theorie des Geldes und der Umlaufsmittel* (1912). Simultaneously with Professor Mises a distinguished Italian economist, Professor Marco Fanno, made in an exceedingly interesting and now very rare book on *Le Banche e il Mercato Monetario* (Rome: Athenaeum, 1913), an independent attempt to develop Wicksell's theory further. A revised shorter German version of the views of this author is now available in his contribution to the *Beiträge zur Geldtheorie* (Vienna: Springer, 1933).

Considerable elements of Professor Mises's theory and particularly the doctrine of "Forced Saving" seem to have been introduced into America through Professor Schumpeter's *Theorie der Wirtschaftlichen Entwicklung* (Munich: Duncker & Humblot, 1911) and Dr. B.M. Anderson's *Value of Money* (New York: Macmillan, 1917) and gained considerable vogue since. In any case, since the publication of this book in 1917, "Forced Saving" has been discussed by Professors F.W. Taussig, *Principles of Economics,* 3rd ed. (New York: Harper & Row, 1915), pp. 351, 359; F. Knight, *Risk, Uncertainty and Profit* (New York: Houghton Mifflin, 1921), p. 166, note and Index; D. Friday, *Profit, Wages and Prices* (New York: Harcourt, Brace, 1921), pp. 216–17; and A.H. Hansen *Cycles of Prosperity and Depression* (Madison: University of Wisconsin Press, 1921), pp. 104–06. Whether the American author whose views on these problems comes nearest to those expressed in the present book, Mr. M.W. Watkins, whose exceedingly interesting article on "Commercial Banking and the Formation of Capital," *Journal of Political Economy,* 27 (1919), I have only recently become acquainted with, is indebted to the same source I do not know.

In England similar ideas seem to have been developed independently, first by Professor Pigou, *Is Unemployment Inevitable?* (London: Macmillan, 1925), pp. 100–11 and then in much greater detail by Mr. D.H. Robertson, *Banking Policy and the Price Level* (London: P.S. King, 1926), *passim.*

form the main subject of my next two lectures. Here it is only necessary to point out that Professor Mises has improved the Wicksellian theory by an analysis of the different influences which a money rate of interest different from the equilibrium rate exercises on the prices of consumers' goods on the one hand, and the prices of producers' goods on the other. In this way, he has succeeded in transforming the Wicksellian theory into an explanation of the credit cycle which is logically satisfactory.

(8) But this brings me to the next part of my discussion. For it is partly upon the foundations laid by Wicksell and partly upon criticism of his doctrine that what seems to me the fourth of the great stages of the progress of monetary theory is being built. (I ought, perhaps, expressly to warn you that while up to this point of our survey I have been describing developments which have already taken place, what I am about to say about the fourth stage concerns rather what I think it should be than what has already taken definite shape.)

It would take too much time to trace chronologically the steps by which, by degrees, the Wicksellian theory has been transformed into something new. You will be better able to appreciate this change if I turn immediately to the discussion of those deficiencies of his doctrine which eventually made it necessary definitely to break away from certain of the fundamental concepts in the theory which had been taken over by him from his predecessors.

I have mentioned already that, according to Wicksell, the equilibrium rate of interest was a rate which simultaneously restricted the demand for real capital to the amount of savings available *and* secured stability of the price level. His idea is obviously one which is very generally held even at the present time, namely, that as, at an equilibrium rate of interest, money would remain neutral toward prices, therefore in such circumstances there could be no reason at all for a change of the price level.

Nevertheless, it is perfectly clear that, in order that the supply and demand for real capital should be equalized, the banks must not lend more or less than has been deposited with them as savings (and such additional amounts as may have been saved and hoarded). And this means naturally that (always excepting the case just mentioned) they must never allow the effective amount of money in circulation to change.[36] At the same time, it is no less clear that, in order that the price level may remain unchanged, the amount of money in circulation must change as the volume of production increases or decreases. The banks could *either* keep the demand for real capital within the limits set by the supply of savings, *or* keep the price level steady; but they cannot perform both functions at once. Except in a society in which there were no additions to the supply of savings, i.e., a stationary society, to keep the money rate of interest at the level of the equilibrium rate would mean that in times of expansion of production the price level would fall. To keep the general price level steady would mean, in similar circumstances, that the loan rate of interest would have to be lowered below the equilibrium rate. The consequences would be what they always are when the rate of investment exceeds the rate of saving.

It would be possible to cite other cases where the influence of money on prices and production is quite independent of the effects on the general price level. But it seems obvious as soon as one once begins to think about it that almost any change in the amount of money, whether it does influence the price level or not, must *always* influence relative prices. And, as there can be no doubt that it is relative prices which determine the amount and the direction of production, almost any change in the amount of money must necessarily also influence production.

But if we have to recognize that, on the one hand, under a stable price level, relative prices may be changed by monetary influences, and, on the other that relative prices may remain

---

[36] From now onward the term "amount of money in circulation" or even shortly "the quantity of money" will he used for what should more exactly be described as the effective money stream or the amount of money payments made during a unit period of time. The problems arising out of possible divergences between these two magnitudes will only be taken up in Lecture 4.

undisturbed only when the price level changes, we have to give up the generally received opinion that if the general price level remains the same, the tendencies toward economic equilibrium are not disturbed by monetary influences, and that disturbing influences from the side of money cannot make themselves felt otherwise than by causing a change of the general price level.

This doctrine, which has been accepted dogmatically by almost all monetary theorists, seems to me to lie at the root of most of the shortcomings of present-day monetary theory and to be a bar to almost all further progress. Its bearing on various proposals for stabilization is obvious. In these lectures, however, it is in the theoretical foundations of these schemes rather than in the formulation of alternative practical proposals that we are interested. And here, it may be suggested, it is possible very greatly to underestimate the changes in economic theory which are implied once we drop these unjustified assumptions. For when we investigate into all the influences of money on individual prices, quite irrespective of whether they are or are not accompanied by a change of the price level, it is not long before we begin to realize the superfluity of the concept of a general value of money, conceived as the reverse of some price level. And, indeed, I am of the opinion that, in the near future, monetary theory will not only reject the explanation in terms of a direct relation between money and the price level, but will even throw overboard the concept of a general price level and substitute for it investigations into the causes of the changes of relative prices and their effects on production. Such a theory of money, which will be no longer a theory of the value of money in general, but a theory of the influence of money on the different ratios of exchange between goods of all kinds, seems to me the probable fourth stage in the development of monetary theory.

This view of the probable future of the theory of money becomes less startling if we consider that the concept of relative prices includes the prices of goods of the same kind at different moments, and that here, as in the case of interspatial price relationships, only one relation between the two prices can correspond to a condition of "intertemporal" equilibrium, and that this need not, *a priori*, be a relation of identity or the one which would exist under a stable price level. (This has a particular bearing on the problem of money as a standard of deferred payments, because in this function money is to be conceived simply as the medium which effects an intertemporal exchange.) If this view is correct, the question which in my opinion will take the place of the question whether the value of money has increased or decreased will be the question whether the state of equilibrium of the rates of intertemporal exchange is disturbed by monetary influences in favor of future or in favor of present goods.[37]

(9) It will be the object of the following lectures to show how it is possible to solve at least some of the most important problems of monetary theory without recourse to the concept of a value of money in general. It will then remain for you to make up your mind whether we can conceivably entirely dispense with it. For the moment, I wish only to remind you of one further reason why it seems that, in the case of money, in contrast to any other good, the question of its value in general is of no consequence.

We are interested in the prices of individual goods because these prices show us how far the demand for any particular good can be satisfied. To discover the causes why certain needs, and the needs of certain persons, can be satisfied to a greater degree than others is the ultimate object of economics. There is, however, no *need* for money in this sense—the absolute amount of money in existence is of no consequence to the well-being of mankind—and there is, therefore, no objective value of money in the sense in which we speak of the objective value of goods. *What*

---

[37] I have dealt more fully with the difficult question of the conditions of intertemporal equilibrium of exchange in an article "Das intertemporale Gleichgewichtsystem der Preise und die Bewegungen des 'Geldwertes'," *Weltwirtschaftliches Archiv* 28 (1928).

we are interested in is only how the relative values of goods as sources of income or as means of satisfaction of wants are affected by money.

The problem is never to explain any "general value" of money but only how and when money influences the relative values of goods and under what conditions it leaves these relative values undisturbed, or, to use a happy phrase of Wicksell, when money remains *neutral* relatively to goods.[38] Not a money which is *stable* in value but a *neutral* money must therefore form the starting point for the theoretical analysis of monetary influences on production, and the first object of monetary theory should be to clear up the conditions under which money might be considered to be neutral in this sense. We stand as yet at the very beginning of this kind of investigation. And, though I hope that what I say in the next lectures may help a little, I am fully conscious that all results we obtain at this stage should only be regarded as tentative. So far as I am concerned, it is the method of approach more than the details of the results which is of importance in what follows.

---

[38] Cf. the Appendix to Lecture 4.

LECTURE 2

The Conditions of Equilibrium between the Production of Consumers' Goods and the Production of Producers' Goods

> The question of how far, and in what manner, an increase of currency tends to increase capital appears to us so very important, as fully to warrant our attempt to explain it. ... It is not the *quantity* of the circulating medium which produces the effects here described, but the *different distribution* of it ... on every fresh issue of notes ... a larger proportion falls into the hands of those who consume and produce, and a smaller proportion into the hands of those who only consume.
>
> T.R. Malthus
> *Edinburgh Review* 17 (1811): 363 *et seq.*

(1) Before we can attempt to understand the influence of prices on the amount of goods produced, we must know the nature of the immediate causes of a variation of industrial output. Simple as this question may at first appear, contemporary theory offers at least three explanations.

(2) First of these, we may take the view that the main causes of variations of industrial output are to be found in changes in the willingness of individuals to expand effort. I mention this first, because it is probably the theory which has at present the greatest number of adherents in this country. That this point of

view is so widely accepted in England is probably due to the fact that a comparatively great number of economists here are still under the influence of "real cost" theories of value which make this type of explanation of any change in the total value of output the natural one. Mr. D.H. Robertson's stimulating book on *Banking Policy and the Price Level* provides, perhaps, the best example of reasoning based on this assumption. Yet I do not think that this assumption is at all justified by our common experience; it is a highly artificial assumption to which I would only be willing to resort when all other explanations had failed. But its correctness is a question of fact, and I shall make no attempt to refute it directly. I shall only try to show that there are other ways of accounting for changes in industrial output which seem less artificial.

(3) The second type of explanation is the one which "explains" variations of production simply by the changes of the amount of factors of production used. In my opinion this is no explanation at all. It depends essentially upon a specious appeal to facts. Starting from the existence of unused resources of all kinds, known to us in daily experience, it regards any increase of output simply as the consequence of bringing more unused factors into use, and any diminution of output as the consequence of more resources becoming idle. Now, that any such change in the amount of resources employed implies a corresponding change in output is, of course, beyond question. But it is not true that the existence of unused resources is a *necessary* condition for an increase of output, nor are we entitled to take such a situation as a starting point for theoretical analysis. If we want to explain fluctuations of production, we have to give a complete explanation. Of course this does not mean that we have to start for that purpose *ab ovo* with an explanation of the whole economic process. But it does mean that we have to start where general economic theory stops; that is to say, at a condition of equilibrium when no unused resources exist. The existence of such unused resources is itself a fact which needs explanation. It is not

explained by static analysis and, accordingly, we are not entitled to take it for granted. For this reason I cannot agree that Professor Wesley Mitchell is justified when he states that he considers it no part of his task "to determine how the fact of cyclical oscillations in economic activity can be reconciled with the general theory of equilibrium, or how that theory can be reconciled with facts."[39] On the contrary, it is my conviction that if we want to explain economic phenomena at all, we have no means available but to build on the foundations given by the concept of a tendency toward an equilibrium. For it is this concept alone which permits us to explain fundamental phenomena like the determination of prices or incomes, an understanding of which is essential to any explanation of fluctuation of production. If we are to proceed systematically, therefore, we must start with a situation which is already sufficiently explained by the general body of economic theory. And the only situation which satisfies this criterion is the situation in which all available resources are employed. The existence of unused resources must be one of the main objects of our explanation.[40]

(4) To start from the assumption of equilibrium has a further advantage. For in this way we are compelled to pay more attention to causes of changes in the industrial output whose importance might otherwise be underestimated. I refer to changes in the methods of using the existing resources. Changes in the direction given to the existing productive forces are not only the main cause of fluctuations of the output of individual industries; the output of industry as a whole may also be increased or decreased to an enormous extent by changes in the use made of existing resources. Here we have the third of the contemporary

---

[39] *Business Cycles: The Problem and Its Setting* (New York: National Bureau of Economic Research, 1927), p. 462.

[40] I have dealt more fully with the relation between pure economic theory and the explanation of business fluctuations in my book, *Monetary Theory and the Trade Cycle*, chaps. 1 and 2.

explanations of fluctuations which I referred to at the beginning of the lecture. What I have here in mind are *not* changes in the methods of production made possible by the progress of technical knowledge, but the increase of output made possible by a transition to more capitalistic methods of production, or, what is the same thing, by organizing production so that, at any given moment, the available resources are employed for the satisfaction of the needs of a future more distant than before. It is to this effect of a transition to more or less "roundabout" methods of production that I wish particularly to direct your attention. For, in my opinion, it is only by an analysis of this phenomenon that in the end we can show how a situation can be created in which it is temporarily impossible to employ all available resources.

The processes involved in any such transition from a less to a more capitalistic form of production are of such a complicated nature that it is only possible to visualize them clearly if we start from highly simplified assumptions and work through gradually to a situation more like reality. For the purpose of these lectures, I shall divide this investigation into two parts. Today I shall confine myself to a consideration of the conditions under which an equilibrium between the production of producers' goods and the production of consumers' goods is established, and the relation of this equilibrium to the flow of money; I reserve for the next lecture a more detailed explanation of the working of the price mechanism during the period of transition, and of the relation between changes in the price system and the rate of interest.

(5) My first task is to define the precise meaning of certain terms. The term *production* I shall always use in its widest possible sense, that is to say, all processes necessary to bring goods into the hands of the consumer. When I mean land and labor, I shall speak of *original means of production*. When I use the phrase *factors of production* without further qualification this will cover capital also, that is to say this term will include all factors from which we derive *income* in the form of wages, rent, and interest.

When I use the expression *producers' goods*, I shall be designating all goods existing at any moment which are not consumers' goods, that is to say, *all* goods which are directly or indirectly used in the production of consumers' goods *including*, therefore, the original means of production, as well as instrumental goods and all kinds of unfinished goods. Producers' goods which are not original means of production, but which come between the original means of production and consumers' goods, I shall call *intermediate products*. None of these distinctions coincides with the customary distinction between durable and nondurable goods, which I do not need for my present purpose. I shall, however, have to use this distinction and to add a new one, which stands in some relation to it, in my next lecture.

(6) I have already pointed out that it is an essential feature of our modern, "capitalistic," system of production that at any moment a far larger proportion of the available original means of production is employed to provide consumers' goods for some more or less distant future than is used for the satisfaction of immediate needs. The *raison d'être* of this way of organizing production is, of course, that by lengthening the production process we are able to obtain a greater quantity of consumers' goods out of a given quantity of original means of production. It is not necessary for my present purpose to enter at any length into an explanation of this increase of productivity by roundabout methods of production. It is enough to state that within practical limits we may increase the output of consumers' goods from a given quantity of original means of production indefinitely, provided we are willing to wait long enough for the product. The thing which is of main interest for us is that any such change from a method of production of any given duration to a method which takes more or less time implies quite definite changes in the organization of production, or, as I shall call this particular aspect of organization, to distinguish it from other more familiar aspects, changes in the *structure of production*. In order to get a clear view of what is actually implied by these changes in the

structure of production it is useful to employ a schematic representation.[41] For this purpose, I find it convenient to represent the successive applications of the original means of production which are needed to bring forth the output of consumers' goods accruing at any moment of time, by the hypotenuse of a right-angled triangle, such as the triangle in Fig. 1.

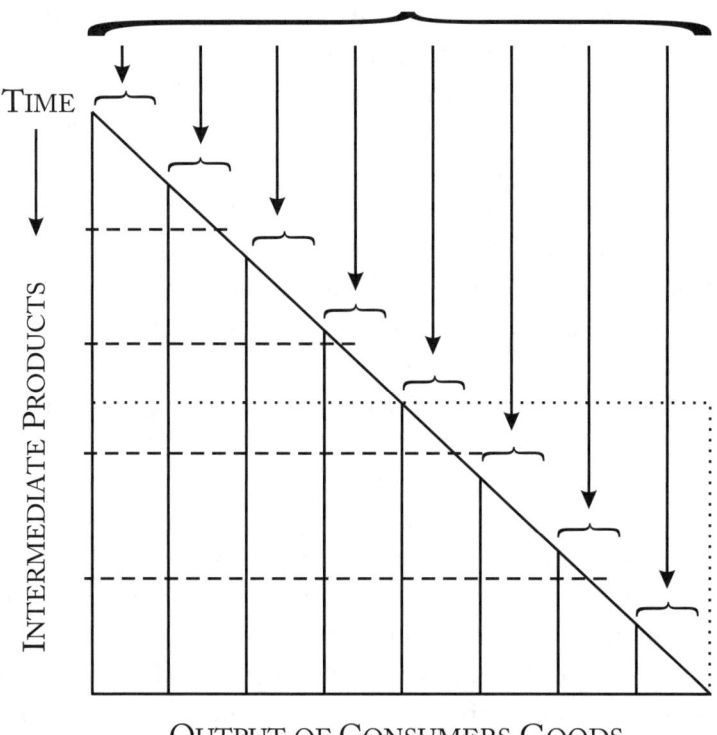

FIG. 1

---

[41] The following diagrams were originally the result of an attempt to replace the somewhat clumsy tables of figures, used for the same purpose in my "'Paradox' of Saving," by a more easily grasped form of representation. Later I noticed that similar triangular figures had been used as representations of the capitalistic process of production not only by W.S. Jevons, *Theory of*

The value of these original means of production is expressed by the horizontal projection of the hypotenuse, while the vertical dimension, measured in arbitrary periods from the top to the bottom, expresses the progress of time, so that the inclination of the line representing the amount of original means of production used means that these original means of production are expended continuously during the whole process of production. The bottom of the triangle represents the value of the current output of consumers' goods. The area of the triangle thus shows the totality of the successive stages through which the several units of original means of production pass before they become ripe for consumption. It also shows the total amount of intermediate products which must exist at any moment of time in order to secure a continuous output of consumers' goods. For this reason we may conceive of this diagram not only as representing the successive stages of the production of the output of any given moment of time, but also as representing the processes of production going on simultaneously in a stationary society. To use a happy phrase of J.B. Clark's, it gives a picture of the "synchronized process of production."[42,43]

Political Economy, 4th ed. (London: Macmillan, 1911), pp. 230–07, but particularly also by K. Wicksell, *Lectures on Political Economy* (New York: Macmillan, 1935), vol. 1, p. 152 *et seq.*, and, following him, G. Akerman, *Realkapital und Kapitalzins*, part 1 (Stockholm, 1923). Dr. Marschak has recently made the very appropriate suggestion to designate these triangular figures as the "Jevonian Investment Figures."

[42] The methodological bearing of the concept of a synchronized production is particularly well brought out by Hans Mayer in his article "Produktion," *Handwörterbuch der Staatswissenschaften*, 4th ed., vol. 6 (Jena: Gustav Fischer, 1925), p. 1115 *et seq.*

[43] So long as we confine ourselves to the real aspects of the capital structure, the triangular figures may be taken to represent not only the stock of goods in process but also the stock of durable instruments existing at any moment of time. The different installments of future services which such goods are expected to render will in that case have to be imagined to belong to different "stages" of production corresponding to the time interval which will elapse

Now it should be clear without further explanation that the proportion between the amount of intermediate products (represented by the area of the triangle) which is necessary at any moment of time to secure a continuous output of a given quantity of consumers' goods, and the amount of that output,[44] must grow with the

---

before these services mature. (For a more detailed discussion of the problems arising out of the two different aspects, of actual duration of production and the durability of goods, in which time enters in the productive process, cf. my article "On the Relationship between Investment and Output," *Economic Journal* [June 1934].) But as soon as the diagrammatic representations are used to show the successive transfers of the intermediate products from stage to stage in exchange for money, it becomes evidently impossible to treat durable goods in the same way as goods in process, since it is impossible to assume that the individual services embodied in any durable goods will regularly change hands as they approach a stage nearer to the moment when they will actually be consumed. For this reason, it has been necessary, as has been pointed out in the preface, to abstract from the existence of durable goods so long as the assumption is made that the total stock of intermediate products as it gradually proceeds toward the end of the process of production is exchanged against money at regular intervals.

[44] It would be more exact to compare the stock of intermediate products existing *at a moment* of time not with the output of consumers' goods *during a period* of time, but rather with the rate at which consumers' goods mature at the same moment of time. Since, however, this output at a moment of time would be infinitely small, that proportion could only be expressed as a differential quotient of a function which represents the flow of intermediate products at the point where this flow ends, i.e., where the intermediate products become consumers' goods. This relationship is essentially the same as that between the total quantity of water in a stream and the rate at which this water passes the mouth of this stream. (This *simile* seems to be more appropriate than the more familiar one which considers capital as a "stock" and only income as a "flow." Cf. on this point N.J. Polak, *Grundzüge der Finanzierung* [Berlin, 1926], p. 13.) It is convenient to treat the quantity of intermediate products at any point of this stream as a function of time $f(t)$ and accordingly the total quantity of intermediate products in the stream, as an integral of this function over a period r equal to the total length of the process of production. If we apply this to any process of production beginning at the moment x, the total quantity of intermediate products in the

length of the roundabout process of production. As the average time interval between the application of the original means of production and the completion of the consumers' goods increases, production becomes more capitalistic, and *vice versa*. In the case we are contemplating, in which the original means of production are applied at a constant rate throughout the whole process of production, this average time is exactly half as long as the time which elapses between the application of the first unit of original means of production and the completion of the process. Accordingly, the total amount of intermediate products may also be represented by a rectangle half as high as the triangle, as indicated by the dotted line in the diagram. The areas of the two figures are necessarily equal, and it sometimes assists the eye to have a rectangle instead of a triangle when we have to judge the relative magnitude represented by the area of the figure. Furthermore, it should be noticed that, as the figure represents values and not physical production, the surplus return obtained by the roundabout methods of production is not represented in the diagram. In this lecture I have intentionally neglected interest. We shall have to take that into consideration next time; until then we may assume that the intermediate products remain the property of the owners of the original means of production until they have matured into consumers' goods and are sold to consumers. Interest is then received by the owners of the original means of production together with wages and rent.

(7) A perfectly continuous process of this sort is somewhat unwieldy for theoretical purposes: moreover such an assumption

---

stream will be expressed by $\int_{x}^{x+r} f(t) \cdot dt$, and the output of consumers' goods at a moment of time by $f(x+r)$. In the diagrams used in the text, the function $f(t)$ is represented by the hypotenuse, its concrete value $f(x+r)$ by the horizontal side and the integral by the area of the triangle. There is of course no reason to assume that the function $f(t)$ will be linear, i.e., that the amount of original factors applied during successive stages of the process is constant, as is assumed in the diagrams. On these and some connected points, see the article on "Investment and Output," quoted in the preceding footnote.

is not perhaps sufficiently realistic. It would be open to us to deal with the difficulties by the aid of higher mathematics. But I, personally, prefer to make it amenable to a simpler method by dividing the continuous process into distinct periods, and by substituting for the concept of a continuous flow the assumption that goods move intermittently in equal intervals from one stage of production to the next. In this way, in my view, the loss in precision is more than compensated by the gain in lucidity.

Probably the simplest method of transforming the picture of the continuous process into a picture of what happens in a given period is to make cross sections through our first figure at intervals corresponding to the periods chosen, and to imagine observers being posted at each of these cross cuts who watch and note down the amount of goods flowing by. If we put these cross sections, as indicated by the broken lines in Fig. 1, at the end of each period, and represent the amount of goods passing these lines of division in a period by a rectangle of corresponding size, we get the new illustration of the same process given in Fig. 2.

It is convenient for the purposes of exposition to count only that part of the total process of production which is completed during one of these periods, as a separate stage of production. Each of the successive shaded blocks in the diagram will then represent the product of the corresponding stage of production as it is passed on to the next while the differences in the length of the successive blocks correspond to the amount of original means of production used in the succeeding stage. The white block at the bottom represents the output of consumers' goods during the period. In a stationary state, which is still the only state I am considering, this output of consumers' goods is necessarily equal to the total income from the factors of production used, and is exchanged for this income. The proportion of the white area to the shaded area, in this diagram 40:80 or 1:2, expresses the proportion between the output of consumers' goods and the output of intermediate products (or between the amount of consumption

Prices and Production

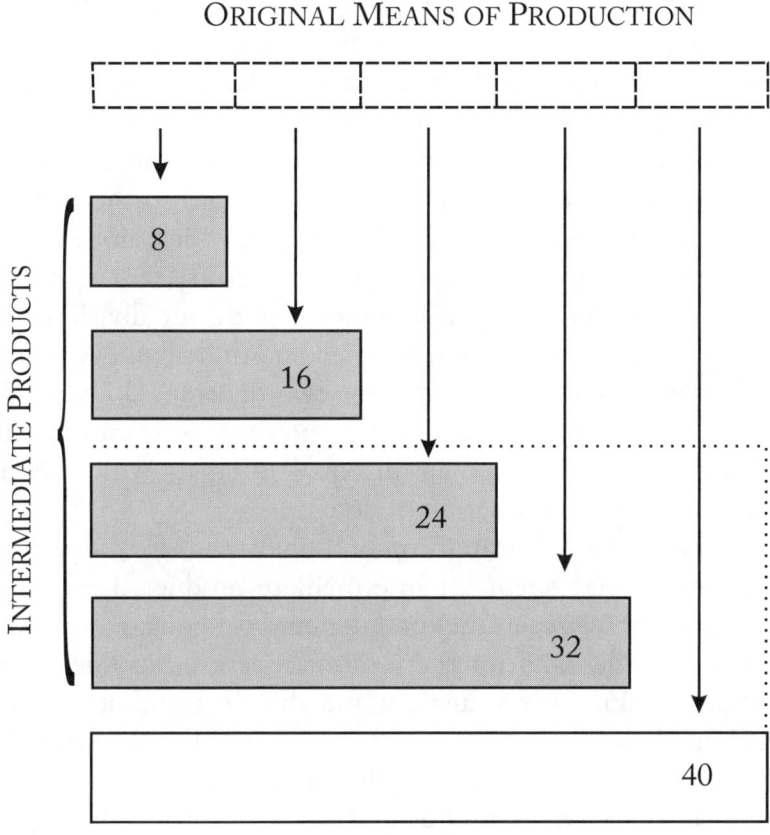

Fig. 2

and the amount of new and renewed investment during any period of time).

So far, I have used this schematic illustration of the process of production only to represent the movements of goods. It is just as legitimate to use it as an illustration of the movement of money. While goods move downward from the top to the bottom of our diagram, we have to conceive of money moving in the opposite direction, being paid first for consumers' goods and thence moving upward until, after a varying number of intermediary movements, it is paid out as income to the owners of the factors of production, who in turn use it to buy consumers' goods. But in order to trace the relation between actual money payments, or the proportional quantities of money used in the different stages of production, and the movements of goods, we need a definite assumption in regard to the division of the total process among different firms, which alone makes an exchange of goods against money necessary. For this does not by any means necessarily coincide with our division into separate stages of production of equal length. I shall begin with the simplest assumption, that these two divisions do coincide, that is to say that goods moving toward consumption do change hands against money in equal intervals which correspond to our unit production periods.

In such a case, the proportion of money spent for consumers' goods and money spent for intermediate products is equal to the proportion between the total demand for consumers' goods and the total demand for the intermediate products necessary for their continuous production; and this, in turn, must correspond, in a state of equilibrium, to the proportion between the output of consumers' goods during a period of time and the output of intermediate products of all earlier stages during the same period. Given the assumptions we are making, all these proportions are accordingly equally expressed by the proportion between the area of the white rectangle and the total shaded area. It will be noticed that the same device of the dotted line as was used in the earlier figure is employed to facilitate the comparison of the two areas. The dotted rectangle shows that, in the kind of production represented by Fig. 2, which actually takes four successive stages, the average length of the roundabout process is only two stages, and the amount of intermediate products is therefore twice as great as the output of customers' goods.

(8) Now if we adopt this method of approach, certain fundamental facts at once become clear. The first fact which

emerges is that the amount of money spent on producers' goods during any period of time may be far greater than the amount spent for consumers' goods during the same period. It has been computed, indeed, that in the United States, payments for consumers' goods amount only to about one-twelfth of the payments made for producers' goods of all kinds.[45] Nevertheless, this fact has not only very often been overlooked, it was even expressly denied by no less an authority than Adam Smith. According to Smith: "The value of goods circulated between the different dealers never can exceed the value of those circulated between dealers and consumers; whatever is bought by the dealer being ultimately destined to be sold to the consumers."[46] This proposition clearly rests upon a mistaken inference from the fact that the total expenditure made in production must be covered by the return from the sale of the ultimate products; but it remained unrefuted, and quite recently in our own day it has formed the foundation of some very erroneous doctrines.[47] The solution of the difficulty is, of course, that most goods are exchanged several times against money before they are sold to the consumer, and on the average exactly as many times as often as the total amount spent for producers' goods is larger than the amount spent for consumers' goods.

---

[45] Cf. M.W. Holtrop, *De Omloopssnelheid van het Geld* (Amsterdam: H.J. Paris, 1928), p. 181.

[46] *Wealth of Nations*, book 2, chap. 1, ed. E. Cannan (London: Methuen, 1904), p. 305. It is interesting to note that this statement of Adam Smith is referred to by Thomas Tooke as a justification of the erroneous doctrines of the Banking School. Cf. *An Inquiry into the Currency Principle*, p. 71.

[47] Cf. W.T. Foster and W. Catchings, *Profits*, Publications of the Pollak Foundation for Economic Research, No. 8 (Boston and New York: Houghton Mifflin, 1925), and a number of other books by the same authors and published in the same series. For a detailed criticism of their doctrines, cf. my article, "The 'Paradox' of Saving."

Another point which is of great importance for what follows, and which, while often overlooked in current discussion,[48] is quite obvious if we look at our diagram, is the fact that what is generally called the capital equipment of society—the total of intermediate products in our diagram—is not a magnitude which, once it is brought into existence, will necessarily last forever independently of human decisions. Quite the contrary: whether the structure of production remains the same depends entirely upon whether entrepreneurs find it profitable to re-invest the usual proportion of the return from the sale of the product of their respective stages of production in turning out intermediate goods of the same sort. Whether this is profitable, again, depends upon the prices obtained for the product of this particular stage of production on the one hand and on the prices paid for the original means of production and for the intermediate products taken from the preceding stage of production on the other. The continuance of the existing degree of capitalistic organization depends, accordingly, on the prices paid and obtained for the product of each stage of production; and these prices are, therefore, a very real and important factor in determining the direction of production.

The same fundamental fact may be described in a slightly different way. The money stream which the entrepreneur representing any stage of production receives at any given moment is always composed of net income which he may use for consumption

---

[48] J.S. Mill's emphasis on the "perpetual consumption and reproduction of capital," like most of his other penetrating, but often somewhat obscurely expressed observations on capital, has not had the deserved effect, although it directs attention to the essential quality of capital which distinguishes it from other factors of its production. More recently the misplaced emphasis which some authors, particularly Professors J.B. Clark, J. Schumpeter, and F.H. Knight, have put on the tautological statement that so long as stationary conditions prevail capital is *ex definitione* permanent, has further contributed to obscure the problem.

Prices and Production 237

without disturbing the existing method of production, and of parts which he must continuously reinvest. But it depends entirely upon him whether he redistributes his total money receipts in the same proportions as before. And the main factor influencing his decisions will be the magnitude of the profits he hopes to derive from the production of his particular intermediate product.

(9) And now at last we are ready to commence to discuss the main problem of this lecture, the problem of how a transition from less to more capitalistic methods of production, or *vice versa*, is actually brought about, and what conditions must be fulfilled in order that a new equilibrium may be reached. The first question can be answered immediately: a transition to more (or less) capitalistic methods of production will take place if the total demand for producers' goods (expressed in money) increases (or decreases) relatively to the demand for consumers' goods. This may come about in one of two ways: either as a result of changes in the volume of voluntary saving (or its opposite), or as a result of a change in the quantity of money which alters the funds at the disposal of the entrepreneurs for the purchase of producers' goods. Let us first consider the case of changes in voluntary saving, that is, simple shifts of demand between consumers' goods and producers' goods.[49]

As a starting point, we may take the situation depicted in Fig. 2, and suppose that consumers save and invest an amount of

---

[49] I am deliberately discussing here the "strong case" where saving implies a reduction in the demand for *all* consumers' goods, although this is a highly unlikely case to occur in practice, since it is in this case that many people find it so difficult to understand how a general decrease in the demand for consumers' goods should lead to an increase of investment. Where, as will regularly be the case, the reduction in the demand for consumers' goods affects only a few kinds of such goods, these special difficulties would, of course, be absent.

money equivalent to one-fourth of their income of one period. We may assume further that these savings are made continuously, exactly as they can be used for building up the new process of production. The proportion of the demand for consumers' goods to the demand for intermediate products will then ultimately be changed from 40:80 to 30:90, or 1:2 to 1:3. The additional amounts of money available for the purchase of intermediate products must now be so applied that the output of consumers' goods may be sold for the reduced sum of thirty now available for that purpose. It should now be sufficiently clear that this will only be the case if the average length of the roundabout processes of production and, therefore, in our instance, also the number of successive stages of production, is increased in the same proportion as the demand for intermediate products has increased relatively to the demand for consumers' goods, i.e., from an average of two to an average of three (or from an actual number of four to an actual number of six) stages of production. When the transition is completed, the structure of production will have changed from that shown in Fig. 2 to the one shown in Fig. 3. (It should be remembered that the relative magnitudes in the two figures are values expressed in money and not physical quantities, that the amount of original means of production used has remained the same, and that the amount of money in circulation and its velocity of circulation are also supposed to remain unchanged.)

If we compare the two diagrams, we see at once that the nature of the change consists in a stretching of the money stream flowing from the consumers' goods to the original means of production. It has, so to speak, become longer and narrower. Its breadth at the bottom stage, which measures the amount of money spent during a period of time on consumers' goods and, at the same time, the amount of money received as income in payment for the use of the factors of production, has permanently decreased from forty to thirty. This means that the price of a unit of the factors of production, the total amount of which

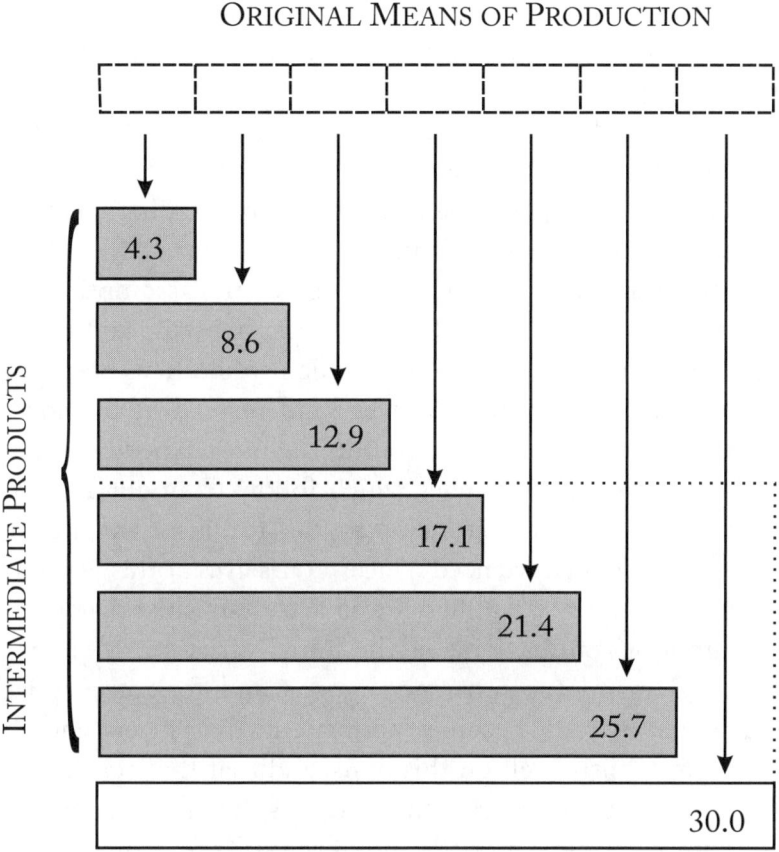

FIG. 3

(if we neglect the increase of capital) has remained the same, will fall in the same proportion, and the price of a unit of consumers' goods, the output of which has increased as a consequence of the more capitalistic methods of production, will fall in still greater proportion. The amount of money spent in each of the later stages of production has also decreased, while the amount used in the earlier stages has increased, and the total spent on intermediate products has increased also because of the addition of a new stage of production.[50]

Now it should be clear that to this change in the distribution of the amounts of money spent in the different stages of production there will correspond a similar change in the distribution of the total amount of goods existing at any moment. It should also be clear that the effect thus realized—given the assumptions we are making—is one which fulfills the object of saving and investing, and is identical with the effect which would have been produced if the savings were made in kind instead of in money. Whether it has been brought about in the most expeditious way, and whether the price changes which follow from our assumptions provide a suitable stimulus to the readjustment are not questions with which we need concern ourselves at this juncture. Our present purpose is fulfilled if we have established that, under the assumptions we have made, the initial variation in the proportional demand for consumers' goods and for intermediate products, respectively, becomes permanent, that a new equilibrium may establish itself on this basis, and that the fact that the amount of money remains unchanged, in spite of the increase of the output of consumers' goods and of the still greater increase of the total turnover of goods of all kinds and stages, offers no fundamental difficulties to such an increase of production, since total expenditure on the factors of production, or total costs, will still be covered by the sums received out of the sales of consumers' goods.

---

[50] To avoid misunderstandings I have now substituted the terms "earlier" and "later" stages used by Professor Taussig in this connection, for the expression "higher" and "lower," which are unequivocal only with reference to the diagrams but are liable to be confused with such expressions as "highly finished" products, particularly as A. Marshall has used the terms in this reverse sense (cf. *Industry and Trade* [London: Macmillan, 1919], p. 219).

Prices and Production 241

But now the question arises: does this remain true if we drop the assumptions that the amount of money remains unchanged and that, during the process of production, the intermediate products are exchanged against money at equal intervals of time?

(10) Let us begin by investigating the effects of a change in the amount of money in circulation. It will be sufficient if we investigate only the case most frequently to be encountered in practice: the case of an increase of money in the form of credits granted to producers. Again we shall find it convenient to start from the situation depicted in Fig. 2 and to suppose that the same change in the proportion between the demand for consumers' goods and the demand for intermediate products, which in the earlier instance was supposed to be produced by voluntary saving, is now caused by the granting of additional credits to producers. For this purpose, the producers must receive an amount of forty in additional money. As will be seen from Fig. 4, the changes in the structure of production, which will be necessary in order to find employment for the additional means which have become available, will exactly correspond to the changes brought about by saving. The total services of the original means of production will now be expended in six instead of in four periods; the total value of intermediate goods produced in the different stages during a period will have grown to three times instead of twice as large as the value of consumers' goods produced during the same period; and the output of each stage of production, including the final one, measured in physical units will accordingly be exactly as great as in the case represented in Fig. 3. The only difference at first apparent is that the money values of these goods have grown by one-third compared with the situation depicted in Fig. 3.

There is, however, another and far more important difference which will become apparent only with the lapse of time. When a change in the structure of production was brought about by saving, we were justified in assuming that the changed distribution of demand between consumers' goods and producers' goods

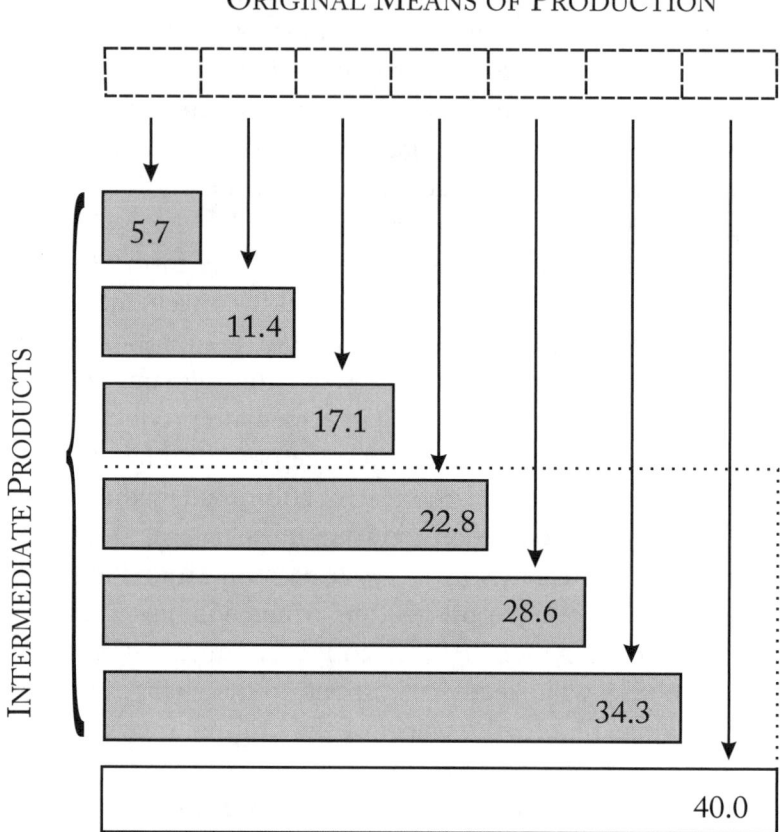

Fig. 4

would remain permanent, since it was the effect of voluntary decisions on the part of individuals. Only because a number of individuals had decided to spend a smaller share of their total money receipts on consumption and a larger share on production was there any change in the structure of production. And since, after the change had been completed, these persons would get a greater proportion of the increased total real income, they would have no reason again to increase the *proportion* of their money receipts spent for consumption.[51] There would accordingly exist no inherent cause for a return to the old proportions.

In the same way, in the case we are now considering, the use of a larger proportion of the original means of production for the manufacture of intermediate products can only be brought about by a retrenchment of consumption. But now this sacrifice is not voluntary, and is not made by those who will reap the benefit from the new investments. It is made by consumers in general who, because of the increased competition from the entrepreneurs who have received the additional money, are forced to forgo part of what they used to consume. It comes about not because they want to consume less, but because they get fewer goods for their money income. There can be no doubt that, if their money receipts should rise again, they would immediately attempt to expand consumption to the usual proportion. We shall see in the next lecture why, in time, their receipts will rise as a consequence of the increase of money in circulation. For the moment, let us assume that this happens. But if it does, then at once the money stream will be redistributed between consumptive and productive uses according to the wishes of the individual concerned, and the artificial distribution, due to the injection of the new money, will, partly at any rate, be reversed. If we assume that the old proportions are adhered to, then the structure of production too will have to return to the old proportion, as shown in Fig. 5. That is to say production will become less capitalistic, and that part of the new capital which was sunk in equipment adapted only to the more capitalistic processes will be lost. We shall see in the next lecture that such a transition to less capitalistic methods of production necessarily takes the form of an economic crisis.

---

[51] It is important to bear in mind that, though the total money income would diminish, the total real income would increase.

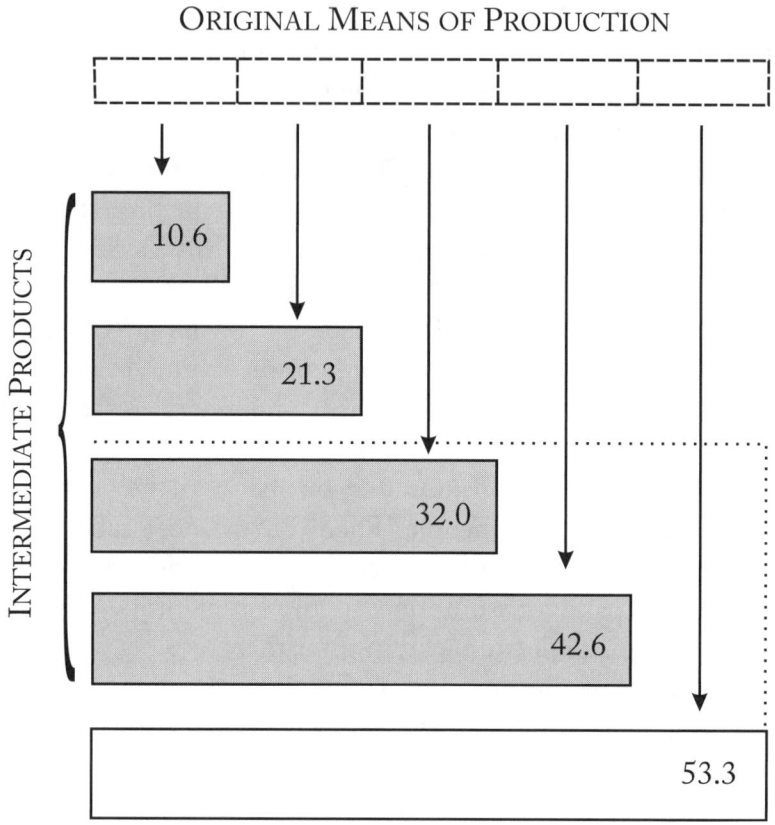

FIG. 5

But it is not necessary that the proportion between the demand for consumers' goods and the demand for intermediate products should return exactly to its former dimensions as soon as the injection of new money ceases. Insofar as the entrepreneurs have already succeeded, with the help of the additional money, in completing the new processes of longer duration,[52] they will, perhaps,

---

[52] It should, however, be remembered that a process cannot be regarded as completed in this sense, just because an entrepreneur at any one stage of

receive increased money returns for their output, which will put them in a position to continue the new processes, i.e., to expend permanently a larger share of their money receipts upon intermediate products without reducing their own consumption. It is only in consequence of the price changes caused by the increased demand for consumers' goods that, as we shall see, these processes too become unprofitable.

But for the producers who work on a process where the transition to longer roundabout processes is not yet completed when the amount of money ceases to increase the situation is different. They have spent the additional money which put them in a position to increase their demand for producers' goods and in consequence it has become consumers' income; they will, therefore, no longer be able to claim a larger share of the available producers' goods, and they will accordingly have to abandon the attempt to change over to more capitalistic methods of production.

(11) All this becomes easier to follow if we consider the simpler case in which an increase in demand for consumers' goods of this sort is brought about directly by additional money given to consumers. In recent years, in the United States, Messrs. Foster and Catchings have urged that, in order to make possible the sale of an increased amount of consumers' goods produced with the help of new savings, consumers must receive a proportionately larger money income. What would happen if their proposals were carried out? If we start with the situation which would establish itself as a consequence of new savings if the amount of money remained unchanged (as shown in Fig. 3), and then assume that consumers receive an additional amount of money sufficient to compensate for the relative increase of the demand for intermediate products

---

production has succeeded in completing his section of it. A complete process, in the sense in which this concept is used in the text, comprises *all* the stages of any one line of production, whether they are part of one firm or divided between several. I have further elaborated this point in my article on "Capital and Industrial Fluctuations."

caused by the savings (i.e., an amount of 15) and spend it on consumers' goods, we get a situation in which the proportion between the demand for consumers' goods, and the demand for producers' goods, which, in consequence of the new savings, had changed from 40:80 to 30:90 or from 1:2 to 1:3 would again be reduced to 45:90 or 1:2. That this would mean a return to the less capitalistic structure of production which existed before the new savings were made, and that the only effect of such an increase of consumers' money incomes would be to frustrate the effect of saving follows clearly from Fig. 6. (The difference from the original situation

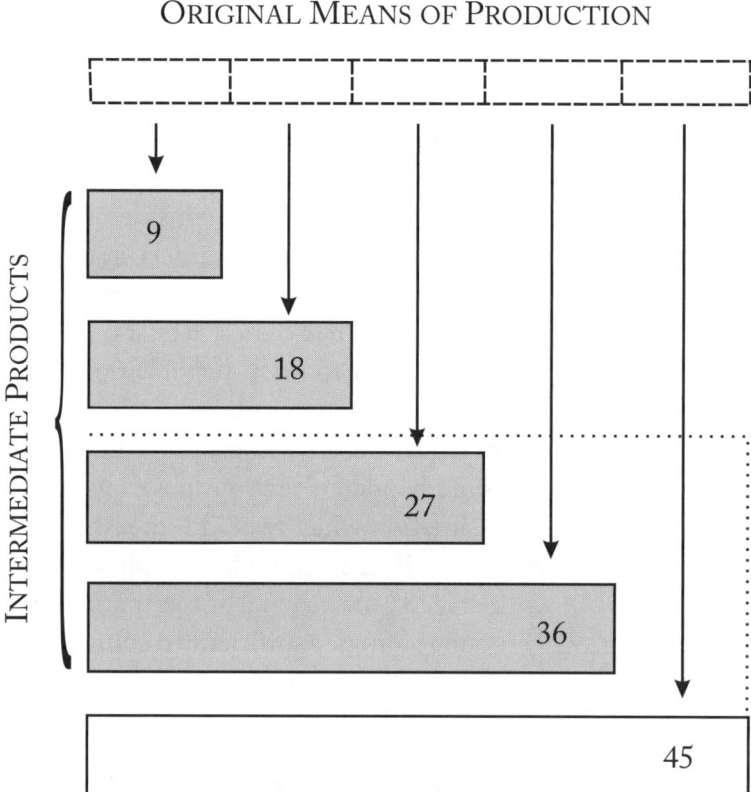

FIG. 6

depicted in Fig. 2 is again only a difference in money values and not a difference in the physical quantities of goods produced or in their distribution to the different stages of production.)

(12) It is now time to leave this subject and to pass on to the last problem with which I have to deal in this lecture. I wish now to drop the second of my original assumptions, the assumption, namely, that, during the process of production, the intermediate products are exchanged against money between the firms at successive stages of production in equal intervals. Instead of this very artificial assumption, we may consider two possible alternatives: we may suppose (a) that in any line of production the whole process is completed by a single firm, so that no other money payments take place than the payments for consumers' goods and the payments for the use of the factors of production: or we may suppose (b) that exchanges of intermediate products take place, but at very irregular intervals, so that in some parts of the process the goods remain for several periods of time in the possession of one and the same firm, while in other parts of the process they are exchanged once or several times during each period.

(13) (a) Let us consider first the case in which the whole process of production in any line of production is completed by a single firm. Once again we may use Fig. 1 to illustrate what happens. In this case the base of the triangle represents the total payments for consumers' goods and the hypotenuse (or, more correctly, its horizontal projection) represents the amounts of money paid for the original means of production used. No other payments would be made, and any amount of money received from the sale of consumers' goods could immediately be spent for the original means of production. It is of fundamental importance to remember that we can assume only that any *single* line of production is in this way integrated into one big firm. It would be entirely inappropriate in this connection to suppose that the production of *all* goods is concentrated in one enterprise. For, if this were the case, of course the manager of this firm could, like the economic dictator of a communistic society, arbitrarily

decide what part of the available means of production should be applied to the production of consumers' goods and what part to the production of producers' goods. There would exist for him no reason to borrow and, for individuals, no opportunity to invest savings. Only if *different* firms compete for the available means of production will saving and investing in the ordinary sense of the words take place, and it is therefore such a situation which we must make the starting point of our investigation.

Now, if any of these integrated industries decides to save and invest part of its profits in order to introduce more capitalistic methods of production, it must not immediately pay out the sums saved for the original means of production. As the transition to more capitalistic methods of production means that it will be longer until the consumers' goods produced by the new process are ready, the firm will need the sums saved to pay wages, etc., during the interval of time between the sale of the last goods produced by the old process, and the getting ready of the first goods produced by the new process. So that, during the whole period of transition, it must pay out less to consumers than it receives in order to be able to bridge the gap at the end of this period, when it has nothing to sell but has to continue to pay wages and rent. Only when the new product comes on the market and there is no need for further saving will it again currently pay out all its receipts.

In this case, therefore, the demand for consumers' goods, as expressed in money, will be only temporarily reduced, while in the case where the process of production was divided between a number of independent stages of equal length, the reduction of the amount available for the purchase of consumers' goods was a permanent one. In the present case, the prices of the consumers' goods will, accordingly, fall only in inverse proportion as their quantity has increased, while the total paid as income for the use of the factors of production will remain the same. These conclusions are, however, only provisional as they do not take account of the relative position of the one firm considered to all other firms which will certainly be affected by a change of relative prices and interest rates which are necessarily connected with such a process. Unfortunately, these influences are too complicated to allow for treatment within the scope of these lectures, and I must ask you, therefore, to suspend judgment upon the ultimate effects of the price changes which will take place under these conditions.

But there is one point to which I must particularly direct your attention. The reason in this case why the unchanged amount of money used in production remains sufficient, in spite of the fact that a larger amount of intermediate products now exists, whereas in the former case, the use of an increased amount of intermediate products required the use of an increased quantity of money is this: in the former case the intermediate products passed from one stage of production to the next by an exchange against money. But in the present case this exchange is replaced by internal barter, which makes money unnecessary. Of course, our division of the continuous process of production into separate stages of equal length is entirely arbitrary: it would be just as natural to divide it into stages of different lengths and then speak of these stages as exhibiting so many more or less instances of internal barter. But the procedure which has been adopted serves to bring out a concept, which I shall need in a later lecture, the concept of the relative volume of the flow of goods during any period of time, as compared with the amount of goods exchanged against money in the same period. If we divide the path traversed by the elements of any good from the first expenditure of original means of production until it gets in the hands of the final consumer into unit periods, and then measure the quantities of goods which pass each of these lines of division during a period of time, we secure a comparatively simple measure of the flow of goods without having recourse to higher mathematics. Thus, we may say that, in the instance we have been considering, money has become more efficient in moving goods, in the sense that a given amount of exchanges against money has now become sufficient to make possible the movement of a greater volume[53] of goods than before.

(14) (b) Perhaps this somewhat difficult concept becomes more intelligible if I illustrate it by supposing that two of the independent firms which we have supposed to represent the successive stages of production in our Figs. 2 and 6 are combined into one firm. This is the second of the alternative possibilities I set out to consider. Once this has happened, the passage of the intermediate products from the one to the next stage of production will take place without money payments being necessary, and the flow of goods from the moment they enter the earlier of the two stages until they leave the later will be effected by so much less money. A corresponding amount of money will thus be released and may be used for other purposes. The reverse effect will, of course, be witnessed if the two firms separate again. An increased amount of money payments will be required to effect the same movement of goods and the proportion of money payments to the flow of goods advancing toward consumption will have increased.

(15) Unfortunately, all names which might be used to designate this kind of monetary effectiveness have already been appropriated for designating different concepts of the velocity of money. Until somebody finds a fitting term, therefore, we shall have to speak somewhat clumsily of the proportion between the amount of goods exchanged against money and the total flow of

---

[53] Even if this total of goods moving toward consumption during each period is not actually exchanged against money in each period, it is not an imaginary, but a real and important magnitude, since the value of this total is a magnitude which continually rests within our power to determine. It probably stands in close relation to what is commonly called free capital, and it is certainly the supply of this factor which—together with new saving—determines the rate of interest; the capital which remains invested in durable instruments affects the interest rate from the demand side only, i.e., by influencing opportunities for new investment.

goods or of the proportion of the total movements of goods which is effected by exchange against money.

Now this proportion must on no account be confused with the proportion of the volume of money payments to the physical volume of trade. The proportion I have in mind may remain the same while the volume of trade increases relatively to the total of money payments and the price level falls, if only the same proportion of the total flow of goods is exchanged against money, and it may change though the proportion of the total of money payments to the physical volume of trade remains the same. It is, therefore, not necessarily influenced either by changes in the amount of money or by changes in the physical volume of trade; it depends only upon whether, in certain phases of the process of production, goods do or do not change hands.

So far I have illustrated this concept only by instances from the sphere of production. It may be applied also to the sphere of consumption. Here, too, sometimes a larger and sometimes a smaller share of the total output of consumers' goods is exchanged for money before it is consumed. Accordingly, here, too, we may speak about the proportion which the total output of consumers' goods in a period of time bears to the output which is sold for money. And this proportion may be different in the different stages of production. But in its effect upon the structure of production, the efficiency of a given amount of money spent in any stage of production (including the last stage—consumption) is determined by the proportion in that stage; and any change in that proportion has the same effects as an alteration in the amount of money spent in this particular stage of production.

So much for the complications which arise when we drop the assumption that production is carried on in independent stages of equal length. It has been necessary to discuss them here at some length in order to clear the way for an investigation, into which I wish to enter in the last lecture, in connection with the arguments for and against an elastic money supply. But for the tasks which I shall have to face tomorrow, it will be expedient again to make use of the simplest assumption and to suppose that production is carried on in independent stages of equal length, as we did in our schematic representations, and that this proportion is not only the same in all stages of production, but also that it remains constant over time.

LECTURE 3

The Working of the Price Mechanism in the Course of the Credit Cycle

> The first effect of the increase of productive activity, initiated by the policy of the banks to lend below the natural rate of interest is . . . to raise the prices of producers' goods while the prices of consumers' goods rise only moderately. . . . But soon a reverse movement sets in: prices of consumers' goods rise and prices of producers' goods fall, i.e., the loan rate rises and approaches again the natural rate of interest.
>
> L. v. Mises
> *Theorie des Geldes und der Umlaufsmittel* (1912), p. 431

(1) In the last lecture I dealt with the problems of changes in the structure of production consequent upon any transition to more or less capitalistic methods of production, in terms of the total sums of money available for the purchase of the product of each stage of production. It might seem, therefore, that now I come to the problem of explaining those changes in relative prices which bring it about that goods are directed to new uses—the central problem of these lectures[54]—the explanation

---

[54] As has already been mentioned in the first lecture, the effects of a divergence between the money rate and the equilibrium rate of interest on relative prices were originally briefly discussed by Professor Mises. On the actual working of the price mechanism which brings about the changes in the structure of production, his work contains, however, hardly more than the sentences quoted at the beginning of this lecture. It seems that most people have found them difficult to understand and that they have remained completely unintelligible

should run in terms of sectional price levels, that is to say, in terms of changes in the price levels of the goods of the different stages of production. But to do this would mean that at this stage of the explanation I should fall back upon just that method of using price averages which I condemned at the outset.

At the same time, it should by now be clear that, at this stage of the explanation, a treatment in terms of price averages would not be adequate to our purposes. What we have to explain is why certain goods which have thus far been used in one stage of production can now be more profitably used in another stage of production. Now this will only be the case if there are changes in the proportions in which the different producers' goods may be profitably used in any stage of production, and this in turn implies that there must be changes in the prices offered for them in different stages of production.

(2) At this point, it is necessary to introduce the new[55] distinction between producers' goods to which I alluded in the last

---

to all who were not very familiar with Böhm-Bawerk's theory of interest, on which they are based. The main difficulty lies in Professor Mises's short statement that the rise of the prices of consumers' goods is the cause of the crisis, while it seems natural to assume that this would rather make production more profitable. This is the main point which I have here tried to clear up. So far, the most exhaustive previous exposition of these interrelationships, which anticipates in some points what is said in the following pages, is to be found in R. Strigl, "Die Produktion unter dem Einfluss einer Kreditexpansion," *Schriften des Vereins für Sozialpolitik* 173, no. 2 (Munich, 1928), esp. p. 203 *et seq*. More recently, Professor Strigl has further developed his views on the subject in a book, *Kapital und Produktion* (Vienna: Springer, 1934). Some references to earlier anticipations of the ideas developed in this lecture will now be found in an additional note at the end of this lecture.

[55] Since the publication of the first edition of this book my attention has been drawn to the fact that this distinction is clearly implied in some of Böhm-Bawerk's discussions of these problems. Cf. his *Positive Theorie des Kapitalzinses*, 3rd ed. (Jena: Gustav Fischer, 1921), pp. 195 and 199.

lecture: the distinction between producers' goods which may be used in all, or at least many, stages of production, and producers' goods which can be used only in one, or at the most, a few, stages of production. To the first class belong not only almost all original means of production, but also most raw materials and even a great many implements of a not very specialized kind—knives, hammers, tongs, and so on.[56] To the second class belong most highly specialized kinds of machinery or complete manufacturing establishments, and also all those kinds of semi-manufactured goods which can be turned into finished goods only by passing a definite number of further stages of production. By adapting a term of von Wieser's, we may call the producers' goods which can be used only in one or a few stages of production, producers' goods of a specific character, or more shortly "specific" goods, to distinguish them from producers' goods of a more general applicability, which we may call "nonspecific" goods.[57] Of course, this distinction is not absolute, in the sense that we are always in a position to say whether a certain good is

---

[56] This class will, in particular, comprise most of the goods which at one and the same time belong to different stages. "Of course," says Marshall (*Principles of Economics*, 1st ed. [London: Macmillan, 1891], p. 109n.),

> a good many belong to several orders at the same time. For instance, a railway train may be carrying people on a pleasure excursion, and so far it is a good of the first order; if it happens to be carrying at the same time some tins of biscuits, some milling machinery and some machinery that is used for making milling machinery, it is at the same time a good of the second, third and fourth order.
>
> In cases like this a transfer of its services from a later to an earlier stage (or, to use Menger's terminology, from a lower to a higher order) is, of course, particularly easy. A plant manufacturing equipment for the production of consumers' goods as well as for the production of further machinery will sometimes be used mainly for the former and sometimes mainly for the latter purpose.

[57] Cf. Friedrich von Wieser, *Social Economics*, trans. A. Ford Hinrichs (New York: Adelphi, 1927), book 1, chap. 15.

specific or not. But we should be able to say whether any given good is *more or less* specific as compared with another good.

(3) It is clear that producers' goods of the same kind which are used in different stages of production cannot, for any length of time, bring in different returns or obtain different prices in these different stages. On the other hand, it is no less clear that temporary differences between the prices offered in the different stages of production are the only means of bringing about a shift of producers' goods from one stage to another. If such a temporary difference in the relative attractiveness of the different stages of production arises, the goods in question will be shifted from the less to the more attractive stages until, by the operation of the principle of diminishing returns, the differences have been wiped out.

Now, if we neglect the possibility of changes in technical knowledge, which may change the usefulness of any particular producers' goods, it is obvious that the immediate cause of a change in the return obtained from producers' goods of a certain kind used in different stages of production must be a change in the price of the product of the stage of production in question. But what is it which brings about variations of the relative price of such products? At first glance it might seem improbable that the prices of the successive stages of one and the same line of production should ever fluctuate relatively to one another because they are equally dependent upon the price of the final product. But, in regard to what was said in the last lecture concerning the possibility of shifts between the demand for consumers' goods and the demand for producers' goods, and the consequent changes in the relation between the amount of the original means of production expended and the output of consumers' goods, and how an elongation of the process of production increases the return from a given quantity of original means of production—this point should present no difficulty.

Now, so far I have not expressly referred to the price margins which arise out of these relative fluctuations of the prices of the products of successive stages of production. This has been because I have intentionally neglected interest, or, what amounts to the same thing, I have treated interest as if it were a payment for a definitely given factor of production, like wages or rent. In a state of equilibrium these margins are entirely absorbed by interest. Hence my assumption concealed the fact that the total amount of money received for the product of any stage will regularly exceed the total paid out for all goods and services used in this stage of production. Yet that margins of this kind must exist is obvious from the consideration that, if it were not so, there would exist no inducement to risk money by investing it in production rather than let it remain idle. To investigate the relationship of these margins to the peculiar advantages of the roundabout methods of production would lead us too far into the problems of the general theory of interest. We must therefore be content to accept it as one of the definite conclusions of this theory that—other things remaining the same—these margins must grow smaller as the roundabout processes of production increase in length and *vice versa.* There is one point, however, which we cannot take for granted. The fact that in a state of equilibrium those price margins and the amounts paid as interest coincide does *not* prove that the same will also be true in a period of transition from one state of equilibrium to another. On the contrary, the relation between these two magnitudes must form one of the main objects of our further investigations.

The close interrelation between these two phenomena suggests two different modes of approach to our problem: either we may start from the changes in the relative magnitude of the demand for consumers' goods and the demand for producers' goods, and examine the effects on the prices of individual goods and the rate of interest; or we may start from the changes in the rate of interest as an immediate effect of the change in the demand for producers' goods and work up to the changes in the price system which are necessary to establish a new equilibrium between price margins and the rate of interest. It will be found that whichever of these two alternatives we choose as a starting point, our investigation will, in the end, lead us to those aspects of the problem which are the starting point for the other. For the purposes of this lecture, I choose the first as being more in line with my previous argument.

(4) I begin, as I began in the last lecture, with the supposition that consumers decide to save and invest a larger proportion of their income. The immediate effect of the increase in the demand for producers' goods and the decrease in demand for consumers' goods will be that there will be a relative rise in the prices of the former and a relative fall in the prices of the latter. But the prices of producers' goods will not rise equally, nor will they rise without exception. In the stage of production immediately preceding that in which the final touches are given to consumers' goods, the effect of the fall in the prices of consumers' goods will be felt more strongly than the effect of the increase of the funds available for the purchase of producers' goods of all kinds. The price of the product of this stage will, therefore, fall, but it will fall less than the prices of consumers' goods. This means a narrowing of the price margin between the last two stages. But this narrowing of the price margin will make the employment of funds in the last stage less profitable relatively to the earlier stages, and therefore some of the funds which had been used there will tend to be shifted to the earlier stages. This shift of funds will tend to narrow the price margins in the preceding stages, and the tendency thus set up toward a cumulative rise of the prices of the products of the earlier stages will very soon overcome the tendency toward a fall. In other words, the rise of the price of the product of any stage of production will give an extra advantage to the production of the preceding stage, the products of which will not only rise in price because the demand for producers' goods in general has risen, but also because, by the rise of prices in the preceding stages, profits to be obtained in this stage have become comparatively higher than in the later stages. The final effect will be that, through the fall of prices in the later stages of production and the rise of prices in

the earlier stages of production, price margins between the different stages of production will have decreased all around.

This change of relative prices in the different stages of production must inevitably tend to affect the prospects of profits in the different stages, and this, in turn, will tend to cause changes in the use made of the available producers' goods. A greater proportion of those producers' goods which can be used in different stages of production—the nonspecific goods—will now be attracted to the earlier stages, where, since the change in the rate of saving, relatively higher prices are to be obtained. And the shifting of goods and services of this type will go on until the diminution of returns in these stages has equalized the profits to be made in all stages. In the end, the returns and the prices obtained for these goods in the different stages of production will be generally higher and a larger proportion of them will be used in the earlier stages of production than before. The general narrowing of the price margins between the stages of production will even make it possible to start production in new and more distant stages which have not been profitable before, and in this way, not only the average time which elapses between the application of the first unit of original mean of production and the completion of the final product, but also the absolute length of the process of production—the number of its stages—will be increased.[58]

But while the effect on the prices of nonspecific producers' goods has been a general rise, the effect on the prices of goods of a more specific character—those goods which can only be used

---

[58] This lengthening of the structure of production need, however, by no means takes exclusively or even mainly the form that the methods used in any individual line of production are changed. The increased prices in the earlier stages of production (the lowered rate of interest) will favor production in the lines using much capital and lead to their expansion at the expense of the lines using less capital. In this way the aggregate length of the investment structure of society might in the extreme case take place without a change of the method employed in any one line of production.

in one or a very few stages of production—will be different. If a good of this sort is only adapted to a comparatively late stage of production, the relative deficiency of the nonspecific producers' goods required in the same stage of production will lower its return, and if it is itself a product, its production will be curtailed. If, on the other hand, the good belongs to a relatively early stage of production, its price and the amount of it produced will increase. At the same time, the additional stages of production which have been started as a consequence of this transition to more capitalistic methods of production will probably require new goods of a specific character. Some of these will be new products, some natural resources which formerly it was not profitable to use.

Exactly the reverse of all these changes will take place if the demand for consumers' goods increases relatively to the demand for producers' goods. This will cause not only an increase of the difference between the prices of consumers' goods or products of the last stage of production, and the prices of the products of the previous stage, but also an all round increase of the price margins between the products of the successive stages of production. Prices in the later stages will rise relatively to prices in the earlier stages, producers' goods of a nonspecific character will move from the earlier stages to the later, and the goods of specific character in the earlier stages of production will lose part of their value or become entirely useless, while those in the later stages of production will increase in value. I shall discuss certain exceptions to this parallelism later on.

It will, perhaps, facilitate the understanding of these complications if we think of production in its successive stages as a fan, the sticks of which correspond to the prices of the different stages. If more demand is concentrated toward the one extreme—consumers' goods—the fan opens, the differences between the stages become larger, and goods gravitate toward the stages where higher prices are obtained, that is, toward the stages nearer consumption. The most distant stages are abandoned, and within the remaining stages more goods are concentrated toward the one end. The opening of the price fan is thus accompanied by a reduction of the number of stages of production, i.e., of the number of sticks.[59] If, however, a shift of demand from consumers' goods toward producers' goods takes place, the price fan will close, i.e., the differences between the stages will become smaller and goods will tend to gravitate toward the higher stages where prices are now relatively higher, and new and hitherto unused possibilities of further extension of the process of production will be exploited. The closing of the price fan has brought a greater number of stages of production within the range of practical possibilities and thus initiated the transition to longer roundabout methods of production.

(5) A more exact representation of this process can be given by means of a diagram. This has the special advantage of making quite clear a point which is of considerable importance but on which a merely verbal explanation is likely to mislead. It is necessary in such an exposition, if one wants to avoid too cumbersome expressions, to speak of actual changes in the relative prices of goods in the different stages, where it would be more correct to speak of tendencies toward such a change, or of changes in the demand function for the particular commodity. Whether and to what extent such changes in demand will lead to an actual change in price will of course depend on the elasticity of supply, which in the particular case depends in turn in every stage on the degree of specificity of the intermediate products and the factors from which they are made.

The way in which this shifting of the demand curves for any single factor in the different stages of production operates can be

---

[59] At this point the simile becomes liable to mislead and it is important to keep in mind all the time that the "fan" refers to price relationships only, but that the length of the structure of production will move in the reverse direction compared with the width of the fan. When the price fan opens, the structure of production is shortened, and *vice versa*.

illustrated in the following way. In Fig. 7 below the successive curves represent the marginal productivity of different quantities of one factor in the successive stages of production, the earlier stages being shown on the left and the later stages toward the right. To make the main point come out clearer it has been assumed that the physical quantity of the product due to every additional unit of the factor decreases at the same rate in all stages and that in consequence the general shape of the curves is the same.

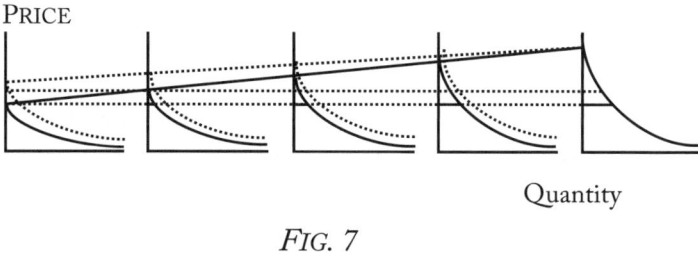

FIG. 7

The value of the marginal product attributable to every unit of factors will, however, be equal to the value of the physical product which is due to it only in the very last stage where no interval of time elapses between the investment of the factors and the completion of the product. If we assume, then, the curve on the right to represent not only the physical magnitude but also the value of the marginal product of successive units of factors applied in that stage, the other curves representing the physical marginal product of the factors invested in earlier stages will have to be somewhat adjusted if they are to represent the discounted value of the marginal product of successive units of factors applied in the respective stages. And if we assume the points to which these curves refer, to be equidistant stages as were those discussed before, the adjustment necessary at any given rate of interest can be shown by drawing a discount curve (or a family of discount curves) connecting every point on the curve on the right with the corresponding points of the curves further on the left, and lowering each of these curves by the amount indicated by the discount curves. (Since every point on these curves will have to be adjusted separately, i.e., will have to be lowered not by the same amount but by the same percentage, this will involve a change not only of the position but also of the shape of these curves.) The set of fully drawn curves in the above diagram shows the position at a given rate of interest indicated by the one discount curve which is also fully drawn. And since these curves show the discounted value of the marginal product of one kind of factor which must of course be the same in the different stages of production, they enable us to determine how much of this factor will be used in every stage if either its price or the total quantity of it to be used in this process is known. This distribution of the factor between the different stages at an arbitrarily assumed price is shown by the fully drawn horizontal lines.

Assume now that the rate of interest is reduced. The new position is indicated by the dotted discount curve and the correspondingly changed shape and position of the marginal productivity curves for the individual stages. Under these conditions the old distribution of factors between the stages would evidently not represent an equilibrium position but one at which the discounted value of the marginal product would be different in every stage. And if the total quantity of the factor which is available remains the same the new equilibrium distribution will apparently be one at which not only the price of the factor will be higher but at which also a considerably greater quantity of it is used in the earlier stages and correspondingly less in the later stages.

This accounts for the change in the price and the distribution of factors which can be used in different stages. To what extent and in what proportion the prices of different factors will be affected by a given change in the rate of interest will depend on the stages in which they can be used and on the shape of their marginal productivity curves in these stages. The price of a factor which can be used in most early stages and whose marginal productivity there falls very slowly will rise more in consequence of a fall in the rate of interest than the price of a factor which can only be used in relatively lower stages of reproduction or whose marginal productivity in the earlier stages falls very rapidly.

It is essentially this difference between the price changes of the different factors which accounts for the changes of the relative prices of the intermediate products at the successive stages. At first it might seem as if, since relative prices of the different intermediate products must correspond to their respective costs, they could change only to the relatively small extent to which the direct interest element in their cost changes. But to think of interest only as a direct cost factor is to overlook its main influence on production. What is much more important is its effect on prices through its effect on demand for the intermediate products and for the factors from which they are produced. It is in consequence of these changes in demand and the changes in cost which it brings about by raising the prices of those factors which are in strong demand in early stages compared to those which are less demanded there, that the prices of the intermediate products are adjusted.

(6) As the initial changes in relative prices which are caused by a change of the relative demand for consumers' goods and producers' goods give rise to a considerable shifting of goods to other stages of production, definite price relationships will only establish themselves after the movements of goods have been completed. For reasons which I shall consider in a moment, this process may take some time and involve temporary discrepancies between supply and demand. But there is one medium through which the expected ultimate effect on relative prices should make itself felt immediately, and which, accordingly, should serve as a guide for the decisions of the individual entrepreneur: the rate of interest on the loan market. Only in comparatively few cases will the people who have saved money and the people who want to use it in production be identical. In the majority of cases, therefore, the money which is directed to new uses will first have to

pass into other hands. The question of *who* is going to use the additional funds available for investment in producers' goods will be decided on the loan market. Only at a lower rate of interest than that formerly prevailing will it be possible to lend these funds, and how far the rate of interest will fall will depend upon the amount of the additional funds and the expectation of profits on the part of the entrepreneurs willing to expand their production. If these entrepreneurs entertain correct views about the price changes which are to be expected as a result of the changes in the method of production, the new rate of interest should correspond to the system of price margins which will ultimately be established. In this way, from the outset, the use of the additional funds which have become available will be confined to those entrepreneurs who hope to obtain the highest profits out of their use, and all extensions of production, for which the additional funds would not be sufficient, will be excluded.

(7) The significance of these adjustments of the price mechanism comes out still more clearly when we turn to investigate what happens if the "natural" movement of prices is disturbed by movements in the supply of money, whether by the injection of new money into circulation or by withdrawal of part of the money circulating. We may again take as our two typical cases (a) the case of additional money used first to buy producers' goods and (b) the case of additional money used first to buy consumers' goods. The corresponding cases of a diminution of the amount of money we may neglect because a diminution of the demand for consumers' goods would have essentially the same effects as a proportional increase of the demand for producers' goods, and *vice versa*.[60] I have already outlined in the last lecture the general tendencies involved in such cases. My present task is

---

[60] As I have tried to show in another place ("Capital and Industrial Fluctuations," p. 164) it is even conceivable, although highly unlikely to occur in practice, that hoarding of money income before spent on consumers' goods, might give rise to some additional investment.

to fill in the details of that rough sketch and to show what happens in the interval before a new equilibrium is attained.

As before, I commence with the supposition that the additional money is injected by way of credits to producers. To secure borrowers for this additional amount of money, the rate of interest must be kept sufficiently below the equilibrium rate to make profitable the employment of just this sum and no more. Now the borrowers can only use the borrowed sums for buying producers' goods, and will only be able to obtain such goods (assuming a state of equilibrium in which there are no unused resources) by outbidding the entrepreneurs who used them before. At first sight it might seem improbable that these borrowers who were only put in a position to start longer processes by the lower rate of interest should be able to outbid those entrepreneurs who found the use of those means of production profitable when the rate of interest was still higher. But when it is remembered that the fall in the rate will also change the relative profitableness of the different factors of production for the existing concerns, it will be seen to be quite natural that it should give a relative advantage to those concerns which use proportionately more capital. Such old concerns will now find it profitable to spend a part of what they previously spent on original means of production, on intermediate products produced by earlier stages of production, and in this way they will release some of the original means of production they used before. The rise in the prices of the original means of production is an additional inducement. Of course it might well be that the entrepreneurs in question would be in a better position to buy such goods even at the higher prices, since they have done business when the rate of interest was higher, though it must not be forgotten that they too will have to do business on a smaller margin. But the fact that certain producers' goods have become dearer will make it profitable for them to replace these goods by others. In particular, the changed proportion between the prices of the original means of production and the rate of interest will make it profitable for them to spend part of what they have till now spent on original means of production on intermediate products or capital. They will, e.g., buy parts of their products, which they used to manufacture themselves, from another firm, and can now employ the labor thus dismissed in order to produce these parts on a large scale with the help of new machinery. In other words, those original means of production and nonspecific producers' goods which are required in the new stages of production are set free by the transition of the old concerns to more capitalistic methods which is caused by the increase in the prices of these goods. In the old concerns (as we may conveniently, but not quite accurately, call the processes of production which were in operation before the new money was injected), a transition to more capitalistic methods will take place; but in all probability it will take place without any change in their total resources: they will invest less in original means of production and more in intermediate products.

Now, contrary to what we have found to be the case when similar processes are initiated by the investment of new savings, this application of the original means of production and nonspecific intermediate products to longer processes of production will be effected without any preceding reduction of consumption. Indeed, for a time, consumption may even go on at an unchanged rate after the more roundabout processes have actually started, because the goods which have already advanced to the lower stages of production, being of a highly specific character, will continue to come forward for some little time. But this cannot go on. When the reduced output from the stages of production, from which producers' goods have been withdrawn for use in higher stages, has matured into consumers' goods, a scarcity of consumers' goods will make itself felt, and the prices of those goods will rise. Had saving preceded the change to methods of production of longer duration, a reserve of consumers' goods would have been accumulated in the form of increased stocks, which could now be sold at unreduced prices, and would thus serve to bridge the interval of time between the moment when the last products of the old shorter process come onto the market and the moment when the first products of the new longer processes are ready. But as things are, for some time, society as a whole will have to put up with an involuntary reduction of consumption.

But this necessity will be resisted. It is highly improbable that individuals should put up with an unforeseen retrenchment of their real income without making an attempt to overcome it by spending more money on consumption. It comes at the very moment when a great many entrepreneurs know themselves to be in command—at least nominally—of greater resources and expect greater profits. At the same time incomes of wage earners will be rising in consequence of the increased amount of money available for investment by entrepreneurs. There can be little doubt that in the face of rising prices of consumers' goods these increases will be spent on such goods and so contribute to drive up their prices even faster. These decisions will not change the amount of consumers' goods immediately available, though it may change their distribution between individuals. But—and this is the fundamental point—*it will mean a new and reversed change of the proportion between the demand for consumers' goods and the demand for producers' goods in favor of the former.* The prices of consumers' goods will therefore rise relatively to the prices of producers' goods. And this rise of the prices of consumers' goods will be the more marked because it is the consequence not only of an increased demand for consumers' goods but an increase in the demand as measured in money. All this must mean a return to shorter or less roundabout methods of production if the increase in the demand for consumers' goods is not compensated by a further proportional injection of money by new bank loans granted to producers. And at first this is probable. The rise of the prices of consumers' goods will offer prospects of temporary extra profits to entrepreneurs. They will be all the more ready to borrow at the prevailing rate of interest. And, so long as the banks go on progressively increasing their loans it will, therefore, be possible to continue the prolonged methods of production or perhaps even to extend them still further. But for obvious reasons the banks cannot continue indefinitely to extend credit; and even if they could, the other effects of a rapid and continuous rise of prices would, after a while, make it necessary to stop this process of inflation.[61]

Let us assume that for some time, perhaps a year or two, the banks, by keeping their rate of interest below the equilibrium rate, have expanded credit, and now find themselves compelled to stop further expansion. What will happen? (Perhaps it should be mentioned at this point that the processes I shall now describe are processes which would also take place if existing capital is encroached upon, or if, in a progressive society, after a temporary increase in saving, the rate should suddenly fall to its former level. Such cases, however, are probably quantitatively less important.)

Now we know from what has been said already that the immediate effect of the banks' ceasing to add to their loans is that the absolute increase of the amount of money spent on consumers' goods is no longer compensated by a proportional increase in the demand for producers' goods. The demand for consumers' goods will for some time continue to increase because it will necessarily always lag somewhat behind the additional expenditure on investment which causes the increase of money incomes. The effects of such a change will, therefore, be similar to what would happen in the second case we have to consider, the case of an increase of money by consumers' credits. At this point, accordingly, the two cases can be covered by one discussion.

(8) Speaking generally, it might be said that the effects of a relative increase in the demand for consumers' goods are the reverse of the effects of an increase in the relative demand for

---

[61] For a fuller discussion of the reasons why this process of expansion must ultimately come to an end, whether the banks are restricted by reserve regulations, etc., or not, and of some of the points alluded to in the next paragraphs, see my article on "Capital and Industrial Fluctuations," p. 161.

producers' goods. There are, however, two important differences which make a detailed account necessary.

The first effect of the rise of the prices of consumers' goods is that the spread between them and the prices of the goods of the preceding stage becomes greater than the price margins in the higher stages of production. The greater profits to be obtained in this stage will cause producers' goods in use elsewhere which may be used in this stage to be transferred to it, and the all-around increase of price margins between the stages of production which will follow will cause a widespread transfer of nonspecific producers' goods to lower stages. The new demand for these goods will cause a relative rise of their prices, and this rise will tend to be considerable because, as we have seen, there will be a temporary rise in the price of consumers' goods, due to the transient discrepancy between demand and supply, greater than will be the case after the supply of consumers' goods has caught up with demand. These temporary scarcity prices of consumers' goods will, furthermore, have the effect that at first production will tend to shrink to fewer stages than will be necessary after equilibrium prices of consumers' goods have established themselves.

Very soon the relative rise of the prices of the original factors and the more mobile intermediate products will make the longer processes unprofitable. The first effect on these processes will be that the producers' goods of a more specific character, which have become relatively abundant by reason of the withdrawal of the complementary nonspecific goods, will fall in price. The fall of the prices of these goods will make their production unprofitable; it will in consequence be discontinued. Although goods in later stages of production will generally be of a highly specific character, it may still pay to employ original factors to complete those that are nearly finished. But the fall in the price of intermediate products will be cumulative; and this will mean a fairly sudden stoppage of work in at least all the earlier stages of the longer processes.

But while the nonspecific goods, in particular the services of workmen employed in those earlier stages, have thus been thrown out of use because their amount has proved insufficient and their prices too high for the profitable carrying through of the long processes of production, it is by no means certain that all those which can no longer be used in the old processes can immediately be absorbed in the short processes which are being expanded. Quite the contrary; the shorter processes will have to be started at the very beginning and will only *gradually* absorb all the available producers' goods as the product progresses toward consumption and as the necessary intermediate products come forward. So that, while in the longer processes productive operations cease almost as soon as the change in relative prices of specific and nonspecific goods in favor of the latter and the rise of the rate of interest make them unprofitable, the released goods will find new employment only as the new shorter processes are approaching completion.[62] Moreover, the final adaptation will be further retarded by initial uncertainty as regards the methods of production which will ultimately prove profitable once the temporary scarcity of consumers' goods has disappeared. Entrepreneurs, quite rightly, will hesitate to make investments suited to this over-shortened process, i.e., investments which would enable them to produce with relatively little capital and a relatively great quantity of the original means of production.

---

[62] The reason for this asymmetry between a transition to longer processes of production, which need not bring about any of these peculiar disturbances, and a transition to shorter processes, which will regularly be accompanied by a crisis, will perhaps become more evident if it is considered that in the former case there will necessarily be time to amortize the capital invested in the existing structure before the new process is completed, while in the latter case this will evidently be impossible and therefore a loss of capital and a reduction of income inevitable. (In all these discussions it is assumed that technical knowledge remains the same; a shortening of the structure of production which is due to technical progress has an altogether different significance from that due to an increase of consumption.)

It seems something of a paradox that the self-same goods whose scarcity has been the cause of the crisis would become unsaleable as a consequence of the same crisis. But the fact is that when the growing demand for finished consumers' goods has taken away part of the nonspecific producers' goods required, those remaining are no longer sufficient for the long processes, and the particular kinds of specific goods required for the processes which would just be long enough to employ the total quantity of those nonspecific producers' goods do not yet exist. The situation would be similar to that of a people of an isolated island, if, after having partially constructed an enormous machine which was to provide them with all necessities, they found out that they had exhausted all their savings and available free capital before the new machine could turn out its product. They would then have no choice but to abandon temporarily the work on the new process and to devote all their labor to producing their daily food without any capital. Only after they had put themselves in a position in which new supplies of food were available could they proceed to attempt to get the new machinery into operation.[63] In the actual world, however, where the accumulation of capital has permitted a growth of population far beyond the number which could find employment without capital, as a general rule the single workman will not be able to produce enough for a living without the help of capital and he may, therefore, temporarily become unemployable. And the same will apply to all goods and services whose use requires the cooperation of other goods and services which, after a change in the structure of production of this kind, may not be available in the necessary quantity.

In this connection, as in so many others, we are forced to recognize the fundamental truth, so frequently neglected nowadays, that the machinery of capitalistic production will function

---

[63] Cf. the very similar example now given by C. Landauer, *Planwirtschaft und Verkehrswirtschaft* (Leipzig: Duncker & Humblot, 1931), p. 47.

smoothly only so long as we are satisfied to consume no more than that part of our total wealth which under the existing organization of production is destined for current consumption. Every increase of consumption, if it is not to disturb production, requires previous new saving, even if the existing equipment with durable instruments of production should be sufficient for such an increase in output. If the increase of production is to be maintained continuously, it is necessary that the amounts of intermediate products in all stages is proportionately increased; and these additional quantities of goods in process are of course no less capital than the durable instruments. The impression that the already existing capital structure would enable us to increase production almost indefinitely is a deception. Whatever engineers may tell us about the supposed immense unused capacity of the existing productive machinery, there is in fact no possibility of increasing production to such an extent. These engineers and also those economists who believe that we have more capital than we need, are deceived by the fact that many of the existing plant and machinery are adapted to a much greater output than is actually produced. What they overlook is that durable means of production do not represent all the capital that is needed for an increase of output and that in order that the existing durable plants could be used to their full capacity it would be necessary to invest a great amount of other means of production in lengthy processes which would bear fruit only in a comparatively distant future. The existence of unused capacity is, therefore, by no means a proof that there exists an excess of capital and that consumption is insufficient: on the contrary, it is a symptom that we are unable to use the fixed plant to the full extent because the current demand for consumers' goods is too urgent to permit us to invest current productive services in the long processes for which (in consequence of "misdirections of capital") the necessary durable equipment is available.

(9) Here then we have at last reached an explanation of how it comes about at certain times that some of the existing resources cannot be used, and how, in such circumstances, it is impossible to

sell them at all—or, in the case of durable goods, only to sell them at very great loss. To provide an answer to this problem has always seemed to me to be the central task of any theory of industrial fluctuations; and, though at the outset I refused to base my investigation on the assumption that unused resources exist, now that I have presented a tentative explanation of this phenomenon, it seems worthwhile, rather than spending time filling up the picture of the cycle by elaborating the process of recovery, to devote the rest of this lecture to further discussion of certain important aspects of this problem. Now that we have accounted for the existence of unused resources, we may even go so far as to assume that their existence to a greater or lesser extent is the regular state of affairs save during a boom. And, if we do this, it is imperative to supplement our earlier investigation of the effects of a change in the amount of money in circulation on production, by applying our theory to such a situation. And this extension of our analysis is the more necessary since the existence of unused resources has very often been considered as the only fact which at all justifies an expansion of bank credit.

If the foregoing analysis is correct, it should be fairly clear that the granting of credit to consumers, which has recently been so strongly advocated as a cure for depression, would in fact have quite the contrary effect; a relative increase of the demand for consumers' goods could only make matters worse. Matters are not quite so simple so far as the effects of credits granted for productive purposes are concerned. In theory it is at least possible that, during the acute stage of the crisis when the capitalistic structure of production tends to shrink more than will ultimately prove necessary, an expansion of producers' credits might have a wholesome effect. But this could only be the case if the quantity were so regulated as exactly to compensate for the initial, excessive rise of the relative prices of consumers' goods, and if arrangements could be made to withdraw the additional credits as these prices fall and the proportion between the supply of consumers' goods and the supply of intermediate products adapts itself to the proportion between the demand for these goods. And even these credits would do more harm than good if they made roundabout processes seem profitable which, even after the acute crisis had subsided, could not be kept up without the help of additional credits. Frankly, I do not see how the banks can ever be in a position to keep credit within these limits.

And, if we pass from the moment of actual crisis to the situation in the following depression, it is still more difficult to see what lasting good effects can come from credit expansion. The thing which is needed to secure healthy conditions is the most speedy and complete adaptation possible of the structure of production to the proportion between the demand for consumers' goods and the demand for producers' goods as determined by voluntary saving and spending. If the proportion as determined by the voluntary decisions of individuals is distorted by the creation of artificial demand, it must mean that part of the available resources is again led into a wrong direction and a definite and lasting adjustment is again postponed. And, even if the absorption of the unemployed resources were to be quickened in this way, it would only mean that the seed would already be sown for new disturbances and new crises. The only way permanently to "mobilize" all available resources is, therefore, not to use artificial stimulants—whether during a crisis or thereafter—but to leave it to time to effect a permanent cure by the slow process of adapting the structure of production to the means available for capital purposes.

(10) And so, at the end of our analysis, we arrive at results which only confirm the old truth that we may perhaps prevent a crisis by checking expansion in time, but that we can do nothing to get out of it before its natural end, once it has come. In the next lecture I shall be dealing with some of the problems connected with a monetary policy suitable for the prevention of crises. Meanwhile, although so far our investigation has not produced a preventive for the recurrence of crises, it has, I hope, at least provided a guide to the maze of conflicting movements during the credit cycle which may prove useful for the diagnosis of

the situation existing at any moment. If this is so, certain conclusions with regard to the methods commonly used in current statistical analysis of business fluctuations seem to follow immediately. The first is that our explanation of the different behavior of the prices of specific and nonspecific goods should help to substitute for the rough empirical classification of prices according to their sensitiveness, a classification based on more rational considerations. The second, that the average movements of general prices show us nothing of the really relevant facts; indeed, the index numbers generally used will, as a general rule, fail even to attain their immediate object because, being for practical reasons almost exclusively based on prices of goods of a nonspecific character, the data used are never random samples in the sense required by statistical method, but always a biased selection which can only give a picture of the peculiar movements of prices of goods of this class. And the third is that for similar reasons every attempt to find a statistical measure in the form of a general average of the total volume of production, or the total volume of trade, or general business activity, or whatever one may call it, will only result in veiling the really significant phenomena, the changes in the structure of production to which I have been drawing your attention in the last two lectures.

APPENDIX TO LECTURE 3

A Note on the History of the Doctrines Developed in the Preceding Lecture

The central idea of the theory of the trade cycle which has been expounded in the preceding lecture is by no means new. That industrial fluctuations consist essentially in alternating expansions and contractions of the structure of capital equipment has often been emphasized. At one time, at the beginning of the second half of the last century, such theories even enjoyed considerable vogue and the financial journalists of those days frequently used a terminology which, intelligently interpreted, seems to imply essentially the same argument as that used here. The creation of "fictitious capital," it was said, leads to the conversion of too much circulating into fixed capital which ultimately brings about a scarcity of disposable or floating capital which makes it impossible to continue or to complete the new undertakings and so causes the collapse. The reason why these theories did not prove more fruitful seems to have been that the concepts employed, particularly the concepts of the different kinds of capital, were too uncertain in their meaning to give a clear idea of what was really meant. But even if for this reason their popularity in the 'sixties and 'seventies was of a transient nature, they are of considerable interest as an expression of a fairly long and continuous strand of thought which occasionally came very near to modern ideas and in some instances leads very directly to some of the best known theories of today.

I have made no special study of the development of these doctrines (which they would well deserve), and I can therefore do no more than give a brief sketch of the main lines of development as I see them. It seems that all these doctrines trace back to Ricardo's doctrine of the conversion of circulating into fixed capital, developed in the chapter "On Machinery" in the third edition of his *Principles*. A relatively early attempt to apply these ideas to the explanation of crises was made in 1839 by the American Condy Raguet.[64] But the author who mainly developed and widely popularized it was James Wilson, the first editor of *The Economist*.[65] It seems to be from him that a host of English and French writers adopted it. In England it was particularly the group of economists connected with the Manchester Statistical Society who took up the idea. Mr. T.S. Ashton in his recent Centenary History of this Society[66] quotes several extremely interesting extracts from lectures given to this society by T.H. Williams in 1857 and John Mills in 1867 which show clearly the great importance which they all attached to the "excessive conversions of floating into fixed capital"; and he particularly draws attention to a significant passage in W.S. Jevons's early tract on the *Serious Fall in the Value of Gold*, published in 1863 soon after he came to Manchester, where he says that the remote cause of the commercial tides "seems to lie in the *varying proportions which the capital devoted to permanent and remote investment bears*

---

[64] Condy Raguet, *A Treatise on Currency and Banking* (London: Grigg & Elliot, 1839), p. 62 *et seq.*

[65] James Wilson, *Capital, Currency and Banking* (London: The Economist, 1847), articles 11, 13, and 16, particularly p. 152 *et seq.*; articles 1, 13, and 17 in the second edition (London: D.M. Aird, 1859).

[66] T.S. Ashton, "Economic and Social Investigations in Manchester, 1833–1933," *A Centenary History of the Manchester Statistical Society* (London: P.S. King & Son, 1934), p. 72 *et seq.*

to that which is but temporarily invested soon to reproduce itself."[67] From the author who later on was to be the first to provide the basis for that modern theory of capital which now enables us to give more definite meaning to these ideas, this statement is of special interest and makes one wonder whether it may not be due to his early preoccupation with the problem of the trade cycle that he was led to a correct appreciation of the role the time element played in connection with capital.

A little later Bonamy Price developed these ideas in considerable detail[68] and from him they were taken over in France, where other authors like J.G. Courcelle-Seneuil and V. Bonnet[69] had been working on similar lines, by Yves Guyot, who not inappropriately summarized this theory by saying the "Commercial and financial crises are produced, not by over-production, but by over-consumption."[70]

In the German literature similar ideas were introduced mainly by the writings of Karl Marx. It is on Marx that M. v. Tougan-Baranovsky's work is based which in turn provided the starting point for the later work of Professor Spiethoff and Professor Cassel. The extent to which the theory developed in these lectures corresponds with that of the two last-named authors, particularly with that of Professor Spiethoff, need hardly be emphasized.

Another contemporary author who is evidently indebted to the same strand of thought and whose views on these problems

---

[67] W.S. Jevons, *A Serious Fall in the Value of Gold Ascertained and its Social Effects set Forth* (London: Edward Stanford, 1863), p. 10, in the reprint in the *Investigations in Currency and Finance* (London: Macmillan, 1884), p. 28.

[68] Bonamy Price discussed these problems on numerous occasions. Cf. however, particularly his *Chapters on Practical Political Economy* (London: Kegan Paul, 1878), pp. 110–24.

[69] On these authors, cf. E. v. Bergmann, *Geschichte der nationalökonomischen Krisentheorien* (Stuttgart: Kohlhammer, 1895), where the reader will find references to still further authors belonging to the same category.

[70] Yves Guyot, *La Science Économique,* English translation, *Principles of Social Economy* (London: Sonnenschein, 1884), p. 249.

are even more closely related to those taken in these lectures, but with whose work on this point I have unfortunately only became acquainted since he has collected his earlier scattered articles in book form, is Professor C. Bresciani-Turroni. His monumental study of the German inflation (*Le Vicende del Marco Tedesco* [Milano: Università Bocconi, 1931]) appears to me to be one of the most important contributions to the study of money which have appeared in recent years. Particularly the chapters on the influence of inflation on production and on the scarcity of capital after the stabilization (chapters 5 and 10, an abridged German version of the latter appeared in the *Wirtschaftstheorie der Gegenwart*, ed. by H. Mayer, vol. 2 [Vienna: Springer, 1931]) seem to me of extraordinary interest and to contain a wealth of concrete illustrations of these difficult theoretical questions which is not to be found elsewhere. Few other foreign books on economic problems would equally deserve being made available in an English translation.

In view of the importance which so many theories of the trade cycle attach to the interrelationships between the different forms of "capital" one might expect that investigations in this field should have received considerable help from the theory of capital. That this has hitherto been the case only to a very limited degree is mainly due to the rather unsatisfactory state of this theory which was mainly concerned with barren terminological debates or the question whether capital was to be regarded as a separate factor of production and how this factor was to be defined, instead of making its main task the general question of the *way* in which production was carried on. It would not be surprising if it would ultimately be that theory of the trade cycle, which consciously utilizes the results of the only satisfactory theory of capital which we yet possess, that of Böhm-Bawerk, which should prove to be successful. It must be admitted, however, that, so far, the further elaboration of the ideas of Böhm-Bawerk, apart from two notable exceptions, have not helped us much further with the problems of the trade cycle. The two exceptions are Knut Wicksell and his pupil, Professor G. Akerman. Particularly the difficult but important investigations in the *Realkapital und Kapitalzins* of the latter author (two parts, 1923 and 1924), which I did not yet know at the time when I wrote these lectures, seems to me to deserve particular attention as one of the few attempts to clear up the difficult problems which arise out of the existence of very durable capital goods. It seems, however, not improbable that in the future the relationship between the theory of capital and the theory of the trade cycle may be reversed and that the former will be benefited by the progress of the latter. Only by studying the changes of the capitalistic structure of production will we learn to understand the factors which govern it, and it seems that the trade cycle is the most important manifestation of these changes. It is therefore not surprising that the study of the problems of the trade cycle should lead to the study of the theory of capital. As has been suggested before, this may have been the case with Jevons, and more recently it has certainly been true of Professor Spiethoff (cf. already his "Vorbemerkungen zu einer Theorie der Überproduktion," *Schmollers Jahrbuch* 26 [1902], particularly p. 299 and his essay on "Die Lehre vom Kapital" in *Die Entwicklung der Deutschen Volkswirtschaft im 19. Jahrhundert* 1 [1908]).

LECTURE 4

The Case For and Against an "Elastic" Currency

> The notion common . . . to 90 per cent, of the writings of monetary cranks is that every batch of goods is entitled to he born with a monetary label of equivalent value round its neck, and to carry it round its neck until it dies.
>
> D.H. Robertson
> *Economica* 23 (June 1928): 142

(1) If the considerations brought forward in the last lecture are at all correct, it would appear that the reasons commonly advanced as a proof that the quantity of the circulating medium should vary as production increases or decreases are entirely unfounded. It would appear rather that the fall of prices proportionate to the increase in productivity, which necessarily follows when, the amount of money remaining the same, production increases, is not only entirely harmless but is in fact the only means of avoiding misdirections of production. So far as an increase of production caused by a transition to more capitalistic methods of production is concerned, this result bears some resemblance to the theory underlying certain proposals for stabilizing the value of money so as to keep, not the prices of consumers' goods, but incomes, or the prices of the factors of production constant, the prices of consumers' goods being allowed

to fall as costs fall and *vice versa*.⁷¹ Complete invariability of the effective money stream would, as we have seen, however, have the further effect that any transition to more capitalistic methods of production would also make a reduction of money income necessary, except in the case of complete vertical integration of production. This necessity, which in view of the notorious rigidity of wages is certainly very undesirable, could however only be avoided without causing misdirections of production, if it were possible to inject the required additional quantities of money in such a way into the economic system that the proportion between the demand for consumers' goods and the demand for producers' goods would not be affected. This is no doubt a task which cannot be solved in practice. But apart from the special difficulties which may arise from the existence of rigidities I believe that the conclusion stated above holds here not only for this case of the transition to more capitalistic methods of production but also for an increase of production caused by the absorption of unused resources. Furthermore, by another chain of reasoning—which is too long and complicated to reproduce here, and which I have sketched elsewhere⁷²—it might be shown to apply in principle even to the particularly difficult case of an increase of production caused by the growth of population, the discovery of new natural resources, and the like. But however that may be, our result is in sufficient contrast to generally received opinions to require further elucidation.

---

[71] That there is no harm in prices falling as productivity increases has been pointed out again and again, e.g., by A. Marshall, N.G. Pierson, W. Lexis, F.Y. Edgeworth, F.W. Taussig, L. Mises, A.C. Pigou, D.H. Robertson, and G. Haberler. (For more detailed references see my article on "The 'Paradox' of Saving," p. 179.) Cf. also the stabilization proposal made by Dr. Maurice Leven, mentioned by W.J. King in the *Journal of the American Statistical Association* (March 1928), supplement, p. 146, and the article by R.G. Hawtrey "Money and Index Numbers."

[72] In the article, "Das intertemporale Gleichgewichtssystem der Preise und die Bewegungen des 'Geldwertes'."

(2) We can best observe how deeply the notion that it is the "natural" thing for the quantity of money to fluctuate with fluctuations in the volume of production is ingrained in the minds of many modern economists if we look at the use they make of it in their theoretical analysis. Professor Cassel, for instance, who is of course the outstanding representative of this point of view, discussing the treatment of price problems[73] in a recent article, writes as follows: "The simplest assumption is, then, that a country has a paper currency so regulated as to keep the general level of prices constant." And again—to quote another well-known authority—Professor Pigou is expressing the same opinion when he argues[74] that if countries with paper currencies will regulate them with a view to keeping the general price level in some sense stable, there will be no impulses from the side of money which can properly be called "autonomous." Both statements imply that changes in the quantity of the circulating medium which are only just sufficient to keep the general price level steady exert *no* active influence on the formation of prices, and that, accordingly, a money so regulated would remain "neutral" toward prices in the sense in which I have used the word. I see no foundation at all for this hypothesis, although by most it seems to be considered as an obvious platitude requiring no further justification. Everything that has been said in the earlier lectures seems to me to prove that changes in the volume of the circulation which are supposed to be justified by changes in the volume of production will have effects which are just as disturbing as those changes of the circulation which cause changes in the general price level. *Prima facie*, I suggest that we should expect rather that, to be neutral in this sense, the supply of money should be invariable. The question is, can this be true? Are there not many other reasons besides a change in the volume of production which experience suggests justify changes

---

[73] *Economic Journal* 38 (December 1929): 589.

[74] *Industrial Fluctuations,* 2nd ed. (London: Macmillan, 1929), p. 101.

in the quantity of money in circulation if serious disturbances are to be avoided?

I suppose that, to most economists, the idea of a circulating medium which does not vary in amount will seem perfectly absurd. We have all been brought up upon the idea that an elastic currency is something highly to be desired, and it is considered a great achievement of modern monetary organization, particularly of the recent American Federal Reserve system, to have secured it. It does not seem open to doubt that the amount of money necessary to carry on the trade of a country fluctuates regularly with the seasons, and that central banks should respond to these changes in the "demand for money," that not only *can* they do this without doing harm, but that they *must* do so if they are not to cause serious disturbances. It is also a fact which has been established by long experience, that in times of crisis central banks should give increased accommodation and extend thereby their circulation in order to prevent panics, and that they can do it to a great extent without effects which are injurious. How are we to reconcile all this with the conclusions of my earlier lectures?

(3) To begin with certain terminological elucidations. It should be fairly clear that the magnitude which in the course of my theoretical analysis I have called "quantity of money in circulation" and that commonly referred to under the same name in dealing with the practical problems mentioned before are not identical, but different in two respects. When, in the course of analysis, I speak of changes in the quantity of money, this is always meant to include that *total* of all kinds of media of exchange (including all so-called "substitutes" for money) used in either a *closed* economic system (i.e., in a country which has no communication with the outside world) or in the world as a whole. But when dealing with practical problems we speak of the quantity of money in circulation, we always mean the quantity of any particular kind or kinds of media of exchange used within one or several countries which form a part of a larger economic unit. Now, as we shall see, it follows from the definition of the

quantity of money in circulation in open communities that the quantity of money thus defined will always be liable to fluctuations even if we suppose that the quantity included in the more comprehensive theoretical concept remains unchanged. It is probably this fact which makes it so difficult even theoretically to conceive the possibility or usefulness of an invariable circulation.

The fact that the monetary circulation of any one country, whatever we include under the heading money, will always show natural fluctuations in conforming with an increase or decrease of the volume of local production is probably the main reason why elasticity is generally considered a self-evident necessity for the amount of money in general. But the question we have to answer is just this. Do the reasons which make fluctuations of the circulation of *any single* country necessary apply when we are considering the quantity of money as a whole?[75] The answer is simple. The increase or decrease of the quantity of money circulating within any one geographical area serves a function just as definite as the increase or decrease of the money incomes of particular individuals, namely the function of enabling the inhabitants to draw a larger or smaller share of the total product of the world. The relative magnitude of the total incomes of all individuals in an "open" community will always stand in a definite proportion to the share of the total product of the world which the people of that community command. And, if the money circulating within that nation regularly increases as a consequence of an increase of its product, this is only one of the steps in the process of adjustment which are necessary to enable that nation to procure a larger portion of the product of the world for itself. What appears to be an *absolute* increase of the amount of money in circulation consequent upon an increase of production, if viewed from the standpoint of a single country, proves to be

---

[75] For a more detailed discussion of this problem, see my article "Das intertemporale Gleichgewichtsystem der Preise und die Bewegungen des 'Geldwertes'," sect. 12.

nothing but a change in the *relative local distribution* of the money of all nations, which is a necessary condition of a change in the distribution of the product of the world as a whole. The same thing would happen, and would be just as necessary to restore equilibrium, if the product of this country were not absolutely increased but the products of all other countries were absolutely diminished. The fact that the increase of the product of any one country is regularly accompanied by an increase of the quantity of money circulating there, is therefore not only no proof that the same would be necessary for an isolated community, it rather shows by contrast how useless would be an increase of its monetary circulation either for such a community or for the world as a whole. While for any single country among others an increase of its possession of money is only a means of obtaining more goods, for the world as a whole the increase of the amount of money only means that somebody has to give up part of his additional product to the producers of the new money.

(4) The second source of the prevalent belief that, in order to prevent dislocation, the quantity of the circulating medium must adapt itself to the changing needs of trade arises from a confusion between the demand for *particular kinds of currency* and the demand for money *in general*.[76] This occurs especially in connection with the so-called seasonal variations of the demand for currency which in fact arises because, at certain times of the year, a larger proportion of the total quantity of the circulating medium is required in *cash* than at other times. The regularly recurring increase of the "demand for money" at quarter days, for instance, which has played so great a role in discussions of central bank policy since attention was first drawn to it by the evidence of J. Horsley Palmer and J.W. Gilbart before the parliamentary committees of 1832 and 1841, is mainly a demand to exchange

---

[76] This confusion is particularly obvious in the writings of Thomas Tooke. Cf. T.E. Gregory, introduction to Tooke and Newarch's *A History of Prices and the State of the Circulation* (London: P.S King, 1928), p. 87 *et seq*.

money held in the form of bank deposits into bank notes or coin.[77] The same thing is true in regard to the "increased demand for money" in the last stages of a boom and during a crisis. When, toward the end of a boom period, wages and retail prices rise, notes and coin will be used in proportionately greater amounts, and entrepreneurs will be compelled to draw a larger proportion of their bank deposits in cash than they used to do before. And when, in a serious crisis, confidence is shaken, and people resort to hoarding, this again only means that they will want to keep a part of their liquid resources in cash which they used to hold in bank money, etc. All this does not necessarily imply a change in the total quantity of the circulating medium, if only we make this concept comprehensive enough to comprise everything which serves as money, even if it does so only temporarily.

(5) But at this point we must take account of a new difficulty which makes this concept of the total quantity of the circulating medium somewhat vague, and which makes the possibility of ever actually fixing its magnitude highly questionable. There can be no doubt that besides the regular types of the circulating medium, such as coin, bank notes and bank deposits, which are generally recognized to be money or currency, and the quantity of which is regulated by some central authority or can at least be imagined to be so regulated, there exist still other forms of media of exchange which occasionally or permanently do the service of money. Now while for certain practical purposes we are accustomed to distinguish these forms of media of exchange from money proper as being mere substitutes for money, it is clear that, *ceteris paribus,* any increase or decrease of these money substitutes will have exactly the same effects as an increase or decrease of the quantity of money proper, and should therefore, for the purposes of theoretical analysis, be counted as money.

---

[77] On this point, see, however, the recent discussion by F. Machlup, *Börsenkredit, Industriekredit und Kapitalbildung* (Vienna: Springer, 1931), particularly chaps. 8 and 9.

In particular, it is necessary to take account of certain forms of credit not connected with banks which help, as is commonly said, to economize money, or to do the work for which, if they did not exist, money in the narrower sense of the word would be required. The criterion by which we may distinguish these circulating credits from other forms of credit which do not act as substitutes for money is that they give to somebody the means of purchasing goods without at the same time diminishing the money-spending power of somebody else. This is most obviously the case when the creditor receives a bill of exchange which he may pass on in payment for other goods. It applies also to a number of other forms of commercial credit, as, for example, when book credit is simultaneously introduced in a number of successive stages of production in the place of cash payments, and so on. The characteristic peculiarity of these forms of credit is that they spring up without being subject to any central control, but once they have come into existence their convertibility into other forms of money must be possible if a collapse of credit is to be avoided. But it is important not to overlook the fact that these forms of credits owe their existence largely to the expectation that it will be possible to exchange them at the banks against other forms of money when necessary, and that, accordingly, they might never come into existence if people did not expect that the banks would in the future extend credit against them. The existence of this kind of demand for more money, too, is therefore no proof that the quantity of the circulating medium must fluctuate with the variations in the volume of production. It is only a proof that once additional money has come into existence in some form or other, *convertibility* into other forms must be possible.

(6) Before proceeding to investigate whether there exist any genuine reasons which would make changes in the amount of the circulation necessary in order to keep money entirely neutral toward the economic process (i.e., to prevent it from exercising any active influence on the formation of prices), it is useful to ask

whether, under the circumstances just described, it is at all conceivable that the quantity of the circulating medium *can* be kept invariable, and by what means a monetary authority could attain that end. I may say at once that, in spite of the qualifications that I shall introduce later, this question seems to me not merely a question of theoretical interest, but also a question the answer to which may prove very important in the shaping of a more rational monetary policy.

The credit system of a country has very often been compared to an inverted pyramid, a simile which serves very well for our purpose. The lowest part of the pyramid corresponds of course to the cash basis of the credit structure. The section immediately above corresponds to central bank credit in its various forms, the next part corresponds to the credits of commercial banks, and on these finally is built the total of business credits outside the banks. Now it is only in regard to the two lower parts, cash and central bank credit, that an immediate control can be exercised by the central monetary authority. So far as the third part, the credits of the commercial banks, are concerned, it is at least conceivable that a similar control could be exercised. But the uppermost section of the pyramid—private credits—can be controlled only indirectly through a change in the magnitude of their basis, i.e., in the magnitude of bank credit. The essential thing is that the proportion between the different parts of the pyramid is not constant but variable, in other words that the angle at the apex of the pyramid may change. It is a well-known fact that, during a boom, the amount of central bank credits erected upon a given cash basis increases, and likewise the amount of credits of the commercial banks based on a given amount of central bank credit, and even the amount of private credits based on a given amount of central bank credit. This is certainly true on the continent of Europe, where the possibility of rediscounting takes to a large extent the place of actual cash reserves. So that, even if central banks should succeed in keeping the basis of the credit structure unchanged during an upward swing of a cycle, there can be no doubt that the total quantity of the circulating medium would nonetheless increase. To prevent expansion, therefore, it would not be sufficient if central banks, contrary to their present practice, refrained from *expanding* their own credits. To compensate for the change in the proportion between the base furnished by the credit and the superstructure erected upon it, it would be necessary for them actually to *contract* credit proportionally. It is probably entirely utopian to expect anything of that kind from central banks so long as general opinion still believes that it is the duty of central banks to accommodate trade and to expand credit as the increasing demands of trade require. Unfortunately, we are very far from the more enlightened times when, as John Fullarton complained, "the words 'demand' and 'legitimate demand' could not even be mentioned in Parliament in connection with this subject unaccompanied by a sneer."[78] Nonetheless, I am strongly convinced that, if we want to prevent the periodic misdirections of production caused by additional credit, something very similar to the policy outlined above, absurd as it may seem to those accustomed to present-day practice, would be necessary. I do not delude myself that, in the near future, there will be any opportunity of experimenting with such a policy. But this is no excuse for not following the implications of our theoretical arguments right through to their practical consequences. On the contrary, it is highly important that we should become fully conscious of the enormous difficulties of the problem of the elimination of disturbing monetary influences, difficulties which monetary reformers are always so inclined to underrate. We are still very far from the point when either our theoretical knowledge or the education of the general public provides justification for revolutionary reform or hope of carrying such reforms to a successful conclusion.

---

[78] John Fullarton, *On the Regulation of Currencies*, 2nd ed. (London: John Murray, 1845), p. 206.

(7) As a matter of fact, the course of our argument so far understates rather than overstates the real difficulties. I think that I have shown that changes in the physical volume of production offer no sufficient reason for variations in the supply of money. Nonetheless there do seem to me to exist other causes whose operation may necessitate such changes if the "natural" price system or the equilibrium of the economic process is not to be disturbed. So far, I have been able to neglect these causes, since what I have said has been subject to an assumption, which I expressly introduced at the outset, the assumption, namely, that the proportion between the total flow of goods and the part which takes the form of an exchange against money, or the rate at which goods are exchanged against money, remains constant. But this assumption must now be removed.

Now it will be remembered that the proportion in question is not necessarily changed by changes in the physical volume of production while the amount of money in circulation remains the same, nor by a variation of the quantity of money in circulation, while the physical volume of production remains the same; it changes only if movements of goods which before have been effected without the use of money now require the transfer of money, or if movements of goods which before could only be effected by means of money payments can now be effected without the use of money. It will be remembered further that changes in that proportion are caused by certain changes of the business organization, as the amalgamation of two firms into one, or the division of one firm into two, by the extension of the money economy into spheres where before everybody had only consumed his own product, or where barter had predominated, and the like. The question to which we must now address our attention is this: will not such changes in the proportions of money transactions to the total flow of goods make a corresponding change in the quantity of the circulating medium necessary?

The answer to that question depends upon whether, without such a corresponding change in the quantity of money, the change in business organization, would cause shifts in the directions of demand and consequential shifts in the direction of production not justified by changes in the "real" factors. That the simple fact that a money payment is inserted at a point in the movement of goods from the original means of production to the final stage where none has been necessary before (or the reverse) is no "real" cause in the sense that it would justify a change in the structure of production, is a proposition which probably needs no further explanation. If, therefore, we can show that, without a corresponding change in the amount of the circulation, it has such an effect, this would provide sufficient reason, in these circumstances, to consider a change in the amount of money to be necessary.

(8) Let us examine what happens when a firm which represents two different stages of production, say spinning and weaving, is divided into two independent firms. The movement of the yarn from the spinning to the weaving factory, which before required no money, will now be effected by a purchase against money. The new weaving firm, which before, as part of the larger concern, had to keep money only for the payment of wages, etc., will now require additional money balances to buy the yarns. The new owner, whom we will assume to have bought the weaving mill from the old firm, will therefore need additional capital beyond what was needed to buy the existing plant and equipment and to replace the cash balances kept by the former owner for that mill, in order to effect these new payments. If no new money is added to the amount already circulating, he will either have to take this sum from other employments where it cannot be replaced, causing an absolute reduction of the demand for capital goods, and consequently a shrinkage of the structure of production; or he will have to use new savings for that purpose, which would thus cease to be available for lengthening the roundabout processes—that is to say, to use a phrase of Mr. Robertson's, they would become "abortive." The effects would be the same as if, other things remaining the same, the total amount

of money in circulation had been reduced by a corresponding sum used before for productive purposes. The two cases are so far alike that the change in the proportion between the demand for consumers' goods and the demand for producers' goods, which in the second case as in the first is not determined by "real" causes, will not be permanent: the old proportion will tend to re-establish itself. But if, from the outset, the demand of the new entrepreneur for the additional cash balances had been satisfied by the creation of new money, this change in the total quantity of circulation would not have caused a change in the direction of the demand, and would only have helped to preserve the existing equilibrium.

It would be easy to show, if time permitted, that in the contrary case, the merger of two firms, and in a number of similar changes in business organization, money is set free and that this money, if not withdrawn from circulation, would have the same effects as if so much money were added to the circulation. But I think that what I have already said on this point will be sufficient to justify the conclusion that changes in the demand for money caused by changes in the proportion between the total flow of goods to that part of it which is effected by money, or, as we may tentatively call that proportion, of *the coefficient of money transactions,* should be justified by changes in the volume of money if money is to remain neutral toward the price system and the structure of production.

All this assumes a greater importance if we remember that this coefficient of money transactions may not only change in time, but that, at the same moment of time, it may be different in different parts of an economic system, for instance because goods change hands at shorter intervals in the lower stages of production than they do in the higher stages. If this is the case, any transfer of money from one part of the economic system to another or from one stage of production to another where the coefficient of money transactions is different will also make a corresponding change of the amount of money in circulation necessary. If, for instance, money is transferred from a lower to a higher stage of production where the interval between two successive stages is twice as long, and, accordingly, only half as much money is needed to hold the same quantity of goods in that stage, half the money so transferred would become free. In the opposite case an addition of new money of an equal amount would be necessary. In such a situation, therefore, the transition to more or less capitalistic methods of production may also require a change in the quantity of money, *not* because the physical magnitude of the goods-stream has changed, but because money has been transferred from a sphere where the coefficient of money transactions has been higher to one where it is lower, or *vice versa*.

(9) And this is not the only exception to which our original maxim of policy, that the quantity of money should remain invariable, may be deemed to be subject.

The case just discussed is, in fact, only a special aspect of a more general and very familiar phenomenon which, so far, has been entirely neglected in these lectures. I refer to changes in what is commonly called the velocity of circulation. Up to this point I have treated the quantity of money in circulation and the number of payments effected during a given period of time as equivalent concepts, a method of procedure which implied the assumption that the velocity of circulation is constant. That is to say, the whole of my argument applies directly only to the *amount of payments* made during a period of time. It applies indirectly to the *amount of money* if we assume the "velocity of circulation" to be constant. So long as we make that assumption, or so long as we are speaking only of the volume of payments made during a period of time, the case just discussed seems to me the only exception to the general rule that, in order that money should remain neutral toward prices, the amount of money or the amount of money payments should remain invariable. But the situation becomes different as soon as we take into account the possibility of changes in methods of payment which make it possible for a given amount of money to effect a larger or smaller number of payments during a period of time than before. Such a change in the "velocity of circulation" has rightly always been considered as equivalent to a change in the amount of money in circulation, and though, for reasons which it would go too far to explain here, I am not particularly enamored of the concept of an average velocity of circulation,[79] it will serve as sufficient justification of the general statement that any change in the velocity of circulation would have to be compensated by a reciprocal change in the amount of money in circulation if money is to remain neutral toward prices.

(10) Even now our difficulties are not at an end. For, in order to eliminate all monetary influences on the formation of prices and the structure of production, it would not be sufficient merely quantitatively to adapt the supply of money to these changes in demand, it would be necessary also to see that it came into the hands of those who actually require it, i.e., to that part of the system where that change in business organization or the habits of payment had taken place. It is conceivable that this could be managed in the case of an increase of demand. It is clear that it would be still more difficult in the case of a reduction. But quite apart from this particular difficulty which, from the point of view of pure theory, may not prove insuperable, it should be clear that only to satisfy the legitimate demand for money in this sense, and otherwise to leave the amount of the circulation unchanged, can never be a practical maxim of currency policy. No doubt the statement as it stands only provides another, and probably clearer, formulation of the old distinction between the demand for additional money as money which is justifiable, and the demand for additional money as capital which is not justifiable. But the difficulty of translating it into the language of practice

---

[79] Cf. L. v. Mises, *Theorie des Geldes und der Umlaufsmittel*, 2nd ed. (Munich and Leipzig: Duncker & Humblot, 1924), p. 3 *et seq*.

still remains. The "natural" or equilibrium rate of interest which would exclude all demands for capital which exceed the real supply capital, is incapable of ascertainment, and, even if it were not, it would not be possible, in times of optimism, to prevent the growth of circulatory credit outside the banks.

Hence the only practical maxim for monetary policy to be derived from our considerations is probably the negative one that the simple fact of an increase of production and trade forms no justification for an expansion of credit, and that—save in an acute crisis—bankers need not be afraid to harm production by over-caution. Under existing conditions, to go beyond this is out of the question. In any case, it could be attempted only by a central monetary authority for the whole world: action on the part of a single country would be doomed to disaster. It is probably an illusion to suppose that we shall ever be able entirely to eliminate industrial fluctuations by means of monetary policy. The most we may hope for is that the growing information of the public may make it easier for central banks both to follow a cautious policy during the upward swing of the cycle, and so to mitigate the following depression, and to resist the well-meaning but dangerous proposals to fight depression by "a little inflation."

(11) Anybody who is skeptical of the value of theoretical analysis if it does not result in practical suggestions for economic policy will probably be deeply disappointed by the small return of so prolonged an argument. I do not, however, think that effort spent in clearing up the conditions under which money would remain neutral toward the economic process is useless because these conditions will never be given in the real world. And I would claim for these investigations at least two things. The first is that, as I have said in my first lecture, monetary theory is still so very far from a state of perfection that even some of the most fundamental problems in this field are yet unsolved, that some of the accepted doctrines are of very doubtful validity. This applies in particular to the widespread illusion that we have simply to stabilize the value of money in order to

eliminate all monetary influences on production and that, therefore, if the value of money is assumed to be stable, in theoretical analysis, we may treat money as nonexistent. I hope to have shown that, under the existing conditions, money will always exert a determining influence on the course of economic events and that, therefore, no analysis of actual economic phenomena is complete if the role played by money is neglected. This means that we have definitely to give up the opinion which is still widely prevalent, that, in the words of John Stuart Mill, "there cannot, in short, be intrinsically a more insignificant thing, in the economy of society, than money" which "like many other kinds of machinery only exerts a distinct and independent influence of its own when it gets out of order."[80] It means also that the task of monetary theory is a much wider one than is commonly assumed; that its task is nothing less than to cover a second time the whole field which is treated by pure theory under the assumption of barter, and to investigate what changes in the conclusions of pure theory are made necessary by the introduction of indirect exchange. The first step toward a solution of this problem is to release monetary theory from the bonds which a too narrow conception of its task has created.

The second conclusion to be drawn from the results of our considerations follows from the first: so long as we do not see more clearly about the most fundamental problems of monetary theory and so long as no agreement is reached on the essential theoretical questions, we are also not yet in a position drastically to reconstruct our monetary system, in particular to replace the semiautomatic gold standard by a more or less arbitrarily managed currency. Indeed, I am afraid that, in the present state of knowledge, the risks connected with such an attempt are much greater than the harm which is possibly done by the gold standard. I am not

---

[80] Mill, *Principles of Political Economy,* book 3, chap. 7, para. 3, ed. Ashley, p. 488.

even convinced that a good deal of the harm which is just now generally ascribed to the gold standard will not by a future and better informed generation of economists be recognized as a result of the different attempts of recent years to make the mechanism of the gold standard inoperative. And there is still another and perhaps no less important reason why it seems dangerous to me to overstress at the present moment the urgency of a change in our monetary system; it is the danger of diverting public attention from other and more pressing causes of our difficulties. I must say a last word on that point because it will help to prevent a misunderstanding which I am particularly anxious to avoid. Though I believe that recurring business depressions can only be explained by the operation of our monetary institutions, I do not believe that it is possible to explain in this way every stagnation of business. This applies in particular to the kind of prolonged depression through which some European countries are passing today. It would be easy to demonstrate by the same type of analysis which I have used in the last two lectures that certain kinds of state action, by causing a shift in demand from producers' goods to consumers' goods, may cause a continued shrinking of the capitalist structure of production, and therefore prolonged stagnation. This may be true of increased public expenditure in general or of particular forms of taxation or particular forms of public expenditure. In such cases, of course, no tampering with the monetary system can help. Only a radical revision of public policy can provide the remedy.

APPENDIX TO LECTURE 4

Some Supplementary Remarks on "Neutral Money"

The term "neutral money," as mentioned in Lecture I, was apparently first used by Wicksell, but more or less incidentally, and without the intention to introduce it as a technical term. It was only comparatively recently that it came to be more widely used, apparently first in Holland, probably owing to the influence of Mr. J.G. Koopmans, who has for years been investigating this problem. The first results of Mr. Koopmans' studies have, however, appeared only recently, since the present book was first published.[81] But Mr. Koopmans has carried his investigations considerably further than was possible in the present essay, and to anyone who is interested in that problem I can only warmly recommend Mr. Koopmans's study, with which I find myself in general agreement.

A short but earlier discussion of the problem is to be found in a German work by Mr. W.G. Behrens.[82] Mr. Behrens also points out correctly that this is only a new name for the problem which

---

[81] J.G. Koopmans, "Zum Problem des 'Neutralen' Geldes," in *Beiträge zur Geldtheorie,* ed. F.A. Hayek (Vienna: Springer, 1933).

[82] Walter G. Behrens, *Das Geldschöpfungsproblem* (Jena: Gustav Fischer, 1928), particularly pp. 228, 286, 312 *et seq.*

had been discussed by Carl Menger and Professor Mises under the (in my opinion rather unfortunate) name of the invariability of the "*innere objektive Tauschwert*" of money, or shortly of the "*innere Geldwert.*" And it may also be added that it was essentially for the same purpose that L. Walras and the later economists of the Lausanne School used the concept of a "*numéraire*" as distinguished from that of "*monnaie.*"

It is not intended here to go further into the extremely difficult theoretical problems which this concept raises. There is, however, one respect in which recent discussions devoted to it have shown a certain ambiguity of the concept, which it seems desirable to clear up. It is frequently assumed that the concept of neutrality provides a maxim which is immediately applicable to the practical problems of monetary policy.

But this need by no means be the case, and the concept was certainly not primarily intended for that purpose. It was destined in the first instance to provide an instrument for theoretical analysis, and to help us to isolate the active influences, which money exercised on the course of economic life. It refers to the set of conditions, under which it would be *conceivable* that events in a monetary economy would take place, and particularly under which, in such an economy, relative prices would be formed, as if they were influenced only by the "real" factors which are taken into account in equilibrium economics. In this sense the term points, of course, only to a problem, and does not represent a solution. It is evident that such a solution would be of great importance for the questions of monetary policy. But it is not impossible that it represents only one ideal, which in practice competes with other important aims of monetary policy.

The necessary starting point for any attempt to answer the theoretical problem seems to me to be the recognition of the fact that the identity of demand and supply, which must necessarily exist in the case of barter, ceases to exist as soon as money becomes the intermediary of the exchange transactions. The problem then becomes one of isolating the one-sided effects of money—to repeat an expression which on an earlier occasion I had unconsciously borrowed from Wieser[83]—which will appear when, after the division of the barter transaction into two separate transactions, one of these takes place without the other complementary transaction. In this sense demand without corresponding supply, and supply without a corresponding demand, evidently seem to occur in the first instance when money is spent out of hoards (i.e., when cash balances are reduced), when money received is not immediately spent, when additional money comes on the market, or when money is destroyed. So this formulation of the problem leads immediately to the solution of a constant money stream, with the exceptions sketched in the last lecture. The argument has, however, been developed systematically only by Mr. J.G. Koopmans in the essay mentioned above.

In order to preserve, in the case of a money economy, the tendencies toward a stage of equilibrium which are described by general economic theory, it would be necessary to secure the existence of all the conditions, which the theory of neutral money has to establish. It is however very probable that this is practically impossible. It will be necessary to take into account the fact that the existence of a generally used medium of exchange will always lead to the existence of long-term contracts in terms of this medium of exchange, which will have been concluded in the expectation of a certain future price level. It may further be necessary to take into account the fact that many other prices possess a considerable degree of rigidity and will be particularly difficult to reduce. All these "frictions" which obstruct the smooth adaptation of the price system to changed conditions, which would be necessary if the money supply were to be kept neutral, are of course of the greatest importance for all practical problems of monetary policy. And it may be necessary to seek for

---

[83] Cf. F. v. Wieser, "Der Geldwert und seine Veränderungen," *Zeitschrift für Volkswirtschaft, Sozialpolitik und Verwaltung* 13 (1904), p. 54, also reprinted in the same author's *Gesammelte Abhandlungen* (Tübingen: Mohr, 1929), p. 178.

a compromise between two aims which can be realized only alternatively: the greatest possible realization of the forces working toward a state of equilibrium, and the avoidance of excessive frictional resistances. But it is important to realize fully that in this case the elimination of the active influences of money has ceased to be the only, or even a fully realizable, purpose of monetary policy; and it could only cause confusion to describe this practical aim of monetary policy by the same name, which is used to designate the theoretically conceivable situation, in which one of the two competing aims was fully obtained.

The true relationship between the theoretical concept of neutral money, and the practical ideal of monetary policy is, therefore, that the former provides one criterion for judging the latter; the degree to which a concrete system approaches the condition of neutrality is one and perhaps the most important, but not the only criterion by which one has to judge the appropriateness of a given course of policy. It is quite conceivable that a distortion of relative prices and a misdirection of production by monetary influences could only be avoided if, first, the total money stream remained constant, and second, all prices were completely flexible, and, third, all long term contracts were based on a correct anticipation of future price movements. This would mean that, if the second and third conditions are not given, the ideal could not be realized by any kind of monetary policy.

APPENDIX

Capital and Industrial Fluctuations: A Reply to a Criticism[84]

A sympathetic criticism of the kind to which the views of the present author have been subjected by Messrs. Hansen and Tout in a recent issue of *Econometrica*[85] offers a welcome opportunity of clearing up some points upon which I have obviously not yet been sufficiently explicit. The critical comments of the two authors are mostly directed against points where real difficulties present themselves; and while I think I can answer their main objections, it is probable that I can do so more profitably by means of a further systematic development of my thesis than by wasting time on the comparatively unimportant discussion of whether these developments were already implied in my earlier statements, or whether the interpretation put upon these by Messrs. Hansen and Tout can or cannot be justified from the admittedly sketchy and incomplete exposition in the preceding lectures.

---

[84] Reprinted from *Econometrica* 2, no. 2 (April 1934).
[85] A. Hansen and H. Tout, "Annual Survey of Business Cycle Theory: Investment and Saving in Business Cycle Theory," *Econometrica* 1, no. 2 (April 1933).

Messrs. Hansen and Tout have stated my theory in the following series of propositions:

> Thesis Number 1. That depression is brought about by a shrinkage in the structure of production (i.e., a shortening of the capitalistic process). In Hayek's view, the phenomenon of depression *is* a shrinkage in the structure of production. Dynamic forces may bring about various effects on economic life, but unless they have the specific effect of shortening the process of production, depression will not follow therefrom. Nor does depression ever assume any other form than that of a shrinkage in the structure of production. In short, depression may be defined as a shortening of the capitalistic process of production.
>
> Thesis Number 2. The leading cause (there are, however, others) which brings about, either directly or indirectly, a shortening in the process of production, is the phenomenon of *forced* saving.
>
> Thesis Number 3. An elongation of the process of production caused by *voluntary* saving tends to remain intact; or at least, there is no inherent reason why such an elongation *must* necessarily be followed by a shrinkage in the structure of production.
> An increase in voluntary saving would cause an enlarged demand for producers' goods in relation to consumers' goods, and this would raise the prices of goods in the higher stages of production in relation to those of the lower stages. The consequent narrowing of the price margins or, in other words, the lower rate of interest, would thus make possible a permanent elongation of the process of production.
>
> Thesis Number 4. A lengthening of the process of production caused by forced saving (the money supply not having been held neutral) cannot possibly be permanently

maintained, but must necessarily be followed by a shortening in the process of production.

An increase in money supply (bank credit) made available to entrepreneurs would cause an increase in the demand for producers' goods in relation to consumers' goods, and this would raise the prices of goods of the higher order in relation to those of the lower order. The consequent elongation of the process of production could not, however, be maintained, because a reversal in the price relationship of higher and lower order goods would appear as soon as the money supply ceased to increase owing to the fact that spending and saving habits had not changed. Thus, a shrinkage in the artificially elongated process of production would inevitably occur.

Thesis Number 5. An increase in consumer demand occasioned by an increase in the supply of money (over and above what may be necessary to hold money neutral) inevitably brings about a shortening in the process of production, and so causes depression.

An increased supply of money made available directly to consumers would cause an increase in the demand for consumers' goods in relation to producers' goods, and would thus raise the prices of goods of the lower order in relation to those of the higher order, and this would inevitably bring about a shortening in the process of production.

Thesis Number 6. That excessive public expenditures and taxation, by increasing the ratio of spending to saving, will force a shortening in the process of production and so cause prolonged depression or business stagnation.

An increase in spending would cause an increased demand for consumers' goods in relation to producers' goods, and this would raise the prices of goods in the lower order in relation to those of the higher order. The consequent widening of the price margins between the lower and higher order goods, or, in other words, a higher rate of interest, would, therefore, bring about a shortening of the process of production.

Thesis Number 7. That the supply of money should be kept constant, except for such increases and decreases as may be necessary (1) to offset changes in the velocity of circulation, (2) to counteract such changes in the coefficient of money transactions as are occasioned by the amalgamation of firms, and the like, and (3) to provide for any changes in non-monetary means of payment, such as book credit, that may be taking place. (A distinction is thus made between a "constant" money supply and a "neutral" money supply.)

Thesis Number 8. That any change in money supply (other than that necessary to hold money neutral) is harmful because it necessarily brings about, eventually, a shortening in the process of production, (a) If the increased money supply goes to entrepreneurs, the process of production is first elongated, but, subsequently, necessarily shortened, returning to its previous status, or to a still shorter process. (b) If the increased money goes first to consumers, the shortening of the process of production takes place at once, and the process remains permanently shortened.

Thesis Number 9. That an increase in production and trade forms no justification for an increase in bank credit.

Thesis Number 10. That a period of depression should not be counteracted by any inflation of the money supply, though, in theory, there is the possibility that during the acute stages of the crisis, while the capitalistic structure is tending to shrink more than will ultimately prove necessary, a nicely regulated increase might prove beneficial. The impossibility of such skilful management makes this an unimportant exception.

I

With one exception, I fully agree that this formulation of my views is a fair and accurate summary of my position. Even the unimportant exception is probably only a slip of the pen, and is satisfactorily cleared up in the later discussion. But, as it may have confused some readers, I should like to emphasize at the outset that I should never say, as stated in thesis number 2, that forced saving can ever *directly* bring about a shortening of the process of production. Forced saving means essentially a lengthening of the process of production and the crucial point is that, in my view, it is these elongations which are likely to be partly or wholly *reversed* as soon as the cause of the forced saving *disappears*.

The first major difficulty which Messrs. Hansen and Tout discuss is connected with what they call my thesis number 1, namely, that the phenomenon of depression is equivalent to a shrinkage of the structure of production. Their difficulty here seems to me to turn on the distinction between a completed and an uncompleted structure, which I have probably failed to make sufficiently clear, and which is closely connected with the distinction between the effects of mere fluctuations in the rate of saving (or, more correctly, in the rate of investment) and the peculiar instability of capital created by means of forced saving. The best way of making these distinctions clear is probably to start with a general discussion of the effects of fluctuations in the means available for investment on the structure of production in general, and on the profitableness of the early stages in particular. From this discussion it will, I think, appear that, contrary to the opinion of Messrs. Hansen and Tout, it is not the mere fluctuations in the rate of investment which tend to make the earlier stages unprofitable but only, on the one hand, particularly violent fluctuations of this sort, and, on the other, fluctuations which make the net investment negative. Finally, concluding this part of the discussion, it will appear that, in the case of "forced savings," it is not only impossible to keep the rate of investment constant, but that there will exist, as a necessary consequence of the "forced saving," strong forces which tend to make the rate of investment negative.

II

Any lengthening of the process of production can only be completed over a period of time corresponding to the interval between the moment when the factors which are being shifted to an earlier stage are being invested, and the moment when their product matures. If the new, longer process is to be completed and maintained, this requires not only that the investment in the earlier stage must be constantly maintained, but also (except in a few rare cases, like the aging of wine and the growing of trees) that further complementary investments must be made in the later stages.

From this it follows that, in any progressive society, the particular forms in which investments are being made are determined by the expectation that, for some time to come, a similar stream of funds for investment will be forthcoming; and that, at any moment of time, only a fraction of the funds available for new investment will be used to start new processes, while the rest will be required to complete the processes already under way. On the simplifying assumption that the *total* length of the marginal processes which are made possible by an increase in the supply of investable funds, is always greater than the total length of any process already used, this situation can be represented by the following diagram. The curvilinear[86] triangle ABC represents, in the same way as the triangle I have used in the preceding lectures, the stock of capital belonging to processes already completed. (The area of the curvilinear triangle $AB'C'$ shows the stock of capital before the additions were begun.) The fully drawn stripes, beginning between C and D, represent incomplete processes started at different moments in the past—and now in different

---

[86] The reasons which make a curvilinear triangle of the kind shown in the text a more appropriate representation than the simplified form used in Lecture 2 are probably obvious. *See p. 228.*

Prices and Production

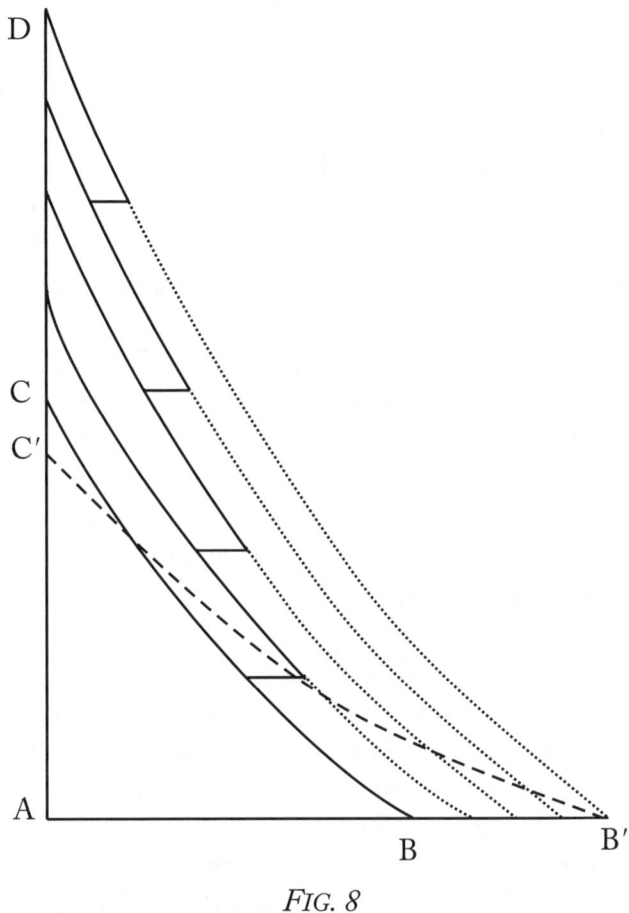

Fig. 8

stages of completion. The part of these stripes which is dotted represents the additional investment which is required to complete the processes. During every successive period of investment, part of the fund available will be used to start new processes, part to advance processes which are already under way, and part to complete the most advanced processes.

If at any moment savings fall by no more than had previously been used to start new processes, the completion of the processes already under way will not be endangered. And since, at any moment, some of the unfinished processes will be completed, the amount of saving may continually fall off at a certain rate, and may reach zero at the moment when all the processes under way are completed. There is, therefore, at any moment, a maximum rate at which the rate of saving may fall off, without interfering with the new processes already started. It is only when the decrease in saving is faster than this rate, at which the need for capital for the purpose of completing processes under way decreases, that the incomplete structure cannot be completed and some of the investments made in the earlier stages have to be abandoned.

Such an abandonment of early stages will, of course, mean that the average period for which the current supply of original factors is being invested, is shortened even if, at the same time, a good deal of investment in new forms in later stages is taking place. In this case, however, investment in new forms need *not* mean *net* investment, since the losses on the abandoned earlier stages have to be offset against it.

III

It is only another way of stating the same conclusions if one says that the total demand for producers' goods will fall off in consequence of a decrease in the demand for new producers' goods only if the latter declines faster than the replacement demand increases, in consequence of the preceding growth of the stock of producers' goods. And this brings me to a discussion of the famous argument according to which any increase in the demand for productive equipment must lead to surplus capacity of plant producing that equipment, as soon as the demand for it ceases to increase. Although this is rarely recognized, this is a typical instance where an expansion of an earlier stage of production can be maintained only if the further increase of capital makes it possible to complete the structure by adequate increases of capital in the later stages.[87]

---

[87] A top-heavy structure of this kind is, therefore, an uncompleted structure in the sense that its earlier stages will be permanently employed only after they have helped to increase the equipment in later stages to such a magnitude that

From the very outset, it is important in this connection carefully to avoid a confusion which arises from the failure to distinguish between fluctuations in the demand for productive equipment of a particular industry, which arise from fluctuations in the demand for the product of that industry, and fluctuations in the demand for new producers' goods in general, which are connected with fluctuations in the supply of funds available for new investment. Here I am mainly concerned with the latter type of fluctuation. How far what is to be said about this particular case is also applicable to the former depends upon the degree to which the concrete capital equipment in earlier stages is specialized to the production of equipment for a particular industry, or whether it can be more generally used. On this question of fact, I can only refer to an interesting article which was recently published by Mr. Seltzer,[88] who seems to show that the mobility of capital in this sense is far greater than is commonly supposed. Some other considerations on this point can be more appropriately discussed after I have dealt with the first type of fluctuation.

At first, therefore, I shall assume that the increase in investment is due to an increase in the supply of capital, and that the plant required to provide the new equipment is not adapted to the requirements of one industry only, but can be used fairly widely. The question then is whether, on the expectation of a continued growth of capital at about the same rate, it will appear profitable to expand the plant in the industries producing that equipment to a point where *any* decline in the current supply of new capital will make full use of that plant unprofitable.

The answer to this question is simply this: as long as the supply of capital does not decrease by more than the amount which

---

its replacement demand will fully use the capacity of the earlier stages. (The essential thing here, however, is not capacity in a technical sense, but sufficient employment to make amortization of plant at current prices possible.)

[88] "The Mobility of Capital," *Quarterly Journal of Economics* 46 (1932).

has so far been used to construct the new plant[89] making that equipment, there is no reason why the demand for new equipment should fall off. In other words, the effect of a decrease in saving will simply be that the beginning of new roundabout processes will be stopped but, if the decrease does not exceed a certain rate, there is no reason why the already existing plant should not be continuously used to add to the equipment in later stages. And as the replacement demand due to earlier additions to this equipment will continue to rise, the supply of new savings may even continue to fall at a certain rate without affecting the employment of the plant producing this equipment. The situation is, therefore, completely analogous to the case of fluctuations in the rate of saving already discussed: it need not have any harmful effects, so long as the decline in the rate of saving does not exceed the amount, which will permit the processes already begun to be completed.

---

[89] It is assumed here that the construction of this additional plant for making the equipment in question can be carried out either with the help of similar plant already in existence, or of some other plant which can *also* be used to produce equipment for later stages. This, of course, will always be the case since no capital is created without the help of some capital already in existence, which if it is a question of adding an earlier stage of production to those already existing, must, *ex definitione,* mean that these capital goods have hitherto been used in later stages. It may be mentioned here, since this has occasionally been a cause of confusion, that any given capital good need not, and usually will not, belong to any one given "stage" of production only. If it is used to produce other capital goods employed in different stages, and still more if it helps to produce durable goods, or is itself durable, it belongs to as many different "stages" as different periods of time elapse from the moment in which we consider it, to the moments when the different final products which it has helped to produce are consumed. This, however, so far from making the concept of stages useless, is only a necessary distinction in order to explain the different ways in which the value of individual capital goods will be affected by changes in the supply of capital, the rate of interest, or other factors affecting the structure of production.

IV

The confusion on this point seems to result from a very common mistake—that of applying what is true of a single industry to industry as a whole. While, of course, the relative magnitude of the demand for equipment for a particular industry will depend upon the demand for the product of that industry, it is certainly not true to say that the demand for capital goods in general is directly determined by the magnitude of the demand for consumers' goods. While it is true that some contemporary economists have come so much under the influence of the underconsumptionist fallacy that they are prepared to say that the savings will never lead to a corresponding increase in investment, because they involve a decline in the demand for consumers' goods, and are therefore only a harmful and undesirable phenomenon, I certainly need not discuss this with economists who accept as much of my fundamental position as do Messrs. Hansen and Tout. But, if one accepts the proposition that the magnitude of the total demand for producers' goods is not a simple derivative of the demand for consumers' goods, but that any given demand for consumers' goods can lead to methods of production involving very different demands for producers' goods, and that the particular method of production chosen will depend upon the proportion of the total wealth *not* required for immediate consumption, then we must certainly take the fluctuations in the supply of free capital, and not the fluctuations in the demand for consumers' goods, as the starting point for this kind of analysis.

There is, therefore, no reason to suppose that a general increase in the demand for new capital goods, which is due to an increase in the supply of saving, must lead to a decrease in the demand for capital goods, as soon as the rate of saving begins to decline. And since I am still abstracting from the case where investment is financed by the creation of credit ("forced saving") or any other purely monetary changes, it is difficult to see what factors can affect the *total* demand for new capital goods, other than the supply of savings. Only if we assume that changes in the rate of interest which can be earned on new capital lead to hoarding or dishoarding, would a new cause of change be introduced. But this is one of the cases of monetary changes in the demand for consumers' goods which I shall have to discuss later on.

On this point, my argument so far amounts to this: that insofar as we abstract from monetary changes, the demand for consumers' goods can only change inversely with the demand for producers' goods, and in consequence, so far from having a cumulative effect in the same direction as the latter, will tend to offset it in the opposite direction.

There is, however, still the case of mere shifts of demand between different kinds of consumers' goods, which of course will have some effect on the demand for particular kinds of capital goods. An unexpected shift of this kind will undoubtedly have the effect that provision made for the supply of new equipment in the industry from which demand has turned away, will now prove excessive or, in other words, it will now become unprofitable to complete the longer processes in the expected way. But the total demand for new equipment will not be changed, and whether the equipment-producing plant already in existence will continue to be used or whether a new plant will have to be built, will depend upon the technical considerations already mentioned.

V

So much for the pure or barter theory of the subject (in the sense of the usual assumption of theory that money exists to facilitate exchange but exercises no determining influence on the course of things or, in other words, remains neutral—an assumption which is almost always made though not expressed in these terms). The discussion of the active influence which may be exercised by money in this connection is best begun with the peculiar effect of forced savings, which will lead us to another of the points of discussion, namely, the effect of monetary changes on the demand for consumers' goods. For the peculiar characteristic of forced saving, which distinguishes its effects from those of voluntary saving, is simply that it leads necessarily to an increase in the means available for the purchase of consumers' goods. For this reason, my thesis number 4 about the impermanence of capital accumulated by forced saving is directly bound up with my thesis number 5 as to the effects of a direct increase in the monetary demand for consumers' goods, which Messrs. Hansen and Tout, quite consistently, also reject.

The reason why forced saving will always lead to a subsequent increase in the money available for the purchase of consumers' goods, is fairly obvious and will probably not be contested. Entrepreneurs are in this case enabled to attract factors of production from later to earlier stages, not by a corresponding transfer of funds from consumers' to producers' goods, but by additional money handed to them. This means that they will bid up the prices of these factors without there being a corresponding fall in the prices of other factors. Total money income will therefore increase, and this increase will in turn lead to an increase in the amount of money expended on consumers' goods. This increase in the expenditure on consumers' goods will necessarily follow in time upon the increase in the demand for factors. This lag will mean that, for some time after the demand for factors (or producers' goods) has ceased to increase (or when its rate of increase begins to slow down), the demand for consumers' goods will continue to increase at a faster rate; and so long as the increase in the demand for producers' goods is slowing down—and for some time afterwards—the monetary proportion between the demand for producers' goods and the demand for consumers' goods will change in favor of the latter.

The question turns, therefore, upon the effect of such a relative increase in the monetary demand for consumers' goods. The reply, in the particular case in question, however, is simplified, in comparison with the general problem, because, on our assumptions, two relevant points are given. We have in this particular case to assume that: (a) since it is the situation at the end of a boom, there are no unemployed resources, and (b) since the rate of credit expansion for productive purposes tends to be slowed down in spite of a continued rise in the monetary demand for consumers' goods, we cannot assume that the continued rise in this demand will lead to a renewed credit expansion. The much more difficult case of an increase in the monetary demand for consumers' goods, where these assumptions do not necessarily hold, as well as the problem why the rate of credit expansion cannot be sufficiently high to avoid this type of reaction, will be considered later on.

The relative rise in the price of consumers' goods will not only improve the competitive position of their producers on the market for original factors, but will also make it profitable for these to increase their output by the more rapid, even if more expensive, method of employing relatively more labor (original factors) in proportion to capital. And while their demand for all the non-specific factors of production (which can also be used in the latest stages of production) will continue to drive up the prices of these factors, the prices of the intermediate products specific to earlier stages of production will tend to fall relatively to their costs. And since the effect of this will not only tend to increase cumulatively toward the earlier stages but will also cause a shift of free capital toward the more profitable earlier stages, it is easy to see how more and more of the earlier stages will tend to become unprofitable, until unemployment finally arises and leads to a fall in the prices of the original factors of production as well as in the prices of consumers' goods.

VI

Before I turn to the aspects of the situation where unemployed factors and unused lending capacity of all banks exist, and where perhaps delay in making the necessary adjustments has led to prolonged unprofitability causing deflation and a rapid general fall of prices, a little more must be said about the rate of credit expansion which would have to continue uninterruptedly if a reaction of the kind just discussed is to be avoided.

Hansen and Tout merely speak of a *steady* rate of credit expansion as a sufficient condition for a continuous and undisturbed rate of capital growth. I am not quite sure what "steady" means in this context. But if it refers, as is probably the case, to a constant rate of increase in the total media of circulation, I think it can be shown that this is not sufficient to maintain a constant rate of forced saving; while it seems that any attempt to make the rate of credit expansion great enough to secure a constant rate of forced saving will inevitably be frustrated by counteracting forces which come into operation as soon as the process of inflation exceeds a certain speed.

A constant rate of forced saving (i.e., investment in excess of voluntary saving) requires a rate of credit expansion which will enable the producers of intermediate products, during each successive unit of time, to compete successfully with the producers of consumers' goods[90] for constant additional quantities of the original factors of production. But as the competing demand from the producers of consumers' goods rises (in terms of money) in consequence of, and in proportion to, the preceding increase of expenditure on the factors of production (income), an increase of credit which is to enable the producers of intermediate products to attract additional original factors, will have to be, not only absolutely but even relatively, greater than the last increase which is now reflected in the increased demand for consumers' goods. Even in order to attract only as great a proportion

---

[90] I am compelled here—as I was in the preceding lecture—to speak, for the sake of brevity, in terms of competition between the producers of intermediate products and the producers of consumers' goods (the present and future goods of Böhm-Bawerk's exposition) instead of speaking more correctly of competition between a continuous range of entrepreneurs in all "stages" of production, which leads to all original factors being invested for a shorter or longer average period.

of the original factors, i.e., in order merely to maintain the already existing capital, every new increase would have to be proportional to the last increase, i.e., credit would have to expand progressively at a constant *rate*. But in order to bring about constant additions to capital, it would have to do more: it would have to increase at a *constantly increasing rate*. The rate at which this rate of increase must increase would be dependent upon the time lag between the first expenditure of the additional money on the factors of production and the re-expenditure of the income so created on consumers' goods.

It is true that in the preceding lectures I have not only discussed in detail what rate of credit expansion is required to maintain a given rate of forced saving, but have simply assumed that that rate—whatever it was—could not be permanently maintained for institutional reasons, such as traditional banking policies or the operation of the gold standard. But I think it can be shown without great difficulty that even if these obstacles to credit expansion were absent, such a policy would, sooner or later, inevitably lead to a rapid and progressive rise in prices which, in addition to its other undesirable effects, would set up movements which would soon counteract, and finally more than offset, the "forced saving."

That it is impossible, either for a simple progressive increase of credit which only helps to maintain, and does not add to, the already existing "forced saving," or for an increase in credit at an increasing rate, to continue for a considerable time without causing a rise in prices, results from the fact that in neither case have we reason to assume that the increase in the supply of consumers' goods will keep pace with the increase in the flow of money coming on to the market for consumers' goods. Insofar as, in the second case, the credit expansion leads to an ultimate increase in the output of consumers' goods, this increase will lag considerably and increasingly (as the period of production increases) behind the increase in the demand for them. But whether the prices of consumers' goods will rise faster or slower, all other prices, and particularly the prices of the original factors of production, will rise even faster. It is only a question of time when this general and progressive rise of prices becomes very rapid. My argument is not that such a development is *inevitable* once a policy of credit expansion is embarked upon, but that it *has to be* carried to that point if a certain result—a constant rate of forced saving, or maintenance without the help of voluntary saving of capital accumulated by forced saving—is to be achieved.

Once this stage is reached, such a policy will soon begin to defeat its own ends. While the mechanism of forced saving continues to operate, the general rise in prices will make it increasingly more difficult, and finally practically impossible, for entrepreneurs to maintain their existing capital intact. Paper profits will be computed and consumed, the failure to reproduce the existing capital will become quantitatively more and more important, and will finally exceed the additions made by forced saving.

It is important in this connection to remember that the entrepreneur necessarily and inevitably thinks of his capital in terms of money, and that, under changing conditions, he has no other way of thinking of its quantity than in value terms, which practically means in terms of money. But even if, for a time, he resists the temptation of paper profits (and experience teaches us that this is extremely unlikely) and computes his costs in terms of some index number, the rate of depreciation has only to become fast enough, and such an expedient will be ineffective. And since the gist of my argument is that, for the purpose under discussion, the rate of credit expansion and depreciation has to increase at an increasing rate, it will in time reach any desired magnitude.

VII

For these reasons, it seems to me that the hope of Messrs. Hansen and Tout based on a steady rate of forced saving is illusory. Whether there may not exist conditions under which temporary forced saving may take place without the evil consequences of a crisis, is quite another matter. That this will be possible only if the rate of forced saving is comparatively small, is probably obvious. Another condition which we already know is that the fluctuations in investment to which it gives rise keep well within the limits we have described. In another place,[91] I have tried to show that, if these conditions are combined with a third, namely, the presence of a relatively high rate of voluntary saving, which provides the means of taking over, as it were, the real capital which has been created but cannot be maintained by means of forced saving, the loss of this capital may be avoided. But in this case, the only one I know where such a loss will be avoided, the forced saving will only mean an anticipation but no net increase of the circulation of capital, because it can only be maintained if an equivalent amount of saving is to be forthcoming later. For this reason, I am even more doubtful than before whether forced saving can ever be a blessing as Messrs. Hansen and Tout think. This is quite irrespective of the question whether there is any sense in which the economist can legitimately say (as I have occasionally said myself) that such decisions made against the will of those concerned may be "beneficial." But that touches the much wider problem of whether we possess any gauge by which to measure the satisfaction derived by those concerned, except their own preferences, shown in their decisions—a question which I cannot even begin to discuss here.

8

It will be impossible within the compass of this article to discuss the further points made by Messrs. Hansen and Tout in the same orbit as those more fundamental problems already taken up. Particularly, the next and very important point as to the effect of an expansion of consumers' demand at a time when the productive forces are not fully employed, and banks are in a position to expand credits to producers, could be answered completely only

---

[91] "Stand und Zukunftsaufgaben der Konjunkturforschung," p. 110.

in connection with a fully developed theory of the process going on during a depression. But, if it be assumed that these two conditions exist as a consequence of a preceding crisis (and a definite assumption as regards the reason *why* these conditions exist is essential for any answer), and if the explanation of the crisis which I have just discussed is accepted, it is difficult to see how the same phenomenon, which has brought about the crisis, i.e., the rise in the relative demand for consumers' goods, should also be the cure for it. The scarcity of capital, which, of course, is nothing else but the relatively high price of consumers' goods, could only be enhanced by giving the consumers more money to spend on final products. At least so long as there are no further monetary complications, particularly so long as it is not assumed that the expectation of a further fall in prices has led to hoarding, I see no way of getting over this difficulty. But before I proceed to the relation between these secondary monetary complications, and the underlying real maladjustments which have caused it, I must try to clear away what seems to me to be a confusion which has led Messrs. Hansen and Tout to apply their denial of the capital-destroying effect of additions to consumers' credits not only to the peculiar situation of an advanced depression but also generally.

The essence of the confusion on this point seems to me to lie in the contrast which my critics try to establish in several places between what they call "nominal" changes in the relative monetary demand for consumers' goods and producers' goods, and the "real changes in the demand for consumers' goods occasioned by a fundamental modification in time preference for present and future goods." It seems to me that to assume that this rate of time preference can have any effect other than through the relative demand for these two classes of goods, or can have any immediate effects different from those of any other cause affecting that relative demand, is an attempt to establish a purely mystical connection. The mere fact that even without a monetary change, any change in the distribution of the command over existing resources will under a given set of individual time preferences lead to quite different proportions between capital and income, should suffice to make this quite clear.[92]

Nor can I see how the two authors can combine their acceptance of the idea that forced saving can be brought about by monetary causes, without a change in the rate of time preference, with a general denial that monetary causes may also lead to "forced dis-saving." In principle, any change in the relative demand for the two categories of goods, whether brought about by actual shifts of monetary demand from one to the other, or merely by unilateral increases or decreases without corresponding changes on the other side, will *tend* to lead to corresponding changes in the relative amounts produced. The differences between these two cases (a shift and a unilateral change) are, *first*, that the shift of an amount of money from the demand for consumers' goods to the demand for producers' goods changes the proportion between the two much more effectively than a mere unilateral increase or decrease by the same amount; and, *second*, that the changes in the quantity of money, which are implied in the second type of change, will lead to further changes which may counteract or offset the tendency created by the change in relative demand. This will be particularly true if a change in relative demand is accompanied by an absolute reduction in demand and if, at the same time, costs (i.e., the prices of

---

[92] This fact is partly realized by the authors who, however, seem to underestimate its importance, mainly because they think only of the effects of a change in the distribution of *income;* and while this is obviously the only factor which will affect *new savings*, the total supply of free capital depends even more on turnover or amortization of existing capital. Any change in that stock of existing capital, brought about by monetary causes, will, by means of the consequent redistribution of the command over resources, tend to affect the relative demand for producers' and consumers' goods. If the monetary causes have led to a destruction of capital, this change will necessarily be permanent. If they have led to the creation of additional capital goods, the effect on relative demand *may* be, at least to some extent, permanently to increase the relative demand for capital goods.

the original factors of production) are rigid. In this case, deflationary tendencies are likely to set in, which may more than counterbalance the effect of the changed relative demand. But, in spite of these further complications which seem likely to arise, the principle seems to me to be true, and to comprise even what seems to Messrs. Hansen and Tout a *reductio ad absurdum* of the argument, namely that a unilateral decrease in the demand for consumers' goods may lead to a lengthening of the structure of production. Although I fully admit that, because of the probable complications, this case is very unlikely to materialize, I do not think that it is entirely impractical. Would Messrs. Hansen and Tout deny that, e.g., increased hoarding on the part of a class of very small rentiers who reduced their consumption of agricultural products, might not lead, via the reduction of wages, first in agriculture and then generally, to an increase in the real quantity of labor corresponding to a constant amount of money invested in industry, and therefore of capital?

IX

The analysis of this and similar cases would help to bring out an important distinction which Messrs. Hansen and Tout tend to overlook: the distinction between the tendencies set up directly by a given monetary change, and the effects of the further monetary changes which may, and perhaps even probably will, but need not, be induced by this first change. A sharp dividing line is the more necessary here since the tendency in current discussions is either to take these secondary monetary changes for granted, without ever mentioning them, or to fail to demonstrate why, and under what conditions, they should follow the first change.

These considerations bring me back to the problem of the relation between the demand for consumers' goods and the prices of capital goods. I should not deny that there may be conditions where, e.g., the expectation of a general price fall has led to extensive hoarding, and where any change in this expectation may lead to such dishoarding of funds available for investment as to outbalance the initial effect of the increase in the demand for consumers' goods.[93] Nor is it inconceivable that a similar situation may prevail as regards bank lending. There can also be no doubt that, in connection with these secondary monetary complications, *general* price movements, apart from the changes in relative prices, will be of the greatest importance, and that anything which stops or reverses the general price movement may lead to induced monetary changes, the effect of which on the demand for consumers' goods, and producers' goods, may be stronger than the initial change in the quantity of money.

But one has to be careful not to fall into the error apparently made by Messrs. Hansen and Tout—that of assuming that, in all cases, where the prices of consumers' goods and producers' goods move in the same direction (e.g., upward), this may not be accompanied by changes in their relative height, which would produce exactly the same effect as if there were no general price movement. Their general proposition that changes in the relative prices of consumers' goods and producers' goods will not have the same effect when they are accompanied by a universal movement in the same direction as when they find expression in an absolute movement in different direction, is only true under the following assumptions: (1) that the expected general price movement is relatively great compared with the relative price changes; (2) that, at the same time, the general movement does not exceed the limits beyond which—as experience has shown at least in cases of considerable inflation—costs begin to move more rapidly than prices; (3) that money rates of interest do not adapt themselves to the expected rate of general price change.[94]

---

[93] Cf. "Stand und Zukunftsaufgaben der Konjunkturforschung," my contribution to the *Festschrift für Arthur Spiethoff*.

[94] It is a curious fact that the discussion of the supposedly different effect of changes in the relative demand which are due to changes in the supply of money leads the two authors to argue—in effect, if not explicitly, and on what

Further, it is necessary to be careful to make clear the special assumptions under which these further complications are likely to arise. The deflationary tendencies, which are assumed to exist in most of the reasoning of the kind discussed, are not a necessary consequence of any crisis and depression, but are probably due to resistances to the necessary readjustments, caused by rigidity of prices, the existence of long term contracts, etc., I am far from underrating the importance of these phenomena. What I am pleading for is only that, for analytical purposes, these tendencies should carefully be kept separate and not confused with one another. Only in this way can we hope ultimately to unravel the tangle of different forces at work during a depression, and to arrive at that detailed explanation of the depression which I cannot even attempt here. But to deny the existence of certain tendencies merely because they are likely to be counteracted by others, does not seem to me to be a promising procedure.

X

The objections raised by Messrs. Hansen and Tout to what they call my theses 7, 8, 9, and 10, are partly based on arguments

---

seems to me to be wrong grounds—what they had previously denied, namely that capital accumulated by means of "forced saving" will not be permanent. If it were true that when, after a change in the supply of money, "equilibrium is finally established, the relation (between the prices of consumers' goods and the prices of producers' goods) will be found unaltered unless the effects of the transition period have been such as to change permanently the time preference of the income receivers" (p. 143), then, no doubt, the greater part of the real capital created by means of forced saving would be lost. But I think it will be clear by now why I should be very reluctant to use this argument in defense of my position.

Messrs. Hansen and Tout think that such a permanent change in the time preference of the income receivers "is not unlikely, since an increase or decrease in money supply is likely to increase the real income of the community." This seems to show conclusively that what they have in mind is not the effect on the quantity and distribution of resources, but on individual time preferences.

which I have already discussed and partly introduce further complications which any program of practical policy has to face and which I admit I have not investigated sufficiently. But it is obviously impossible to develop my ideas further, in this connection, or to try to make good these deficiencies here.

There are only two more points upon which I wish to touch. The first is that the concept of neutral money was meant in the first place to be an instrument of theoretical analysis and not necessarily a tool of practical policy. Its purpose was to bring out clearly the conditions under which we could expect the economic process in a money economy to correspond perfectly to the picture drawn by the theory of equilibrium and, incidentally, to show what we should have to consider as the peculiar active effects caused by monetary changes. In a sense, of course, this would also set up an ideal of policy. But it is by no means inconceivable that considerations other than the direct monetary influences on prices, such as the existence of long term contracts in fixed sums of money, the rigidity of prices, and such like institutional factors, may make such an attempt entirely impracticable, because it would set up frictions of a new kind. In that case, the task of monetary policy would be to find a workable compromise between the different incompatible aims. But, in this case, one would have to be clear that certain important determining and disturbing influences arising from monetary causes would remain in existence, and that we should always have to remain conscious of this fact. Or, in other words, that even under the best practicable monetary system, the self-equilibrating mechanism of prices might be seriously disturbed by monetary causes.

The second point is that up to 1927, I should indeed have expected that—because during the preceding boom period prices did not rise but rather tended to fall—the subsequent depression would be very mild.

But, as is well known, in that year an entirely unprecedented action was taken by the American monetary authorities, which makes it impossible to compare the effects of the boom on the subsequent depression with any previous experience. The authorities succeeded, by means of an easy-money policy, inaugurated as soon as the symptoms of an impending reaction were noticed, in prolonging the boom for two years beyond what would otherwise have been its natural end. And when the crisis finally occurred, for almost two more years, deliberate attempts were made to prevent, by all conceivable means, the normal process of liquidation. It seems to me that these facts have had a far greater influence on the character of the depression than the developments up to 1927, which from all we know, might instead have led to a comparatively mild depression in and after 1927.

MONETARY NATIONALISM AND INTERNATIONAL STABILITY

Originally published by Longmans, Green in London, 1937; The Graduate Institute of International Studies, Publication no. 18, Geneva, 1937; reprinted by Augustus M. Kelley in New York, 1964 and 1971.

Preface

The five lectures which are here reproduced are necessarily confined to certain aspects of the wide subject indicated by the title. They are printed essentially as they were delivered and, as is explained in the first lecture, limitations of time made it necessary to choose between discussing the concrete problems of the present policy of monetary nationalism and concentrating on the broader theoretical issues on which the decision between an international standard and independent national currencies must ultimately be based. The first course would have involved a discussion of such technical questions as the operations of exchange equalization accounts, forward exchanges, the choice and adjustment of parities, cooperation between central banks, etc., etc. The reader will find little on these subjects in the following pages. It appeared to me more important to use the time available to discuss the general ideas which are mainly responsible for the rise of monetary nationalism and to which it is mainly due that policies and practices which not long ago would have been frowned upon by all responsible financial experts are now generally employed throughout the world. The immediate influence of the theoretical speculation is probably weak, but that it has had a profound influence in shaping those views which today dominate monetary policy is not open to serious question. It seemed to me better therefore to concentrate on these wider issues.

This decision has permitted me a certain freedom in the discussion of alternative policies. In discussing the merits of various systems I have not felt bound to confine myself to those which may today be considered practical politics. I have no doubt that to those who take the present trend of intellectual development for granted much of the discussion in the following pages will appear highly academic. Yet fundamentally the alternative policies here considered are no more revolutionary or impracticable than the deviations from traditional practice which have been widely discussed and which have even been attempted in recent years—except that at the moment not so many people believe in them. But while the politician—and the economist when he is advising on concrete measures—must take the state of opinion for granted in deciding what changes can be contemplated here and now, these limitations are not necessary when we are asking what is best for the human race in general. I am profoundly convinced that it is academic discussion of this sort which in the long run forms public opinion and which in consequence decides what will be practical politics some time hence. I regard it therefore not only as the privilege but as the duty of the academic economist to take all alternatives into consideration, however remote their realization may appear at the moment.

And indeed I must confess that it seems to me in many respects the future development of professional and public opinion on these matters is much more important than any concrete measure which may be taken in the near future. Whatever the permanent arrangements in monetary policy, the spirit in which the existing institutions are administered is at least as important as these institutions themselves. And just as, long before the breakdown of the international gold standard in 1931, monetary policy all over the world was guided by the ideas of monetary nationalism which eventually brought its breakdown, so at the present time there is grave danger that a restoration of the external apparatus of the gold standard may not mean a return to a really international currency. Indeed I must admit that—although I am a convinced believer in the international gold standard—I regard the prospects of its restoration in the near future not without some concern. Nothing would be more fatal from a long run point of view than if the world attempted a formal return to the gold standard before people had become willing to work it, and if, as would be quite probable under these circumstances, this were soon followed by a renewed collapse. And although this would probably be denied by the advocates of monetary nationalism, it seems to me as if we had reached a stage where their views have got such a hold on those in responsible positions, where so much of the traditional rules of policy have either been forgotten or been displaced by others which are, unconsciously perhaps, part of the new philosophy, that much must be done in the realm of ideas before we can hope to achieve the basis of a stable international system. These lectures were intended as a small contribution to this preparatory work which must precede a successful reconstruction of such a system.

It was my good fortune to be asked to deliver these lectures at the *Institut Universitaire de Hautes Etudes Internationales* in Geneva. I wish here to express my profound gratitude for the opportunity thus afforded and for the sympathetic and stimulating discussion which followed the lectures. My thanks are particularly due to the directors of the institute, Professors Rappard and Mantoux, not only for arranging the lectures but also for undertaking their publication in the present series.

I am also indebted to a number of my friends and colleagues at the London School of Economics, particularly to Dr. F. Benham, Mr. F. Paish, Professor Robbins, and Mr. G.H. Secord, who have read the manuscript and offered much valuable advice as regards the subject matter and the form of exposition of these lectures. This would certainly have been a much bigger and much better book if I had seen my way to adopt and incorporate all their suggestions. But at the moment I do not feel prepared to undertake the larger investigation which my friends rightly think the subject deserves. I alone must therefore bear the blame for the sketchy treatment of some important points and for any shortcomings which offend the reader.

I hope however it will be born in mind that these lectures were written to be read aloud and that this forbade any too extensive discussion of the more intricate theoretical points involved. Only at a few points have I, added a further explanatory paragraph or restored sections which would not fit into the time available for the lecture. That this will not suffice to provide satisfactory answers to the many questions I have raised I have no doubt.

F.A. von Hayek
London School of Economics and Political Science
May 1937

Lecture 1

National Monetary Systems

1. Theoretical Character of these Lectures

When I was honored with the invitation to deliver at the *Institut* five lectures "on some subject of distinctly international interest," I could have little doubt what that subject should be. In a field in which I am particularly interested I had been watching for years with increasing apprehension the steady growth of a doctrine which, if it becomes dominant, is likely to deal a fatal blow to the hopes of a revival of international economic relations. This doctrine, which in the title of these lectures I have described as monetary nationalism, is held by some of the most brilliant and influential economists of our time. It has been practiced in recent years to an ever-increasing extent, and in my opinion it is largely responsible for the particular intensification of the last depression, which was brought about by the successive breakdown of the different currency systems. It will almost certainly continue to gain influence for some time to come, and it will probably indefinitely postpone the restoration of a truly international currency system. Even if it does not prevent the restoration of an international gold standard, it will almost inevitably bring about its renewed breakdown soon after it has been re-established.

When I say this I do not mean to suggest that a restoration of the gold standard of the type we have known is necessarily desirable, nor that much of the criticism directed against it may not be justified. My complaint is rather that most of this criticism is not concerned with the true reasons why the gold standard, in the form in which we knew it, did not fulfill the functions for which it was designed; and further that the only alternatives which are seriously considered and discussed, completely abandon what seems to me the essentially sound principle—that of an international currency system—which that standard is supposed to embody.

But let me say at once that when I describe the doctrines I am going to criticize as monetary nationalism I do not mean to suggest that those who hold them are actuated by any sort of narrow nationalism. The very name of their leading exponent, Mr. J.M. Keynes, testifies that this is not the case. It is not the motives which inspire those who advocate such plans, but the consequences which I believe would follow from their realization, which I have in mind when I use this term. I have no doubt that the advocates of these doctrines sincerely believe that the system of independent national currencies will reduce rather than increase the causes of international economic friction; and that not merely one country but all will in the long run be better off if there is established that freedom in national monetary policies which is incompatible with a single international monetary system.

The difference then is not one about the ultimate ends to be achieved. Indeed, if it were, it would be useless to try to solve it by rational discussion. The fact is rather that there are genuine differences of opinion among economists about the consequences of the different types of monetary arrangements we shall have to consider, differences which prove that there must be inherent in the problem serious intellectual difficulties which have not yet been fully overcome. This means that any discussion of the issues involved will have to grapple with considerable technical difficulties, and that it will have to grapple with wide problems of general theory if it is to contribute anything to their solution. My aim throughout will be to throw some light on a very practical and topical problem. But I am afraid my way will have to lead for a considerable distance through the arid regions of abstract theory.

There is indeed another way in which I might have dealt with my subject. And when I realized how much purely theoretical argument the other involved I was strongly tempted to take it. It would have been to avoid any discussion of the underlying ideas and simply to take one of the many concrete proposals for independent national currency systems now prevalent and to consider its various probable effects. I have no doubt that in this form I could give my lectures a much more realistic appearance and could prove to the satisfaction of all who have already an unfavorable opinion of monetary nationalism that its effects are pernicious. But I am afraid I would have had little chance of convincing anyone who has already been attracted by the other side of the case. He might even admit all the disadvantages of the proposal which I could enumerate, and yet believe that its advantages outweigh the defects. Unless I can show that these supposed advantages are largely illusory, I shall not have got very far. But this involves an examination of the argument of the other side. So I have come rather reluctantly to the conclusion that I cannot shirk the much more laborious task of trying to go to the root of the theoretical differences.

2. Monetary Nationalism and National Monetary Systems

But it is time for me to define more exactly what I mean by monetary nationalism and its opposite, an international monetary system. By monetary nationalism I mean the doctrine that a country's share in the world's supply of money should *not be* left to be determined by the same principles and the same mechanism as those which determine the relative amounts of money in its different regions or localities. A truly international monetary system would be one where the whole world possessed a homogeneous currency such as obtains within separate countries and where its flow between regions was left to be determined by the results of the action of all individuals. I shall have to define later what exactly I mean by a homogeneous currency. But I should like to make it clear at the outset that I do not believe that the gold standard as we knew it conformed to that ideal and that I regard this as its main defect.

Now from this conception of monetary nationalism there at once arises a question. The monetary relations between small adjoining areas are alleged to differ from those between larger regions or countries; and this difference is supposed to justify or demand different monetary arrangements. We are at once led to ask what is the nature of this alleged difference? This question is somewhat connected but not identical with the question of what constitutes a national monetary system, in what sense we can speak of different monetary systems. But, as we shall see, it is very necessary to keep these questions apart. For if we do not, we shall be confused between differences which are inherent in the underlying situation and which may make different monetary arrangements desirable, and differences which are the consequence of the particular monetary arrangements which are actually in existence. For reasons which I shall presently explain, this distinction has not always been observed. This has led to much argument at cross-purposes, and it is therefore necessary to be rather pedantic about it.

3. A Homogeneous International Currency

I shall begin by considering a situation where there is as little difference as is conceivable between the money of different countries, a case indeed where there is so little difference that it becomes doubtful whether we can speak of different "systems." I shall assume two countries only, and I shall assume that in each of the two countries of which our world is assumed to consist, there is only one sort of widely used medium of exchange, namely coins consisting of the same metal. It is irrelevant for our purpose whether the denomination of these coins in the two countries is the same, so long as we assume, as we shall, that the two sorts of coins are freely and without cost interchangeable at the mints. It is clear that the mere difference in denomination, although it may mean an inconvenience, does not constitute a relevant difference in the currency systems of the two countries.[1]

In starting from this case we follow a long established precedent. A great part of the argument of the classical writers on money proceeded on this assumption of a "purely metallic currency." I wholly agree with these writers that for certain purposes it is a very useful assumption to make. I shall however not follow them in their practice of assuming that the conclusions arrived

---

[1] Since these lines were written a newly published book has come to my hand in which almost the whole argument in favor of monetary nationalism is based on the assumption that different national currencies are different commodities and that consequently there ought to be variable prices of them in terms of each other (C.R. Whittlesey, *International Monetary Issues* [New York: McGraw-Hill, 1937]). No attempt is made to explain why or under what conditions and in what sense the different national moneys ought to be regarded as different commodities, and one can hardly avoid the impression that the author has uncritically accepted the difference of denomination as proof of the existence of a difference in kind. The case illustrates beautifully the prevalent confusion about differences between the currency systems which can be made an argument for national differentiations and those which are a consequence of such differentiations. That it is "only a difference in nomenclature" (as Professor Gregory has well put it) whether we express a given quantity of gold as pounds, dollars, or marks, and that this no more constitutes different commodities than the same quantity of cloth becomes a different commodity when it is expressed in meters instead of in yards, ought to be obvious. Whether different national currencies are in any sense different commodities depends on what we make them, and the real problem is whether we should create differentiations between the national currencies by using in each national territory a kind of money which will be generally acceptable only within that territory, or whether the same money should be used in the different national territories.

from these assumptions can be applied immediately to the monetary systems actually in existence. This belief was due to their conviction that the existing mixed currency systems not only could and should be made to behave in every respect in the same way as a purely metallic currency, but that—at any rate in England since the Bank Act of 1844—the total quantity of money was *actually* made to behave in this way. I shall argue later that this erroneous belief is responsible for much confusion about the mechanism of the gold standard as it existed; that it has prevented us from achieving a satisfactory theory of the working of the modern mixed system, since the explanation of the role of the banking system was only imperfectly grafted upon, and never really integrated with, the theory of the purely metallic currency; and that in consequence the gold standard or the existence of an international system was blamed for much which in fact was really due to the mixed character of the system and not to its "internationalism" at all.

For my present purpose, however, namely to find whether and in what sense the monetary mechanism of one country can or must be regarded as a unit or a separate system, even when there is a minimum of difference between the kind of money used there and elsewhere, the case of the "purely metallic currency" serves extraordinarily well. If there are differences in the working of the national monetary systems which are not merely an effect of the differences in the monetary arrangements of different countries, but which make it desirable that there *should* be separate arrangements for different regions, they must manifest themselves even in this simplest case.

It is clear that in this case the argument for a national monetary system cannot rest on any peculiarities of the national money. It must rest, and indeed it does rest, on the assumption that there is a particularly close connection between the prices— and particularly the wages—within the country which causes them to move to a considerable degree up and down together compared with prices outside the country. This is frequently regarded as sufficient reason why, in order to avoid the necessity that the "country as a whole" should have to raise or lower its prices, the quantity of money in the country should be so adjusted as to keep the "general price level" within the country stable. I do not want to consider this argument yet. I shall later argue that it rests largely on an illusion, based on the accident that the statistical measures of prices movements are usually constructed for countries as such; and that insofar as there are genuine difficulties connected with general downward adjustments of many prices, and particularly wages, the proposed remedy would be worse than the disease. But I think I ought to say here and now that I regard it as the only argument on which the case for monetary nationalism can be rationally based. All the other arguments have really nothing to do with the existence of an international monetary system as such, but apply only to the particular sorts of international systems with which we are familiar. But since these arguments are so inextricably mixed up in current discussion with those of a more fundamental character it becomes necessary, before we can consider the main arguments on its merits, to consider them first.

4. The Mixed or National Reserve System

The homogeneous international monetary system which we have just considered was characterized by the fact that each unit of the circulating medium of each country could equally be used for payments in the other country and for this purpose could be bodily transferred into that other country and be bodily transformed into the currency of that country. Among the systems which need to be considered only an international gold standard with exclusive gold circulation in all countries would conform to this picture. This has never existed in its pure form, and the type of gold standard which existed until fairly recently was even further removed from this picture than was generally realized. It was never fully appreciated how much the operation of the system which actually existed diverged from the ideal pure gold standard. For the points of divergence were so familiar that they were usually taken for granted. It was the design of the Bank Act of 1844 to make the mixed system of gold and other money behave in such a way that the quantity of money would change exactly as if only gold were in circulation; and for a long time, argument proceeded as if this intention had actually been realized. And even when it was gradually realized that deposits subject to check were no less money than bank notes, and that since they were left out of the regulation, the purpose of the act had really been defeated, only a few modifications of the argument were thought necessary. Indeed in general this argument is still presented as it was originally constructed, on the assumption of a purely metallic currency.

In fact however with the coming of modern banks a complete change had occurred. There was no longer one homogeneous sort of money in each country, the different units of which could be regarded as equivalent for all relevant purposes. There had arisen a hierarchy of different kinds of money within each country, a complex organization which possessed a definite structure, and which is what we really mean when we speak of the circulating medium of a country as a "system." It is probably much truer to say that it is the difference between the different kinds of money which are used in any one country, rather than the differences between the moneys used in different countries, which constitutes the real difference between different monetary systems.

We can see this if we examine matters a little more closely. The gradual growth of banking habits, that is, the practice of keeping liquid assets in the form of bank balances subject to check, meant that increasing numbers of people were satisfied to hold a form of the circulating medium which could be used directly only for payments to people who banked with the same institution. For all payments beyond this circle they relied on the ability of the bank to convert the deposits on demand into another sort of money which was acceptable in wider circles; and for this purpose the banks had to keep a "reserve" of this more widely acceptable or more liquid medium.

But this distinction between bank deposits and "cash" in the narrower sense of the term does not yet exhaust the classification of different sorts of money, possessing different degrees of liquidity, which are actually used in a modern community. Indeed, this development would have made little difference if the banks themselves had not developed in a way which led to their organization into banking "systems" on national lines. Whether there existed only a system of comparatively small local unit banks, or whether there were numerous systems of branch banks which covered different areas freely overlapping and without respect to national boundaries, there would be no reason why all the monetary transactions within a country should be more closely knit together than those in different countries. For any excess payments outside their circle the customers of any single bank, it is true, would be dependent on the reserve kept for this purpose for them by their bank, and might therefore find that their individual position might be affected by what other members of this circle did. But at most the inhabitants of some small town would in this way become dependent on the same reserves and thereby on one another's action,[2] never all the inhabitants of a big area or a country.

It was only with the growth of centralized national banking systems that all the inhabitants of a country came in this sense to be dependent on the same amount of more liquid assets held for them collectively as a national reserve. But the concept of centralization in this connection must not be interpreted too narrowly as referring only to systems crowned by a central bank of the familiar type, nor even as confined to branch banking systems where each district of a country is served by the branches of the same few banks. The forms in which centralization, in the sense of a system of national reserves which is significant here,

---

[2] Compare on this and the following L. Robbins, *Economic Planning and International Order* (London: Macmillan, 1937), pp. 274 *et seq.*

may develop, are more varied than this and they are only partly due to deliberate legislative interference. They are partly due to less obvious institutional factors.

For even in the absence of a central bank and of branch banking, the fact that a country usually has one financial center where the stock exchange is located and through which a great proportion of its foreign trade passes or is financed tends to have the effect that the banks in that center become the holders of a large part of the reserve of all the other banks in the country. The proximity of the stock exchange puts them in a position to invest such reserves profitably in what, at any rate for any single bank, appears to be a highly liquid form. And the greater volume of transactions in foreign exchange in such a center makes it natural that the banks outside will rely on their town correspondents to provide them with whatever foreign money they may need in the course of their business. It was in this way that long before the creation of the Federal Reserve System in 1913, and in spite of the absence of branch banking, there developed in the United States a system of national reserves under which in effect all the banks throughout their territory relied largely on the same ultimate reserves. And a somewhat similar situation existed in Great Britain before the growth of joint stock banking.

But this tendency is considerably strengthened if instead of a system of small unit banks there are a few large joint stock banks with many branches; still more if the whole system is crowned by a single central bank, the holder of the ultimate cash reserve. This system, which today is universal, means in effect that additional distinctions of acceptability or liquidity have been artificially created between three main types of money, and that the task of keeping a sufficient part of the total assets in liquid form for different purposes has been divided between different subjects. The ordinary individual will hold only a sort of money which can be used directly only for payments to clients of the same bank; he relies upon the assumption that his bank will hold for all its clients a reserve which can be used for other payments.

The commercial banks in turn will only hold reserves of such more liquid or more widely acceptable sort of money as can be used for interbank payments within the country. But for the holding of reserves of the kind which can be used for payments abroad, or even those which are required if the public should want to convert a considerable part of its deposits into cash, the banks rely largely on the central bank.

This complex structure, which is often described as the one-reserve system, but which I should prefer to call the system of national reserves, is now taken so much for granted that we have almost forgotten to think about its consequences. Its effects on the mechanism of international flows of money will be one of the main subjects of my next lecture. Today I only want to stress two aspects which are often overlooked. In the first place I would emphasize that bank deposits could never have assumed their present predominant role among the different media of circulation, that the balances held on current account by banks could never have grown to ten times and more of their cash reserves, unless some organ, be it a privileged central bank or be it a number of or all the banks, had been put in a position to create in case of need a sufficient number of additional bank notes to satisfy any desire on the part of the public to convert a considerable part of their balances into hand-to-hand money. It is in this sense and in this sense only that the existence of a national reserve system involves the question of the regulation of the note issue, alone.

The second point is that nearly all the practical problems of banking policy, nearly all the questions with which a central banker is daily concerned, arise out of the coexistence of these different sorts of money within the national monetary system. Theoretical economists frequently argue as if the quantity of money in the country were a perfectly homogeneous magnitude and entirely subject to deliberate control by the central monetary authority. This assumption has been the source of much mutual misunderstanding on both sides. And it has had the effect that the fundamental dilemma of all central banking policy has hardly ever been really faced: the only effective means by which a central bank can control an expansion of the generally used media of circulation is by making it clear in advance that it will not provide the cash (in the narrower sense) which will be required in consequence of such expansion, but at the same time it is recognized as the paramount duty of a central bank to provide that cash once the expansion of bank deposits has actually occurred and the public begins to demand that they should be converted into notes or gold.

I shall be returning to this problem later. But in the next two lectures my main concern will be another set of problems. I shall argue that the existence of national reserve systems is the real source of most of the difficulties which are usually attributed to the existence of an international standard. I shall argue that these difficulties are really due to the fact that the mixed national currencies are not sufficiently international, and that most of the criticism directed against the gold standard *qua* international standard is misdirected. I shall try to show that the existence of national reserve systems alters the mechanism of the international money flows from what it would be with a homogeneous international currency to a much greater degree than is commonly realized.

5. Independent National Currencies

But before I can proceed to this major task I must shortly consider the third and most efficient cause which may differentiate the circulating media of different countries and constitute separate monetary systems. Up to this point I have only mentioned cases where the ratio between the monetary units used in the different countries was given and constant. In the first case this was secured by the fact that the money circulating in the different countries was assumed to be homogeneous in all essential respects, while in the second and more realistic case it was assumed that, although different kinds of money were used in the different countries, there was yet in operation an effective if somewhat complicated mechanism which made it always possible to convert at a constant rate money of the one country into money of the other. To complete the list there must be added the case where these ratios are variable: that is, where the rate of exchange between the two currencies is subject to fluctuations.

With monetary systems of this kind we have of course to deal with differences between the various sorts of money which are much bigger than any we have yet encountered. The possession of a quantity of money current in one country no longer gives command over a definite quantity of money which can be used in another country. There is no longer a mechanism which secures that an attempt to transfer money from country to country will lead to a decrease in the quantity of money in one country and a corresponding increase in the other. In fact an actual transfer of money from country to country becomes useless because what is money in the one country is not money in the other. We have here to deal with things which possess different degrees of usefulness for different purposes and the quantities of which are fixed independently.

Now I think it should be sufficiently clear that any differences between merely interlocal and international movements of money which only arise as a consequence of the variability of exchange rates cannot themselves be regarded as a justification for the existence of separate monetary systems. That would be to confuse effect and cause—to make the occasion of difference the justification of its perpetuation. But since the adoption of such a system of "flexible parities" is strongly advocated as a remedy for the difficulties which arise out of other differences which we have already considered, it will be expedient if in the following lectures I consider side by side all three types of conditions under which differences between the national monetary systems may arise. We shall be concerned with the way in which in each case redistributions of the relative amounts of money in the different countries are effected. I shall begin with the only case which can truly be described as an international monetary standard, that of a homogeneous international currency. Consideration of this case will help me to show what functions change in the relative quantities of money in different regions and countries may be conceived to serve; and how such changes are spontaneously brought about. I shall then proceed to the hybrid "mixed" system which until recently was the system generally in vogue and which is meant when, in current discussion, the traditional gold standard is referred to. As I said at the beginning, I shall not deny that this system has serious defects. But while the monetary nationalists believe that these defects are due to the fact that it is still an international system and propose to remove them by substituting the third or purely national type of monetary system for it, I shall on the contrary attempt to show that its defects lie in the impediments which it presents to the free international flow of funds. This will then lead me first to an examination of the peculiar theory of inflation and deflation on which monetary nationalism is based; then to an investigation of the consequences which we should have to expect if its proposals were acted upon; and finally to a consideration of the methods by which a more truly international system could be achieved.

LECTURE 2
The Function and Mechanism of International Flows of Money

1. The Functions of Redistributions of the World's Stock of Money

At the end of my first lecture I pointed out that the three different types of national monetary systems which we have been considering differed mainly in the method by which they effected international redistributions of money. In the case of a homogeneous international currency such a redistribution is effected by actual transfers of the corresponding amounts of money from country to country. Under the "mixed" system represented by the traditional gold standard—better called "gold nucleus standard"—it is brought about partly by an actual transfer of money from country to country, but largely by a contraction of the credit superstructure in the one country and a corresponding expansion in the other. But although the mechanism and, as we shall see, some of the effects, of these two methods are different, the final result, the change in the relative value of the total quantities of money in the different countries, is brought about by a corresponding change in the quantity of money, the number of money units, in each country. Under the third system, however, the system of independent currencies, things are different. Here the adjustment is brought about, not by a change in the number of money units in each country, but by changes in their relative value. No money actually passes from country to country, and whatever redistribution of money between persons may be involved by the redistribution between countries has to be brought about by corresponding changes inside each country.

Before, however, we can assess the merits of the different systems it is necessary to consider generally the different reasons why it may become necessary that the relative values of the total quantities of money in different countries should alter. It is clear that changes in the demand for or supply of the goods and services produced in an area may change the value of the share of the world's income which the inhabitants of that area may claim. But changes in the relative stock of money, although of course closely connected with these changes of the shares in the world's income which different countries can claim, are not identical with them. It is only because people whose money receipts fall will in general tend to reduce their money holdings also and *vice versa*, that changes in the size of the money stream in the different countries will as a rule be accompanied by changes in the same direction in the size of the money holdings. People who find their income increasing will generally at first take out part of the increased money income in the form of a permanent increase in their cash balances, while people whose incomes decrease will tend to postpone for a while a reduction of their expenditure to the full extent, preferring to reduce their cash balances.[3] To this extent changes in the cash balances serve, as it were, as cushions which soften the impact and delay the adaptation of the real incomes to the changed money incomes, so that in the interval, money is actually taken as a substitute for goods.

---

[3] For a full description of this mechanism cf. R.G. Hawtrey, *Currency and Credit*, 3rd ed. (New York: Longmans, Green, 1928), chap. 4, pp. 41–63.

But given existing habits, it is clear that changes in the relative size of money incomes—and the same applies to the total volume of money transactions—of different countries make corresponding changes in the money stocks of these countries inevitable; changes which, although they need not be in the same proportion, must at any rate be in the same direction as the changes in incomes. If the share in the world's production which the output of a country represents rises or falls, the share of the total which the inhabitants of the country can claim will fully adapt itself to the new situation only after money balances have been adjusted.[4]

Changes in the demand for money on the part of a particular country may of course also occur independently of any change in the value of the resources its inhabitants can command. They may be due to the fact that some circumstances may have made its people want to hold a larger or smaller proportion of their resources in the most liquid form, i.e., in money. If so, then for a time they will offer to the rest of the world more commodities, receiving money in exchange. This enables them, at any later date, to buy more commodities than they can currently sell. In effect they decide to lend to the rest of the world that amount of money's worth of commodities in order to be able to call it back whenever they want it.

2. The Mechanism under a System of Purely Metallic Currencies

The function which is performed by international movements of money will be seen more clearly if we proceed to consider such movement in the simplest case imaginable—a homogeneous international or "purely metallic" currency. Let us suppose that

---

[4] Perhaps, instead of speaking of the world's output, I should have spoken about the share in the command over the world's resources, since of course it is not only the current consumable product but equally the command over resources which will yield a product only in the future which is distributed by this monetary mechanism.

somebody who used to spend certain sums on products of country A now spends them on products of country B. The immediate effect of this is the same whether this person himself is domiciled in A or in B. In either case there will arise an excess of payments from A to B—an adverse balance of trade for A—either because the total of such payments has risen or because the amount of payments in the opposite direction has fallen off. And if the initiator of this change persists in his new spending habits, this flow of money will continue for some time.

But now we must notice that, because of this, in A somebody's money receipts have decreased, and in B somebody's money receipts have increased. We have long been familiar with the proposition that counteracting forces will in time bring the flow of money between the countries to a stop. But it is only quite recently that the exact circumstances determining the route by which this comes about have been satisfactorily established.[5] In both countries the change in the money receipts of the people first affected will be passed on and disseminated. But how long the outflow of money from A to B will continue depends on how long it takes before the successive changes in money incomes set up in each country will bring about new and opposite changes in the balance of payments.

This result can be brought about in two ways in each of the two countries. The reduction of money incomes in country A may lead to a decrease of purchases from B, or the consequent fall of the prices of some goods in A may lead to an increase of exports to B. And the increase of money incomes in country B may lead to an increase of purchases from A or to a rise in the prices of some commodities in B and a consequent decrease of exports to A. But how long it will take before in this way the flow

---

[5] Cf. particularly F.W. Paish, "Banking Policy and the Balance of International Payments" *Economica* n.s. 3, no. 2 (November 1936); K.F. Maier, *Goldwanderungen* (Jena: Gustav Fischer, 1936); and P.B. Whale, "The Working of the Pre-War Gold Standard," *Economica* 4, no. 13 (February 1937).

of money from A to B will be offset will depend on the number of links in the chains which ultimately lead back to the other country, and on the extent to which at each of these points the change of incomes leads first to a change in the cash balances held before it is passed on in full strength. In the interval, money will continue to flow from A to B; and the total which so moves will correspond exactly to the amounts by which, in the course of the process just described, cash balances have been depleted in the one country and increased in the other.

This part of the description is completely general. But we cannot say how many incomes will have to be changed, how many individual prices will have to be altered upward or downward in each of the two countries, in consequence of the initial changes. For this depends entirely on the concrete circumstances of each particular case. In some countries and under some conditions the route will be short because some of the first people whose incomes decrease cut down their expenditure on imported goods, or because the increase of incomes is soon spent on imported goods.[6] In other cases the route may be long, and external payments will be made to balance only after extensive price changes have occurred, which induce further people to change the direction of their expenditure.

The important point in all this is that what incomes and what prices will have to be altered in consequence of the initial change will depend on whether and to what extent the value of a particular factor or service, directly or indirectly, depends on the particular change in demand which has occurred, and not on whether it is inside or outside the same "currency area." We can see this more clearly if we picture the series of successive changes of money incomes, which will follow on the initial shift of demand, as single chains, neglecting for the moment the successive ramifications which will occur at every link. Such a chain may either

---

[6] Cf. on this particularly the article by F.W. Paish just quoted.

very soon lead to the other country or first run through a great many links at home. But whether any particular individual in the country will be affected will depend on whether he is a link in that particular chain, that is, whether he has more or less immediately been serving the individuals whose income has first been affected, and not simply on whether he is in the same country or not. In fact this picture of the chain makes it clear that it is not impossible that most of the people who ultimately suffer a decrease of income in consequence of the initial transfer of demand from A to B may be in B and not in A. This is often overlooked because the whole process is presented as if the chain of effects came to an end as soon as payments between the two countries balance. In fact however each of the two chains—that started by the decrease of somebody's income in A, and that started by the increase of another persons income in B—may continue to run on for a long time after they have passed into the other country, and may have even a greater number of links in that country than in the one where they started. They will come to an end only when they meet, not only in the same country but in the same individual, so finally offsetting each other. This means that the number of reductions of individual incomes and prices (not their aggregate amount) which becomes necessary in consequence of a transfer of money from A to B may actually be greater in B than in A.

This picture is of course highly unrealistic because it leaves out of account the infinite ramifications to which each of these chains of effects will develop. But even so it should, I think, make it clear how superficial and misleading the kind of argument is which runs in terms of *the* prices and *the* incomes of the country, as if they would necessarily move in unison or even in the same direction. It will be prices and incomes of particular individuals and particular industries which will be affected, and the effects will not be essentially different from those which will follow any shifts of demand between different industries or localities.

This whole question is of course the same as that which I discussed in my first lecture in connection with the problem of what constitutes one monetary system, namely the question of whether there exists a particularly close coherence between prices and incomes, and particularly wages, in any one country which tends to make them move as a whole relatively to the price structure outside. As I indicated then, I shall not be able to deal with it more completely until later on. But there are two points which I think will have become clear now and which are important for the understanding of the contrast between the working of the homogeneous international currency we are considering and the mixed system to which I shall presently proceed.

In the first place it already appears very doubtful whether there is any sense in which the terms inflation and deflation can be appropriately applied to these interregional or international transfers of money. If, of course, we *define* inflation and deflation as changes in the quantity of money, or the price level, *within a particular territory*, then the term naturally applies. But it is by no means clear that the consequences which we can show will follow if the quantity of money in a closed system changes will also apply to such redistributions of money between areas. In particular there is no reason why the changes in the quantity of money within an area should bring about those merely temporary changes in relative prices which, in the case of a real inflation, lead to misdirections of production—misdirections because eventually the inherent mechanism of these inflations tends to reverse these changes in relative prices. Nor does there seem to exist any reason why, to use a more modern yet already obsolete terminology, saving and investment should be made to be equal within any particular area which is part of a larger economic system.[7] But all these questions can be really answered only when I come to discuss the two conflicting views about the main significance of inflation and deflation which underlie most of the current disputes about monetary policy.

---

[7] Cf. J.M. Keynes, *A Treatise on Money* (London: Macmillan, 1930), vol. 1, chap. 4.

The second point which I want particularly to stress here is that with a homogeneous international currency there is apparently no reason why an outflow of money from one area and an inflow into another should necessarily cause a rise in the rate of interest in the first area and a fall in the second. So far I have not mentioned the rate of interest, because there seems to be no general ground why we should expect that the causes which lead to the money flows between two countries should affect the rate of interest one way or the other. Whether they will have such an effect and in what direction will depend entirely on the concrete circumstances. If the initial change which reduces the money income of some people in one country leads to an immediate reduction of their expenditure on consumers' goods, and if in addition they use for additional investments the surplus of their cash balances which they no longer regard worth keeping, it is not impossible that the effect may actually be a fall in the rate of interest.[8] And, conversely, in the country toward whose product an additional money stream is directed, this might very well lead to a rise in the rate of interest. It seems that we have been led to regard what happens to be the rule under the existing mixed systems as due to causes much more fundamental than those which

---

[8] Although it is even conceivable that a fall in incomes might bring about a temporary rise in investments, because the people who are now poorer feel that they can no longer afford the luxury of the larger cash balances they used to keep before, and proceed to invest part of them, this is neither a very probable effect nor likely to be quantitatively significant. Much more important, however, may be the effect of the fall of incomes on the demand for investment. Particularly if the greater part of the existing capital equipment is of a very durable character a fall in incomes may for some time almost completely suspend the need for investment and in this way reduce the rate of interest in the country quite considerably. Another case where the same cause which would lead to a flow of money from one country to another would at the same time cause a fall in the rate of interest in the first would be if in one of several countries where population used to increase at the same rate, this rate were considerably decreased.

actually operate. But this leads me to the most important difference between the case of a "purely metallic" and that of a "mixed" currency. To the latter case, therefore, I now turn.

3. The Mechanism under a Regime of Mixed Currencies

If in the two countries concerned there are two separate banking systems, whether these banking systems are complete with a central bank or not, considerable transfers of money from the one country to the other will be effected by the actual transmission of only a part of the total, the further adjustment being brought about by an expansion or contraction of the credit structure according as circumstances demand. It is commonly believed that nothing fundamentally is changed but something is saved by substituting the extinction of money in one region and the creation of new money in the other for the actual transfer of money from individual to individual. This is however a view which can be held only on the most mechanistic form of the quantity theory and which completely disregards the fact that the incidence of the change will be very different in the two cases. Considering the methods available to the banking system to bring about an expansion or contraction, there is no reason to assume that they can take the money to be extinguished exactly from those persons where it would in the course of time be released if there were no banking system, or that they will place the additional money in the hands of those who would absorb the money if it came to the country by direct transfer from abroad. There are on the contrary strong grounds for believing that the burden of the change will fall entirely, or to an extent which is in no way justified by the underlying change in the real situation, on investment activity in both countries.

To see why and how this will happen it is necessary to consider in some detail the actual organization of the banking systems and the nature of their traditional policies. We have seen that where bank deposits are used extensively this means that all those who hold their most liquid assets in this form rely on their banks to provide them whenever needed with the kind of money which is acceptable outside the circle of the clients of the bank. The banks in turn, and largely because they have learned to rely on the assistance of other (note issuing) banks, particularly the central bank, have come themselves to keep only very slender cash reserves, that is, reserves which they can use to meet any adverse clearing balance to other banks or to make payments abroad. These are indeed not meant to do more than to tide over any temporary and relatively small difference between payments and receipts. They are altogether insufficient to allow the banks ever to reduce these reserves by the full amount of any considerable reduction of their deposits. The very system of proportional reserves, which so far as deposits are concerned is today universally adopted and even in the case of bank notes applies practically everywhere outside Great Britain, means that the cash required for the conversion of an appreciable part of the deposits has to be raised by compelling people to repay loans.

We shall best see the significance of such a banking structure with respect to international money flows if we consider again the effects which are caused by an initial transfer of demand from country A to country B. The main point here is that, with a national banking system working on the proportional reserve principle, unless the adverse balance of payments corrects itself very rapidly, the central bank will not be in a position to let the outflow of money go on until it comes to its natural end. It cannot, without endangering its reserve position, freely convert all the bank deposits or banknotes which will be released by individuals into money which can be transferred into the other countries. If it wants to prevent an exhaustion or dangerous depletion of its reserves it has to speed up the process by which payments from A to B will be decreased or payments from B to A will be increased. And the only way in which it can do this quickly and effectively is generally and indiscriminately to bring pressure on those who have borrowed from it to repay their loans. In this way it will set up additional chains of successive reductions of outlay, first on the part of those to whom it would have lent and then on the part of all others to whom this money would gradually have passed. So that leaving aside for the moment the effects which a rise in interest rates will have on international movements of short-term capital we can see that the forces which earlier or later will reduce payments abroad and, by reducing prices of home products, stimulate purchases from abroad will be intensified. And if sufficient pressure is exercised in this way, the period during which the outflow of money continues, and thereby the total amount of money that will actually leave the country before payments in and out will balance again, may be reduced to almost any extent.

The important point, however, is that in this case the people who will have to reduce their expenditure in order to produce that result will not necessarily be the same people who would ultimately have to do so under a homogeneous international currency system, and that the equilibrium so reached will of its nature be only temporary. In particular, since bank loans, to any significant extent, are only made for investment purposes, it will mean that the full force of the reduction of the money stream will have to fall on investment activity. This is shown clearly by the method by which this restriction is brought about. We have seen before that under a purely metallic currency an outflow of money need not actually bring about a rise in interest rates. It may, but this is not necessary and it is even conceivable that the opposite will happen. But with a banking structure organized on national lines, that is, under a national reserve system, it is inevitable that it will bring a rise in interest rates, irrespective of whether the underlying real change has affected either the profitability of investment or the rate of savings in such a way as to justify such a change. In other words, to use an expression which has given rise to much dispute in the recent past but which should be readily understood in this connection, the rise of the bank rate under such circumstances means that it has to be deliberately raised above the equilibrium or "natural" rate of interest.[9] The reason for this is not, or need not be, that the initiating change has affected the relation between the supply of investable funds and the demand for them, but that it tends to disturb the customary proportion between the different parts of the credit structure and that the only way to restore these proportions is to cancel loans made for investment purposes.

To some extent, but only to some extent, the credit contraction will, as I have just said, by lowering prices induce additional payments from abroad and in this form offset the outflow of money. But to a considerable extent its effect will be that certain international transfers of money which would have taken the place of a transfer of goods and would in this sense have been a final payment for a temporary excess of imports will be intercepted, so that consequently actual transfers of goods will have to take place. The transfer of only a fraction of the amount of money which would have been transferred under a purely metallic system, and the substitution of a multiple credit contraction for the rest, as it were, deprives the individuals in the country concerned of the possibility of delaying the adaptation by temporarily paying for an excess of imports in cash.

That the rise of the rate of interest in the country that is losing gold, and the corresponding reduction in the bank rate in the country which is receiving gold, need have nothing to do with changes in the demand for or the supply of capital appears also from the fact that, if no further change intervenes, the new rates will have to be kept in force only for a comparatively short

---

[9] This has been rightly pointed out, but has hardly been sufficiently explained, in an interesting article by J.C. Gilbert on "The Present Position of the Theory of International Trade," *The Review of Economic Studies* 3, no. 1 (October 1935), particularly pp. 23–26. To say that money rates of interest in a particular country may be made to deviate from the equilibrium rate by monetary factors peculiar to that country is of course not to say that the equilibrium rate in that country is independent of international conditions.

period, and that after a while a return to the old rates will be possible. The changes in the rates serve the temporary purpose of speeding up a process which is already under way. But the forces which would have brought the flow of gold to an end earlier or later in any case do not therefore cease to operate. The chain of successive reductions of income in country A set up by the initiating changes will continue to operate and ultimately reduce the payments out of the country still further. But since payments in and payments out have in the meantime already been made to balance by the action of the banks, this will actually reverse the flow and bring about a favorable balance of payments. The banks, wanting to replenish their reserves, may let this go on for a while, but once they have restored their reserves, they will be able to resume at least the greater part of their lending activity which they had to curtail.

This picture is admittedly incomplete because I have been deliberately neglecting the part played by short-term capital movements. I shall discuss these in my fourth lecture. At present my task merely is to show how the existence of national banking systems, based on the collective holding of national cash reserves, alters the effects of international flows of money. It seems to me impossible to doubt that there is indeed a very considerable difference between the case where a country, whose inhabitants are induced to decrease their share in the world's stock of money by ten percent, does so by actually giving up this ten percent in gold, and the case where, in order to preserve the accustomed reserve proportions, it pays out only one percent in gold and contracts the credit superstructure in proportion to the reduction of reserves. It is as if all balances of international payments had to be squeezed through a narrow bottleneck as special pressure has to be brought on people who would otherwise not have been affected by the change to give up money which they would have invested productively.

Now the changes in productive activity which are made necessary in this way are not of a permanent nature. This means not only that in the first instance many plans will be upset, that equipment which has been created will cease to be useful and that people will be thrown out of employment. It also means that the revised plans which will be made are bound soon to be equally disappointed in the reverse direction and that the readjustment of production which has been enforced will prove to be a misdirection. In other words, it is a disturbance which possesses all the characteristics of a purely monetary disturbance, namely that it is self-reversing in the sense that it induces changes which will have to be reversed because they are not based on any corresponding change in the underlying real facts.

It might perhaps be argued that the contraction of credit in the one country and the expansion in the other brings about exactly the same effects that we should expect from a transfer of a corresponding amount of capital from the one country to the other, and that since the amount of money which would otherwise have to be transferred would represent so much capital, there can be no harm in the changes in the credit structure. But the point is exactly that not every movement of money is in this sense a transfer of capital. If a group of people want to hold more money because the value of their income rises, while another group of people reduce their money holdings because the value of their income falls, there is no reason why in consequence the funds available for investment in the first group should increase and those available in the second group should decrease. It is, on the other hand, quite possible that the demand for such funds in the first group will rise and in the second group will fall. In such a case, as we have seen, there would be more reason to expect that the rate of interest will rise in the country to which the money flows rather than in the country from which the money comes.

The case is of course different when the initiating cause is not a shift in demand from one kind of consumers' goods to another kind of consumers' goods, but when funds which have been invested in one type of producers' goods in one country are transferred to investment in another type of producers' goods in another country. Then indeed we have a true movement of capital and we should be entitled to expect it to affect interest rates in the usual manner. What I am insisting on is merely that this need not be the general rule and that the fact that it is generally the case is not the effect of an inherent necessity but due to purely institutional reasons.

4. The Role of Central Bank Policy

There are one or two further points which I must shortly mention before I can conclude this subject. One is the rather obvious point that the disturbing effects of the organization of the world's monetary system on the national reserve principle are of course considerably increased when the rate of multiple expansion or contraction, which will be caused by a given increase or decrease of gold, is different in different countries. If this is the case, and it has of course always been the case under the gold standard as we knew it, it means that every flow of gold from one country to another will mean either an inflation or a deflation from the world point of view, accordingly as the rate of secondary expansion is greater or smaller in the country receiving gold than in the country losing gold.

The second point is one on which I am particularly anxious not to be misunderstood. The defects of the mixed system which I have pointed out are not defects of a particular kind of policy, or of special rules of central bank practice. They are defects inherent in the system of the collective holding of proportional cash reserves for national areas, whatever the policy adopted by the central bank or the banking system. What I have said provides in particular no justification for the common infringements of the "rules of the game of the gold standard," except, perhaps, for a certain reluctance to change the discount rate too frequently or too rapidly when gold movements set in. But all the attempts to substitute other measures for changes in the discount rate as a means to "protect reserves" do not help, because it is the necessity of "protecting" reserves rather than letting them go (i.e., using the conversion into gold as the proper method of reducing internal circulation), not the methods by which it has to be done, which is the evil. The only real cure would be if the reserves kept were large enough to allow them to vary by the full amount by which the total circulation of the country might possibly change; that is, if the principle of Peel's Act of 1844 could be applied to all forms of money, including in particular bank deposits. I shall come back to this point in my last lecture. What I want to stress, however, is that in the years before the breakdown of the international gold standard the attempts to make the supply of money of individual countries independent of international gold movements had already gone so far that not only had an outflow or inflow of gold often no effect on the internal circulation but that sometimes the latter moved actually in the opposite direction. To "offset" gold movements, as was apparently done by the Bank of England,[10] by replacing the gold lost by the central bank by securities bought from the market, is of course not to correct the defects of the mixed system, but to make the international standard altogether ineffective.

One should probably say much more on this subject. But I am afraid I must conclude here. I hope that what I have said today has at least made one point clear which I made yesterday; namely that many objections which are raised against the gold standard as we knew it, are not really objections against the gold standard, or against any international standard as such, but objections against the mixed system which has been in general vogue. It should be clear too that the main defect of this system was that it was not sufficiently international. Whether and how these defects can be remedied I can consider only at the end of this course. But before I can do this I shall yet have to consider the more completely nationalist systems which have been proposed.

---

[10] Cf. *Minutes of Evidence taken before the Committee on Finance and Industry* (London, 1931), vol. 1, Q. 363. Sir Ernest Harvey: "You will find if you look at a succession of Bank Returns that the amount of gold we have lost has been almost entirely replaced by an increase in the Bank's securities."

Lecture 3

Independent Currencies

1. National Stabilization and International Shifts of Demand

When the rates of exchange between currencies of different countries are variable, the consequences which will follow from changes which under an international system would lead to flows of money from country to country, will depend on the monetary policies adopted by the countries concerned. It is therefore necessary, before we can say anything about those effects, to consider the aims which will presumably guide the monetary policy of countries which have adopted an independent standard. This raises immediately the question whether there is any justification for applying any one of the principles according to which we might think that the circulation in a closed system should be regulated, to a particular country or region which is part of the world economic system.

Now it should be evident that a policy of stabilization, whether it be of the general price level or the general level of money incomes, is one thing if it is applied to the whole of a closed system and quite another if the same policy is applied to each of the separate regions into which the total system can be more or less arbitrarily divided. In fact, however, this difficulty is generally ignored by the advocates of monetary nationalism, and it is simply assumed that the criteria of a good monetary policy which are applicable to a closed system are equally valid for a single country. We shall have to consider later the theoretical problems here involved. But for the moment we can confine ourselves to an examination of the working of the mechanism which brings about relative changes in the value of the total money holdings of the different nations when each nation follows independently the objective of stabilizing its national price level, or income stream, or whatever it may be, irrespective of its position in the international system.

The case which has figured most prominently in these discussions in recent years, and which is apparently supposed to represent the relative positions of England and the United States, is that of two countries with unequal rates of technological progress, so that, in the one, costs of production will tend to fall more rapidly than in the other. Under a regime of fixed parities this would mean that the fall in the prices of some products produced in both countries could be faster than the fall in their cost in the country where technological progress is slower, and that in consequence it would become necessary to reduce costs there by scaling down money wages, etc. The main advantage of a system of movable parities is supposed to be that in such a case the downward adjustment of wages could be avoided and equilibrium restored by reducing the value of money in the one country relative to the other country.

It is, however, particularly important in this connection not to be misled by the fact that this argument is generally expressed in terms of averages, that is, in terms of general levels of prices and wages. A change in the level of prices or of costs in one country relatively to that of another means that, in consequence of changes in relative costs, the competitive position of a particular industry or perhaps group of industries in the one country has deteriorated. In other words, the lower prices in the one country will lead to a transfer of demand from the other country to it. The case is therefore essentially similar to that which we have been considering in the last lecture, and it will be useful to discuss it in the same terms. We shall therefore in the first instance again consider the effects of a simple shift of demand if rates of exchange are allowed to vary and if the monetary authorities in each country aim either at stability of some national price level, or—what amounts very much to the same thing for our purpose—at a constant volume of the effective money stream within the country. Only occasionally, where significant differences arise, I shall specially refer to the case where the shift of demand has been induced by unequal technological progress.

Now of course no monetary policy can prevent the prices of the product immediately affected from falling relatively to the prices of other goods in the one country, and a corresponding rise taking place in the other.[11] Nor can it prevent the effects of the change of the income of the people affected in the first instance from gradually spreading. All it can do is to prevent this from leading to a change in the *total* money stream in the country; that is, it must see that there will be offsetting changes of other prices so that the price level remains constant. It is on this assumption that we conduct our investigations. For purposes of simplicity, too, I assume that at the outset a state of full employment prevails.

2. The Position in the Country Adversely Affected

It will be convenient to concentrate first on the country from which demand has turned away and from which under an international monetary system there would in consequence occur an outflow of money. But in the present case not only would a real outflow of money be impossible, but it would also be contrary to the intentions of the monetary authorities to sell additional quantities

---

[11] Where the shift of demand has been induced by a reduction of cost and a consequent fall of prices in the one country, this will only be a relative rise and will of course only partly counteract this fall in the price of the final product, but may bring about an actual rise in the prices of the factors used in their production.

of foreign exchange against national money and to cancel the national money so received. The monetary authorities might hold some reserves of foreign exchange to even out what they regarded as merely temporary fluctuations of exchange rates. But there would be no point in using them in the case of a change which they would have to regard as permanent. We can, therefore, overlook the existence of such reserves and proceed as if only current receipts from abroad were available for outward payments.

On this assumption it is clear that the immediate effect of the adverse balance of payments will be that foreign exchange rates will rise. But the full amount that importers used to spend on buying foreign exchange is not likely to be spent on the reduced supply of foreign exchange; since with the higher price of imported goods some of the money which used to be spent on them will probably be diverted to home substitutes.[12] The foreign exchanges will therefore probably rise less than in proportion to the fall in supply. But *via* the sale of foreign exchange at the higher rate those who continue to export successfully will receive greater amounts of the national currency. For those whose sales abroad have not been unfavorably affected by the initial change in question this will mean a net gain, and the price of their products will correspondingly rise in terms of the national currency. And those whose exports have fallen in price will find that this reduced price in terms of the foreign currency will now correspond to a somewhat greater amount in the national currency than what they could obtain before the exchange depreciation, although not as much as they received before the first change took place.

This impact effect of the rise of exchange rates on relative prices in terms of the national currency will however be temporary.

---

[12] The assumption that the demand for the commodities in question is elastic, that is, that the total expenditure upon them will be reduced when their prices rise and *vice versa*, will be maintained throughout this discussion. To take at every step the opposite case into account would unduly lengthen the argument without affecting the conclusion.

The relative costs of the different quantities of the different commodities which are being produced have not changed, and it is not likely that they will go on being produced in these quantities if their prices have changed. Moreover all the changes in the direction of the money streams caused by the rise in exchange rates will continue to work. More is being spent on home goods, and this, together with the increased profitability of those export industries which have not been adversely affected by the initial change, will tend to bring about a rise of all prices except those which are affected by the decreased demand from the declining industry and from the people who draw their income from it.

It seems therefore that the argument in favor of depreciation in such cases is based on a too simplified picture of the working of the price mechanism. In particular it seems to be based on the assumption (underlying much of the classical analysis of these problems) that relative prices within each country are uniquely determined by (constant) relative cost. If this were so, a proportional reduction of all prices in a country relatively to those in the rest of the world would indeed be sufficient to restore equilibrium. In fact, however, there can be little doubt that the changes in the relative quantities of goods to be produced by the different industries which will become necessary in consequence of the initial change, can be brought about only by changes in the relative prices and the relative incomes of the different kinds of resources within the country.

Without following the effects in all their complicated detail it must be clear that the ultimate result of depreciation can only be that, instead of prices and incomes in the industry originally affected falling to the full extent, a great many other prices and incomes will have to rise to restore the proportions appropriate to cost conditions and the relative volume of output now required. Even disregarding the absolute height of prices, the final positions will not be the same as that which would have been reached if exchanges had been kept fixed; because in the course of the different process of transition all sorts of individual profits and losses will have been made which will affect that final position. But roughly speaking and disregarding certain minor differences, it can be said that the same change in relative prices which, under fixed exchanges, would have been brought about by a reduction of prices in the industry immediately affected is now being brought about largely by a corresponding rise of all other prices.

Two points, however, need special mention. One is that the decrease of the comparative advantage of the export industry originally affected cannot be changed in this way; and that to this extent a contraction of the output of this industry will remain unavoidable. The other is that, at least in certain respects, the process which brings about the rise in prices will be of a definitely inflationary character. This will show itself partly by some industries becoming *temporarily* more profitable so that there will be an inducement to expand production there, although this increase will soon be checked and even reversed by a rise in cost; and partly by some of the cash released by importers finding its way, *via* the repayment of loans, to the banks, who will be able to increase their loans to others and, in order to find lenders, will relax the terms on which they will be ready to lend. But this too will prove a merely temporary effect, since as soon as costs begin generally to rise it will become apparent that there are really no funds available to finance additional investments. In this sense the effects of this redistribution of money will be of that self-reversing character which is typical of monetary disturbances. This leads, however, already to the difficult question of what constitutes an inflation or deflation within a national area. But before we can go on to this it is necessary to consider what happens in the converse case of the country which has been put in a more favorable condition by the change.

3. The Position in the Country Favorably Affected

Let us first assume that the monetary authorities here as in the other country aim at a constant price level and a constant income stream. The industry which directly benefits from the initial shifts in demand will then find that, because of the fall of foreign exchanges, the increase of their receipts in terms of the national currency will not be as large as would correspond to the increase of their sales in terms of foreign money, while the other export industries will see their receipts actually reduced. Similarly those home industries whose products compete with imports which are now cheaper in terms of the national currency will have to lower their prices and will find their incomes reduced. In short, if the quantity of money in the country, or the price level, is kept constant, the increase of the aggregate value of the products of one industry due to a change in international demand will mean that there has to be a compensating reduction of the prices of the products of other industries. Or, in other words, part of the price reduction which under a regime of stable exchanges would have been necessary in the industry and in the country from which demand has turned away, will under a regime of independent currencies and national stabilization have to take place in the country toward which demand has turned, and in industries which have not been directly affected by the shift in demand.

This at least should be the case if the principle of national stabilization were consistently applied. But it is of course highly unlikely that it ever would be so applied. That in order to counteract the effects of a severe fall of prices in one industry in a country other prices in the country should be allowed to rise, appears fairly plausible. But that in order to offset a rise of prices of the products of one industry which is due to an increase in international demand, prices in the other industries should be made to fall sounds far less convincing. I find it difficult to imagine the president of a central bank explaining that he has to pursue a policy which means that the prices of many home industries have to be reduced, by pointing out that an increase of international demand has led to an increase of prices in an important export industry, and it seems fairly certain what would happen to him if he tried to do so.

Indeed, if we take a somewhat more realistic point of view, there can be little doubt what will happen. While, in the country where in consequence of the changes in international demand some prices will tend to fall the price level will be kept stable, it will certainly be allowed to rise in the country which has been benefited by the same shift in demand. It is not difficult to see what this implies if all countries in the world act on this principle. It means that prices would be stabilized only in that area where they tend to fall lowest relatively to the rest of the world, and that all further adjustments are brought about by proportionate increases of prices in all other countries. The possibilities of inflation which this offers if the world is split up into a sufficient number of very small separate currency areas seem indeed very considerable. And why, if this principle is once adopted, should it remain confined to average prices in particular national areas? Would it not be equally justified to argue that no price of any single commodity should ever be allowed to fall and that the quantity of money in the world should be so regulated that the price of that commodity which tends to fall lowest relatively to all others should be kept stable, and that the prices of all other commodities would be adjusted upwards in proportion? We only need to remember what happened, for instance, a few years ago to the price of rubber to see how such a policy would surpass the wishes of even the wildest inflationist. Perhaps this may be thought an extreme case. But, once the principle has been adopted, it is difficult to see how it could be confined to "reasonable" limits, or indeed to say what "reasonable" limits are.

4. Causes of the Recent Growth of Monetary Nationalism

But let us disregard the practical improbability that a policy of stabilization will be followed in the countries where, with stable exchanges, the price level would rise, as well as in the countries where in this case it would have to fall. Let us assume that, in the countries which benefit from the increase of the demand, the prices of other goods are actually lowered to preserve stability of the national price level and that the opposite action will be taken in the countries from which demand has turned away. What is the justification and significance of such a policy of national stabilization?

Now it is difficult to find the theoretical case for national stabilization anywhere explicitly argued. It is usually just taken for granted that any sort of policy which appears desirable in a closed system must be equally beneficial if applied to a national area. It may therefore be desirable before we go on to examine its analytical justification, to trace the historical causes which have brought this view to prominence. There can be little doubt that its ascendancy is closely connected with the peculiar difficulties of English monetary policy between 1925 and 1931. In the comparatively short space of the six years during which Great Britain was on a gold standard in the post war period, it suffered from what is known as overvaluation of the pound. Against all the teaching of "orthodox" economics—already a hundred years before Ricardo had expressly stated that he "should never advise a government to restore a currency, which was depreciated 30 p.c., to par"[13]—in 1925 the British currency had been brought back to its former gold value. In consequence, to restore equilibrium, it was necessary to reduce *all* prices and costs in proportion as the value of the pound had been raised. This process, particularly because of the notorious difficulty of reducing money wages, proved to be very painful and prolonged. It deprived England of real participation in the boom which led up to the crisis of 1929, and, in the end, its results proved insufficient to secure the maintenance of the restored parity. But all this was not due to an initial shift in the conditions of demand or to any of the

---

[13] In a letter to John Wheatley, dated September 18, 1821, reprinted in *Letters of David Ricardo to Hutches Trower and Others*, ed. J. Bonar and J. Hollander (Oxford: Clarendon Press, 1899), p. 160.

causes which may affect the condition of a particular country under stable exchanges. It was an *effect* of the change in the external value of the pound. It was not a case where with given exchange rates the national price or cost structure of a country as a whole had got out of equilibrium with the rest of the world, but rather that the change in the parities had suddenly upset the relations between all prices inside and outside the country.

Nevertheless this experience has created among many British economists a curious preoccupation with the relations between national price and cost and particularly wage levels, as if there were any reason to expect that as a rule there would arise a necessity that the price and cost structure of one country as a whole should change relatively to that of other countries. And this tendency has received considerable support from the fashionable pseudo-quantitative economics of averages with its argument running in terms of national "price levels," "purchasing power parities," "terms of trade," the "multiplier," and what not.

The purely accidental fact that these averages are generally computed for prices in a national area is regarded as evidence that in some sense all prices of a country could be said to move together relatively to prices in other countries.[14] This has strengthened the belief that there is some peculiar difficulty about the case where "the" price level of a country had to be changed relatively to its given cost level and that such adjustment had better be avoided by manipulations of the rate of exchange.

---

[14] The fact that the averages of (more or less arbitrarily selected) groups of prices move differently in different countries does of course in no way prove that there is any tendency of the price structure of a country to move as a whole relatively to prices in other countries. It would however be a highly interesting subject for statistical investigation, if a suitable technique could be devised, to see whether, and to what extent, such a tendency existed. Such an investigation would of course involve a comparison not only of some mean value of the price changes in different countries, but of the whole frequency distribution of relative price changes in terms of some common standard. And it should be supplemented by similar investigations of the relative movements of the price structure of different parts of the same country.

Now let me add immediately that of course I do not want to deny that there may be cases where some change in conditions might make fairly extensive reductions of money wages necessary in a particular area if exchange rates are to be maintained, and that under present conditions such wage reductions are at best a very painful and long drawn out process. At any rate in the case of countries whose exports consist largely of one or a few raw materials, a severe fall in the prices of these products might create such a situation. What I want to suggest, however, is that many of my English colleagues, because of the special experience of their country in recent times, have got the practical significance of this particular case altogether out of perspective: that they are mistaken in believing that by altering parities they can overcome many of the chief difficulties created by the rigidity of wages and, in particular, that by their fascination with the relation between "the" price level and "the" cost level in a particular area they are apt to overlook the much more important consequences of inflation and deflation.[15]

5. The Significance of the Concepts of Inflation and Deflation Applied to a National Area

As I have already suggested at an earlier point, the difference of opinion here rests largely on a difference of view on the meaning and consequence of inflation and deflation, or rather in the importance attached to two sorts of effects which spring from changes in the quantity of money. The one view stresses

---

[15] The propensity of economists in the Anglo-Saxon countries to argue exclusively in terms of national price and wage levels is probably mainly due to the great influence which the writings of Professor Irving Fisher have exercised in these countries. Another typical instance of the dangers of this approach is the well-known controversy about the reparations problem, where it was left to Professor Ohlin to point out against his English opponents that what mainly mattered were not so much effects on total price levels but rather the effects on the position of particular industries.

what I have called before the self-reversing character of the effects of monetary changes. It emphasizes the misdirection of production caused by the wrong expectations created by changes in relative prices which are necessarily only temporary, of which the most conspicuous is of course the trade cycle. The other view emphasizes the effects which are due to the rigidity of certain money prices, and particularly wages. Now the difficulties which arise when money wages have to be lowered cannot really be called monetary disturbances; the same difficulties would arise if wages were fixed in terms of some commodity. It is only a monetary problem in the sense that this difficulty might to some extent be overcome by monetary means when wages are fixed in terms of money. But the problem left unanswered by the authors who stress this second aspect is whether the difficulty created by the rigidity of money wages can be overcome by monetary adjustments without setting up new disturbances of the first kind. And there are in fact strong reasons to believe that the two aims of avoiding so far as possible downward adjustments of wages and preventing misdirections of production may not always be reconcilable.

This difference in emphasis is so important in connection with the opinions about what are the appropriate principles of national monetary policy because, if one thinks principally in terms of the relation of prices to given wages and particularly if one thinks in terms of national wage "levels," one is easily led to the conclusion that the quantity of money should be adjusted for each group of people among whom a given system of contracts exists. (To be consistent, of course, the argument should be applied not only to countries but also to particular industries, or at any rate to "noncompeting groups" of workers in each country.) On the other hand, there is no reason why one should expect the self-reversing effects of monetary changes to be connected with the change of the quantity of money in a particular area which is part of a wider monetary system. If a decrease or increase of demand in one area is offset by a corresponding change in demand in another area, there is no reason why the changes in the quantity of money in the two areas should in any sense misguide productive activity. They are simply manifestations of an underlying real change which works itself out through the medium of money.

To illustrate this difference let me take a statement of one of the most ardent advocates of monetary nationalism, Mr. R.F. Harrod of Oxford. Mr. Harrod is not unfamiliar with what I have called the self-reversing effects of monetary changes. At any rate in an earlier publication he argued that "if industry is stimulated to go forward at a pace which cannot be maintained, you are bound to have periodic crises and depressions."[16] Yet for some reason he seems to think that these misdirections of industry will occur even when the changes in the quantity of money of a particular country take place in the course of the normal redistributions of money between countries. In his *International Economics* there appears the following remarkable passage which seems to express the theoretical basis, or as I think the fallacy, underlying monetary nationalism more clearly than any other statement I have yet come across. Mr. Harrod is discussing the case of unequal economic progress in different countries with a common standard and concludes that "the less progressive countries would thus be afflicted with the additional inconvenience of a deflationary monetary system. Inflation would occur just where it is most dangerous, namely in the rapidly advancing countries. This objection appears in one form or another in all projects for

---

[16] *The International Gold Problem*, ed. Royal Institute of International Affairs (London: Oxford University Press, 1931), p. 29. Cf. also, in the light of this statement, the remarkable passage in the same author's *International Economics*. Cambridge Economic Handbooks no. 8 (London: Nisbet, 1933), p. 150, where it is argued that "the only way to avoid a slump is to engineer a boom," although only two lines later a boom is still "defined as an increase in the rate of output which cannot be maintained in the long period."

a common world money."[17] And the lesson which Mr. Harrod derives from these considerations is that "the currencies of the more progressive countries must be made to appreciate in terms of the others."[18]

It is interesting to inquire in what sense inflation and deflation are here represented as *additional* inconveniences, superimposed, as it were, on the difficulties created by unequal economic progress. One might think at first that what Mr. Harrod has in mind are the *extra* difficulties caused by the secondary expansions and contractions of credit which are made necessary by the national reserve systems which I have analyzed in an earlier lecture. But this interpretation is excluded by the express assertion that this difficulty appears under *all* forms of a common world money. It seems that the terms inflation and deflation are here used simply as equivalents to increases and decreases of money demand relatively to given costs. In this sense the terms could equally be applied to shifts in demand between different industries and would really mean no more than a change in demand relatively to supply. But the objection to this is not only that the terms inflation and deflation are here unnecessarily applied to phenomena which can be described in simpler terms. It is rather whether in this case there is any reason to expect any of the special consequences which we associate with monetary disturbances, that is, whether there really is any "additional inconvenience" caused by monetary factors proper. We might ask whether in this case there will be any of the peculiar self-reversing effects which are typical of purely monetary causes; in particular whether "inflation" as used here with reference to the increase of money in one country at the expense of another, "stimulates industry to go forward at a pace which cannot be maintained"; and whether deflation in the same sense implies a temporary and avoidable contraction of production.

---

[17] *International Economics*, p. 170.
[18] Ibid., p. 174.

The answer to these questions is not difficult. We know that the really harmful effects of inflation and deflation spring, not so much from the fact that all prices change in the same direction and in the same proportion, but from the fact that the relation between individual prices changes in a direction which cannot be maintained; or in other words, that it temporarily brings about a distribution of spending power between individuals which is not stable. We have seen that the international redistributions of money are part of a process which at the same time brings about a redistribution of relative amounts of money held by the different individuals in each country, a redistribution within the nation which would also have to come about if there were no international money. The difference, however, in the latter case, the case of free currencies, is that here first the relative value of the total amounts of money in each country is changed and that the process of internal redistribution takes places in a manner different from that which would occur with an international monetary standard. We have seen before that the variation of exchange rates will in itself bring about a redistribution of spending power in the country, but a redistribution which is in no way based on a corresponding change in the underlying real position. There will be a temporary stimulus to particular industries to expand, although there are no grounds which would make a lasting increase in output possible. In short, the successive changes in individual expenditure and the corresponding changes of particular prices will not occur in an order which will direct industry from the old to the new equilibrium position. Or, in other words, the effects of keeping the quantity of money in a region or country constant when under an international monetary system it would decrease are essentially inflationary, while to keep it constant if under an international system it would increase at the expense of other countries would have effects similar to an absolute deflation.

I do not want to suggest that the practical importance of the deflationary or inflationary effects of a policy of keeping the quantity of money in a particular area constant is very great. The practical arguments which to me seem to condemn such a policy I have already discussed. The reason why I wanted at least to mention this more abstract consideration is that, if it is correct, it shows particularly clearly the weakness of the theoretical basis of monetary nationalism. The proposition that the effects of keeping the quantity of money constant in a territory where with an international currency it would decrease are inflationary and *vice versa*[19] is of course directly contrary to the position on which monetary nationalism is based. Far from admitting that changes in the relative money holdings of different nations which go parallel with changes in their share of the world's income are harmful, we believe that such redistributions of money are the only way of effecting the change in real income with a minimum of disturbance. And to speak in connection with such changes of national inflation or deflation can only lead to a serious confusion of thought.[20]

Before I leave this subject I should like to supplement these theoretical reflections by a somewhat more practical consideration.

---

[19] Without giving disproportionate space to what is perhaps a somewhat esoteric theoretical point, it is not possible to give here a complete proof of this proposition. A full discussion of the complicated effects would require almost a separate chapter. But a sort of indirect proof may be here suggested. It would probably not be denied that if, without any other change, the amount of money in one currency area were decreased by a given amount and at the same time the amount of money in another currency area increased by a corresponding amount, this would have deflationary effects in the first area and inflationary effects in the second. And most economists (the more extreme monetary nationalists only excepted) would agree that no such effects would occur if these changes were made simultaneous with corresponding changes in the relative volume of transactions in the two countries. From this it appears to follow that if such a change in the relative volume of transactions in the two countries occurs but the quantity of money in each country is kept constant, this must have the effect of a relative inflation and deflation, respectively.

[20] See on this point also Robbins, *Economic Planning and International Order*, pp. 281 *et seq*.

While the whole idea of a monetary policy directed to adjust everything to a "given" wage level appears to me misconceived on purely theoretical grounds, its consequences seem to me to be fantastic if we imagine it applied to the present world where this supposedly given wage level is at the same time the subject of political strife. It would mean that the whole mechanism of collective wage bargaining would in the future be used exclusively to raise wages, while any reduction—even if it were necessary only in one particular industry—would have to be brought about by monetary means. I doubt whether such a proposal could ever have been seriously entertained except in a country and in a period where labor has been for long on the defensive.[21] It is difficult to imagine how wage negotiations would be carried on if it became the recognized duty of the monetary authority to offset any unfavorable effect of a rise in wages on the competitive position of national industries on the world market. But of one thing we can probably be pretty certain: that the working class would not be slow to learn that an engineered rise of prices is no less a reduction of wages than a deliberate cut of money wages, and that in consequence the belief that it is easier to reduce by the round-about method of depreciation the wages of all workers in a country than directly to reduce the money wages of those who are affected by a given change, will soon prove illusory.

---

[21] It is interesting to note that those countries in Europe where, up to 1929, wages had been rising relatively most rapidly were on the whole those most reluctant to experiment with exchange depreciation. The recent experience of France seems also to suggest that a working-class government may never be able to use exchange depreciation as an instrument to lower real wages.

LECTURE 4

International Capital Movements

1. Definition and Classification of Capital Movements

For the purposes of this lecture, by international capital movements I shall mean the acquisition of claims on persons or of rights to property in one country by persons in another country, or the disposal of such claims or property rights in another country to people in that country. This definition is meant to exclude from capital movements the purchase and sale of commodities which pass from one country to the other at the same time as they are paid for and change their owners. But it also excludes any net movement of gold (or other international money) insofar as these movements are payments for commodities or services received (or "unilateral" payments) and therefore involve a transfer of ownership in that money without creating a new claim from one country to the other. This is of course not the only possible definition of capital movements, and strong arguments could be advanced in favor of a more comprehensive definition, which in effect would treat every transfer of assets from country to country as a capital movement. The reason which leads me to adopt here the former definition is that only on that definition is it possible to distinguish between those items in international transactions which are, and those which are not, capital items.

The first kind of capital item of this sort and the one which will occupy us in this lecture more than any other is the acquisition, or sale, of amounts of the national money of one country by inhabitants of the other.[22] The form which this kind of transaction today predominantly takes is the holding of balances with the banks of one country on the part of banks and individuals in the other country. Such balances will to some extent be held even if there is a safe and stable international standard, since, rather than actually send money, it will as a rule be cheaper for the banks to provide out of such balances those of their customer's requirements which arise out of the normal day-to-day differences between payments and receipts abroad. And if it is possible to hold such balances either in the form of interest-bearing deposits or in the form of bills of exchange, there will be a strong inducement to hold such earning assets as substitutes for the sterile holdings of international money. It was in this way that what is called the gold exchange standard tended more and more to supplant the gold standard proper. In the years immediately preceding 1931 this assumed very great significance.

If there exists a system of fluctuating exchanges, or a system where people are not altogether certain about the maintenance of the existing parities, these balances become even more important. There are two new elements which enter in this case. In the first place it will then no longer be sufficient if banks and others who owe debts in different currencies keep one single liquidity reserve against all their liabilities. It will become necessary for them to keep separate liquid assets in each of the different currencies in

---

[22] This is not to be interpreted as meaning that I subscribe to the view that all money is in some sense a "claim." The statement in the text applies strictly only to credit money and particularly to bank deposits, which will be mainly considered in what follows. But it would not apply to the acquisition of gold by foreigners for export. The gold coins so acquired would thereby cease to be "national" money in the sense in which this term is here used, that is, they would not be assets belonging to the country where they have been issued.

which they owe debts, and to adjust them to the special circumstances likely to affect liabilities in each currency. We get here new artificial distinctions of liquidity created by the multiplicity of currencies and involving all the consequential possibilities of disturbances following from changes in what is now called "liquidity preference." Second there will be the chance of a gain or loss on these foreign balances due to changes in the rates of exchange. Thus the anticipation of any impending variation of exchange rates will tend to bring about temporary changes of a speculative nature in the volume of such balances. Whether these two kinds of motives must really be regarded as different, or whether they are better treated as essentially the same, there can be no doubt that variability of exchange rates introduces a new and powerful reason for short-term capital movements, and a reason which is fundamentally different from the reasons which exist under a well-secured international standard.

Foreign bank balances and other holdings of foreign money are of course only part, although probably the most important part, of the volume of short-term foreign investment. It is here that the impact effect of any change in international indebtedness arising out of current transactions will show itself; and it is here that there will be the most ready response to changes in the relative attractiveness of holding assets in the different countries. Once we go beyond this field it becomes rather difficult to say what can properly be called movements of short-term capital. In fact, with the exception of nonfunded, long-term loans, almost any form of international investment may have to be regarded as short-term investment, including in particular all investments in marketable securities.[23] But for the monetary problems with which we are here

---

[23] Even the intentions of the lender or investor would hardly provide a sufficient criterion for a distinction between what are short- and what are long-term capital movements, since it may very well be clear in a particular case to the outside observer that circumstances will soon lead the investors to change their intentions.

concerned it is mainly the short-term credits which are of importance, because it is here that we have to deal with large accumulated funds which are apt to change their location at comparatively slight provocation. Compared with these "floating" funds, the supply of capital for long-term investment, limited as it will be to a certain part of new savings, will be relatively small.

Now the chief question which we shall have to consider is the question to what extent under different monetary systems international capital movements are likely to cause monetary disturbances, and to what extent and by what means it may be possible to prevent such disturbances. It will again prove useful if we approach this task in three stages, beginning with a consideration of the mechanism and function of international capital movements under a homogeneous standard. Then we shall go on to inquire how this mechanism and the effects are modified if we have "mixed" currency systems organized on the national reserve principle but with fixed exchange rates. And finally we shall have to see what will be the effects of the existence of variable exchange rates and the way in which fluctuations of the exchange and capital movements mutually influence one another.

2. Their Mechanism under a Homogeneous International Currency

If exchange rates were regarded as invariably fixed we should expect capital movements to be guided by no other considerations except expected net yield, including of course adjustments which will have to be made for the different degrees of risk inherent in the different sorts of investments. This does not mean that there would not be frequent changes in the flow of capital from country to country. There might of course be a permanent tendency on the part of one country to absorb part of the current savings of another at terms more favorable than those at which these savings could be invested in the country were they are made. Quite apart from these flows of capital for more or less permanent investment however, there would be periodic or occasional short-term lending to make up for temporary differences between imports and exports of commodities and services.

Now there is of course no reason why exports and imports should move closely parallel from day to day or even from month to month. If in all transactions payment had to be made simultaneously with the delivery of the goods, this would mean, in external trade no less than in internal, a restriction of the possible range of transactions similar in kind to what would occur if all transaction had to take the form of barter. The possibility of credit transactions, the exchange of present goods against future goods, greatly widens the range of advantageous exchanges. In international trade it means in particular that countries may import more than they export in some seasons because they will export more than they import during other seasons. Whether this is made possible by the exporter directly crediting the importer with the price, or whether it takes place by some credit institution in either country providing the money, it will always mean that the indebtedness of the importing country to the exporting increases temporarily, that is, that net short-term lending takes place.

At this point it is necessary especially to be on guard against a form of stating these relations which suggests that short-term lending is made necessary by, or is in any sense a consequence of, a passive balance of trade—that the loans are made so to speak with the purpose of covering a deficit in the balance of trade. We shall get a more correct picture if we think of the great majority of the individual transactions in both ways being credit transactions so that it is the excess lending in one direction during any given period which has made possible a corresponding excess of exports in the same direction. If we look on the whole process in this way we can see how considerable a part of trade is only made possible by short-term capital movements. We can see also how misleading it may be to think of capital movements as exclusively directed by previous changes in the relative rates of interest in the different money markets. What directs the use of the available credit and therefore decides in what direction the balance of indebtedness will shift at a particular moment is in the first instance the relation between prices in different places. It is of course true that where each country habitually finances its exports and borrows its imports, any absolute increase of exports will tend to bring about an increase in the demand for loans and therefore a rise in the rate of interest in the exporting country. But in such a case the rise in the rate of interest is rather the effect of this country lending more abroad, than a cause of a flow of capital to the country. And although this rise in money rates may lead to a flow of funds in the reverse direction, that will be more a sign that the main mechanism for the distribution of funds works imperfectly than a part of this mechanism. There is no more reason to say that the international redistribution of short-term capital is brought about by changes in the rates of interest in the different localities than there would be for saying that the seasonal transfers of funds from say agriculture to coal mining are brought about by a fall of the rate of interest in agriculture and a rise in coal mining or *vice versa*.

Changes in short-term international indebtedness must therefore be considered as proceeding largely concurrently with normal fluctuations in international trade; and only certain remaining balances will be settled by a flow of funds, largely of an interbank character, induced by differences in interest rates to be earned. It is of course not to be denied that, apart from changes in international indebtedness which are more directly connected with international trade, there may also be somewhat sudden and considerable flows of funds which may be caused either by the sudden appearance of very profitable opportunities for investment, or by some panic which causes an insistent demand for cash. In this last case indeed it is true that the flow of short-term funds may transmit monetary disturbances to parts of the world which have nothing to do with the original cause of the disturbance, as say a war scare in South America might conceivably lead to a general rise in interest rates in London. But, apart from such special cases, it is difficult to see how under a homogeneous international standard, capital movements—and particularly short-term capital movements—should be a source of instability or lead to any changes in productive activity which are not justified by corresponding changes in the real conditions.

3. Under National Reserve Systems

This conclusion has, however, to be somewhat modified if, instead of a homogeneous international currency, we consider a world consisting of separate national monetary and banking systems, even if we still leave the possibility of variations in exchange rates out of account.

It is of course a well-known fact that one of the main purposes of changes in the discount rate of central banks is to influence the international movements of short-term capital.[24] A central bank which is faced with an outflow of gold will raise its discount rate in the hope that by attracting short-term credits it will offset the gold outflow. To the extent that it succeeds, it will postpone the necessity of more drastic credit contraction at home, and—if the cause of the adverse balance of trade is transitory—it may perhaps altogether avoid it. But it is by no means evident that it will attract the funds just from where the gold would tend to flow, and it may well be that it only passes on the necessity of credit contraction to another country. And if for some reason all or the majority of central banks should at a particular moment feel that they ought to become more liquid and for this purpose raise their discount rates, the sole effect will be a kind of general tug-of-war in which all central banks—trying to prevent an outflow of funds and if possible to attract funds—

---

[24] If this effect was disregarded in the discussion of changes in the discount rates in the two proceeding lectures, this was done to make the effects discussed there stand out more clearly; but this must not be taken to mean that this effect on capital movements is not, at any rate in the short run, perhaps the most important effect of these changes.

only succeed in bringing about a violent contraction of credit at home. But although the fact that central banks react to all major gold movements with changes in the rate of discount may mean that changes in the volume and direction of short-term credits will be more frequent and violent if we have a number of banking systems organized on national lines, it is again not the fact that the system is international, but rather that it creates impediments to the free international flow of funds which must be regarded as responsible for these disturbances. Again we must be careful not to ascribe this difficulty to the existence of central banks in particular, although in a sense the growth of the sort of credit structure to which they are due was only made possible by the existence of some such institutions. The ultimate source of the difficulty is the differentiation between moneys of different degrees of acceptability or liquidity, the existence of a structure consisting of superimposed layers of reserves of different degrees of liquidity, which makes the movement of short-term money rates, and in consequence the movement of short-term funds, much more dependent on the liquidity position of the different financial institutions than on changes in the demand for capital for real investment. It is because with "mixed" national monetary systems, the movements of short-term funds are frequently due, not to changes in the demand for capital for investment, but to changes in the demand for cash as liquidity reserves, that short-term international capital movements have such a bad reputation as causes of monetary disturbances. And this reputation is not altogether undeserved.

But now the question arises whether this defect can be removed not by making the medium of circulation in the different countries more homogeneous, but rather, as the monetary nationalists wish, by severing even the remaining tie between the national currencies, the fixed parities between them. This question is of particular importance since the idea that the national monetary authorities should never be forced by an outflow of capital to take any action which might unfavorably affect economic activity at home is probably the main source of the demand for variable exchanges. To this question therefore we must now turn.

4. Under Independent National Currencies

The chief questions which we shall have to consider here are three: will the volume of short-term capital movement be larger or smaller when there exists uncertainty about the future of exchange rates? Are the national monetary authorities in a position either to prevent capital movements which they regard as undesirable, or to offset their effects? And, finally, what further measures, if any, are necessary if the aims of such a policy are to be consistently followed?

We have already partly furnished the answer to the first question. Although the contrary has actually been asserted, I am altogether unable to see why, under a regime of variable exchanges, the volume of short-term capital movements as well as the frequency of changes in their direction should be anything but greater.[25] Every suspicion that exchange rates were likely to change in the near future would create an additional powerful

---

[25] The only argument against this view which I find at all intelligible is that, under the gold standard, movements to one of the gold points will create a certain expectation that the movement will soon be reversed and thus provides a special inducement to speculative shifts of funds. But while this is perfectly true, it only shows that the defects of the traditional gold standard were due to the fact that it was not a homogeneous international currency. If the same arrangements applied to international as to infranational payments the problem would disappear. This would be the case either if within the country as much as between countries the costs of transfers of money were not borne by some institution like the central banks and consequently (as in the United States before the establishment of the Federal Reserve System) rates of exchange between the different towns were allowed to fluctuate, and if at the same time gold were freely obtainable near the frontier as well as in the capital, or on the other hand, if the system of par clearance were applied to international as well as national payments. On the last point compare below, Lecture 5, p. 413.

motive for shifting funds from the country whose currency was likely to fall or to the country whose currency was likely to rise. I should have thought that the experience of the whole post-war period and particularly of the last few years had so amply confirmed what one might have expected *a priori* that there could be no reasonable doubt about this.[26] There is only one point which perhaps still deserves to be stressed a little further. Where the possible fluctuations of exchange rates are confined to narrow limits above and below a fixed point, as between the two gold points, the effect of short-term capital movements will be on the whole to reduce the amplitude of the actual fluctuations, since every movement away from the fixed point will, as a rule, create the expectation that it will soon be reversed. That is, short-term capital movements will, on the whole, tend to relieve the strain set up by the original cause of a temporarily adverse balance of payments. If exchanges, however, are variable, the capital movements will tend to work in the same direction as the original cause and thereby to intensify it. This means that if this original cause is already a short-term capital movement, the variability of exchanges will tend to multiply its magnitude and may turn what originally might have been a minor inconvenience into a major disturbance.

Much more difficult is the answer to the second question: can the authorities control these movements; since what the monetary authorities can achieve in a particular direction will largely depend on what other consequences of their action they are willing to put

---

[26] Since it is being more and more forgotten that the period before 1931 was, on pre-war standards, already one of marked instability—and uncertainty about the future—of exchange rates, it is perhaps worth stressing that in particular the accumulation of foreign balances in London during that period was almost entirely a consequence of the fact that Sterling was regarded as relatively the most safe of the European currencies. Cf. on this T.E. Gregory, *The Gold Standard and Its Future*, 3rd ed. (New York: E.P. Dutton, 1932), pp. 48 *et seq*.

up with. In this particular case, the question is mainly whether they would be willing to let exchange rates fluctuate to any degree or whether they would not feel that although moderate fluctuations of exchange rates were not worth the cost of preventing them, yet they must not be allowed to exceed certain limits, since the unsettling effects from large fluctuations would be worse than the measures by which they could be prevented. In practice we must probably assume that even if the authorities are prepared to allow a slow and gradual depreciation of exchanges, they would feel bound to take strong action to counteract it as soon as it threatened to lead to a flight of capital or a strong rise of prices of imported goods.

The theory that by keeping exchange rates flexible a country could prevent dear money abroad from affecting home conditions is of course not a new one. It was for instance argued by the opponents of the introduction of the gold standard in Austria in 1892 that the paper standard insulated and protected Austria from disturbances originating on the world markets. But I doubt whether it has ever been carried quite as far as by some of our contemporary monetary nationalists—for instance Harrod, who declared that he could not accept exchange stabilization "if thereby a country is committed to an interior monetary policy which involves raising the bank rate of interest."[27] The modern idea apparently is that never under any circumstances must an outflow of capital be allowed to raise interest rates at home, and the advocates of this view seem to be satisfied that if the central banks are not committed to maintain a particular parity they will have no difficulty either in preventing an outflow of capital altogether or in offsetting its effect by substituting additional bank credit for the funds which have left the country.

It is not easy to see on what this confidence is founded. So long as the outward flow of capital is not effectively prevented by

---

[27] Cf. *Report of the Proceedings of the Meeting of Economists* held at the Antwerp Chamber of Commerce on July 11–13, 1935, published by the Antwerp Chamber of Commerce, p. 107.

other means, a persistent effort to keep interest rates low can only have the effect of prolonging this tendency indefinitely and of bringing about a continuous and progressive fall of the exchanges. Whether the outward flow of capital starts with a withdrawal of balances held in the country by foreigners, or with an attempt on the parts of nationals of the country to acquire assets abroad, it will deprive banking institutions at home of funds which they were able to lend, and at the same time lower the exchanges. If the central bank succeeds in keeping interest rates low in the first instance by substituting new credits for the capital which has left the country, it will not only perpetuate the conditions under which the export of capital has been attractive; the effect of capital exports on the rates of exchange will, as we have seen, tend to become self-inflammatory and a "flight of capital" will set in. At the same time the rise of prices at home will increase the demand for loans because it means an increase in the "real" rate of profit. And the adverse balance of trade, which must necessarily continue while part of the receipts from exports is used to repay loans or to make new loans abroad, means that the supply of real capital and therefore the "natural" or "equilibrium" rate of interest in the country will rise. It is clear that under such conditions the central bank could not, merely by keeping its discount rate low, prevent a rise of interest rates without at the same time bringing about a major inflation.

5. The Control of International Capital Movements

If this is correct it would be only consistent if the advocates of monetary nationalism should demand that monetary policy proper should be supplemented by a strict control of the export of capital. If the main purpose of monetary management is to prevent exports of capital from disturbing conditions of the money market at home, this clearly is a necessary complement of central banking policy. But those who favor such a course seem hardly to be conscious of what it involves. It would certainly not be sufficient in the long run merely to prohibit the more conspicuous forms of sending money abroad. It is of course true that if there are no impediments to the export of capital the most convenient and therefore perhaps the quantitatively most important form which the export of capital will take is the actual transfer of money from country to country. And it is conceivable that this might be pretty effectively prevented by mere prohibition and control. To make even this really effective would of course involve not only a prohibition of foreign lending and of the import of securities of any description, but could hardly stop short of a full-fledged system of foreign-exchange control. But exchange control designed to prevent effectively the outflow of capital would really have to involve a complete control of foreign trade, since of course any variation in the terms of credit on exports or imports means an international capital movement.

To anyone who doubts the importance of this factor, I strongly recommend the very interesting memorandum on international short-term indebtedness which has recently been published by Mr. F.G. Conolly of the staff of the Bank for International Settlements in the recent joint publication of the Carnegie Endowment and the International Chamber of Commerce.[28] I will quote only one paragraph. "It has been the experience of every country whose currency has come under pressure," writes Mr. Conolly,

> that importers tend not only to refuse to utilize the normal period of credit but to cover their requirements for months in advance; they prefer to utilize the home currency while it retains its international value rather than run the risk of being forced to pay extra for the foreign currency necessary for their purchases. Exporters, on the other hand, tend to

---

[28] *The Improvement of Commercial Relations between Nations: The Problem of Monetary Stabilization.* Separate Memoranda from the Economists consulted by the Joint Committee of the Carnegie Endowment and the International Chamber of Commerce and practical Conclusions of the Expert Committee appointed by the Joint Committee (Paris, 1936), pp. 352 *et seq.*

allow foreign currencies, the proceeds of exports already made, to lie abroad and to finance their current operations as far as possible by borrowing at home. Thus a double strain falls on the exchange market; the normal supply of foreign currencies from export dries up while the demands from importers greatly increase. For a country with a large foreign trade the strain on the exchange market due to the effects of this change over in trade financing may be very considerable.[29]

What Mr. Conolly here describes amounts, of course, to an export of capital which could only be prevented by controlling the terms of every individual transaction of the country's foreign trade, an export of capital which may be equally formidable whether the country carries on its foreign trade "actively" or "passively,"[30] that is, whether it normally provides the capital to finance the trade herself or borrows it. Indeed to anyone who has had any experience of foreign-exchange control there should be no doubt possible that an export of capital can only be prevented by controlling not only the volume of exports and imports so that they will always balance, but also the terms of credit of all these transactions.

At first indeed—and so long as discrepancies between national rates of interest are not too big and people have not yet fully learned to adapt themselves to fluctuating exchanges—much less thoroughgoing measures may be quite effective. I can already hear some of my English friends point out to me the marvelous discipline of the City of London which on a slight hint from the bank that capital exports would be undesirable will refrain from acting against the general interest. But we need only visualize how big the discrepancies between national interest rates would become if capital movements were for a time

---

[29] Ibid., p. 360

[30] Cf. N.G. Pierson, "The Problem of Value in a Socialist Community," *Collectivist Economic Planning* (London: Routledge and Kegan Paul, 1935).

effectively stopped in order to realize how illusionary must be the hopes that anything but the strictest control will be able to prevent them.

But let us disregard for the moment the technical difficulties inherent in any effective control of international capital movements. Let us assume that the monetary authorities are willing to go any distance in creating new impediments to international trade and that they actually succeed in preventing any unwanted change in international indebtedness. Will this successfully insulate a country against the shocks which may result from changes in the rates of interest, abroad? Or will these not still transmit themselves via the effect such a change of interest rates will have on the relative prices of the internationally traded securities and commodities? It is probably obvious that so long as there is a fairly free international movement of securities, no great divergence in the movement of rates of interest in the different countries can persist for any length of time. But monetary nationalists would probably not hesitate at any rate to attempt to inhibit these movements. It is not so generally recognized however that commodity movements will have a similar effect and perhaps this needs a few more words of explanation.

It will probably not be denied that a considerable rise in the rate of interest will lead to a fall in the prices of some commodities relatively to those of others, particularly of those which are largely used for the production of capital goods and of those of which large stocks are held, compared with those which are destined for more or less immediate consumption. And surely, in the absence of immediate adjustments in tariffs or quotas, such a fall will transmit itself to the prices of similar commodities in the country in which interest rates at first are not allowed to rise. But if the prices of the goods which are largely used for investment fall relatively to the prices of other goods, this means an increased profitability of investment compared with current production, consequently an increased demand for loans at the existing rates of interest; and, unless the central bank is willing to allow an indefinite expansion of credit, it will be compelled by the rise of interest rates abroad to raise its own rate of interest, even if any outflow of capital has been effectively prevented. Although the supply of capital may not change, the kind of goods which under the changed circumstances it will be most profitable to import and export will still alter the demand for capital with the same effects.[31]

The truth of the whole matter is that for a country which is sharing in the advantages of the international division of labor it is not possible to escape from the effects of disturbances in these international trade relations by means short of severing all the trade ties which connect it with the rest of the world. It is of course true that the fewer the points of contact with the rest of the world the less will be the extent to which disturbances originating outside the country will affect its internal conditions. But it is an illusion that it would be possible, while remaining a member of the international commercial community, to prevent disturbances from the outside world from reaching the country by following a national monetary policy such as would be indicated if the country were a closed community. It is for this reason that the ideology of monetary nationalism has proved—and if it remains influential will prove to an even greater extent in the future—to be one of the main forces destroying what remnants of an international economic system we still have.

There are two more points which I should like specially to emphasize before I conclude for today. One is that up to this point I have, following the practice of the monetary nationalists, considered mainly the disturbing effects on a country of changes in the demand for capital originating abroad. But there is of course another side to this picture. What from the point of view of the country to which the effects are transmitted from abroad

---

[31] Cf. on this L. Robbins, *The Great Depression* (London: Macmillan, 1934), p. 175.

is a disturbance is from the point of view of the country where the original change takes place a stabilizing effect. To have to give up capital because somewhere else a sudden more urgent demand has arisen is certainly unsettling. But to be able to obtain capital at short notice if a sudden unforeseen need arises at home will certainly tend to stabilize conditions at home. It is more than unlikely that fluctuations on the national capital market would be smaller if the world were cut up into watertight compartments. The probability is rather that in this case fluctuations within each national territory would be much more violent and disturbing than they are now.

Closely connected with this is the second point, on which I can touch only even more shortly. I have already mentioned the probability that the restrictions on capital movements involved in a policy of monetary nationalism would tend to increase the differences between national interest rates. This would of course be due to the fact that while instability of exchange rates would tend to increase the volume and frequency of irregular flows of short-term funds, it would to an even greater degree decrease the volume of international long-term investment. Although by some this is regarded as a good thing, I doubt whether they fully appreciate what it would mean. The purely economic effects, the restriction of international division of labor which it implies, and the reduction in the total volume of investment to which it would almost certainly lead, are bad enough. But even more serious seem to me the political effects of the intensification of the differences in the standard of life between different countries to which it would lead. It does not need much imagination to visualize the new sources of international friction which such a situation would create.[32] But this leads me beyond the proper scope of these lectures, and I must confine myself to drawing your attention to it without attempting to elaborate it any further.

---

[32] Cf. on this Robbins, *Economic Planning and International Order*, pp. 68 *et seq.*

LECTURE 5

The Problems of a Really International Standard

1. Gold as the International Standard

I have now concluded the negative part of my argument, the case against independent national currencies. While I cannot hope in the space of these few lectures completely to have refuted the theoretical basis of monetary nationalism, I hope at least to have shown three things: that there is no rational basis for the separate regulation of the quantity of money in a national area which remains a part of a wider economic system; that the belief that by maintaining an independent national currency we can insulate a country against financial shocks originating abroad is largely illusory; and that a system of fluctuating exchanges would on the contrary introduce new and very serious disturbances of international stability. I do not want now further to add to this except that I might perhaps remind you that my argument throughout assumed that such a system would be run as intelligently as is humanly possible. I have refrained from supporting my case by pointing to the abuses to which such a system would almost certainly lend itself, to the practical impossibility of different countries agreeing on what degree of depreciation is justified, to the consequent danger of competitive depreciation, and the general return to mercantilist policies of restriction which now, as in earlier centuries, are the inevitable reaction to debasement in other countries.[33]

We must recognize, therefore, that independent regulation of the various national currencies cannot be regarded as in any sense a substitute for a rationally regulated world monetary system. Such a system may today seem an unattainable ideal. But this does not mean that the question of what we can do to get as near the ideal as may be practicable does not present a number of important problems. Of course some "international" systems would be far from ideal. I hope I have made it clear in particular that I do not regard the sort of international system which we have had in the past as by any means completely satisfactory. The monetary nationalists condemn it because it is international; I, on the other hand, ascribe its shortcomings to the fact that it is not international enough. But the question of how we can make it more satisfactory, that is, more genuinely international, I have not yet touched upon. It is a question which raises exceedingly difficult problems; I can survey them only rapidly in this final lecture.

The first, but by no means the most important or most interesting question which I must consider is the question of whether the international standard need be gold. On purely economic grounds it must be said that there are hardly any arguments which can be advanced for, and many serious objections which can be raised against, the use of gold as the international money. In a securely established world state with a government immune to the temptations of inflation it might be absurd to spend enormous effort in extracting gold out of the earth if cheap tokens

---

[33] I feel I must remind the reader here that limitations of time made it impossible for me to dwell in these lectures on the tremendously important practical effects of a policy of monetary nationalism on commercial policy as long as I should have wished. Although this is well-trodden ground, it cannot be too often reiterated that without stability of exchange rates it is vain to hope for any reduction of trade barriers.

would render the same service as gold with equal or greater efficiency. Yet in a world consisting of sovereign nation-states, there seem to me to exist compelling political reasons why gold (or the precious metals) alone and no kind of artificial international currency, issued by some international authority, could be used successfully as the international money. It is essential for the working of an international standard that each country's holdings of the international money should represent for it a reserve of exchange medium which in all eventualities will remain universally acceptable in international transactions. And so long as there are separate sovereign states there will always loom large among these eventualities the danger of war, or of the breakdown of the international monetary arrangements for some other reason. And since people will always feel that against these emergencies they will have to hold some reserve of the one thing which by age-old custom civilized as well as uncivilized people are ready to accept—that is, since gold alone will serve one of the purposes for which stocks of money are held—and since to some extent gold will always be held for this purpose, there can be little doubt that it is the only sort of international standard which in the present world has any chance of surviving. But, to repeat, while an international standard is desirable on purely economic grounds, the choice of gold with all its undeniable defects is made necessary entirely by political considerations.

What should be done if the well-known defects of gold should make themselves too strongly felt, if violent changes in the condition of its production or the appearance of a large new demand for it should threaten sudden changes in its value, is of course a problem of major importance. But it is neither the most interesting nor the most important problem and I do not propose to discuss it here. The difficulties which I want to consider are rather those which were inherent in the international gold standard, even before 1914, and to a still greater degree during its short post-war existence. They are the problems which arise out of the fact that the so-called gold currencies are connected with gold only through the comparatively small national reserves which form the basis of a multiple superstructure of credit money which itself consists of many different layers of different degrees of liquidity or acceptability. It is, as we have seen, this fact which makes the effects of changes in the international flow of money different from merely interlocal shifts, to which is due the existence of separate national monetary systems which to some extent have a life of their own. The homogeneity of the circulating medium of different countries has been destroyed by the growth of separate banking systems organized on national lines. Can anything be done to restore it?

2. The "Perverse Elasticity" of Our Credit Money

It is important here first to distinguish between the need for some "lender of last resort" and the organization of banking on the "national reserve" principle. That an extensive use of bank deposits as money would not be possible, that deposit banking of the modern type could not exist, unless somebody were in a position to provide the cash if the public should suddenly want to convert a considerable part of its holdings of bank deposits into more liquid forms of money, is probably beyond doubt. It is far less obvious why all the banking institutions in a particular area or country should be made to rely on a single national reserve. This is certainly not a system which anybody would have deliberately devised on rational grounds, and it grew up as an accidental by-product of a policy concerned with different problems.[34] The rational choice would seem to lie between either a system of "free banking," which not only gives all banks the right of note issue and at the same time makes it necessary for them to rely on their own reserves, but also leaves them free to choose their field of operation and their correspondents without regard to national

---

[34] Cf. W. Bagehot, and V.G. Smith, *The Rationale of Central Banking* (London, 1936).

boundaries,[35] and on the other hand, an international central bank. I need not add that both of these ideals seem utterly impracticable in the world as we know it. But I am not certain whether the compromise we have chosen, that of national central banks which have no direct power over the bulk of the national circulation but which hold as the sole ultimate reserve a comparatively small amount of gold, is not one of the most unstable arrangements imaginable.

Let us recall for a moment the essential features of the so-called gold standard systems as they have existed in modern times. The most widely used medium of exchange, bank deposits, is not fixed in quantity. Additional deposits may at any time spontaneously spring up (be "created" by the banks), or part of the total may similarly disappear. But while they are predominantly used in actual payments, they are by no means the only forms in which balances can be held to meet such payments. In this function, deposits on current account are only one item—a very liquid one, although by no means the most liquid of all—in a long range of assets of varying degree of liquidity.[36] Overdraft facilities, saving deposits and many types of very marketable securities on the one hand, and bank notes and coin on the other, will at different times and to different degrees compete with bank deposits in this function. And the amounts which will be held on current account to meet expected demands need not therefore fluctuate with the expected magnitude of these payments; they may also change with any change in the views about the ease with which it will be possible to convert these other assets into bank deposits. The supply of bank deposits on the other hand will depend on similar considerations. How much

---

[35] Cf. L. v. Mises, *Geldwertstabilisierung und Konjunkturpolitik* (Jena: Gustav Fischer, 1928).

[36] Cf. particularly J.R. Hicks, "A Suggestion for the Simplification of the Theory of Money," *Economica* n.s. 2, no. 6 (February 1936), and F. Lavington, *The English Capital Market* (London: Methuen, 1921), p. 30.

the banks will be willing to owe in this form in excess of the ready cash they hold will depend on their view as to how easy it will be to convert other assets into cash. It is when general confidence is high, so that comparatively small amounts of bank deposits will be needed for a given volume of payments, that the banks will be more ready to increase the amount of bank deposits. On the other hand, any increase of uncertainty about the future will lead to an increased demand for all the more liquid forms of assets, that is, in particular, for bank deposits and cash, and to a decrease in the supply of bank deposits.

Where there is a central bank, the responsibility for the provision of cash for the conversion of deposits is divided between the banks and the central bank, or one should probably better say shifted from the banks to the central bank, since it is now the recognized duty of the central banks to supply in an emergency—at a price—all the cash that may be needed to repay deposits. Yet while the ultimate responsibility to provide the cash when needed is thus placed on the central bank, until this demand actually arises, the latter has little power to prevent the expansion leading to an increased demand for cash.

But with an international standard a national central bank is itself not a free agent. Up to this point the cash about which I have been speaking is the money created by the central bank which within the country is generally acceptable and is the only means of payment outside the circle of the customers of a particular bank. The central bank, however, has not only to provide the required amounts of the medium generally accepted within the country; it has also to provide the even more liquid, internationally acceptable, money. This means that in a situation where there is a general tendency toward greater liquidity there will be at the same time a greater demand for central bank money and for the international money. But the only way in which the central bank can restrict the demand for and increase the supply of the international money is to curtail the supply of central bank money. In consequence, in this stage as in the preceding one, any increase in the demand for the more liquid type of money will lead to a much greater decrease in the supply of the somewhat less liquid kinds of money.

This differentiation between the different kinds of money into those which can be used only among the customers of a particular bank and those which can be used only within a particular country and finally those which can be used internationally—these artificial distinctions of liquidity (as I have previously called them)—have the effect, therefore, that any change in the relative demand for the different kinds of money will lead to a cumulative change in the total quantity of the circulating medium. Any demand on the banks for conversion of part of their deposits into cash will have the effect of compelling them to reduce their deposits by more than the amount paid out and to obtain more cash from the central bank, which in turn will be forced to take counter-measures and so to transmit the tendency toward contraction to the other banks. And the same applies, of course, *mutatis mutandis* to a decrease in the demand for the more liquid type of assets, which will bring about a considerable increase in the supply of money.

All this is of course only the familiar phenomenon which Mr. R.G. Hawtrey has so well described as the "inherent instability of credit." But there are two points about it which deserve special emphasis in this connection. One is that, in consequence of the particular organization of our credit structure, changes in liquidity preference as between different kinds of money are probably a much more potent cause of disturbances than the changes in the preference for holding money *in general* and holding goods *in general* which have played such a great role in recent refinements of theory. The other is that this source of disturbance is likely to be much more serious when there is only a single bank for a whole region or when all the banks of a country have to rely on a single central bank; since the effect of any change in liquidity preference will generally be confined to the group of people who directly or indirectly rely on the same reserve of more liquid assets.

It seems to follow from all this that the problem with which we are concerned is not so much a problem of currency reform in the narrower sense as a problem of banking reform in general. The seat of the trouble is what has been very appropriately been called the perverse elasticity of bank deposits[37] as a medium of circulation, and the cause of this is that deposits, like other forms of "credit money," are claims for another, more generally acceptable sort of money, that a proportional reserve of that other money must be held against them, and that their supply is therefore inversely affected by the demand for the more liquid type of money.

3. The Chicago Plan of Banking Reform

By far the most interesting suggestion on banking reform which has been advanced in recent years, not because in its present form its seems to be practicable or even theoretically right, but because it goes to the heart of the problem, is the so-called Chicago or 100 percent plan.[38] This proposal amounts in effect to an extension of the principles of Peel's Act of 1844 to bank deposits. The most practicable suggestion yet made for its execution is to give the banks a sufficient quantity of paper money to increase the reserves held against demand deposits to 100 percent and henceforth to require them to maintain permanently such a 100 percent reserve.

In this form, the plan is conceived as an instrument of monetary nationalism. But there is no reason why it should not equally

---

[37] L. Currie, *The Supply and Control of Money in the United States* (Cambridge, Mass.: Harvard University Press, 1934), pp. 130 *et seq.*

[38] On the significance of the "Chicago Plan" compare particularly the interesting and stimulating article by H.C. Simons, "Rule versus Authority in Monetary Policy," *Journal of Political Economy* 44, no. 1 (February 1936), and F. Lutz, *Das Grundproblem der Geldverfassung* (Stuttgart: Kohlhammer, 1936), where references to the further literature on the proposal will be found.

be used to create a homogeneous international currency.[39] A possible, although perhaps somewhat fantastic, solution would seem to be to reduce proportionately the gold equivalents of all the different national monetary units to such an extent that all the money in all countries could be covered 100 percent by gold, and from that date onwards to allow variations in the national circulations only in proportion to changes in the quantity of gold in the country.[40] Such a plan would clearly require as an essential complement an international control of the production of gold, since the increase in the value of gold would otherwise bring about an enormous increase in the supply of gold. But this would only provide a safety valve probably necessary in any case to prevent the system from becoming all too rigid.

The undeniable attractiveness of this proposal lies exactly in the feature which makes it appear somewhat impracticable, in the fact that in effect it amounts, as is fully realized by at least one of its sponsors, to an abolition of deposit banking as we know it.[41] It does provide, instead of the variety of media of circulation which today range according to their degree of acceptability from bank deposits to gold, one single kind of money. And it would do away effectively with that most pernicious feature of our present system: namely that a movement toward more liquid types of money causes an actual decrease in the total supply of money and *vice versa*. The most serious question which it raises, however, is whether by abolishing deposit banking as we know it we would effectively prevent the principle on which it rests from manifesting itself in other forms. It has been well remarked by the most critical among the originators of the scheme that banking is a pervasive phenomenon,[42] and the

---

[39] Cf. Simons, "Rule versus Authority in Monetary Policy," p. 5, note 3.

[40] A perhaps somewhat less impracticable alternative might be international bimetallism at a suitable ratio.

[41] Cf. Simons, "Rule versus Authority in Monetary Policy," p. 16.

[42] Ibid., p. 17.

question is whether, when we prevent it from appearing in its traditional form, we will not just drive it into other and less easily controllable forms. Historical precedent rather suggests that we must be wary in this respect. The Act of 1844 was designed to control what then seemed to be the only important substitute for gold as a widely used medium of exchange and yet failed completely in its intention because of the rapid growth of bank deposits. Is it not possible that if similar restrictions to those placed on bank notes were now placed on the expansion of bank deposits, new forms of money substitutes would rapidly spring up or existing ones would assume increasing importance? And can we even today draw a sharp line between what is money and what is not? Are there not already all sorts of "near-moneys"[43] like saving deposits, overdraft facilities, bills of exchange, etc., which satisfy at any rate the demand for liquid reserves nearly as well as money?

I am afraid all this must be admitted, and it considerably detracts from the alluring simplicity of the 100 percent banking scheme. It appears that for this reason it has now also been abandoned by at least one of its original sponsors.[44] The problem is evidently a much wider one, and I agree with Mr. H.C. Simons that it "cannot be dealt with merely by legislation directed at what we call banks."[45] Yet in one respect, at least the 100 percent proposal seems to me to point in the right direction. Even if, as is probably the case, it is impossible to draw a sharp line between what is to be treated as money and what is not, and if consequently any attempt to fix rigidly the quantity of what is more or less arbitrarily segregated as "money" would create serious difficulties, it yet remains true that, within the field of instruments which are undoubtedly generally used as money, there are unnecessary and purely institutional distinctions of

---

[43] Ibid., p. 17.

[44] Ibid., p. 17.

[45] Ibid.

liquidity which are the sources of serious disturbances and which should as far as possible be eliminated. If this cannot be done for the time being by a general return to the common use of the same international medium in the great majority of transactions, it should at least be possible to approach this goal by reducing the distinctions of liquidity between the different kinds of money actually used, and offsetting as far as possible the effects of changes in the demand for liquid assets on the total quantity of the circulating medium.

4. Exchange Rates and Gold Reserves

This brings me to the more practical question of what can be done to diminish the instability of the credit structure if the general framework of the present monetary system is to be maintained. The aim, as we have just seen, must be to increase the certainty that one form of money will always be readily exchangeable against other forms of money at a known rate, and that such changes should not lead to changes in the total quantity of money. Insofar as the relations between different national currencies are concerned, this leads of course to a demand for reforms in exactly the opposite direction from those advocated by monetary nationalists. Instead of flexible parities or a widening of the "gold points," absolute fixity of the exchange rates should be secured by a system of international par clearance. If all the central banks undertook to buy and sell foreign exchange freely at the same fixed rates, and in this way prevented even fluctuations within the "gold points," the remaining differences in denomination of the national currencies would really be no more significant than the fact that the same quantity of cloth can be stated in yards and in meters. With an international gold settlement fund on the lines of that operated by the Federal Reserve System, which would make it possible to dispense with the greater part of the actual gold movements which used to take place in the past, invariable rates of exchange could be maintained without placing any excessive burden on the central banks.[46] The main aim here would of course be rather to remove one of the main causes of international movements of short-term funds than to prevent such movements or to offset their effects by means which will only increase the inducement to such movements.[47]

But invariability of the exchange rates is only one precondition of a successful policy directed to minimize monetary disturbances. It eliminates one of the institutional differentiations of liquidity which are likely to give rise to sudden changes in favor of holding one sort of money instead of another. But there remains the further distinction between the different sorts of money which constitute the national monetary systems; and, so long as the general framework of our present banking systems is retained, the dangers to stability which arise here can hardly be combated otherwise than by a deliberate policy of the national central banks.

The most important change which seems to be necessary here is that the gold reserves of all the central banks should be made large enough to relieve them of the necessity of bringing about a

---

[46] The founders of the Bank for International Settlements definitely contemplated that the bank might establish such a fund, and article 24 of its statutes specifically states that the bank may enter into special agreements with central banks to facilitate the settlement of international transactions between them.

> For this purpose it may arrange with central banks to have gold earmarked for their account and transferable on their order, to open accounts through which central banks can transfer their assets from one currency to another and to take such other measures as the Board may think advisable within the limits of the powers granted by these Statutes.

[47] In a book which has appeared since these lectures were delivered (Whittlesey, *International Monetary Issues*) the author, after pointing out that a widening of the gold points would have the effects of increasing the volume of short-term capital movements of this sort (p. 116) concludes that "the only way of overcoming this factor would be to eliminate the gold points" (p. 117). But the only way of eliminating the gold points of which he can think is to abolish the gold standard!

change in the total national circulation *in proportion* to the changes in their reserves; that is, that any change in the relative amounts of money in different countries should be brought about by the actual transfer of corresponding amounts from country to country without any "secondary" contractions and expansions of the credit superstructure of the countries concerned. This would be the case only if individual central banks held gold reserves large enough to be used freely without resort to any special measures for their "protection."

Now the present abundance of gold offers an exceptional opportunity for such a reform. But to achieve the desired result not only the absolute supply of gold but also its distribution is of importance. In this respect it must appear unfortunate that those countries which command already abundant gold reserves and would therefore be in a position to work the gold standard on these lines, should use that position to keep the price artificially high. The policy on the part of those countries which are already in a strong gold position, if it aims at the restoration of an international gold standard, should have been, while maintaining constant rates of exchange with all countries in a similar position, to reduce the price of gold in order to direct the stream of gold to those countries which are not yet in a position to resume gold payments. Only when the price of gold has fallen sufficiently to enable those countries to acquire sufficient reserves should a general and simultaneous return to a free gold standard be attempted.

It may seem at first that even if one could start with an appropriate distribution of gold between countries which at first would put each country in a position where it could allow its stock of gold to vary by the absolute amounts by which its circulation would have to increase or decrease, some countries would soon again find their gold stocks so depleted that they would be compelled to take traditional measures for their protection. And it cannot be denied that, so long as the stock of gold of any country is anything less than 100 percent of its total circulation, it is at least conceivable that it may be reduced to a point where in order to protect the remainder, the monetary authorities might have to have recourse to a policy of credit contraction. But a short reflection will show that this is extraordinarily unlikely to happen if a country starts out with a fairly large stock of gold and if its monetary authorities adhere to the main principle not only with regard to decreases but equally with regard to increases in the total circulation.

If we assume the different countries start with a gold reserve amounting to only a third of the total monetary circulation,[48] this would probably provide a margin amply sufficient for any reduction of the country's share in the world's stock of money which is likely to become necessary. That a country's share in the world's income, and therefore its relative demand for money, should fall off by more than this would at any rate be an exceptional case requiring exceptional treatment.[49] If history seems to suggest that such considerable losses of gold are not at all infrequent, this is due to the operation of a different cause which should be absent if the principle suggested were really applied. If under the traditional

---

[48] At the present value of gold the world's stock of monetary gold (at the end of 1936) amounts to 73.5 percent, of all sight liabilities of the central banks *plus* the circulation of government paper money. The percentage would of course be considerably lower if, as would be necessary for this purpose, the comparison were made with the total of sight deposits with commercial banks *plus* bank notes, etc., in the hands of the public. But there can be no doubt that even if the price of gold should be somewhat lowered (say, by one seventh, i.e., from 140 to 120 shillings or from $35 to $30 per ounce) there would still be ample gold available to provide sufficient reserves.

[49] If in spite of this in an individual case the gold reserves of a country should be nearly exhausted, the necessary remedy would be to acquire the necessary amount of gold through an external loan and to give this amount to the central bank in repayment of part of the state debt which presumably will constitute at least part of its non-gold assets (or in payments of any other assets which the bank would have to sell to the government). The main point here is that the acquisition of this gold must be paid for out of taxation and not by the creation of additional credit by the central bank.

gold standard any one country expanded credit out of step with the rest of the world, this did usually bring about an outflow of gold only after a considerable time lag. This in itself would mean that, before equilibrium would be restored by the direct operations of the gold flows, an amount of gold approximately equal to the credit created in excess would have to flow out of the country. If, however, as has often been the case, the country should be tardy in decreasing its circulation by the amount of gold it has lost, that is, if it should try to "offset" the losses of gold by new creations of credit, there would be no limits to the amount of gold which may leave the country except the size of the reserves. Or, in other words, if the principle of changing the total circulation by the full amount of gold imported or exported were strictly applied, gold movements would be much smaller than has been the case in the past, and the size of the gold movements experienced in the past create therefore no presumption that they would be equally large in the future.

5. Credit Policy of the Central Banks

These considerations will already have made it clear that the principle of central banking policy here proposed by no means implies that the central banks should be relieved from all necessity of shaping their credit policy according to the state of their reserves. Quite the contrary. It only means that they should not be compelled to adhere to the mechanical rule of changing their notes and deposits *in proportion* to the change in their reserves. Instead of this they would have to undertake the much more difficult task of influencing the total volume of money in their countries in such a way that this total would change by the same absolute amounts as their reserves. And since the central bank has no direct power over the greater part of the circulating medium of the country, it would have to try to control its volume indirectly. This means that it would have to use its power to change the volume of its notes and deposits so as to make the superstructure of credit built on those move in conformity with its reserves. But as the amount of ordinary bank deposits and other forms of common means of exchange based on a given volume of central bank money will be different at different times, this means that the central bank, in order to make the total amount of money move with its reserves, would frequently have to change the amount of central bank money independently of changes in its reserves and occasionally even in a direction opposite to that in which its reserves may change.

It should perhaps always have been evident that, with a banking system which has grown to rely on the assistance of a central bank for the supply of cash when needed, no sort of control of the circulating medium can be achieved unless the central bank has power and uses this power to control the volume of bank deposits in ordinary times. And the policy to make this control effective will have to be very different from the policy of a bank which is concerned merely with its own liquidity. It will have to act persistently against the trend of the movement of credit in the country, to contract the credit basis when the superstructure tends to expand, and to expand the former when the latter tends to contract.

It is today almost commonplace that, with a developed banking structure, the policy of the central bank can in no way be automatic. It would indeed require the greatest art and discernment for a central bank to succeed in making the credit money provided by the private banks behave as a purely metallic circulation would behave under similar circumstances. But while it may appear very doubtful whether this ideal will ever be fully achieved, there can be no doubt that we are still so far from it that very considerable changes from traditional policy would be required before we shall be able to say that even what is possible has been achieved.

In any case it should be obvious that the existence of a central bank which does nothing to counteract the expansions of banking credit made possible by its existence only adds another link in the chain through which the cumulative expansions and contractions of credit operate. So long as central banks are regarded, and regard themselves, only as "lenders of last resort" which have to provide the cash which becomes necessary in consequence of a previous credit expansion with which, until this point arrives, they are not concerned, so long as central banks wait until "the market is in the bank" before they feel bound to check expansion, we cannot hope that wide fluctuations in the volume of credit will be avoided. Certainly Mr. Hawtrey was right with his now-celebrated statement that "so long as the credit is regulated with reference to reserve proportions, the trade cycle is bound to recur."[50] But I am afraid only one (and that not the more important of the essential corollaries of this proposition) is usually derived from this statement. What is usually emphasized is the fact that concern with reserve proportions will ultimately compel central banks to stop a process of credit expansion and actually to bring about a process of credit contraction. What seems to me much more important is that sole regard to their own reserve proportions will not lead central banks to counteract the increase of bank deposits, even if it means an increase of the credit circulation of the country relatively to the gold reserve, and although it is an increase largely made possible by the certain expectation—on the part of the other banks—that the central bank will in the end supply the cash needed.

On the question of how far central banks are in practice likely to succeed in this difficult task, different opinions are clearly possible. The optimist will be convinced that they will be able to do much more than merely offset the dangers which their existence creates. The pessimist will be skeptical whether on balance they will not do more harm than good. The difficulty of the task, the impossibility of prescribing any fixed rule, and the extent to which the action of the central banks will always be exposed to the pressure of public opinion and political influence certainly justify grave doubts. And though the alternative solution is today

---

[50] *Monetary Reconstruction* (London: Longmans, Green, 1923), p. 144.

probably outside of the realm of practical politics, it is sufficiently important to deserve at least a passing consideration before we leave this subject.

As I have pointed out before, the "national reserve principle" is not insolubly bound up with the centralization of the note issue. While we must probably take it for granted that the issue of notes will remain reserved to one or a few privileged institutions, these institutions need not necessarily be the keepers of the national reserve. There is no reason why the banks of issue should not be entirely confined to the functions of the issue department of the Bank of England, that is, to the conversion of gold into notes and notes into gold, while the duty of holding appropriate reserves is left to individual banks. There could still be in the background—for the case of a run on the banks—the power of a temporary "suspension" of the limitations of the note issue and of the issue of an emergency currency at a penalizing rate of interest.

The advantage of such a plan would be that one tier in the pyramid of credit would be eliminated and the cumulative effects of changes in liquidity preference accordingly reduced. The disadvantage would be that the remaining competing institutions would inevitably have to act on the proportional reserve principle and that nobody would be in a position, by a deliberate policy, to offset the tendency to cumulative changes. This might not be so serious if there were numerous small banks whose spheres of operation freely overlapped over the whole world. But it can hardly be recommended where we have to deal with the existing banking systems, which consist of a few large institutions covering the same field of a single nation. It is probably one of the ideals which might be practical in a liberal world federation but which is impracticable where national frontiers also mean boundaries to the normal activities of banking institutions. The practical problem remains that of the appropriate policy of national central banks.

6. Conclusions

It is unfortunately impossible to say here more about the principles which a rational central banking policy would have to follow without going into some of the most controversial problems of the theory of the trade cycle which clearly fall outside the scope of these lectures. I must therefore confine myself to pointing out that what I have said so far is altogether independent of the particular views on this subject for which I have been accused, I think unjustly, of being a deflationist. Whether we think that the ideal would be a more or less constant volume of the monetary circulation, or whether we think that this volume should gradually increase at a fairly constant rate as productivity increases, the problem of how to prevent the credit structure in any country from running away in either direction remains the same.

Here my aim has merely been to show that whatever our views about the desirable behavior of the total quantity of money, they can never legitimately be applied to the situation of a single country which is part of an international economic system, and that any attempt to do so is likely in the long run and for the world as a whole to be an additional source of instability. This means of course that a really rational monetary policy could be carried out only by an international monetary authority, or at any rate by the closest cooperation of the national authorities and with the common aim of making the circulation of each country behave as nearly as possible as if it were part of an intelligently regulated international system.

But I think it also means that so long as an effective international monetary authority remains a utopian dream, any mechanical principle (such as the gold standard) which at least secures some conformity of monetary changes in the national area to what would happen under a truly international monetary system is far preferable to numerous independent and independently regulated national currencies. If it does not provide a really rational regulation of the quantity of money, it at any rate tends to make it behave on roughly foreseeable lines, which is of the greatest importance. And since there is no means, short of complete autarchy, of protecting a country against the folly or perversity of the monetary policy of other countries, the only hope of avoiding serious disturbances is to submit to some common rules, even if they are by no means ideal, in order to induce other countries to follow a similarly reasonable policy. That there is much scope for an improvement of the rules of the game which were supposed to exist in the past, nobody will deny. The most important step in this direction is that the *rationale* of an international standard and the true sources of the instability of our present system should be properly appreciated. It was for this reason that I felt that my most urgent task was to restate the broader theoretical considerations which bear on the practical problem before us. I hope that by confining myself largely to these theoretical problems I have not too much disappointed the expectations to which the title of these lectures may have given rise. But, as I said at the beginning of these lectures, I do believe that in the long run human affairs are guided by intellectual forces. It is this belief which for me gives abstract considerations of this sort their importance, however slight may be their bearing on what is practicable in the immediate future.

Reflections on the Pure Theory of Money of Mr. J.M. Keynes

Reflections on the Pure Theory of Money of Mr. J.M. Keynes

I

The appearance of any work by Mr. J.M. Keynes must always be a matter of importance; and the publication of the *Treatise on Money*[1] has long been awaited with intense interest by all economists. Nonetheless, in the event, the *Treatise* proves to be so obviously—and, I think, admittedly—the expression of a transitory phase in a process of rapid intellectual development that its appearance cannot be said to have that definitive significance which at one time was expected of it. Indeed, so strongly does it bear the marks of the effect of the recent discovery of certain lines of thought hitherto unfamiliar to the school to which Mr. Keynes belongs, that it would be decidedly unfair to regard it as anything else but experimental—a first attempt to amalgamate those new ideas with the monetary teaching traditional in Cambridge and pervading Mr. Keynes's own earlier contributions. That the new approach, which Mr. Keynes has adopted, which makes the rate of interest and its relation to saving and

---

This article was originally published in two parts. Part one first appeared in *Economica* 33 (August 1931): 270–95; part two in *Economica* 35 (February 1932): 22–44.

[1] J.M. Keynes, *A Treatise on Money*, 2 vols. (London: Macmillan, 1930).

investing the central problem of monetary theory, is an enormous advance on this earlier position, and that it directs the attention to what is really essential, seems to me to be beyond doubt. And even if, to a Continental economist, this way of approach does not seem so novel as it does to the author, it must be admitted that he has made a more ambitious attempt to carry the analysis into the details and complications of the problem than any that has been attempted hitherto. Whether he has been successful here, whether he has not been seriously hampered by the fact that he has not devoted the same amount of effort to understanding those fundamental theorems of "real" economics on which alone any monetary explanation can be successfully built, as he has to subsidiary embellishments, are questions which will have to be examined later.

That such a book is theoretically stimulating goes without saying. At the same time, it is difficult to suppress some concern as regards the immediate effect which its publication in its present form may have on the development of monetary theory. It was, no doubt, the urgency which he attributes to the practical proposals which he holds to be justified by his theoretical reasoning, which led Mr. Keynes to publish the work in what is avowedly an unfinished state. The proposals are indeed revolutionary, and cannot fail to attract the widest attention: they come from a writer who has established an almost unique and well-deserved reputation for courage and practical insight; they are expounded in passages in which the author displays all his astonishing qualities of learning, erudition and realistic knowledge, and in which every possible effort is made to verify the theoretical reasoning by reference to available statistical data. Moreover, most of the practical conclusions seem to harmonize with what seems to the man in the street to be the dictates of common sense, and the favorable impression thus created will probably not be diminished at all by the fact that they are based on a part of the work (books 3 and 4) which is so highly technical and complicated that it must forever remain entirely unintelligible to those who are not experts. But it is this part on which everything else depends. It is here that all the force and all the weakness of the argument are concentrated, and it is here that the really original work is set forth. And here, unfortunately, the exposition is so difficult, unsystematic, and obscure, that it is extremely difficult for the fellow economist who disagrees with the conclusions to demonstrate the exact point of disagreement and to state his objections. There are passages in which the inconsistent use of terms produces a degree of obscurity which, to anyone acquainted with Mr. Keynes's earlier work, is almost unbelievable. It is only with extreme caution and the greatest reserve that one can attempt to criticize, because one can never be sure whether one has understood Mr. Keynes aright.

For this reason, I propose in these reflections to neglect for the present the applications, which fill almost the whole of volume 2, and to concentrate entirely on the imperative task of examining these central difficulties. I address myself expressly to expert readers who have read the book in its entirety.[2]

II

Book 1 gives a description and classification of the different kinds of money which in many respects is excellent. Where it gives rise to doubts or objections, the points of difference are not of sufficient consequence to make it necessary to give them space which will be much more urgently needed later on. The most interesting and important parts consist in the analysis of the factors which determine the amounts of money which are held by different members of the community, and the division of the total money in circulation into "income deposits" and "business

---

[2] If at any point my own analysis seems to English readers to take too much for granted, perhaps I may be permitted to refer to my *Prices and Production* (London: Routledge and Sons, 1931) in chaps. 2 and 3; also included in this volume, of which I have attempted to provide a broad outline of the general theoretical considerations which seem to me indispensable in any approach to this problem.

deposits" according to the purpose for which it is held. This distinction, by the way, has turned up again and again in writings on money since the time of Adam Smith (whom Mr. Keynes quotes), but so far it has not proved of much value.

Book 2 is a highly interesting digression into the problem of the measurement of the value of money, and forms in itself a systematic and excellent treatise on that controversial subject. Here it must be sufficient to say that it deals with the problem in the most up-to-date manner, treating index-numbers on the lines developed chiefly by Dr. Haberler in his *Sinn der Indexzahlen,* as expressions of the changes in the price sum of definite collections of commodities—its main addition to the existing knowledge of this subject being an excellent and very much needed criticism of certain attempts to base the method of index numbers on the theory of probability. For an understanding of what follows, I need only mention that Mr. Keynes distinguishes as relatively less important for the purposes of monetary theory the currency standard in its two forms, the cash transactions standard and the cash balances standard (and the infinite number of possible secondary price levels corresponding, not to the general purchasing power of money as a whole, but to its purchasing power for special purposes), from the "labor power" of money and the purchasing power of money proper, which are fundamental in a sense in which price levels based on other types of expenditure are not, because "human effort and human consumption are the ultimate matters from which alone economic transactions are capable of deriving any significance" (vol. 1, p. 134).

III

It is in books 3 and 4 that Mr. Keynes proposes "a novel means of approach to the fundamental problem of monetary theory" (Preface). He begins with an elaborate catalogue of the terms and concepts he wants to use. And here, right at the beginning, we encounter a peculiarity which is likely to prove a stumbling block to most readers, the concept of entrepreneur's profits. These are expressly excluded from the category of money income, and form a separate category of their own. I have no fundamental objection to this somewhat irritating distinction, and I agree perfectly when he defines profits by saying that "when profits are positive (or negative) entrepreneurs will—insofar as their freedom of action is not fettered by existing bargains with the factors of production which are for the time being irrevocable—seek to expand (or curtail) their scale of operations" and hence depicts profits as the mainspring of change in the existing economic system. But I cannot agree with his explanation of why profits arise, nor with his implication that only changes in "total profits" in his sense can lead to an expansion or curtailment of output. For profits in his view are considered as a "purely monetary phenomenon" in the narrowest sense of that expression. The cause of the emergence of those profits which are "the mainspring of change" is not a "real" factor, not some maladjustment in the relative demand for and supply of cost goods and their respective products (i.e., of the relative supply of intermediate products in the successive stages of production) and, therefore, something which could arise also in a barter economy, but simply and solely spontaneous changes in the quantity and direction of the flow of money. Indeed, throughout the whole of his argument the flow of money is treated as if it were the only independent variable which could cause a positive or negative difference between the prices of the products and their respective costs. The structure of goods on which this flow impinges is assumed to be relatively rigid. In fact, of course, the original cause may just as well be a change in the relative supply of these classes of goods, which then, in turn, will affect the quantities of money expended on them.[3]

---

[3] The difference between Mr. Keynes's viewpoint and my own here is not, as may seem in the first instance, due to any neglect on my part of the fact that Mr. Keynes is dealing only with a short-run problem. It is Mr. Keynes, rather, with his implied assumption that the real factors are in equilibrium, who is unconsciously introducing a long-run view of the subject.

But though many readers will feel that Mr. Keynes's analysis of profit leaves out essential things, it is not at all easy to detect the flaw in his argument. His explanation seems to flow necessarily from the truism that profits can arise only if more money is received from the sale of goods than has been expended on their production. But, obvious as this is, the conclusion drawn from it becomes a fallacy if only the prices of finished consumption goods and the prices paid for the factors of production are contrasted. And, with the quite insufficient exception of *new* investment goods, this is exactly what Mr. Keynes does. As I shall repeatedly have occasion to point out, he treats the process of the current output of consumption goods as an integral whole in which only the prices obtained at the end for the final products and the prices paid at the beginning for the factors of production have any bearing on its profitableness. He seems to think that sufficient account of any change in the relative supply (and therefore in the value) of intermediate products in the successive stages of that process is provided for by his concept of (positive or negative) investment, i.e., the net addition to (or diminution from) the capital of the community. But this is by no means sufficient if only the total or net increment (or decrement) of investment goods in all stages is considered and treated as a whole, and the possibility of fluctuations between these stages is neglected; yet this is just what Mr. Keynes does. The fact that his whole concept of investment is ambiguous, and that its meaning is constantly shifting between the idea of any surplus beyond the reproduction of the identical capital goods which have been used up in current production and the idea of any addition to the total value of the capital goods, renders it still less adequate to account for that phenomenon.

When I come to the concept of investment I shall quote evidence of this confusion. For the present, however, let us assume that the concept of investment includes, as, in spite of some clearly contradictory statements of Mr. Keynes it probably should include, only the net addition to the value of all the existing capital goods.

If we take a situation where, according to that criterion, no investment takes place, and therefore the total expenditure on the factors of production is to be counted as being directed toward the current production of consumers' goods, it is quite conceivable that—to take an extreme case—there may be no net difference between the total receipts for the output and the total payments for the factors of production, and no net profits for the entrepreneurs as a whole, *because* profits in the lower stages of production are exactly compensated by the losses in the higher stages. Yet, in that case, it will not be profitable for a time for entrepreneurs as a whole to continue to employ the same quantity of factors of production as before. We need only consider the quite conceivable case that in each of the successive stages of production there are more intermediate products than are needed for the reproduction of the intermediate products existing at the same moment in the following stage, so that, in the lower stages (i.e., those nearer consumption) there is a shortage, and in the higher stages there is an abundance, as compared with the current demand for consumers' goods. In this case, all the entrepreneurs in the higher stages of production will probably make losses; but even if these losses were exactly compensated, or more than compensated, by the profits made in the lower stages, in a large part of the complete process necessary for the continuous supply of consumption goods it will not pay to employ all the factors of production available. And while the losses of the producers of those stages are balanced by the profits of those finishing consumption goods, the diminution of their demand for the factors of production cannot be made up by the increased demand from the latter because these need mainly semi-finished goods and can use labor only in proportion to the quantities of such goods which are available in the respective stages. In such a case, profits and losses are originally not the effect of a discrepancy between the receipts for consumption goods and the expenditure on the factors of production, and therefore they are not explained by Mr. Keynes's analysis. Or, rather, there are no total profits in Mr. Keynes's sense in this case, and yet there occur those very effects which he regards as only conceivable as the consequence of the emergence of net total profits or losses. The explanation of this is that while the definition of profits which I have quoted before serves very well when it is applied to individual profits, it becomes misleading when it is applied to entrepreneurs as a whole. The entrepreneurs making profits need not necessarily employ more original factors of production to expand their production, but may draw mainly on the existing stocks of intermediate products of the preceding stages while entrepreneurs suffering losses dismiss workmen.

But this is not all. Not only is it possible for the changes which Mr. Keynes attributes only to changes in "total profits") to occur when "total profits" in his sense are absent: it is also possible for "total profits" to emerge for causes other than those contemplated in his analysis. It is by no means necessary for "total profits" to be the effect of a difference between *current* receipts and *current* expenditure. Nor need every difference between current receipts and current expenditure lead to the emergence of "total profits." For even if there is neither positive nor negative investment, yet entrepreneurs may gain or lose in the aggregate because of changes in the value of capital which existed before—changes due to new additions to or subtractions from existing capital.[4] It is such changes in the value of existing intermediate products (or "investment," or capital, or whatever one likes to call it) which act as a balancing factor between current receipts and current expenditure. Or to put the same thing another way, profits cannot be explained as the difference between expenditure in one period and receipts in the *same* period or a period of equal length because *the result of the expenditure in one period will very often have to be sold in a period which is either longer or shorter than the first period.* It is indeed the essential characteristic of positive or negative investment that this must be the case.

---

[4] Of course such changes need not only affect entrepreneurs. They may also affect other owners of capital.

It is not possible at this stage to show that a divergence between current expenditure and current receipts will always tend to cause changes in the value of existing capital which are by no means constituted by that difference, and that because of this, the effects of a difference between current receipts and current expenditure (i.e., profits in Mr. Keynes's sense), may lead to a change in the value of existing capital which may more than balance the money profits. We shall have to deal with this matter in detail when we come to Mr. Keynes's explanation of the trade cycle, but before we can do that, we shall have to analyze his concept of investment very closely. It should, however, already be clear that even if his concept of investment does not refer, as has been assumed, to changes in the value of existing capital but to changes in the physical quantities of capital goods—and there can be no doubt that in many parts of his book Mr. Keynes uses it in this sense—this would not remedy the deficiencies of his analysis. At the same time there can be no doubt that it is the lack of a clear concept of investment—and of capital—which is the cause of this unsatisfactory account of profits.

There are other very mischievous peculiarities of this concept of profits which may be noted at this point. The derivation of profits from the difference between receipts for the total output and the expenditure on the factors of production implies that there exists some normal rate of remuneration of invested capital which is more stable than profits. Mr. Keynes does not explicitly state this, but he includes the remuneration of invested capital in his more comprehensive concept of the "money rate of efficiency earnings of the factors of production" in general, a concept on which I shall have more to say later on. But even if it be true, as it probably is, that the rate of remuneration of the original factors of production is relatively more rigid than profits, it is certainly not true in regard to the remuneration of invested capital. Mr. Keynes obviously arrives at this view by an artificial separation of the function of the entrepreneurs as owners of capital and their function as entrepreneurs in the narrow sense. But these two functions cannot be absolutely separated even in theory, because the essential function of the entrepreneurs, that of assuming risks, necessarily implies the ownership of capital. Moreover, *any new chance to make entrepreneurs' profits is identical with a change in the opportunities to invest capital, and will always be reflected in the earnings (and value) of capital invested.* (For similar reasons it seems to me also impossible to mark off entrepreneurs' profits as something fundamentally different from, say, the extra gain of a workman who moves first to a place where a scarcity of labor makes itself felt and, therefore, for some time obtains wages higher than the normal rate.)

Now this artificial separation of entrepreneurs' profits from the earnings of existing capital has very serious consequences for the further analysis of investment: it leads not to an explanation of the changes in the demand price offered by the entrepreneurs for new capital, but only to an explanation of changes in their aggregate demand for "factors of production" in general. But, surely, an explanation of the causes which make investment more or less attractive should form the basis of any analysis of investment. *Such an explanation can, however, only be reached by a close analysis of the factors determining the relative prices of capital goods in the different successive stages of production*—for the difference between these prices is the only source of interest. But this is excluded from the outset if only *total* profits are made the aim of the investigation. Mr. Keynes's aggregates conceal the most fundamental mechanisms of change.

IV

I pass now to the central and most obscure theme of the book, the description and explanation of the processes of investment. It seems to me that most of the difficulties which arise here are a consequence of the peculiar method of approach adopted by Mr. Keynes, who, from the outset, analyses complex dynamic processes without laying the necessary foundations by adequate static analysis of the fundamental process. Not only does he fail to concern himself with the conditions which must be given to secure the continuation of the existing capitalistic (i.e., roundabout) organization of production—the conditions creating an equilibrium between the depreciation and the renewal of existing capital—not only does he take the maintenance of the existing capital stock more or less as a matter of course (which it certainly is not—it requires quite definite relationships between the prices of consumption goods and the prices of capital goods to make it profitable to keep capital intact): he does not even explain the conditions of equilibrium at any given rate of saving, nor the effects of any change in the rate of saving. Only when money comes in as a disturbing factor by making the rate at which additional capital goods are produced different from the rate at which saving is taking place does he begin to be interested.

All this would do no harm if his analysis of this complicating moment were based on a clear and definite theory of capital and saving developed elsewhere, either by himself or by others. But this is obviously not the case. Moreover, he makes a satisfactory analysis of the whole process of investment still more difficult for himself by another peculiarity of his analysis, namely by completely separating the process of the reproduction of the old capital from the addition of new capital, and treating the former simply as a part of current production of consumption goods, in defiance of the obvious fact that the production of the same goods, whether they are destined for the replacement of or as additions to the old stock of capital, must be determined by the same set of conditions. New savings and new investment are treated as if they were something entirely different from the reinvestment of the quota of amortization of old capital, and as if it were not the same market where the prices of capital goods needed for the current production of consumption goods and of additional capital goods are determined. Instead of a "horizontal" division between capital goods (or goods of higher stages or orders) and consumption goods (or goods of lower stages)—which one would have thought would have recommended itself on the grounds that in each of these groups and subgroups production will be regulated by similar conditions—Mr. Keynes attempts a kind of vertical division, counting that part of the production of capital goods which is necessary for the continuation of the current production of consumption goods as a part of the process of producing consumption goods, and only that part of the production of capital goods which *adds* to the existing stock of capital as production of investment goods. But this procedure involves him, as we shall see, in serious difficulties when he has to determine what is to be considered as additional capital—difficulties which he has not clearly solved. The question is whether any increase of the value of the existing capital is to be considered as such an addition—in this case, of course, such an addition could be brought about without any new production of such goods—or whether only additions to the physical quantities of capital goods are counted as such an addition—a method of computation which becomes clearly impossible when the old capital goods are not replaced by goods of exactly the same kind, but when a transition to more capitalistic methods brings it about that other goods are produced in place of those used up in production.

This continual attempt to elucidate special complications without first providing a sufficient basis in the form of an explanation of the more simple equilibrium relations becomes particularly noticeable in a later stage of the investigation when Mr. Keynes tries to incorporate into his system the ideas of Wicksell. In Wicksell's system these are necessary outgrowths of the most elaborate theory of capital we possess, that of Böhm-Bawerk. It is *a priori* unlikely that an attempt to utilize the conclusions drawn from a certain theory without accepting that theory itself should be successful. But, in the case of an author of Mr. Keynes's intellectual caliber, the attempt produces results which are truly remarkable.

Mr. Keynes ignores completely the general theoretical basis of Wicksell's theory. But, nonetheless, he seems to have felt that such a theoretical basis is wanting, and accordingly he has sat down to work one out for himself. But for all this, it still seems to him somewhat out of place in a treatise on money, so instead of presenting his theory of capital here, in the forefront of his exposition, where it would have figured to most advantage, he relegates it to a position in volume 2 and apologizes for inserting it (vol. 2, p. 95). But the most remarkable feature of these chapters (27–29) is not that he supplies at least a part of the required theoretical foundation, but that he discovers anew certain essential elements of Böhm-Bawerk's theory of capital, especially what he calls (as has been done before in many discussions of Böhm-Bawerk's theory—I mention only Taussig's *Wages and Capital* as one of the earliest and best known instances) the "true wages fund" (vol. 2, pp. 127–29) and earlier (vol. 1, p. 308) Böhm-Bawerk's formula for the relation between the average length of the roundabout process of production and the amount of capital.[5] Would not Mr. Keynes have made his task easier if he had not only accepted one of the descendants of Böhm-Bawerk's theory, but had also made himself acquainted with the substance of that theory itself?

V

We must now consider in more detail Mr. Keynes's analysis of the process of investment. Not the least difficult part of this task is to find out what is really meant by the expression investment as

---

[5] According to Böhm-Bawerk (*Positive Theory of Captial*, 3rd. ed. [Jena: Gustav Fischer, 1921], p. 535; English translation [New York: Macmillan, 1923], p. 328) the stock of capital must be as great as $\frac{x+1}{2}$ the amount of consumption goods consumed during a period of time if x stands for the total length of the production process and if the original factors of production are applied at a steady rate. Mr. Keynes calls the magnitude which Böhm-Bawerk called x, 2r − 1 and, as $\frac{(2r-1)+1}{2}$ = r, comes to the conclusion that the working capital (to which, for unaccountable reasons, he confines his formula) amounts to r times the earnings per unit of time.

it is used here. It is certainly no accident that the inconsistencies of terminology, to which I have alluded before, become particularly frequent as soon as investment is referred to. I must mention here some of the most disturbing instances, as they will illustrate the difficulties in which every serious student of Mr. Keynes's book finds himself involved.

Perhaps the clearest expression of what Mr. Keynes thinks when he uses the term investment is to be found where he defines it as "the act of the entrepreneur whose function it is to make the decisions which determine the amount of the non-available output" consisting "in the positive act of starting or maintaining some process of production or of withholding liquid goods. It is measured by the net addition to wealth whether in the form of fixed capital, working capital or liquid capital" (vol. 1, p. 172). It is perhaps somewhat misleading to use the term investment for the act as well as the result, and it might have been more appropriate to use in the former sense the term "investing." But that would not matter if Mr. Keynes would confine himself to these two senses, for it would not be difficult to keep them apart. But while the expression "net addition to wealth" in the passage just quoted clearly indicates that investment means the increment of the value of existing capital— since wealth cannot be measured otherwise than as value— somewhat earlier, when the term "value of investment" occurs for the first time (vol. 1, p. 126), it is expressly defined as "not the increment of value of the total capital, but the value of the increment of capital during any period." Now, in any case, this would be difficult as, if it is not assumed that the old capital is always replaced by goods of exactly the same kind so that it can be measured as a physical magnitude, it is impossible to see how the increment of capital can be determined otherwise than as an increment of the value of the total. But, to make the confusion complete, side by side with these two definitions of investment as the increment of the value of existing capital and the value of the increment, four pages after the passage just quoted, he defines the "Value of the Investment" not as an increment at all but as the "value of the aggregate of Real and Loan Capital" and contrasts it with the increment of investment which he now defines as "the net increase of the items belonging to the various categories which make up the aggregate of Real and Loan Capital" while "the value of the increment of investment" is now "the sum of the values of the additional items."

These obscurities are not a matter of minor importance. It is because he has allowed them to arise that Mr. Keynes fails to realize the necessity of dealing with the all-important problem of changes in the value of existing capital; and this failure, as we have already seen, is the main cause of his unsatisfactory treatment of profit. It is also partly responsible for the deficiencies of his concept of capital. I have tried hard to discover what Mr. Keynes means by investment by examining the use he makes of it, but all in vain. It might be hoped to get a clearer definition by exclusion from the way in which he defines the "current output of consumption goods" for, as we shall see later, the amount of investment stands in a definite relation to the current output of consumers' goods so that their aggregate cost is equal to the total money income of the community. But here the obscurities which obstruct the way are as great as elsewhere. While on page 135, the cost of production of the current output of consumption goods is defined as total earnings *minus* that part of it which has been earned by the production of investment goods (which a few pages earlier (p. 130) has been defined as "non-available output *plus* the increment of hoards"), there occurs on page 130 a definition of the "output of consumption goods during any period" as "the flow of available output *plus* the increment of Working Capital which will emerge as available output," i.e., as including part of the as yet non-available output which, in the passage quoted before, has been included in investment goods and therefore excluded from the current output of consumption goods. And still a few pages earlier (vol. 1, p. 127) a "flow of consumers' goods" appears as part of the available output, while on the same page "the excess of the flow of increment to unfinished goods in process over the flow of finished goods emerging from the productive prices" (which, obviously, includes "the increment of Working Capital which will emerge as available output" which, in the passage quoted before, is part of the output of consumption goods) is now classed as non-available output. I am afraid it is not altogether my fault if at times I feel helpless in this jungle of differing definitions.

VI

In the preceding sections we have made the acquaintance of the fundamental concepts which Mr. Keynes uses as tools in his analysis of the process of the circulation of money. Now we must turn to his picture of the process itself. The skeleton of his exposition is given in a few pages (vol. 1, pp. 135–40) in a series of algebraic equations which, however, are not only very difficult, but can only be correctly understood in connection with the whole of book 3. In the adjoining diagram, I have made an attempt to give a synoptic view of the process as Mr. Keynes depicts it, which I hope will give an adequate idea of the essential elements of his exposition.

E, which stands at the top and again at the bottom of the diagram, represents (according to the definition which opens book 3) the total earnings of the factors of production. These are to be considered as identically one and the same thing as (a) the community's money income (which includes all wages in the widest sense of the word, the normal remuneration of the entrepreneurs, interest on capital, regular monopoly gains, rents and the like) and (b) "the cost of production." Though the definition does not expressly say so, the use Mr. Keynes makes of the symbol E clearly shows that that "cost of production" refers to current output. But here the first difficulty arises. Is it necessarily true that the E, which was the cost of production of

Reflections on the Pure Theory of Money of Mr. J.M. Keynes

DIAGRAMMATIC VERSION OF MR. KEYNES'S THEORY OF THE CIRCULATION OF MONEY

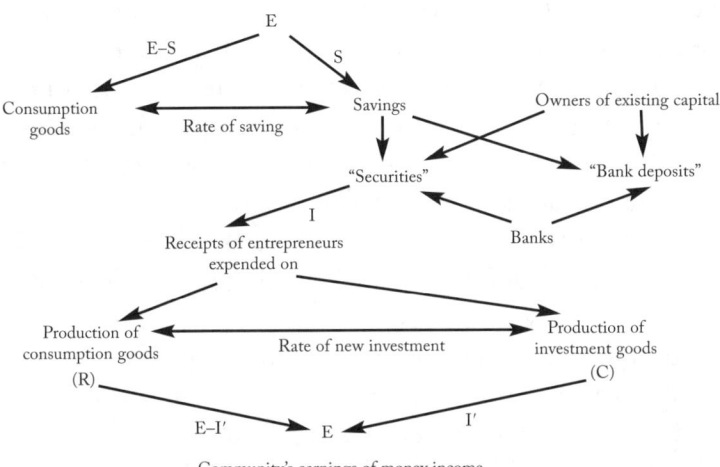

The formulæ on which the above diagram is based are as follows:

$R + C = 0$ (quantity of total current output)

$\frac{E}{0} = W_1$ (rate of efficiency earning) $= \frac{W}{e}$ (rate of earnings per unit of human effort ÷ by the coefficient of efficiency)

Q_1 (Profit on consumption goods) $= (E - S) - (E - I') = I' - S$

P (Price level of consumption goods) $= \frac{E}{0} + \frac{I-S}{R} = W_1 + \frac{Q_1}{R}$ (1)

Q_2 (Profit on investment goods) $= I - I'$

P' (Price level of investment goods*) $= \frac{E}{0} + \frac{I-I'}{C} = W_1 + \frac{Q}{C}$

Q (Profit on total output) $= (E - S) + I - E = I - S$

Π (Price level of total output) $= \frac{E}{0} + \frac{I-S}{0} = W_1 + \frac{Q}{0}$ (2)

(The numbers in brackets denote Mr. Keynes's first and second fundamental equations, respectively.)

There is a disturbing lack of method in Mr. Keynes's choice of symbols, which makes it particularly difficult to follow his algebra. The reader should especially remember that while profits on the production of consumption goods, investment goods, and total profits are denoted by Q1, Q2, and Q, respectively, the symbols for the corresponding price levels are chosen without any parallelism as P, P´, and Π. On the other hand, there is a misleading parallelism between P and P´ and I and I´, where the dash does not stand for a similar relation, but in the former case serves to mark off the price level of investment goods from that of consumption goods, and in the second case to distinguish the cost of production of the increment of new investment goods (I´) from its value (I).

*This formula is not given by Mr. Keynes.

current output, is the same thing as the E which is earned during the period when this current output comes on to the market and which therefore is available to buy that current output? If we take the picture as a crosscut at any moment of time, there can be no doubt that the E at the top and the E at the bottom of our diagram, i.e., income available for the purchase of output and the earnings of the factors of production, will be identical, but that does not prove that the cost of *current output* need necessarily also be the same. Only if the picture were to be considered as representing the process in time as a kind of longitudinal section, and if then the two E's at the top and at the bottom (i.e., current money income and the remuneration of the factors of production which were earned from the production of current output) were still equal, would the assumption made by Mr. Keynes be actually given. But this could only be true in a stationary state: and it is exactly for the analysis of a dynamic society that Mr. Keynes constructs his formulae. And in a dynamic society that assumption does not apply.

But whatever the relations of earnings to the cost of production of current output may be, there can be no doubt that Mr. Keynes is right when he emphasizes the importance of the fact that the flow of the community's earnings of money income shows "a twofold division (1) into the parts which have been earned by the production of consumption-goods and investment-goods, respectively, and (2) into parts which are *expended* on consumption goods and savings respectively" (vol. 1, p. 134) and that these two divisions need not be in the same proportion, and that any divergence between them will have important consequences.

Clearly recipients of income must make a choice: they may spend on consumption goods or they may refrain from doing so. In Mr. Keynes's terminology the latter operation constitutes saving. Insofar as they do save in this sense, they have the further choice between what one would ordinarily call hoarding and investing or, as Mr. Keynes (because he has employed these more familiar terms for other concepts) chooses to call it, between "bank-deposits" and "securities."[6] Insofar as the money saved is converted into "loan or real capital," i.e., is lent to entrepreneurs or used to buy investment goods, this means a choice for what Mr. Keynes calls "securities" while when it is held as money this means a choice for "bank deposits." This choice, however, is not only open to persons saving currently, but also to persons who have saved before and are therefore owners of the whole block of old capital. But even this is not yet the end. There is a third and most important factor which may affect the relation between what is currently saved and what becomes currently available for the purposes of investment: the banks. If the demand of the public for bank deposits increases either because the people who save invest only part of the amounts saved, or because the owners of old capital want to convert part of their "securities" into "bank deposits," the banks may create the additional deposits and use them to buy the "securities" which the public is less anxious to hold, and so make up for the difference between current saving and the buying of securities. The banking system may, of course, also create deposits to a greater or a lesser extent than would be necessary for this purpose and will then itself be one of the three factors causing the divergence between savings and investment in "securities."

On the other hand, entrepreneurs will receive money from two sources: either from the sale of the output of consumption goods, or from the "sale" of "securities" (which means investment

---

[6] Vol. 1, p. 141. Some readers may find it confusing that Mr. Keynes uses "bank deposits "and "savings deposits" interchangeably, in this connection without explaining why a few lines after having introduced the term "bank deposits" in a special technical sense, he substitutes "savings deposits" for it. But as savings deposits are defined (vol. 1, p. 36) as bank deposits "held, not for the purpose of making payments, but as means of employing savings, i.e., as an investment," this substitution is quite consistent with the definition, though it is certainly irritating that the employment of savings "as an investment" in this sense is to be contrasted with their other possible use for "securities" which again means investment, but in another, special sense.

in the ordinary sense), which latter operation may take the form of selling investment goods they have produced or raising a loan for the purpose of holding old or producing new investment goods. I understand—I am not sure whether Mr. Keynes really intends to convey this impression—that the total received from these two sources will be equal to the value of new investment, but in this case it would be identical with the amount of the "securities," and there would then be no reason to introduce this latter term. If, however, I should be mistaken on that point, the symbol I (which stands for the value of new investments) would not belong to the place where I have inserted it in the diagram above.

In regard to this total of money at the disposal of entrepreneurs, these have a further and, as must be conceded to Mr. Keynes, to a certain extent independent choice: they have to decide what part of it shall be used for the current production of consumption goods and what part for the production of new investment goods. But their choice is by no means an arbitrary one; and the way in which changes in the two variables mentioned above and changes in technical knowledge and the relative demand for different consumption goods (those which require more or less capital for their production) influence the relative attractiveness of the two lines is the most important problem of all, a problem which can be solved only on the basis of a complete theory of capital. And it is just here, though, of course, Mr. Keynes devotes much effort to the discussion of this central problem, that the lack of an adequate theoretical basis and the consequent obscurities of his concept of "investment," which I have noted before, make themselves felt. The whole idea that it is possible to draw in the way he does a sharp line of distinction between the production of investment goods and the current production of consumption goods is misleading. *The alternative is not between producing consumption goods or producing investment goods, but between producing investment goods which will yield consumption goods at a more or less distant date in the future.* The process of investment does not consist in producing side by side with what is necessary to continue current production of consumption goods on the old methods, additional investment goods, but rather in producing *other* machinery, for the same purpose but of a greater degree of efficiency, to take the place of the inferior machinery, etc., used up in the current production of consumption goods. And when the entrepreneurs decide to increase their investment, this does not necessarily mean that at that time more original factors of production than before are employed in the production of investment goods, but only that the new processes started will have the effect that, because of their longer duration, *after some time* a smaller proportion of the output will be "available" and a larger "nonavailable." Nor does it mean as a matter of course that even that part of the total amount spent on the factors of production which is not new investment but only reproduction of capital used up in the current production of consumption goods, will become available after the usual time.

VII

But, in addition to all these obscurities which are a consequence of the ambiguity of the concept of investment employed by Mr. Keynes, and which, of course, disturb all the apparent neatness of his mathematical formulae, there is a further difficulty introduced with these formulae. In order to provide an explanation of the changes in the price level (or rather price levels) he needs, in addition to his symbols denoting amounts of money or money values, symbols representing the physical quantities of the goods on which the money is spent. He therefore chooses his units of quantities of goods in such a way that "a unit of each has the same cost of production at the base date" and calls O "the total output of goods in terms of these units in a unit of time, R the volume of liquid consumption-goods and services flowing onto the market and purchased by the consumers, and C the net increment of investment, in the sense that O=R+C" (vol. 1, p. 135). Now these sentences, which are all that is said in explanation of these important magnitudes, give rise to a good deal of doubt. Whatever "cost of production" in the first sentence means (I suppose it means money cost, in which case R would be identical with E-I′ and C with I′ at the base date), *the fact that these units are based on a relation existing at an arbitrarily chosen base date makes them absolutely unsuitable for the explanation of any dynamic process.* There can be no doubt that any change of the proportion between what Mr. Keynes calls production of consumption goods and what he calls production of investment goods will be connected with changes of the quantities of the goods of both types which can be produced with the expenditure of a given amount of costs. *But if, as a consequence of such a change, the relative costs of consumption goods and investment goods change, this means that the measurement in units which are produced at equal cost at some base date is a measurement according to an entirely irrelevant criterion.* It would be nonsense to consider as equivalent a certain number of bottles and an automatic machine for producing bottles because, before the fall in the rate of interest made the use of such a machine profitable, it cost as much to produce the one as the other. But this is exactly what Mr. Keynes would be compelled to do if he only stuck to his definitions. But, of course, he does not, as is shown by the fact that he treats $\frac{E}{0} R$ as identical with E-I′ and $\frac{E}{0} C$ as identical with I′ throughout periods of change—which would only be the case if his units of quantity were neither determined by equality of money cost at the base date (money cost without a fixed base would give no measure of quantities) nor, indeed, by any cost at the base date at all, but by some kind of variable "real cost." This is probably what Mr. Keynes has in mind most of the time, though he never says so—but I cannot see how it will help him in the end. But not only does the division of 0 into its component parts R and C give rise to such difficulties. The use which is made of 0 alone is also not free from objections. We shall see in a moment that $\frac{E}{0}$ (i.e., the total income divided by the total output) forms one of the terms of both his fundamental equations. Mr. Keynes calls this the "money rate of efficiency earnings of the factors of production," or more shortly the "money rate of efficiency earnings." Now let me remind the reader for a moment that E means, as identically one and the same thing, (1) the community's money income, (2) the earnings of the factors of production, and (3) the cost of production, and that it expressly includes interest on capital and therefore in any case interest earned on existing capital goods.[7] I must confess that I am absolutely unable to attach any useful meaning to his concept of "the money rate of efficiency earnings of the factors of production" if capital is to be included among the factors of production and if it is *ex hypothesi* assumed that the amount of capital and therefore its productivity is changing. If the units in which 0 is measured are in any sense cost units, it is surely clear that interest will not stand in the same relation to the cost of production of the capital goods as the remuneration of the other factors of production to their cost of production? Or does there lie at the basis of the concept some attempt to construct a common denominator of real cost so as to include "abstinence"?

Mr. Keynes shows a certain inclination to identify efficiency earnings with efficiency wages (as when he speaks about the prevailing type of contracts between entrepreneurs and the factors of production being that of efficiency-earnings rather than effort-earnings—what does efficiency-earnings or even effort-earnings mean in regard to capital?—or when he speaks about the rate of earnings per unit of human effort (cf. vol. 1, pp. 135, 153, 166 *et seq.*), and in regard to wages the concept of efficiency earnings certainly has some sense if it is identified, as it is on page 166, with piece wages. But even if we assume that all contracts with labor were on the basis of piece wages, it would by no means follow that

---

[7] On page 211 (vol. 1) it is expressly stated in connection with some special problem that "in this case interest is simply the money-rate of earnings of one of the factors of production," but as E includes interest, and the money-rate of efficiency earnings of the factors of production is expressed by this must be true generally and not only in that particular context.

so long as existing contracts continue, efficiency wages would always be $\frac{E}{0}$. Piece rates relate only to a single workman or perhaps a group of workmen and their respective immediate output, but never to output as a whole. If, at unchanged piece rates for the individual workmen, total output rises as a consequence of an improved organization of the total process of production, $\frac{E}{0}$ may change (because 0 is increased) without any corresponding change in the rate of money earnings of the individuals. A type of contract according to which the earnings of factors engaged in the higher stages of production automatically changed as their contribution to the output of the last stage changed not only does not exist, it is inconceivable. There is, therefore, no market where the "money rate of efficiency earnings of the factors of production" is determined, and no price or group of prices which would correspond to that concept. What it amounts to is, as Mr. Keynes himself states in several places (e.g., vol. 1, p. 136), nothing else but the average cost of production of some more or less arbitrarily chosen units of output (i.e., such units as had "equal costs at the base date") which will change with every change of the price of the units of the factors of production (including interest) as well as with every change in the organization of production, and therefore with every change not only in the average price of the factors of production, but also with every change in their relative prices—changes which generally lead to a change in the methods of production and therefore in the amount of output produced with a given amount of factors of production. To call this the "money rate of efficiency earnings of the factors of production" and occasionally even simply "rate of earnings" can have no other effect than to convey the misleading impression that this magnitude is determined solely by the existing contracts with the factors of production.

VIII

Mr. Keynes's picture of the circulation of money shows three points where spontaneous change may be initiated: (1) the rate of saving may change, i.e., the division of the total money income of the community into the parts which are spent on consumption goods and saving respectively; (2) the rate of investment may change, i.e., the proportion in which the factors of production are directed by entrepreneurs to the production of consumption goods and the production of additional investment goods, respectively; (3) banks may pass onto investors more or less money than that part of the savings which is not directly invested (and that part of the old capital which is withdrawn from investment) but converted into bank deposits so that the total of money going to entrepreneurs as investment surpasses or falls short of total savings.

If only (1) changes, i.e., if the rate of saving changes without any corresponding change in (2) and (3) from the position existing before the change in (1) (which is to be taken as an equilibrium position) took place the effect will be that producers of consumption goods receive so much more or less for their output than has been expended on its production as E-S exceeds or falls short of E-1′. (E-S)-(E-I′) or I′-S, i.e., the difference between savings and the cost of investment, will be equal to the profits on the production of consumption goods; and as this magnitude is positive or negative entrepreneurs will be induced to expand or curtail output. Provided that (3) remains at the equilibrium position, i.e., that banks will pass on to the entrepreneurs exactly the amount which is saved and not invested directly, the effect on the production of investment goods will be exactly the reverse of the effect on the production of consumption goods. That is to say (positive or negative) profits made on the production of consumption goods will be exactly balanced by (negative or positive) profits on the production of investment goods. A change in (1) will, therefore, never give rise to total profits, but only to partial profits balanced by equal losses, and only lead to a shift between the production of consumption goods and the production of investment goods which will go on until profits on both sides disappear.

It is easily to be seen that the effect of changes of the type (2) will, if not accompanied by changes in either (1) or (3), be of exactly the same nature as of changes in (1). Positive profits on the one hand and negative profits on the other will soon show that the deviation from the equilibrium position existing before without a corresponding change in (1) is unprofitable and will lead to a re-establishment of the former proportion between the production of consumption goods and the production of investment goods.

Only a change in (3) will lead to total profits. (This is also shown by the formula for total profits, namely $Q=I-S$.) Now the causes why I may be different from S are of a very complex nature, and are investigated by Mr. Keynes in very great detail. We shall have to discuss his analysis of this problem when we come to his theory of the bank rate. For present purposes, it will, however, be more convenient to take the possibility of such a divergence for granted, and only to mention that the fact that more (or less) money is being invested than is being saved is equivalent to so much money being added to (or withdrawn from) industrial circulation, so that the total of profits, or the difference between the expenditure and the receipts of the entrepreneurs, which is the essential element in the second term of the fundamental equations, will be equal to the net addition to (or subtraction from) the effective circulation. It is here, according to Mr. Keynes, that we find the monetary causes working for a change in the price level; and he considers it the main advantage of his fundamental equations that they isolate this factor.

IX

The aim of the fundamental equations is to "exhibit the causal process, by which the price level is determined, and the method of transition from one position of equilibrium to another" (vol. 1, p. 135). What they say is essentially that the purchasing power of money (or the general price level) will deviate from its "equilibrium position," i.e., the average cost of production of the unit of output, only if I´ or I (if the price level in general and not the purchasing power of money, or the price level of consumption goods is concerned) is different from S. This has to be constantly kept in mind lest the reader be misled by occasional statements which convey the impression that this applies to every change in the price level, and not only to changes relatively to cost of production[8] or that the "equilibrium position" is in any way definitely determined by the existing contracts with the factors of production,[9] and not simply the cost of production, or what means the same thing, the "money-rate of efficiency earnings of the factors of production."

The best short explanation of the meaning of the fundamental equations I can find is the following:

> Thus, the long period equilibrium norm of the Purchasing Power of Money is given by the money-rate of efficiency earnings of the Factors of Production; whilst the actual Purchasing Power oscillates below or above this equilibrium level according as the cost of current investment is running ahead of, or falling behind, savings. ... A principal object of this *Treatise* is to show that we have here the clue to the way in which the fluctuations of the price level actually come to pass, whether they are due to oscillations about a steady equilibrium or to a transition from one equilibrium to another. ... Accordingly, therefore, as the banking system is allowing the rate of investment to exceed or fall behind the rate of saving, the price level (assuming that there is no spontaneous change in the rate of efficiency-earnings) will rise or fall. If, however,

---

[8] Cf., e.g., on page 158 of vol. 1, where Mr. Keynes speaks simply of the "condition for the stability of the purchasing power" where he obviously does not mean absolute stability but permanent coincidence with the "equilibrium level."

[9] Cf. on page 138 of vol. 1, where it is said that "these equations tell us that the price of consumption goods is equal to the rate of earnings of the factors of production plus the rate of profits per unit of output of consumption goods."

the prevailing type of contract between the entrepreneurs and the factors of production is in terms of effort-earnings W and not in terms of efficiency-earnings W, (existing arrangements probably lie as a rule somewhere between the two) then it would be $\frac{1}{e}$ P, which would tend to rise or fall, where, as before, e is the coefficient of efficiency. (vol. 1, pp. 152–53)

This says quite clearly that not all changes of the price level need to be started by a divergence between I′ (or I) and S, but that it is only one particular cause of such changes, i.e., the changes in the amount of money in circulation, which is isolated by this form of equation. But the peculiar substitution of the misleading term "the money-rate of efficiency earnings of the Factors of Production" for simply money cost of production seems at places to mislead Mr. Keynes himself. I cannot see any reason whatever why, as indicated in the passage just quoted, and elaborated at length in a later section (pp. 166–70) so long as the second term is in the equilibrium position, i.e., zero, the movement of the price level should be at all dependent upon the prevailing type of contract with the factors of production. So long as the amount of money in circulation, or more exactly E, remains unchanged, the fluctuations in the price level would by no means be determined by the existing contracts, but exclusively by the amount of factors of production available and changes in their efficiency, i.e., by the two factors affecting total output. All Mr. Keynes's reasoning on this point seems to be based on the assumption that existing contracts will be changed by entrepreneurs only under the inducement (or pressure) of positive (or negative) profits *created by a change in the second term*. But to me there seems, on the contrary, no doubt possible that if a change in the coefficient of efficiency (or the amount of the factors of production available) occurs, existing contracts will have to be changed unless there is a change in the second term. *The difference seems to lie in the fact that Mr. Keynes believes that it is possible to adapt the amount of money in circulation to what is necessary for the maintenance of existing contracts without upsetting the equilibrium between saving and investing.* But under the existing monetary organization, where all changes in the quantity of money in circulation are brought about by more or less money being lent to entrepreneurs than is being saved, any change in the circulation *must* be accompanied by a divergence between saving and investing. I cannot see why

> if such spontaneous changes in the rate of earnings as tend to occur require a supply of money which is incompatible with the ideas of the Currency Authority or with the limitations on its powers, then the latter will be compelled, in its endeavour to redress the situation, to bring influences to bear which will upset the equilibrium of Investment and Saving, and so induce the entrepreneurs to modify their offers to the factors of production in such a way as to counteract the spontaneous changes which have been occurring in the rates of earnings. (vol. 1, p. 167)

To me it seems rather that if the currency authority wished to adapt the supply of money to the changed requirements, it could do so only by upsetting the equilibrium between saving and investment. But Mr. Keynes later on expressly allows for such increases in the supply of money as correspond to the increase of output and regards them as not upsetting the equilibrium. But how can the money get into circulation without creating a discrepancy between saving and investment? Is there any justification for the assumption that under these conditions entrepreneurs will borrow more just to go on with current production and not use the additional money for new investment? And even if they do use it only to finance the increased production, does not even this mean new investment in the interval of time until the additional products reach the consumer?

It seems to me that by not clearly distinguishing between stable cost of production per unit of output, stable contracts with the factors of production, and stable total cost (i.e., an invariable E) Mr. Keynes is led to connect two things which have nothing to do with one another: on the one hand the maintenance of a price level which will cover costs of production while contracts with the factors of production are more or less rigid, and on the other hand the maintenance of an equilibrium between saving and investment. But without changes in the quantity of money and therefore without a divergence between I′ and S, not only the purchasing power of money, but also the labor power of money, and therefore contracts with the factors of production would have to change with every change in total output.

There can, of course, be no doubt that every divergence between I or I′ and S is of enormous importance. But that importance does not lie in the direction of its influence on the fluctuations of the *price level*, be it its absolute fluctuations or its fluctuations about an equilibrium position, determined by the existing contracts with the factors of production.

It is true that in this attempt to establish a direct connection between a divergence between I and S, or what amounts to the same thing, a divergence between the natural and the money rate of interest, and the changes in the price level, Mr. Keynes is following the lead of Wicksell. But it is just on this point that—as has been shown by Mr. D.H. Robertson[10] among English economists, and by the present writer[11] on the Continent—Wicksell has claimed too much for his theory. And even if Mr. Keynes substitutes for the absolute stability of the price level which Wicksell had in mind, a not clearly defined equilibrium price level, he is still searching for a more definite relation between the price level and the difference between saving and investment than can be found.

---

[10] D.H. Robertson, *Money*, new revised edition (London: Macmillan, 1928), p. 99.

[11] *Geldtheorie und Konjuncturtheorie* (Vienna: Holder-Pichler-Tempsky, 1929), pp. 61, 131 *et seq.*

X

So far we have been mainly concerned with the tools which Mr. Keynes has created for the explanation of dynamic processes and the trade cycle. It is intended to discuss his actual explanation, beginning with the theory of the bank rate and including the whole of book 4, in a second part of this article.[12]

There is just one word more I feel I should add at this point. It is very likely that in the preceding pages I have quite often clothed my comments in the form of a criticism where I should simply have asked for further explanation and that I have dwelt too much on minor inaccuracies of expression. I hope it will not be considered a sign of inadequate appreciation of what is undeniably in so many ways a magnificent performance that what I have had so far to say was almost exclusively critical. My aim has been throughout to contribute to the understanding of this unusually difficult and important book, and I hope that my endeavor in this direction will be the best proof of how important I consider it. It is even possible that in the end it will turn

---

[12] Considerations of space have compelled the splitting up of this article. But there are other reasons which make me welcome the opportunity of delaying the second part of my criticism. As I had to confess at the beginning of this article, it is sometimes extremely difficult to find out exactly what the meaning of Mr. Keynes's concepts is. On several occasions, I have had to point out that several conflicting definitions are given for the same concept, and on many other points I am by no means certain whether I have understood Mr. Keynes correctly. It is very difficult to follow his subsequent complicated analysis so long as these ambiguities are not cleared up. One has to distinguish at every point the different meanings the exposition assumes according to concepts like investment, etc., are interpreted according to this or to that of the several possible meanings it is given. There have accumulated so many questions of this kind which Mr. Keynes could certainly clear up that it is probably wiser to stop for the moment in the hope that further elucidations will in the meanwhile provide a firmer basis on which discussion may proceed. (Part 2 of this article will probably appear in *Economica* [November 1931].)

out that there exists less difference between Mr. Keynes's views and my own than I am at present inclined to assume. The difficulty may be only that Mr. Keynes has made it so extraordinarily hard really to follow his reasoning. I hope that the reviewer will be excused if, in a conscientious attempt to understand it, he may sometimes have been betrayed into impatience with the countless obstacles which the author has put in the way of a full understanding of his ideas.

XI

Toward the end of his summary of the argument contained in those sections of the *Treatise* which were discussed in the first part of this article, Mr. Keynes writes:

> If the banking system controls the terms of credit in such a way that savings are equal to the value of new investment, then the average price level of output as a whole is stable and corresponds to the average rate of remuneration of the factors of production. If the terms of credit are easier than this equilibrium level, prices will rise, profits will be made.... And if the terms of credit are stiffer than the equilibrium level, prices will fall, losses will be made. ... Booms or slumps are simply the expression of the results of an oscillation of the terms of credit about their equilibrium position.[13]

This brings us to the first and, in many respects, the most important question we have to consider in this second article, viz. Mr. Keynes's theory of the bank rate.

The fundamental concept, upon which his analysis of this subject is based, is Wicksell's idea of a natural, or equilibrium, rate of interest, i.e., the rate at which the amount of new investment corresponds to the amount of current savings—a definition

---

[13] *Treatise on Money,* pp. 183–84 of vol. 1. Unless otherwise stated, all page references in this article are to vol. 1 of the *Treatise.*

of Wicksell's concept on which, probably, all his followers would agree. Indeed, when reading Mr. Keynes's exposition, any student brought up on Wicksell's teaching will find himself on what appears to be quite familiar ground until, his suspicions having been aroused by the conclusions, he discovers that, behind the verbal identity of the definition, there lurks (because of Mr. Keynes's peculiar definition of saving and investment) a fundamental difference. For the meaning attached by Mr. Keynes to the terms "saving" and "investment" differs from that usually associated with them. Hence the rate of interest which will equilibrate "savings" and "investment" in Mr. Keynes's sense is quite different from the rate which would keep them in equilibrium in the ordinary sense.

The most characteristic trait of Mr. Keynes's explanation of a deviation of the actual short-term rate of interest from the "natural" or equilibrium rate is his insistence on the fact that this may happen independently of whether the effective quantity of money does, or does not, change. He emphasizes this point so strongly that he could scarcely expect any reader to overlook the fact that he wishes to demonstrate it. But, at the same time, while he certainly *wants* to establish this proposition, I cannot find any proof of it in the *Treatise*. Indeed, at all the critical points, the assumption seems to creep in that this divergence is made possible by the necessary change in the supply of money.[14]

It is quite certain that his reason for believing that a difference between saving and investment can arise without the banks changing their circulation does not become clear in the first section of the relevant chapter. In this section he distinguishes three different strands of thought in the traditional doctrine only the

---

[14] I do not refer here to certain passages (e.g., on pp. 198, 272; vol. 2, p. 100) where this assumption is quite explicitly expressed; these are probably accounted for by the fact that Mr. Keynes actually believed something of this sort when he first began working on book 3 of the *Treatise* (see his reply to the first part of this article, p. 389).

first and third of which are relevant to this point, so that the second, which is concerned with the effect of the bank rate on international capital movements, may be neglected here. According to Mr. Keynes, the first of these strands of thought "regards Bank Rate merely as a means of regulating the quantity of bank money" (p. 187) while the third strand "conceives of Bank Rate as influencing in some way the rate of investment and, perhaps, in the case of Wicksell and Cassel, as influencing the rate of investment relatively to that of saving" (p. 190). But, as Mr. Keynes himself sees in one place (p. 197), there is no necessary conflict between these two theories. The obvious relation between them, which would suggest itself to any reader of Wicksell—a view which was certainly held by Wicksell himself—is that since, under the existing monetary system, changes in the amount of money in circulation are brought about mainly by the banks expanding or contracting their loans, and since money so borrowed at interest is used mainly for purposes of investment, any addition to the supply of money, not offset by a reverse change in the velocity of circulation, is likely to cause a corresponding excess of investment over saving; and any decrease will cause a corresponding excess of saving over investment. But Mr. Keynes believes that Wicksell's theory was something different from this and, in fact, rather like his own, apparently because Wicksell thought that one and the same rate of interest may serve both to make saving and investment equal *and* to keep the general price level steady. As I have already stated, however, this is a point on which, in my view, Wicksell was wrong. But there can be no doubt that Wicksell was emphatically of the opinion that the possibility of there being a divergence between the market rate and the equilibrium rate of interest is entirely due to the "elasticity of the monetary system" (see *Geldzins und Güterpreise* [Jena: Gustav Fischer, 1898], p. 101, *Vorlesungen* [Jena: Gustav Fischer 1922], p. 221 of vol. 2), i.e., to the possibility of adding money to, or withdrawing it from, circulation.

XII

Mr. Keynes's own exposition of the *General Theory* of the Bank Rate (pp. 200–09) does not, by any means, solve the problem of how a divergence between the bank rate and the equilibrium rate should affect prices and production otherwise than by means of a change in the supply of money. Nowhere more than here is one conscious of the lack of a satisfactory theory as to the effects of a change in the equilibrium rate; and of the confusion which results from the fundamentally different treatment of fixed and working capital. In most parts of his analysis, one is not clear whether he is speaking of the effects of *any* change in the bank rate, or whether what he says applies only to the effect of the bank rate being different from the market rate; nowhere does he make it clear that a central bank is in a position to determine the rate only because it is in a position to increase or decrease the amount of money in circulation.

But the least satisfactory part of this section is the oversimplified account of how a change in bank rate affects investment or, rather, the value of *fixed* capital—since, for some unexplained reason, he here substitutes this latter concept for the former. This explanation consists merely in pointing out that, since "a change in Bank Rate is not calculated to have any effect (except, perhaps, a remote effect of the second order of magnitude) on the prospective yield of fixed capital" and since the conceivable effect on the price of that yield may be neglected, the only "immediate, direct and obvious effect" of a change in the bank rate on the value of fixed capital will be that its given yield will be capitalized at the new rate of interest (p. 202). But capitalization is not so directly an *effect* of the rate of interest; it would be truer to say that both are effects of one common cause, viz. the scarcity or abundance of means available for investment, relative to the demand for those means. Only by changing this relative scarcity will a change in the bank rate also change the demand price for the services of fixed capital. If a change in the bank rate corresponds to a change in the equilibrium rate it is only an expression of that relative scarcity which has come about independently of this action. But if it means a movement away from the equilibrium rate, it will become effective and influence the value of fixed capital only insofar as it brings about a change in the amount of funds available for investment.

It is not difficult to see why Mr. Keynes came to neglect this obvious fact. For it is scarcely possible to see how a change in the rate of interest operates at all if one neglects, as Mr. Keynes neglects in this connection, the part played by the circulating capital which cooperates with the fixed capital; only in this way can one see how a change in the amount of free capital will affect the value of invested capital. To overemphasize the distinction between fixed and circulating capital, which is, at best, merely one of degree, and not by any means of fundamental importance, is a common trait of English economic theory and has probably contributed more than any other cause to the unsatisfactory state of the English theory of capital at the present time. In connection with the present problem it is to be noted that his neglect of working capital not only prevents him from seeing in what way a change in the rate of interest affects the value of fixed capital, but also leads him to a quite erroneous statement about the degree and uniformity of that effect. It is simply not true to state that a change in the rate of interest will have no noticeable effect on the yield of fixed capital; this would be to ignore the effect of such a change on the distribution of circulating capital. The return attributable to any piece of fixed capital, any plant, machinery, etc., is, in the short run, essentially a residuum after operating costs are deducted from the price obtained for the output, and once a given amount has been irrevocably sunk in fixed capital, even the total output obtained with the help of that fixed capital will vary considerably, according to the amount of circulating capital which it pays at the given prices, to use in cooperation with the fixed capital. Any change in the rate of interest will, obviously, materially alter the relative profitableness of the employment of circulating capital in the different stages of production, according as an investment for a longer or shorter period is involved; so that it will always cause shifts in the use of that circulating capital between the different stages of production, and bring about changes in the marginal productivity (the "real yield") of the fixed capital which *cannot* be so shifted. As the price of the complementary working capital changes, the yield and the price of fixed capital will, therefore, vary; and this variation may be different in the different stages of production. The change in the price of working capital, however, will be determined by the change in the total means available for investment in all kinds of capital goods ("intermediate products"), whether of durable or nondurable nature. Any increase of means available for such investment will necessarily tend to lower the marginal productivity of any further investment of capital, i.e., lower the margins of profit derived from the difference between the prices of the intermediate products and the final products by raising the prices of the former relatively to the prices of the latter.

It would appear that Mr. Keynes's failure to see these interrelations is due to the fact that he does not clearly distinguish, in the passage referred to above, between the *gross* and the *net* yield of fixed capital. If he had concentrated on the effects of a change in the rate of interest on the net yield, as being the only relevant phenomenon, he could hardly have failed to see that the effect of such a change on fixed capital is not quite as direct and uniform as he supposes; and he would certainly have remembered also that there exists a tendency for the net money yield of real capital and the rate of interest to become equal. Thus, the process of capitalization at any given rate of interest means merely that, while money is obtainable at a rate of interest lower than the rate of yield on existing capital, borrowed money will be used to purchase capital goods until their price is so enhanced that the rate of yield is lowered to equal the rate of interest, and *vice versa*.

XIII

Although these deficiencies account for the fact that Mr. Keynes has not seen what I think is the true effect of a divergence between bank rate and equilibrium rate of interest, their existence does not give an explanation of Mr. Keynes's own solution to this problem. This has to be sought elsewhere, viz. as already indicated, in Mr. Keynes's peculiar concept of saving. He believes that, in order to maintain equilibrium, new investment must be equal not only to that part of the money income of all individuals which *exceeds* what they spend on consumers' goods *plus* what must be reinvested in order to maintain existing capital equipment (which would constitute saving in the ordinary sense of the word); but also to that portion of entrepreneurs' "normal" incomes by which their actual income (and, therefore, their expenditure on consumption goods) has fallen short of that "normal" income. In other words, if entrepreneurs are experiencing losses (i.e., are earning less than the normal rate), and make up for such losses either by cutting down their own consumption *pari passu,* or by borrowing a corresponding amount from the savers, then, argues Mr. Keynes, not only do these sums make replacement of the old capital possible, but there should also be a further amount of *new* investment corresponding to these sums.[15] And as Mr. Keynes obviously thinks that saving (i.e., the refraining from buying consumers' goods) may, in many cases, actually cause some entrepreneurs to suffer losses which will absorb some of the savings which would otherwise have gone to new investment, this special concept of saving probably explains why he suspects almost *any* increase in saving of being conducive to the creation of a dangerous excess of saving over investment.

---

[15] As regards the inclusion of such sums in Mr. Keynes's concept of saving, cf. *Treatise,* vol. 1, p. 139, and my "Rejoinder," *Economica* 34 (1931): 400. That Mr. Keynes actually wants additional new investments to correspond to savings in this sense has now become quite clear from his definition of net investment, to be found at the top of page 397 of the same issue of *Economica*.

In order to arrive at a clearer understanding of this point, let us try to see what usually happens when people begin to save. The first effect will be that *fewer* consumers' goods are sold at existing prices. This does not mean that their prices must fall, still less that their prices must decline in proportion to the decrease in demand. Actually, the first effect will probably be that the sellers of consumers' goods, being unable to retail as much as before at existing prices, will, rather than sell at a loss, decide to increase temporarily their holdings of these goods and to slow down the process of production.[16] This is not only to be expected for psychological reasons, but it is important to note here that this action on the part of entrepreneurs is not only in their own interest, but is necessary in order to make the desire to save effective. Saving must involve a reduction in consumption, in order that there may be accumulated, in finished or semi-finished form, a stock of consumers' goods, which will serve to bridge the gap between the time when the last products of the former (shorter) process of production are consumed and the time when the first products of the new, more capitalistic, process reach the market.[17] And by holding their goods for some time, entrepreneurs will probably be able (if the saving has led to new investment) to dispose of them at the former price.

If, however, we assume that, for some reason or other, producers of consumers' goods prefer to go on producing at full capacity, selling at a loss in the hope that the demand will ultimately revive and that they will suffer smaller losses than a reduction of output might have involved, then, as Mr. Keynes rightly points out, if production is to be maintained at the same

---

[16] This tendency is likely to be modified only to the extent that the cost of carrying goods makes it advisable to reduce prices so as to dispose of them more quickly. But it must be remembered that these costs, also, will be reduced as a consequence of the fall of interest and that this will act as an inducement to merchants to carry larger stocks.

[17] Cf. vol. 1, p. 283, and my *Prices and Production*, p. 79; p. 261 in this volume.

level, they must make up for their losses in one of four possible ways: they must cut down their own expenditure (or, in Mr. Keynes's terminology, they must save in order to cover their losses); reduce their bank balances; borrow from the people who save; or sell to these people other capital, such as securities. According to Mr. Keynes, it is in these cases that investment will remain below saving and it is, therefore, these cases which we must consider more closely.

The task of finding out whether, in any given situation, saving will or will not exactly correspond to investment in Mr. Keynes's sense, is rendered somewhat difficult because, as I have repeatedly pointed out, he has not provided us with a clear and unequivocal definition of what he means by "investment." But, for the present purpose, we can surmount the difficulty by simply taking his account of what happens when investment falls short of saving and then investigating whether these effects manifest themselves in our particular case. Now, the effect of an excess of saving over investment, according to Mr. Keynes, will be that total incomes will not be sufficient to purchase total output at prices which cover costs. (If I and I′=S, then the rate of efficiency earnings, $W_1 = \frac{E}{O}$, is constant and identical with P and II, the price level of consumption goods and the price level of output as a whole, respectively.) The question now, is whether an excess of saving over investment in Mr. Keynes's sense, caused by a part of savings being used to cover losses in any of the above-mentioned ways, will cause total incomes to fall below total cost of production.

The answer to this question seems to me to be an emphatic negative. Two cases are conceivable according to the way in which production is financed by producers of consumption goods who do not reduce their output but suffer losses and go on producing as much as before. When the same output of consumption goods is made possible by the decreased expenditure of the entrepreneurs, incomes derived from the production of consumption goods will not fall off by more than the initial decline in the demand for consumption goods, as the decreased consumption of the entrepreneurs will to the same extent offset the effects of the initial decrease on incomes. In the other case, where producers of consumption goods do not reduce their own consumption but cover their losses by borrowing or selling capital assets, clearly the income derived from the production of consumption goods will not decline at all.[18] In the former case, therefore, the total income stream will remain the same as when an amount equal to the new savings is being used for new investment and, in the latter case, the same will be true provided that the excess (if any) of saving over what has been lent or paid to the losing entrepreneurs is used for new investment. Mr. Keynes, however, seems to believe that a reduction in entrepreneurs' expenditure on consumption goods constitutes a net decrease in the demand for these goods, different from, and in addition to, that shift of incomes from producers of consumption goods to producers of capital goods, which will always be the initial effect of an increase in saving; and that, in order to prevent undesirable disturbances, this reduction in consumption should be offset by a corresponding amount of additional new investment, to be made possible by increased loans from the banks.

Let us, for the moment, concentrate on this example in which the entrepreneur, who is making losses, cuts down his consumption, this being the only available means of maintaining his capital and of recovering it for reinvestment. If, in spite of the fact that he is making losses, he reinvests it in the same line of production, instead of shifting it to some more profitable employment, then his sacrifice will be in vain because, after the next turnover of this capital, he will be face to face with a new loss

---

[18] I neglect in this connection, as Mr. Keynes neglects, the third possible case where entrepreneurs reduce their balances in order to continue production. The effect here would, obviously, be similar to that of an increase in the quantity of money.

equal in amount to the old. What is wanted in order to make effective not only his efforts to maintain his capital, but also the initial saving, is a reduction in his output, in order to set free the factors which are needed for the new investment. But, so long as he insists upon maintaining his output at the old level, his saving (in Mr. Keynes's sense) not only cannot, but certainly *should not* give rise to any new investment. In the other case, where the losing entrepreneur obtains from other savers the capital necessary to make up for his losses, it is, no doubt, true that these individual savings are wasted, i.e., make no increase of the capital equipment possible. But this is so only because it is *assumed* that the losing entrepreneur is consuming his capital and (since the savings of other people are required to compensate for this) is thus preventing any net saving. But since, on balance, there is no excess of incomes over net earnings, *there is no reason why any new investment should take place;* this is also shown by the fact that, because the production of consumption goods is going on at an unchanged rate, no factors of production can be set free for use in the production of new investment goods. *Any attempt to bring about an increase in investment to correspond to this "saving" which is already required to maintain the old capital, would have exactly the same effect as any other attempt to raise investment above net saving; inflation, forced saving, misdirection of production and, finally, a crisis.* It must be remembered that, so long as entrepreneurs insist on producing consumption goods at the old rate, and selling them below normal cost, no restriction of consumption and, therefore, no real saving is effected; and no stock of consumption goods will be accumulated to bridge the time gap to which we referred above (p. 28).

At the same time, it is, of course, true that under Mr. Keynes's assumption, saving will lead to a fall in the general price level, because this assumption implies that, in spite of the decreased demand for the available part of the output, the money which is not spent on consumers' goods is injected into a higher stage of the process of production of these consumers' goods in order to maintain the output and price there. The only effect of saving, on this assumption, would therefore be that the money would, as it were, skip the last stage of the productive process (consumers' goods), and go directly to the higher stage to maintain the demand there; and the consequence would be that no increase in demand would occur anywhere to offset the decreased demand for consumers' goods, and there would be no rise of other prices to compensate for the effect produced on the price level by the fall in the price of consumption goods.

All this is, however, true only because it is *assumed* from the outset that, in spite of the fact that investment in the production of consumption goods has become less profitable (or even, perhaps, a losing proposition), entrepreneurs insist on investing just as much here as before and (insofar as they do not provide the capital themselves by reducing their consumption) offer to the savers better terms than the producers of capital goods. I cannot help feeling that Mr. Keynes has been misled here by his treatment of interest as part of the "rate of efficiency earnings of the factors of production" which he considers to be fixed by existing contracts, so that capitalists will get the same return wherever they invest and only the incomes of entrepreneurs will be affected. In any case, it seems to me that a complete neglect of the part played by rate of interest is involved in the assumption that, after investment in the production of consumption goods has become relatively less profitable, some other openings for investment which are now more profitable, will not be found.

The most curious fact is that, from the outset, all of Mr. Keynes's reasoning which aims at proving that an increase in saving will not lead to an increase in investment is based on the assumption that, in spite of the decrease in the demand for consumption goods, the available output is not reduced; this means, simply, that he assumes from the outset what he wants to prove. This could be shown by many quotations from the *Treatise* and it would be seen that some of his most baffling conclusions, such as the famous analogy between profits and the widow's cruse and losses and the Danaid jar, are expressly based on the assumption "merely [*sic!*] that entrepreneurs were continuing to produce the same output of investment goods as before" (pp. 139–40). But in his recent "Rejoinder to Mr. D.H. Robertson" (*Economic Journal* [December 1931]: 412), Mr. Keynes admits that he did not, in his book, deal in detail "with the train of events which ensues when, as a consequence of making losses, entrepreneurs reduce their output." This is really a most surprising admission from an author who has set out to study the shifts between available and non-available output and wants to *prove* that saving will not lead to the necessary shifts.

To sum up the somewhat prolonged discussion of this point; in none of the cases which we have considered will there occur those effects which should follow if saving and investment (in the ordinary sense) diverge, viz. total income exceeding or falling short of the cost of total output; and *there is no reason why saving and new investment, in Mr. Keynes's sense, should correspond.* By arbitrarily changing the meaning of familiar concepts, Mr. Keynes has succeeded in making plausible a proposition which nobody would accept were it stated in ordinary terms. In the form stated by Mr. Keynes, this proposition certainly has nothing to do with Wicksell's theory, nor can Wicksell be held responsible for Mr. Keynes's interpretation.

XIV

The point discussed in the last section shows what is, obviously, the main reason for Mr. Keynes's belief that a divergence between saving and investment may arise without a change in the amount of the effective circulation. But there are two further reasons given in the *Treatise*. One of these, although it is (as Mr. Keynes himself points out) of but negligible importance, is indeed a conceivable case in which such a divergence may arise for non-monetary reasons; while the other, which is, no doubt, of great importance, clearly relies on a change in the effective circulation. I shall try to dispose of the less important point here and deal more thoroughly with the second in the next section.

The conceivable case in which saving might exceed investment without a change in the effective circulation is where part of the savings might be permanently absorbed by the security market. If this occurred to any considerable extent, i.e., if Mr. Keynes's business deposits B, or that part of his financial circulation which serves to effect the transfer of securities were to vary by large amounts, this would indeed mean that a corresponding part of the savings would not lead to new investment because of the "Financial Circulation stealing resources from the Industrial Circulation" (p. 254). But since Mr. Keynes himself argues (pp. 244, 249, 256, 267) that the *absolute* variability of business deposits B is, as a rule, only small in proportion to the total quantity of money, and since his utterances have even been interpreted, probably justly, as a denial of the view that security speculation can absorb any credit,[19] we could safely ignore this possibility if Mr. Keynes's later exposition, particularly his "Rejoinder to Mr. D.H. Robertson," did not create the impression that he is now inclined to attach more importance to this point. The particular case, in which security transactions seem to assume this new importance to him, is, however, one of the cases already discussed in the last section and not one of the typical cases which might, at first thought, spring to the mind. It is the case in which the producers of consumption goods cover the losses, which they have suffered as a result of the increased saving, by selling securities. In this case, it might be said that the fall in prices is due to the fact that the money saved finds its way to the producers of consumption goods *via* the purchase of securities instead of *via* the purchase of consumption goods, so that a security transaction has taken the place of a commodity transaction and the total

---

[19] Professor J.H. Williams in *The Quarterly Journal of Economics* 45, no. 4 (August 1931): 569.

stream of money directed to the purchase of commodities (and, therefore, the price level of those commodities) has fallen. What I think about this case has already been said in the last section.

XV

The last and, perhaps, the most important cause of a disequilibrium between saving and investment, given by Mr. Keynes, is a change in the effective circulation—not a change in the *amount* of money, but merely in its effectiveness or in the velocity of circulation. Just as the potential saver has to make a double choice and decide, firstly, whether he will save at all and, second, whether he will invest or hoard what he has saved; so there are, also, two ways in which his decisions may cause savings to exceed investment: either because he saves more than entrepreneurs are willing to use for new investment or because he hoards his savings instead of making them available for investment. The first factor, which is the one discussed above in section 13 and which is only very inadequately characterized in the preceding sentence, is christened by Mr. Keynes "the excess saving factor," while he calls the second, which we must now study, "the excess bearish factor" (p. 145). As already indicated, the problem to be studied here is the problem of hoarding; not, however, the hoarding of cash but the much more complicated and interesting problem of "hoarding" in a society where all current money consists of bank deposits.[20]

It is undeniably true that economists in general still make too much use of the assumption that saving means, in the first instance, that people accumulate cash which they will soon bring to their bank if they do not invest it otherwise. Little attention has been given to the fact that, since a large part of our current

---

[20] It should be remembered, throughout the following discussion, that, in Mr. Keynes's theoretical exposition, it is assumed that bank deposits are the only form of money in general circulation and that the cash, held by the banks as reserve against these deposits, never enters the general circulation (p. 31).

money is now in the form of bank deposits, there is no need for people to bring their savings to the bank; and that, therefore, an increase in the amount of money left at the banks as savings, need not increase the power or willingness of the banks to lend. This is particularly true if people leave their savings on current account—as is often the case where interest is paid on these; and to a considerable extent, also, if they transfer them from current account to deposit account, since this will increase the lending power of the bank only in proportion to the difference, if any, between the percentage of reserve held against current accounts and deposit accounts, respectively.[21] One of the great merits of Mr. D.H. Robertson's work is that he has forcefully drawn attention to this fact—the existence of which makes any practical solution to these problems extremely difficult. I think, however, that it should be theoretically clear that what happens in such a case is essentially the same thing as hoarding (i.e., a decrease in the velocity of circulation of money) and that these particular considerations only show that the practical importance of this phenomenon is much greater than most economists used to suppose.

Mr. Keynes's elaboration of this contribution of Mr. Robertson's is, in many respects, the most interesting part of his theoretical analysis. His contribution consists mainly of a detailed analysis of the causes which will lead people to prefer hoarding to investment or *vice versa;* and, since this depends mainly on the people's expectations about the future price of securities, the analysis becomes an extensive study of the relations between

---

[21] If, for instance, the reserve held against current accounts (demand deposits) is 9 percent, and the reserve held against deposit accounts (time deposits) is only 3 percent, then the transfer of any given amount from current account to deposit account will free two-thirds of the reserves formerly held and enable the bank to create additional demand deposits equal to two-thirds of the amount transferred to deposit account. Mr. Keynes would, therefore, be quite consistent if he thought it desirable that banks should not be compelled to hold any reserves against deposit accounts (see vol. 2, p. 13).

bank credit and the stock market. And even if Mr. Keynes is not quite clear, and his solution of the problem not quite satisfactory, there is no doubt that he is here breaking new ground and that he has opened up new vistas.

At the same time, his exposition of this point, which is contained mainly in chapter 10 (section 3) and chapter 15, is by no means less difficult than the parts of his discussion to which we have already referred, and I doubt whether anybody could gather, from the text of the *Treatise* alone, the exact meaning of the author's theory on this point. For my own part, I must confess that it is only after studying the further elucidation of this point, provided by the author in his "Rejoinder to Mr. D.H. Robertson," that I venture to believe that I see what he is driving at. For the purpose of this discussion, therefore, I shall use his exposition in this rejoinder as much as the original text of the *Treatise*.

Before we can enter upon a discussion of the main problem, however, we must acquaint ourselves with the author's special terminology which, in this connection, is as rich and varied as elsewhere. As mentioned (*Economica*, no. 33, p. 284), his initial terms for the alternatives which are commonly called "hoarding" and "investing" are "bank deposits" and "securities." But, instead of "bank deposits" (or "savings deposits" or "inactive deposits"), the terms "liquid assets," "hoarded money," or "hoards" are frequently used, while the "securities" become "nonliquid assets." "Active deposits" correspond, of course, to "current accounts" or "demand deposits."

Only a part of the total savings-deposits, viz. "savings deposits B," is an alternative to securities in the sense that the holder takes an adverse view of the prospects of the money value of securities. It constitutes what Mr. Keynes calls the "bear position,"

> a "bear" being, therefore, one who, at the moment, prefers to avoid securities and to lend cash; while a "bull" is one who prefers to hold securities and borrow cash. The former anticipates that securities will fall in cash value and the latter that they will rise. (p. 250)

This is quite clear; but when Mr. Keynes goes on to elaborate his concept of the "state of preference for savings deposits" or "state or degree of bearishness" or "degree of propensity to hoard," particularly in his *Economic Journal* article, we find suddenly that it depends not on the expectations with regard to the future price of securities, but on the present price of securities, in the sense that, at any moment of time, a curve expressing the "degree of propensity to hoard" could be drawn in a system of coordinates where the ordinate expresses the "price of nonliquid assets in terms of liquid assets" and the abscissa the quantity of "inactive deposits" or "liquid assets" held by the community (*Economic Journal* 41 [1931]: 412). This curve which, according to the explanation given on pages 250–51 of the *Treatise*, probably has a shape somewhat similar to a parabola with an axis parallel to the abscissa and convex toward the ordinate (though the case discussed here may be one of a shift, or change in the shape, of the curve) is, therefore, based on the assumption that, within certain limits, in a given situation any fall in the price of securities will cause a *decrease* in the propensity to hoard or, in other words, that any such fall in the price level of securities will strengthen the expectation of a future rise. To me, it seems very doubtful whether any change in present security prices will lead, immediately, to a reverse change in the expectations concerning future price movements.

This demand curve for securities or nonliquid assets assumes importance in connection with Mr. Keynes's further assumption that the banking system is in a position to determine the amount of savings deposits, and that "given the volume of savings deposits created by the banking system, the price level of investment goods"[22] (whether new or old) is solely determined by the

---

[22] There is considerable obscurity and contradiction with regard to the relation between the price level of "investment goods" and the price level of "securities." In the passage quoted in the text (and in many other places as, for example, at the top of page 418 in the *Economic Journal* article) the two are, obviously,

disposition of the public toward "hoarding money." If we concede both assumptions: the direct dependence of the demand for securities on their present price, and the power of the banking system to determine the volume of savings deposits, then, indeed, this conclusion certainly follows. But both assumptions are highly questionable.

To the former, it need only be answered that any fall in the price of securities is just as likely to create a fear of a further fall as the expectation of a rise. The second is more difficult to refute because, so far as I can see, Mr. Keynes has merely stated it without making any attempt to prove it. It depends, obviously, on the assumption (which, curiously enough, smacks of the fundamental error of the adherents of the banking principle) that the amount of money (or "deposits") required by the industrial circulation is determined independently of the terms on which the banking system is willing to lend; so that any excess of deposits

---

treated as identical and the sub-section which deals with the determination of the prices of "securities," from which this passage is taken, is headed "The Price-level of New Investment goods" (p. 140). Here "securities" are expressly defined as "loan or real capital" (p. 141) and the conclusion of the section is summarized in the following sentence: "The price level of investments as a whole and hence of new investments, is that price level at which the desire of the public to hold savings deposits is equal to the amount of savings deposits which the banking system is willing and able to create." Essentially the same statement is made on page 413 of Mr. Keynes's *Economic Journal* article, regarding the determination of the price of "nonliquid assets" which, as we know, is only another name for "securities." But on page 253 it is said that, when security prices are rising, "this is *likely*—in general, but not necessarily—to *stimulate* a rise in P´, the price level of *new* investment," and on page 219 the following statement occurs: "Nor does the price of existing securities depend at all closely, over short periods, either on the cost of production *or on the price* of new *fixed capital*" (my italics). This last passage is the more remarkable in view of the fact that, in the sections dealing with the effect of the bank rate on investment, the effect on the production of fixed capital was alone considered—to the exclusion of all other kinds of investment goods (p. 202).

created by the banking system beyond this given amount will necessarily go into "hoards," while any deficiency will come out of these hoards and leave the general industrial circulation unaffected.[23] But this position is not only untenable (which hardly needs proving); it is, also, a curious contradiction of other parts of Mr. Keynes's argument. What can the banking system do to keep savings deposits constant if the public become "bullish" and reduce their savings deposits in order to buy securities? Certainly a reduction in the rate of interest will serve only to stimulate the bull movement. And how could the banking system have any influence on investment at all if all deposits it creates in excess of the given "requirements" of industry become inactive?

The cloud which envelops this part of the activities of the banking system becomes even thicker when Mr. Keynes discusses the function of the banks as intermediaries in the situation in which "two opinions develop between different schools of the public, the one favouring bank deposits more than before and the other favouring securities" (pp. 143, 251). The banking system can do this "by creating deposits, not against securities, but against short-term advances" ("brokers' loans") (Ibid.). Now, to take only one case in which, according to Mr. Keynes, an increase in savings deposits may take place at the expense of the industrial circulation: viz. an abnormal rise in savings deposits accompanied by a rise in security prices; this may indicate a *difference* of opinion as to the prospects of securities, the party on the "bull" tack in effect buying securities and borrowing money *via* the banking system from the party on the "bear" tack (p. 251). I am not sure whether, at this point, Mr. Keynes has in mind the fact that the banks re-lend these savings deposits as "loans for account of others" or whether he thinks that the

---

[23] "The amount of inactive deposits or hoards actually held, is determined by the banking system, since it is equal to the excess of total bank money created over what is required for the active deposits," *Economic Journal* 41 (1931): 413; cf. also Ibid., pp. 414, 415, and 419.

increase in savings deposits will lead the banks to grant additional credits to speculators on their own account. But, be this as it may, I cannot see how this process can, on balance, decrease the amount of active deposits. So long as the preference of one party for savings deposits is offset by a corresponding additional lending to the party preferring securities, any increase in inactive deposits, involved in this process, will *not* mean a corresponding decrease in active deposits.

On the whole, this discussion of the relation between the industrial and the financial circulations accomplishes little beyond showing that any increase in inactive deposits at the expense of active deposits will lead to an excess of saving over investment and that these changes are likely to be affected by changes in expectations as to the future course of security values—a result which is not particularly surprising. What Mr. Keynes says besides this (in particular his *obiter dictum* on the duty of a central bank, pp. 254–56) is so closely bound up with the obscurities just mentioned that it is scarcely possible to follow its meaning.

The "excess bearish factor" discussed in this section is the last of the different causes of "the mysterious difference between saving and investment" which Mr. Keynes discusses. The last major subject of his theoretical analysis which we shall discuss here, is the interaction of these different factors during the credit cycle. Before we turn to this problem, however, a few remarks may be made on a point which fits in better here than at any other place in these reflections.

XVI

The point in question concerns a statement so extraordinary that, if it were not clearly in his book in black and white, one would not believe Mr. Keynes to be capable of making it. In the historical illustrations given in volume 2, he devotes a whole section to what he calls "the Gibson Paradox," i.e., "the extraordinarily close correlation over a period of more than one hundred years between the rate of interest, as measured by the yield of Consols, and the level of prices as measured by the Wholesale Index Number."[24] Keynes reproaches economists in general for not having recognized the significance of this phenomenon and urges that it provides a verification of his theory. Without his theory, he contends, it is incapable of explanation, particularly not by "Professor Irving Fisher's well-known theorem as to the relation between the rate of interest and the appreciation or depreciation of the value of money."[25] According to this theorem, he suggests, we should expect just the contrary. Surely this is a definite fallacy, for it can be shown quite easily that this alleged paradox is nothing but an example of Professor Fisher's theorem. In the case of a sum of money, borrowed today and repayable a year hence, Mr. Keynes thinks that, "if real interest is 5 per cent. per annum and the value of money is falling 2 percent per annum, the lender requires the repayment of 107 a year hence in return for 100 loaned to-day." But the movements to which Mr. Gibson calls attention, so far from being compensatory, are, in fact, aggravating in their effect on the relation between lender and borrower; so that the purchaser of long-dated securities will, if prices rise 2 percent per annum, in a year's time possess a sum which is worth 2 percent less in money terms, money itself being 2 percent less valuable, so that he is 4 percent worse off than before. Now this is exactly what one would expect according to Professor Fisher's theorem, because, in the case of long-dated securities, a sale before the date when they become due is not the fulfillment of a contract in which the owner as lender would be in a position to ask for some compensation for the anticipated fall in the value of money; but, *on the contrary, the buyer is in the position of the lender, who (since the amount of the ultimate repayment is given) will naturally offer less if he expects the value of money*

---

[24] Vol. 2, p. 198.

[25] Ibid., p. 202.

to fall. Only if the present holder, at the time when he bought the securities, foresaw the fall in the value of money (and if he found somebody who also foresaw it and was ready to sell) would he have been able to protect himself by offering less for a security which represented a claim to fixed payments in a depreciating money. But I find it utterly impossible to understand why one should expect, as Mr. Keynes obviously does, that a man holding a fixed-interest security should be in a position to ask more interest if the value of money falls. "Gibson's Paradox" is, therefore, no paradox at all and proves nothing in favor of Mr. Keynes's theory.[26]

XVII

Within the limits of this article, it is impossible to deal, in the same detail with which the fundamental concepts have been discussed, with the last major subject upon which I wish to touch: viz. the explanation of the credit cycle. It is only natural that, when one tries to use all these concepts as tools for the purpose for which they were forged, all the difficulties which have been pointed out, not only recur but increase. To show in detail how they affect the results, would require a discussion many times longer than that contained in the respective sections of the *Treatise*. All I can do is to take up a few central points and leave unexamined not only the more intricate problems which arise out of the combination of the difficulties already noted but also some further important problems connected with the traditional English concept of capital, particularly the overemphasized distinction between fixed and circulating capital, an adequate discussion of which would require a separate article.

---

[26] While reading the proofs of this article, I notice that Professor Irving Fisher himself, in his new *Theory of Interest* (New York: Macmillan, 1930), pp. 417 *et seq.*, uses the very same figures of Mr. Gibson, which are used by Mr. Keynes, as evidence confirming his theory.

The first point which must strike any reader conversant with the writings of Wicksell and of what Mr. Keynes calls the Neo-Wicksell school, is how little use he finally makes of the effects of a monetary disequilibrium on *real* investment—which he has been at such pains to develop. What he is really interested in is merely the shifts in the money streams and the consequent changes in price levels. It seems never to have occurred to him that the artificial stimulus to investment, which makes it exceed current saving, may cause a disequilibrium in the real structure of production which, sooner or later, must lead to a reaction. Like so many others who hold a purely monetary theory of the trade cycle (as, for example, Mr. R.G. Hawtrey in this country and Dr. L.A. Hahn in Germany), he seems to believe that, if the existing monetary organization did not make it impossible, the boom could be perpetuated by indefinite inflation. Though the term "overinvestment" occurs again and again, its implications are never explored beyond the first conclusion that, so long as total incomes less the amount saved exceed the cost of the available output of consumers' goods (because investment is in excess of saving), the price level will have a tendency to rise. In Mr. Keynes's explanation of the cycle, the main characteristic of the boom is taken to be, not the increase in investment, but this consequent increase in the prices of consumers' goods and the profit which is therefore obtained. Direct inflation for consumption purposes would, therefore, create a boom quite as effectively as would an excess of investment over saving. Hence, he was quite consistent when, despairing of a revival of investment brought about by cheap money, he advocated, in his well-known broadcast address,[27] the direct stimulation of the expenditure of consumers on the lines suggested by other purchasing-power theorists such as Messrs. Abbati, Martin, and Foster and Catchings; for, on his theory, the effects of cheap money and increased buying of consumers are equivalent.

---

[27] Cf. his *Essays in Persuasion* (London: Macmillan, 1931), p. 148 *et seq.*

Since, according to this theory, it is the excess of the demand for consumers' goods over the costs of the available supply which constitutes the boom, this boom will last only so long as demand keeps ahead of supply and will end either when the demand ceases to increase or when the supply, stimulated by the abnormal profits, catches up with demand. Then the prices of consumers' goods will fall back to costs and the boom will be at an end, though it need not, necessarily, be followed by a depression; yet, in practice, deflationary tendencies are usually set up which will reverse the process.

This seems to me to be, in broad outline, Mr. Keynes's explanation of the cycle. In essence it is not only relatively simple, but also much less different from the current explanations than its author seems to think; though it is, of course, much more complicated in its details. To me, however, it seems to suffer from exactly the same deficiencies as all the other, less elaborate, purchasing-power theories of the cycle.

The main objections to these theories—I cannot go into details here and must beg permission, therefore, to refer to my other attempts to do so[28]—seem to me to be three in number. *First*, that the original increase in investment can be maintained only so long as it is more profitable to increase the output of capital goods than to bid up the prices of the factors of production in the effort to satisfy the increased demands for consumers' goods. *Second*, that the increase in the demand for consumers' goods, if not offset by a new increase in the amount of money available for investment purposes, so far from giving a new stimulus to investment, will, on the contrary, lead to a decrease in investment because of its effect on the prices of the factors of production. *Third*, that the very fact that processes of investment have been begun but have become unprofitable as a result of the

---

[28] Cf. my *Prices and Production* (London: Routledge and Sons, 1931); and "The Paradox of Saving," *Economica* 32 (May 1931). Both are included in this volume.

rise in the price of the factors and must, therefore, be discontinued, is, of itself, a sufficient cause to produce a decrease of general activity and employment (in short, a depression) without any new monetary cause (deflation). Insofar as deflation is brought about—as it may well be—by this change in the prospects of investment, it is a secondary or induced phenomenon caused by the more fundamental, real, disequilibrium which cannot be removed by new inflation, but only by the slow and painful process of readjustment of the structure of production. While Mr. Keynes has occasional glimpses of the alternative character of an increase in the output of consumers' goods and investment goods,[29] he does not follow up this idea; and, in my view, it is this alone which could lead him to the true explanation of the crisis. But it is not surprising that he fails to do so, for it is precisely in the elucidation of these interrelations that the tools he has created become an altogether inadequate and unsuitable equipment. The achievement of this object is, indeed, impossible with his present concepts of capital and "investment" and without a clear notion of the change in the structure of production involved in any transition to more or less capitalistic methods. An adequate criticism of Mr. Keynes's explanation of the cycle would, therefore, require a somewhat elaborate description of that process. This I have tried to give in the places referred to. All I shall attempt here will be some further explanation of the three points already mentioned. Any increase in investment means that, on the average, a longer time will elapse between the application of the factors and the completion of the process and, what is particularly important in this connection, the period is not lengthened

---

[29] For example, when he says (p. 289) that "the incentive to an increased output of capital goods should diminish, just as the incentive to the production of consumption goods increases," or again in the passage at the top of page 310, which clearly implies that it is the quick, and therefore less capitalistic, production of consumers' goods which has become relatively more profitable as a consequence of their higher prices.

only while new investment is going on; it will have to be permanently longer if the increased capital is to be maintained, i.e., total investment (new and renewed) will have to be constantly greater than before. But if the increase of investment is not the consequence of a voluntary decision to reduce the possible level of consumption for this purpose, there is no reason why it should be permanent and the very increase in the demand for consumers' goods which Mr. Keynes has described will put an end to it as soon as the banking system ceases to provide additional cheap means for investment. Here, his exclusive insistence on new investment and his neglect of the process of reinvestment makes him overlook the all-important fact that an increase in the demand for consumers' goods will not only tend to stop new investment, but may make a complete reorganization of the existing structure of production inevitable—which would involve considerable disturbances and would render it impossible, temporarily, to employ all labor.

XVIII

From Mr. Keynes's reply to the first part of these reflections (see *Economica* [November 1931]: 395), I gather that he considers what I have called changes in the structure of production (i.e., the lengthening or shortening of the average period of production) to be a long-run phenomenon which may, therefore, be neglected in the analysis of a short-period phenomenon, such as the trade cycle. I am afraid that this contention merely proves that Mr. Keynes has not yet fully realized that *any* change in the amount of capital per head of working population is equivalent to a change in the average length of the roundabout process of production and that, therefore, all his demonstrations of the change in the amount of capital during the cycle prove my point (see *Treatise*, vol. 2, chaps. 27–29). Any increase in investment means that, on the average, a longer time will elapse between the application of the factors and the completion of the process and, what is particularly important in this connection, the period is not lengthened only while *new* investment is going on; it will have to be permanently longer if the increased capital is to be maintained, i.e., *total* investment (new and renewed) will have to be constantly greater than before. But if the increase of investment is not the consequence of a voluntary decision to reduce the possible level of consumption for this purpose, there is no reason why it should be permanent and the very increase in the demand for consumers' goods which Mr. Keynes has described will put an end to it as soon as the banking system ceases to provide additional cheap means for investment. Here, his exclusive insistence on new investment and his neglect of the process of reinvestment makes him overlook the all-important fact that an increase in the demand for consumers' goods will not only tend to stop new investment, but may make a complete reorganization of the existing structure of production inevitable—which would involve considerable disturbances and would render it impossible, temporarily, to employ all labor.

So long as the absolute rise in the price of consumption goods is relatively smaller than the rise in the price of investment goods due to a continued expansion of credit, it is true that the upward phase of the cycle will continue. But as soon as the rise in the former overtakes the rise in the latter, this will certainly not mean that "the upward phase of the cycle will have made its appearance" (p. 283). On the contrary it must mean a period of declining investment.[30] And, as all inductive evidence shows, it is the

---

[30] Something like this seems to be going on at the present time in Russia where, after the burden imposed by the Five Years' Plan on the consumer was found to be intolerable, the authorities have decided to change their arrangements and speed up the output of consumers' goods. I should not have been surprised if this had led to unemployment just as in a capitalistic society; and in fact, if I have been informed correctly, this has already taken place. This does not, however, lead to an increase in the figure for unemployment, but only in the numbers of so-called unemployable—since workmen are only dismissed on the pretence of inefficiency.

decline in investment (or in the production of producers' goods) and not the impossibility of selling consumers' goods at remunerative prices, which characterizes the beginning of the slump. Indeed, it is the experience of all depressions and especially of the present one, that the sales of consumption goods are maintained until long after the crisis; industries making consumption goods are the only ones which are prosperous and even able to absorb, and return profits on, new capital during the depression. The decrease in consumption comes only as a result of unemployment in the heavy industries, and since it was the increased demand for the products of the industries making goods for consumption which made the production of investment goods unprofitable, by driving up the prices of the factors of production, it is only by such a decline that equilibrium can be restored.

If the real trouble is that the proportion of the total output which, as a consequence of entrepreneurs' decisions, has become "nonavailable" is too great relative to what consumers are demanding to have "available"; and if, therefore, the production of "nonavailable" output has to be cut down, then, certainly, the resulting unemployment is due to more deep-seated causes than mere deflation and can be cured only by such a reduction of consumption relative to saving as will correspond to the existing proportion between "available" and "nonavailable" output; or by adapting this latter proportion to the former, i.e., by returning to less capitalistic methods of production and thus reducing total output. I do not deny that, during this process, a tendency toward deflation will regularly arise; this will particularly be the case when the crisis leads to frequent failures and so increases the risks of lending. It may become very serious if attempts artificially to "maintain purchasing power" delay the process of readjustment—as has probably been the case during the present crisis. This deflation is, however, a secondary phenomenon in the sense that it is caused by the instability in the real situation; the tendency will persist so long as the real causes are not removed. Any attempt to combat the crisis by credit expansion will, therefore, not only be merely the treatment of symptoms as causes, but may also prolong the depression by delaying the inevitable real adjustments. It is not difficult to understand, in the light of these considerations, why the easy-money policy which was adopted immediately after the crash of 1929 was of no effect.

It is, unfortunately, to these secondary complications that Mr. Keynes, in common with many other contemporary economists, directs most attention. This is not to say that he has not made valuable suggestions for treating these secondary complications. But, as I suggested at the beginning of these reflections, his neglect of the more fundamental "real" phenomena has prevented him from reaching a satisfactory explanation of the more deep-seated causes of depression.

The Mythology of Capital

The Mythology of Capital

> With every respect for the intellectual qualities of my opponent, I must oppose his doctrine with all possible emphasis, in order to defend a solid and natural theory of capital against a mythology of capital.
>
> E. v. Böhm-Bawerk
> *Quarterly Journal of Economics* 11, no. 2 (February 1907): 282

I. Professor Knight's Argument

Professor Knight's crusade against the concept of the period of investment[1] revives a controversy which attracted much attention thirty and forty years ago but was not satisfactorily settled at that time. In his attack, he uses very similar arguments to those which Professor J.B. Clark employed then against Böhm-Bawerk. However, I am not concerned here with a defense of the details of the views of the latter. In my opinion the oversimplified form in which he (and Jevons before him) tried to incorporate the time element into the theory of capital prevented him from cutting himself

---

This article first appeared in the *Quarterly Journal of Economics* 50 (February 1936): 199–228.

[1] The following are the main articles in which Professor Knight has recently discussed the problem in question, and to which I shall refer in the course of this article by the numbers given in brackets []:

[1] "Capitalist Production, Time and the Rate of Return," *Economic Essays in Honour of Gustav Cassel* (London: George Allen and Unwin, 1933): 327–42.

finally loose from the misleading concept of capital as a definite "fund," and is largely responsible for much of the confusion which exists on the subject; and I have full sympathy with those who see in the concept of a single or average period of production a meaningless abstraction which has little if any relationship to anything in the real world. But Professor Knight, instead of directing his attack against what is undoubtedly wrong or misleading in the traditional statement of this theory, and trying to put a more appropriate treatment of the time element in its place, seems to me to fall back on the much more serious and dangerous error of its opponents of forty years ago. In the place of at least an attempt of analysis of the real phenomena, he evades the problems by the introduction of a

---

[2] "Capital Time, and the Interest Rate," *Economica* n.s. 1, no. 3 (August 1934): 257–86.

[3] "Professor Hayek and the Theory of Investment," *Economic Journal* 45, no. 177 (March 1935): 77–94.

In addition, certain other articles by Professor Knight which bear closely on the subject and to some of which I may occasionally refer may also be mentioned.

[4] "Professor Fisher's Interest Theory: A Case in Point," *Journal of Political Economy* 39, no. 2 (April 1931): 176–212.

[5] Article on "Interest," *Encyclopaedia of Social Sciences* 8 (1932), pp. 131–44.

[6] "The Ricardian Theory of Production and Distribution," *The Canadian Journal of Economics and Political Science* 1, no. 1 (February 1935): 3–25.

The classical "Austrian" position has recently been ably and lucidly restated and defended against Professor Knight's criticism by Professor Fritz Machlup in an article, "Professor Knight and the 'Period of Production'," which appeared, together with a comment by Professor Knight, in the *Journal of Political Economy* for October 1935. But this as well as Professor Knight's answer to Mr. Boulding ("The Theory of Investment Once More: Mr. Boulding and the Austrians," in the last issue of this Journal) reached me too late to refer to them in the body of the article. But one or two references to these latest publications have been added in footnotes where I refer to the comment and the reply to Mr. Boulding with the numbers [7] and [8], respectively.

pseudo-concept devoid of content and meaning, which threatens to shroud the whole problem in a mist of words.

It is with profound regret that I feel myself compelled to dissent from Professor Knight on this point, and to return his criticism. Quite apart from the great indebtedness which all economists must feel toward Professor Knight for his contributions to economic theory in general, there is no other author with whom I feel myself so much in agreement, even on some of the central questions of the theory of interest, as with Professor Knight. His masterly expositions of the relationship between the productivity and the "time preference" element in the determination of the rate of interest[2] should have removed, for all time I hope, one of the worst misunderstandings which in the past have divided the different camps of theorists. Under these conditions anything which comes from him carries great weight, particularly when he attaches such importance to it that he tries "to force his views on reluctant minds by varied iteration." It is not surprising that he has already gained some adherents to his views.[3] But this only makes it doubly necessary to refute what seems to me to be a series of erroneous conclusions, founded on one basic mistake, which already in the past has constituted a serious bar to theoretical progress, and which would threaten to balk every further advance in this field, if its pronouncement by an authority like Professor Knight were left uncontradicted.

This basic mistake—if the substitution of a meaningless statement for the solution of a problem can be called a mistake—is the idea of capital as a fund which maintains itself automatically, and

---

[2] Cf. particularly articles [4] and [5] quoted above.

[3] Cf. H.S. Ellis, "Die Bedeutung der Productionsperiode für die Krisentheorie," and P. Joseph and K. Bode, "Bemerkungen zur Kapital und Zinstheorie," both articles in *Zeitschrift für Nationalökonomie* 4 (1935). R. Nurkse, "The Schematic Representation of the Structure of Production," *Review of Economic Studies* 2 (1935). S. Carison, "On the Notion of Equilibrium in Interest Theory," *Economic Studies* 1 (Krakow, 1935).

that, in consequence, once an amount of capital has been brought into existence the necessity of reproducing it presents no economic problem. According to Professor Knight, "all capital is normally conceptually, perpetual,"[4] "its replacement has to be taken for granted as a technological detail,"[5] and in consequence "there is no production process of determinate length, other than zero or 'all history',"[6] but "in the only sense of timing in terms of which economic analysis is possible, *production and consumption are simultaneous.*"[7] Into the reasons why the capital maintains itself thus automatically we are not to inquire, because under the stationary or progressive conditions, which alone are considered, this is "axiomatic."[8] On the other hand it is asserted that "making an item of wealth more durable" or "using a longer period of construction,"[9] i.e., lengthening the time dimension of investment in either of the two possible ways, is only one among an "accurately speaking, infinite number" of possible ways of investing more capital, which are later even described as "really an infinite number of infinities."[10]

---

[4] [2], p. 259; a few pages later (p. 266) the treatment of capital once invested as "perpetual" is even described as the "realistic" way of looking at the matter.

[5] [2], p. 264. At one point Professor Knight does indeed say that "the most important fact requiring clarification is the nature of capital maintenance" ([3], p. 84). But instead of the patient analysis of how and why capital is maintained, which after this we feel entitled to expect, we get nothing but a concept of capital as a mystical entity, an "integrated organic conception" which maintains itself automatically. Professor Knight does not actually use the word "automatic" in this connection, but his insistence on the supposed fact that the replacement of capital "has to be taken for granted as a technological detail can hardly have any other meaning but that it needs no explanation in economic terms and is, therefore, from the point of view of the economist "automatic."

[6] [3], p. 78, cf. also [8], p. 64.

[7] [2], p. 275.

[8] [3], p. 84.

[9] [2], p. 268.

[10] [2], p. 270.

According to Professor Knight, "what the Böhm-Bawerk school's position amounts to is simply selecting these two details which are of the same significance as any of an infinity of other details,"[11] while in fact "additional capital is involved in very different ways for lengthening the cycle and for increasing production without this lengthening."[12] "Time is one factor or dimension among a practically infinite number, and quantity of capital may and does vary quite independently of either of these time intervals."[13]

---

[11] [2], p. 268.

[12] [3], p. 81.

[13] [6], p. 82. An attempt to clear up by correspondence at least some of the differences between us has only had the effect of making the gulf which divides our opinion appear wider than ever. In a letter written after reading an earlier draft of the present paper, Professor Knight emphasizes that he "categorically denies that there is any determinate time interval" ... "which elapses between the time when some product might have been obtained from the available factors and the time the product actually accrues." This can hardly mean anything more than either that no postponement whatever of consumption is possible, or at least that, once such a postponement has taken place, it is impossible to use for current consumption any of the factors which would be needed to maintain or replace the capital goods created by the first investment. I find it difficult to believe that Professor Knight should want to assert either. Quite apart from the fact that such statements would, as it seems to me, stand in flagrant contrast to all empirical evidence, the contrary has been asserted by Professor Knight himself as the first of "the three empirical facts that form the basis of a sound theory of capital." This, in his words ([2], p. 258), is

> the simple "technological" fact that it is possible to increase the volume (time rate) of production after any interval by the use during that interval of a part of existing productive resources—in large part the same resources previously and subsequently used for producing "current consumption income"—to produce, instead of current consumption income, instruments of agencies of various sorts, tangible or intangible, which when produced become "productive" of additional current income. This activity or process we call investment.

Against this I do indeed hold that, first, all the problems which are commonly discussed under the general heading of "capital" do arise out of the fact that part of the productive equipment is nonpermanent and has to be deliberately replaced on economic grounds, and that there is no meaning in speaking of capital as something permanent which exists apart from the essentially impermanent capital goods of which it consists. Second, that an increase of capital will *always* mean an extension of the time dimension of investment, that capital will be required to bring about an increase of output only insofar as the time dimension of investment is increased. This is relevant, not only for the understanding of the transition to more capitalistic methods, but equally if one wants to understand how the limitation of the supply of capital limits the possibilities of increasing output under stationary conditions.

This is not a dispute about words. I shall endeavor to show that, on the one hand, Professor Knight's approach prevents him from seeing at all how the choice of particular methods of production is dependent on the supply of capital, and from explaining the process by which capital is being maintained or transformed, and that, on the other hand, it leads him to undoubtedly wrong conclusions. Nor does this discussion seem necessary solely because of the objections raised by Professor Knight. In

---

In giving permission to quote the above sentence from his letter Professor Knight adds:

> It would induce to clearness to add that it is my view that the interval in question approaches determinateness as we impose stationary or given conditions in a sense so rigid that such an expression as "might have been obtained" loses all meaning." I am afraid this explanation leaves me more perplexed than ever. As I have tried to show in the last section of this paper, all Professor Knight's former argument against the concept of a determinate investment period depends exactly on the most rigid static assumptions of this kind.

many respects his conclusions are simply a consistent development of ideas which were inherent in much of the traditional treatment of the subject,[14] and which lead to all kinds of pseudo-problems and meaningless distinctions that have played a considerable role in recent discussions on the business cycle.

II. On Some Current Misconceptions

Before I can enter upon attempting to refute Professor Knight's assertion, it is necessary to dispose of certain preliminary matters. There are certain ideas which Professor Knight and others seem to associate with the view I hold but which in fact are not relevant to it. I do not want to defend these views but rather to make it quite clear that I regard them as erroneous. Practically all the points to which I now call attention were either implicitly or explicitly contained in that article of mine which Professor Knight attacks.[15] As he has chosen to disregard them, it is necessary to set them out in order.

(1) It should be quite clear that the technical changes involved, when changes in the time structure of production are contemplated, are *not* changes due to changes in technical knowledge. The concept of increasing productivity due to increasing roundaboutness arises only when we have to deal with increases of output which are dependent on a sufficient amount of capital being available, and which were impossible before only because of the insufficient supply of capital. This assumes in particular that the increase of output is not due to changes of technical knowledge. It *excludes* any changes in the technique of production which are made possible by new inventions.

---

[14] For an effective criticism of related earlier views, cf. particularly F.W. Taussig, "Capital, Interest and Diminishing Returns," *Quarterly Journal of Economics* 12 (May 1908): 339–44.

[15] "On the Relationship between Investment and Output," *Economic Journal* (June 1934), cf. particularly p. 212, note 1, and p. 226 for point (2), p. 217 for (3), p. 210, note 1, and p. 227 for (4), p. 230, note for (5), and p. 228 for (6).

(2) It is not true that the periods which it is contended are necessarily lengthened when investment is increased are periods involved in the production of a particular type of product. They are rather *periods for which particular factors are invested*, and it would be better for this reason if the term "period of production" had never been invented and if only the term "period of investment" were used. To give here only one example: it is not only conceivable, but it is probably a very frequent occurrence that an increase in the supply of capital may lead not to a change in the technique of production in any particular line of industry, but merely to a transfer of factors from industries where they have been invested for shorter periods to industries where they are invested for longer periods. In this case, the periods for which one has to wait for any particular type of product have all remained unaltered, but the periods of investment of the factors that have been transferred from one industry to another have been lengthened.[16]

---

[16] A similar case is that where an addition to the supply of capital makes it possible to employ factors (say, labor) which before were unemployed. The first question to ask here is how exactly is it that an increase of capital makes their employment possible. We shall have to assume that without this capital the marginal product of this labor would have been lower than the wage at which they would have been willing to work. In what sense can it now be said that an increase of their marginal product is conditional upon more capital becoming available, i.e., why was it impossible, without this increase of capital, to employ them in the more productive processes? I cannot see that the necessity of previous accumulation can mean anything but an increase of the periods for which either the factors immediately concerned, or some other factors employed in providing the former with equipment, are invested.

In the traditional exposition of the theory of roundabout production, this case, where only total capital, but not necessarily capital per head of those employed, has been increased, has been taken account of by saying that the average period of production (i.e., the average period for which the labor actually employed is invested) will only increase when capital per head increases, but will remain constant when capital is increased by an extension of

(3) It is not proposed, and is in fact inadmissible, to reduce the description of the range of periods for which the different factors are invested to an expression of the type of a single time dimension such as the average period of production. Professor Knight seems to hold that to expose the ambiguities and inconsistencies involved in the notion of an average investment period serves to expel the idea of time from capital theory altogether. But it is not so. In general it is sufficient to say that the investment period of some factors has been lengthened, while those of all others have remained unchanged; or that the investment periods of a greater quantity of factors have been lengthened than the quantity of factors whose investment periods have been shortened by an equal amount; or that the investment period of a given quantity of factors has been lengthened by more than the investment period of another equal amount has been shortened. It is true that in some cases (e.g., when the investment period of one factor is shortened, and at the same time the period for which a greater quantity of another factor is invested is lengthened by a smaller interval) the determination of the net effect of the changes of the investment periods of different factors in different directions raises problems which cannot be so easily answered. But the concept of the average period, which was introduced mainly to solve this difficulty, does not really provide a solution. The obstacle here is that the reinvestment of accrued interest has to be counted equally as the investment of an amount of factors of corresponding value for the same period. In consequence the only way in which an aggregate of waiting can be described, and the amount of waiting involved in different investment structures can be compared, is by means of a process of summation, in the form of a double integral over the function describing the rates, at which the factors that contribute to the product of any moment are applied, and at which interest accrues.

---

its "labor dimension" instead of its "time dimension." Although this mode of expression is sometimes useful, I think it has to be abandoned together with the concept of the average period of production.

It should, however, be especially noted that the assertion that it is conceptually possible to conceive of the aggregate capital of a society in terms of possible waiting periods does not mean that *the total period of production* (or the aggregate of all periods of production) of an economic system is necessarily *a phenomenon capable of measurement*. Whether this is the case (and in my opinion it is very unlikely) is altogether irrelevant for the problem at issue. What is essential is solely that whenever a change occurs in any part of the economic system which involves that more (or less) capital is used in the industry or industries concerned, this always means that some of the factors used there will now bring a return only after a longer (or shorter) time interval than was the case in their former use. As Professor Knight himself rightly says,

> the rate of interest which determines the value of all existing capital goods is determined exclusively at the *margin of growth*, where men are comparing large, short segments of income flow with thinner streams reaching out to the indefinite future.[17]

It is at this margin of growth (of every individual firm and industry) where the extensions of investment occur and where the decisive question arises whether the productivity of investment is a

---

[17] [2], p. 278. Cf. also [8], p. 45. The disagreement here concerns the question whether it is true that men directly and irrevocably exchange "short segments of income flow" against "thinner streams reaching into the indefinite future" or whether it is not essential to take into account that the immediate result of the sacrifice of present income is an equally limited income flow of a different time shape which must be clearly defined as regards size and shape in order to make it possible to decide in the particular case whether the sacrifice is justified. And this limited income stream which is the result of the first investment becomes a permanent income stream only by an infinite series of further decisions when the opportunity of consuming more now and less in the future has to be considered every time. By jumping directly to the desired result, the permanent income stream, Professor Knight slurs over so much that is essential for an understanding of the process that any use of his concept of capital for an analysis of the role of this capital in the course of further changes becomes quite impossible.

function of time and whether the limitation of investment is a limitation of the time we are willing or able to wait for a return.[18]

(4) It is quite erroneous to regard propositions concerning the greater productivity of roundabout methods as depending upon the possibility of identifying the contribution of the "original" factors of the remote past. In order to be able to give an intelligible description of a continuous stationary process in which factors are invested at any one moment, some of whose products will mature at almost any later moment, one of two methods is possible. Either we can concentrate on all factors invested in any one interval, and relate them to the stream of product derived from it. Or we can concentrate on the product maturing during a short interval, and relate it to the factors which have contributed to it. But whichever of the two methods we select, in all cases *only the future time intervals* between the moments when the factors are, or will be invested, and the moment when the product will mature are relevant, and *never the past periods* which have elapsed since the investment of some "original factors." The theory looks forward, not back.[19]

---

[18] As Professor Knight now admits "that insofar as any single investment, negligible in size in comparison with the economic system of which it is a part, represents things consumed and reproduced in a regular cycle, the quantity of capital in that investment does bear a mathematical relation to the length of the cycle" and that in this connection some of his "previously published statements have been too sweeping," there is perhaps some hope that ultimately some sort of agreement can be reached along these lines. (Cf. [7], p. 627.)

[19] Insofar as Professor Knight's aim is merely to drive out the remnants of a cost-of-production theory of value which still disfigure many expositions of the theory of capital (cf. [8], p. 45), I am all with him. But while I fully agree that there is no necessary connection between the present value of capital and the volume of past investment, I do maintain that there is a very close connection between the present and anticipated future values of capital on the one hand and the periods for which resources are invested at present on the other.

(5) It is equally erroneous to regard the theory as depending on any distinction between "original" or "primary" and produced means of production. It makes no fundamental difference whether we describe the range of investment periods for *all* factors existing at the beginning of the period,[20] or whether we just describe the range of periods for which those services of the permanent factors are invested that only become available for investment at successive moments as they accrue. I think it is more convenient to use the second method, and to describe the investment structure by what I have called the investment function of the services of these permanent factors. But whether this distinction—which is based on the fact that some of the productive resources have to be deliberately replaced, while others are regarded as not requiring replacement on economic grounds—is accepted or not, in no case is a distinction between "primary" or "original" and "produced" means of production necessary in order to give the concept of the investment function a definite sense.

(6) Last and closely connected with the preceding point, it is not necessarily the case that all "intermediate products" or "produced means of production" are highly specific, and that in consequence any change in the investment structure can only be

---

[20] A peculiar confusion in this respect occurs in the article of Miss Joseph and Mr. Bode quoted above (p. 174), where it is asserted that if all existing productive resources were taken into account, the period of production would "of course" become zero. It is true that the impossibility of drawing a fundamental distinction between the "original factors" and the "intermediate products" is one of the considerations which invalidate the construction of an "average" period of production. But whether we describe the investment structure by an expression representing the rate at which the product of all resources existing at any one moment will mature during the future, or by an expression representing the rate at which the marginal additions will mature which are due to the services of the permanent factors applied at that moment, is merely a difference of exposition. As will be easily seen, the former is simply the integral of the latter and can be represented by the area of the figure which is bounded by the investment curve which represents the latter.

brought about by investing the "original" factors for longer or shorter periods. This seems frequently to be implied in analysis which follows Böhm-Bawerkian lines. But of course there is no reason why it should be true. The periods for which non-permanent resources are being invested are as likely to be changed as the periods of investment of the services of the permanent resources.[21]

III. Professor Knight's Criticism Based on a Misunderstanding

Most of the critical comments in Professor Knight's articles are due to misunderstandings of one or more of these fundamental points. But while each of them seems to be the source of some confusion, probably none was in this respect quite as fertile as number two. The idea that lengthening the process of production must always have the result that a particular kind of product will now be the result of a longer process, or that a person who invests more capital in his enterprise must therefore necessarily lengthen the period of production in this business, seems to be at the root of his assertion that capital can be used otherwise than to lengthen the time dimension of investment, as well as of his statement that I have practically admitted this.

As a proof of the former contention Professor Knight cites a single concrete example, taken from agriculture. "Taking population as given," he writes,[22]

---

[21] It is perhaps necessary, in order to forestall further misunderstandings, to add as point (7) the main conclusion of the article of mine which Professor Knight attacked. It is that the periods of investment are not in all cases given as technical data but can in many instances only be determined by a process of value imputation. This is particularly true in the case of durable goods, where the technical data only tell us how long we have to wait for a particular unit of its services, but not to what share of the factors invested in it this unit has to be attributed. This attribution, however, involves an imputation purely in value terms.

[22] [3], p. 81.

raising *more* plants of the *same* growth period will also require more "stock," but *will not* affect the length of the cycle, while the *addition* to total production of varieties of *shorter* growth, say yielding two harvests per year instead of one, will involve an increase of capital while *shortening* the average cycle.

Unfortunately Professor Knight only adds that "additional capital is involved in very different ways for lengthening the cycle and for increasing production without this lengthening," but does not tell us how exactly the additional capital is used for increasing production other than by lengthening the period for which some resources are invested. If he had stopped to inquire he would soon have found that even in the cases where his quite irrelevant "cycle" of the particular process remains constant, or is actually shortened, additional capital will be used in order to invest some resources for longer periods than before, and will only be needed if this is the case.

As Professor Knight has not stated why, in his example, either of the two new methods of cultivation will only be possible if new capital becomes available, it will be necessary to review the different possibilities which exist in this respect. Changes in technical knowledge must clearly be excluded and apparently Professor Knight also wants to exclude changes in the amount of labor used, although it is not quite clear what the assumption "taking population as given" exactly means. If it is to mean that the quantity of all labor which contributes in any way to the product is assumed to be constant, and to be invested for a constant period, it is difficult to see how, with unchanged technical knowledge, they should suddenly be able to raise more plants and to use more capital. There seem to be only three possibilities, and all of them clearly imply a lengthening of the period for which some of the factors are invested.

(1) It may be assumed that the additional capital is used to buy instruments, etc., which are now made by people who were before directly employed in raising the crop;

(2) or it may be used to buy instruments to be made by people who before were employed to produce something else and have been attracted to making instruments, and thereby contributing to the output in question, by the new capital which has become available for the instruments;

(3) or that the additional capital is used to employ additional people.

Case (1) clearly contradicts the assumption that the periods for which the units of the given labor forces are invested are not lengthened, since the amount of time that will elapse between the making of the instrument and the maturing of the crop will clearly be longer than the period which elapses between the direct application of labor in raising the crop and its maturity. Cases (2) and (3) seem to be in conflict with the assumption of constant population. But in these cases, too, an increase of stock in society will only take place if the labor drawn to this particular line of production from elsewhere is now invested for a longer period than before. (I take it for granted here that additional capital means capital newly saved, and not merely transferred from elsewhere, since nobody, of course, wants to contend that a mere transfer of capital from one line of industry to another, which is accompanied by a similar transfer of the labor for whose investment the capital is required, need lead to an extension of the period for which any resources are invested.) Only if the labor which is now drawn to the process in question has before been invested for shorter periods than it will either in producing agriculture implements (case (2)), or in directly raising the crop (case (3)), will its diversion to the new use cause a temporary gap in the stream of consumable income, which will fall short of the value of the current services of the factors of production, and therefore require some saving or "new capital."

In Professor Knight's second case, that of additional production of shorter duration, he has again neglected to state why this should only become possible if additional capital becomes available. For the same reasons it seems to me to follow that this new production can be dependent on a new supply of capital coming forward only if the other factors required have before been invested for shorter periods.[23]

Evidently this example in no way proves that a case is conceivable where additional capital is used without having the effect of lengthening the investment period of some factor. Yet this example is the only thing in Professor Knight's article which even attempts a demonstration of his main thesis.

The same failure to see the point here involved at all leads Professor Knight also to misinterpret completely a statement of my own, and to describe it "as very nearly a 'give away'," while in fact it simply refers to this case, where the lengthening of the investment structure is brought about not by lengthening any particular process (choosing a more time-consuming technique in the production of a particular product) but by using a greater share of the total factors of production than before in the relatively more time-consuming processes. What I actually said was that a fall in the rate of interest would lead to the production of a greater quantity of durable goods, and that—explaining this further—"more goods (or, where possible, more durable goods) *of the kind* will be produced simply because the more distant part of the expected services will play a greater role in the considerations of the entrepreneur and will lead him to invest more on account of these more distant returns." Even if this statement was not very fortunately phrased,[24] it should have been evident to anyone who has ever made an effort to understand the different ways in which extensions in the time dimension of investment may take place that it referred to

---

[23] I am afraid I am unable to see to what case the sentence in the same paragraph beginning with "in the third case" refers.

[24] My meaning would have been expressed better if, instead of speaking of the production of more goods of the kind, I had said "a greater quantity of the relatively more durable goods will be produced," or "goods of still greater durability made in place of those produced before."

the case where the periods for which particular factors are invested is being lengthened in consequence of their transfer from a less to a more capitalistic process of production. The production of more goods of the same (relatively durable) kind *does* therefore mean a change in the investment function for society as a whole in the direction of lengthening the time dimension of production.

IV. His Own Position Prevents Him from Giving Any Explanation of How the Limitation of Capital Restricts the Increase of Output

More serious than these misunderstandings about what the "period of production" analysis implies is the failure to see that, without such an analysis, no answer whatever can be given to the fundamental question of how the limitation of the available capital limits the choice among the known methods of production. This question is closely connected with the further problem of whether, and in what sense, the nonpermanent resources existing at any one moment can be regarded as one homogeneous factor of determinate magnitude, as a "fund" of definite size which can be treated as a given datum in the sense in which the "supply of capital" or simply the "existing capital" is usually treated.

It is necessary first to say a few words about the reason why it is only in connection with the nonpermanent resources that the problems which can properly be called problems of capital arise. The very concept of capital arises out of the fact that, where nonpermanent resources are used in production, provision for replacement of the resources used up in production must be made, if the same income is to be enjoyed continually, and that in consequence part of the gross produce has to be devoted to their reproduction. But the fact that it may be regarded as the "normal" case that people will do so, with the aim of obtaining the same income in perpetuity, does not mean that therefore capital itself becomes in any sense perpetual. On the contrary the very problem of capital accounting arises only because and to the extent that the component parts of capital are not permanent, and it has no meaning, in economic analysis, to say that apart from the human decision, which we have yet to explain, the aggregate of all the nonpermanent resources becomes some permanent entity. The problem is rather to say how the existence of a given stock of nonpermanent resources makes possible their replacement by newly produced[25] instruments, and at the same time limits the extent to which this can be done.[26] And this raises

---

[25] I am afraid I feel compelled to disregard the special meaning which Professor Knight wants to attach to the term "production." A concept of production which would compel us to say that a man engaged in the production of some instrument which is to replace some similar existing instrument, and which at some time in the future will contribute to the satisfaction of a desire, either produces not at all or produces not the final product in whose manufacture the instrument he makes is actually used, but a similar product which is consumed at the moment when he applies his labor to the instrument, seems to me an absurd abuse of words. But it is on this "concept" and nothing else that the assertion that production and consumption are simultaneous is based (like J.B. Clark's theorem of the "synchronization" of production and consumption).

[26] On the general subject of the amortization of capital Professor Knight is not only rather obscure but his different pronouncements are clearly inconsistent. In [2], p. 273 he writes:

> In reality most investments not only begin at a fairly early date to yield their income in consumable services ... but in addition they begin fairly soon to yield more than interest on cost in this form, and entirely liquidate themselves in a moderate period of time. This additional flow of consumable services is ordinarily treated as a replacement fund, but is available for consumption or for reinvestment in any form and field of use at the will of the owner.

But in [3], p. 83, in order to support his thesis about the perpetuity of capital, this periodic liquidation is denied:

> It cannot now escape observation that "capital" is an integrated, organic conception, and the notion that the investment in a particular instrument comes back periodically in the form of product, giving the owner freedom to choose whether he will re-invest or not, is largely a fiction and a delusion.

the question in what sense these different capital goods can be said to have a common quality, a common characteristic, which entitles us to regard them as parts of one factor, one "fund," or which makes them to some extent substitutable for each other. What creates the identity which makes it possible to say that one capital good has been effectively replaced by another one, or that the existence of the one makes its replacement by another possible? What is that medium through which the substance, commonly called capital in the abstract, can be said to be transformed from one concrete form into another? Is there such a thing, as is implied in the habitual use of terms by economists? Or is it not conceivable that the thing which they all have in mind is that condition affecting the possibilities of production which cannot be expressed in terms of a substantive quantity?

Although Professor Knight rather overstresses the case where a stock of capital goods is maintained by the preservation or replacement of the same items, his assertion that capital is permanent is of course not based on this assumption. The crucial case on which its meaning must be tested, and the only case where the question arises whether capital as something different from the individual instruments is permanent at all, is the case where capital goods that are worn out are replaced by capital goods of a different kind, which in many cases will not even help to produce the same services to the consumer but will contribute to render altogether different services. What does the assertion that the capital is permanent mean here? It must evidently mean more than that there will always be some capital in existence. If it has any sense it must mean that the quantity of capital is kept constant. But what is the criterion which determines whether the new capital goods intended to replace the old ones are exactly their equivalent, and what assures us that they will always be replaced by such equivalent quantities?

To these questions Professor Knight provides no answer, but, although admitting that he has no exact answer, postulates that the idea must be treated as if it had a definite meaning if we are to get anywhere. "The notion of maintaining any capital quantitatively intact," he writes,[27] "cannot be given exact definition; but this limitation applies to all quantitative analysis in economics, and the notion itself is clear and indispensable, and measurement, even, is fairly accurate."

Now, as I have tried to show in considerable detail in another place,[28] the notion of maintaining capital *quantitatively* intact, far from being either clear or indispensable, presupposes a behavior of the capitalist entrepreneurs which under dynamic conditions will sometimes be impossible and rarely reasonable for them to adopt. To assume that under changing conditions capital will be maintained constant in any quantitative sense is to assume something which will never happen, and any deductions derived from this assumption will therefore have no application to anything in the real world.

In some places[29] Professor Knight does, it is true, come somewhat nearer a realistic assumption by stating that what people aim to maintain constant is not some physical or value dimension of capital, but its "capacity to render service."[30] But even

---

[27] [3], p. 90, footnote.

[28] "The Maintenance of Capital," *Economica* (August 1935).

[29] [3], p. 86, note: "Wealth, which is identical with capital, can be treated quantitatively only by viewing it as capacity to render service." Also [2], p. 267: "As long as capital is maintained by replacing the capital goods, if their life is limited, by others of any form with equal earning capacity in imputed income."

[30] Professor Knight, however, by no means consistently adheres to this view. The idea that the quantity of capital which is to be regarded as "perpetual" is a quantity of value occurs again and again. He says, for example, that "there is 'of course' no product yielded by an agency until after full provision has been made for maintaining it, or the investment in it, intact, in the value sense" ([2], p. 280). And similarly, a few pages later (p. 283): "New investments represent additions to all the investment previously made in past time. The amount of such investment cannot indeed be stated quantitatively in any other way than as the capitalized value of existing income sources under existing conditions."

accepting this assumption it proves in no way that people will also always be capable of maintaining this capacity to render service, and, what is more important, it does not in any way help us to explain in what way this "capacity to render service" is limited, why and how it is possible to transfer it from one concrete manifestation in a capital good into another one. It still leaves us with the impression that there is a sort of substance, some fluid of definite magnitude which flows from one capital good into another, and it gives us no indication of the set of conditions which actually at any given moment allows us to maintain output at a particular figure.

The fact that we possess at any one moment, in addition to those natural resources which are expected to render services permanently without any deliberate replacement, an amount of nonpermanent resources which enable us to consume more than we could if only the former were available, will help us to maintain consumption *permanently* above this level only if by investing some of the services of the permanent resources for some time they will bring a greater return than they would have given if they were used for consumption when they first became available. If this were not the case no existing quantity of "capacity to render service" in a nonpermanent form would enable us to replace it by some new instruments with the same capacity to render service. We might spread the use of the services of these nonpermanent factors over as long a period as we like, but after the end of this period no more would be available for consumption than could be obtained from the current use of the permanent services.

That actually we are able to replace the "capacity to render service" represented by the nonpermanent resources, and by doing so maintain income permanently higher than what could be obtained from the permanent services only, is due to the *two* facts: first, that the existence of the nonpermanent resources allows us to forgo for the present some of the services of the existing resources without reducing consumption below the level at which it might have been kept with the permanent resources only, *and,* second, that by investing certain factors for some time we get a greater product than we would have otherwise got from them. Both these factors, the extent to which any given stock of nonpermanent resources enables us to "wait" and the extent to which investment enables us to increase the product from the factors invested, are variable. And it is for this reason that only a very detailed analysis of the time structure of production, of the relationship between the periods for which individual factors have been invested and the product derived from them, can help us to understand the forces which direct the use of the current resources for the replacement of capital. By stressing this relationship the period-of-production analysis (and to some extent already the older wage-fund and abstinence theories) introduced an element into the theory of capital without which no understanding of the process of maintenance and transformation of capital is possible. But the idea was not sufficiently worked out to make it quite clear how exactly the existence of a given stock of capital goods affected the possibilities of renewed investment.

The Böhm-Bawerkian theory in particular went astray in assuming, with the older views that Professor Knight now wants to revive,[31] that the quantity of capital (or the "possibility to wait") was a simple magnitude, a homogeneous fund of clearly determined size. The particular assumption made by Böhm-Bawerk and his immediate followers, which may have some justification as a first approximation for didactic purposes, but

---

[31] [8], p. 57:
> The basic issue is the old and familiar one of choice between two conceptions of capital. In one view, it consists of "things" of limited life which are periodically worn out or used up and reproduced; in the other, it is a "fund" which is maintained intact tho the things in which it is invested may come and go to any extent. In the second view, which of course is the one advocated here, the capital "fund" may be thought of as either a value or a "capacity" to produce a perpetual flow of value.

which is certainly misleading if it is maintained beyond the first stage, is that the existing stock of capital goods corresponds to a fixed quantity of consumer's goods and is therefore, on the further assumption of a given rate of consumption, uniquely associated with a definite total or average waiting period which it makes possible. The basis of this assumption was apparently the idea that every existing capital good was completely specific in the sense that it could be turned into only one particular quantity of consumers' goods by a process which could in no way be varied. On this assumption any present stock of capital could, of course, be regarded as equivalent to one, and only one, quantity of consumers' goods which would become available over a fixed period of time at a predetermined and invariable rate. This simplified picture of the existing stock of capital, representing a "subsistence fund" of determined magnitude which would provide a support for a definite period and therefore enable us to undertake production processes of a corresponding average length, is undoubtedly highly artificial and of little use for the analysis of more complicated processes.

Actually the situation is so much more complicated and requires a much more detailed and careful analysis of the time element because any existing stock of capital goods is not simply equivalent to a single quantity of consumers' goods due to mature at definitely fixed dates, but may be turned by different combinations with the services of the permanent factors into a great many alternative streams of consumers' goods of different size, time-shape, and composition. In a sense, of course, capital serves as a "subsistence fund," but it is not a fund in the sense that it provides subsistence for a single uniquely defined period of time. The question of which of the many alternative income streams which the existing stock of capital goods potentially represents shall be chosen will depend on which will best combine with the services of the permanent factors which are expected to become available during the future best in this context, meaning that it will combine into a total stream of the most desired time-shape. The role of the existing capital goods in this connection is that they fill the gap in the income stream which would otherwise have been caused by the investment of resources which might have been used to satisfy current needs. And it is only by making their investment for these periods possible that those resources will yield a product sufficient to take the place of the products rendered in the meantime by the already existing capital goods. *But there is no other "identity" between the now existing capital goods and those that will take their place than that the results of current investment,* which leads to the creation of the latter, *dovetail with one of the potential income streams,* which the former are capable of producing, into a total income stream of desired shape. And what limits the possibility of increasing output by investing resources which might serve current needs is again nothing but the possibility of providing in the meantime an income "equivalent" to that which will be obtained from the investment of current resources. ("Equivalent," strictly speaking, means, here, not equal but sufficiently large to make it worthwhile to wait for the increased return that will be obtained from the invested resources because of their investment.)

It should be clear that an analysis of this effect of the existence of capital goods on the direction of the investment of current resources is possible only in terms of the alternative time structures of production which are technically possible with a given equipment. What makes this analysis so particularly difficult, *yet* the more necessary (and at the same time lets the traditional approach in terms of an average investment period appear so hopelessly inadequate except as a first approach), is the fact that the existing capital goods do not represent a particular income stream of unique shape or size (as would be the case if it consisted of goods which were completely "specific"), but a great number of alternative contributions to future income of different magnitude and date. Nothing short of a complete description of these alternative time-shapes can provide a sufficient basis for the explanation of the effect of the existence of the capital goods on current investment and, what means the same thing, of the form and quantity of the new capital goods that will replace the old ones.

In this article, no positive attempt can be made to provide the technical apparatus required for a real solution to these problems. Apart from the particular aspect which I have discussed in the article which Professor Knight attacked, this task must be reserved for a more systematic study. I may mention that most of the serious difficulties which this analysis presents are due to the fact that it has to deal largely with joint-product and joint-demand relationships between goods existing at different moments of time. For the present discussion the task has been only to demonstrate why such an analysis of the time structure is necessary and why no description of capital in terms of mere quantity can take its place. The main fault of the traditional analysis in terms of the period of production was that it tried to argue in terms of a single time dimension in order to retain the connection to the conventional but misleading concept of capital as a definite fund. But it has at least the merit of stressing that element in terms of which the real relationship can be explained.

All the other attempts to state the assumptions as regards the supply of capital in terms of a definite fund and without any reference to the time structure, whether this is attempted by postulating given quantities of "waiting," or "capital disposal,"[32] or a "subsistence fund," or "true capital," or "carrying powers," are just so many evasions of the real problem of explaining how the existence of a given stock of capital limits the possibility of current investment. Without such an analysis they are just so many empty words, harmful as the basis of that noxious mythology of capital which by creating the fiction of a non-existing entity

---

[32] It is not surprising that Professor G. Cassel, to whom we owe this particular version of the mythology of capital, should now have joined forces with Professor Knight. Cf. his book *On Quantitative Thinking in Economics* (Oxford: Clarendon Press, 1935), p. 20.

leads to statements which refer to nothing in the real world. And the concept of capital conceived as a separate factor of determinate magnitude which is to be treated on the same footing with "land" and "labor" belongs to the same category.[33] It is no better to say, as Professor Knight did at an earlier stage, that "time as such" is a factor of production,[34] since no definite "quantity" of time is given in a way which would enable us to distribute this "fund" of time in alternative ways between the different lines of production so that the total of "time" used will always be the same. But it is certainly much worse to attempt, as Professor Knight does now, to eliminate time entirely from the analysis of the capitalist process of production. This inevitably prevents him from giving any answer to the question how the limitation of capital limits the possible size of the product and why and how capital is maintained, and compels him to treat this as a datum. And, as we shall see in the next section, it also leads him into positive errors about the function of interest.

V. An Erroneous Assertion Following from His Fundamental Position: The Value of Capital Goods When Interest Disappears

How the neglect of the fundamental fact that capital consists of items which need to be reproduced, and that these serve as capital only insofar as and to the extent that their existence is a

---

[33] If, as seems generally to be the case, one can never be certain that one will not be carried away occasionally by the construction of a quantitatively fixed "fund" which undoubtedly attaches to the term capital, it would probably be advisable to follow Professor Schumpeter's suggestion and avoid the use of the term altogether. (Cf. article "Kapital," in *Handwörterbuch der Staatswissenschaften*, 4th ed. (1923), vol. 5, p. 582.)

[34] [4], p. 198: "It has long been my contention that the best form of statement to indicate the essential fact on the technical side is simply to say that time as such is a factor of production—the only really distinct, homogeneous 'factor,' as a matter of fact."

condition for taking advantage of more productive time-consuming methods, led to the most erroneous conclusions is well illustrated by Professor Knight's remarkable assertion that "the rate of interest could be zero only if all products known, empirically or in imagination, into the creation of which capital in any way enters, were free goods."[35] This statement seems to me to be about as plausible as if it were asserted that the price of air could fall to zero only if all commodities in the production of which the presence of air were an indispensable condition were free goods. Clearly, unless one of several factors cooperating in the production of a number of goods can be substituted for the others without limit, the fact that this one factor becomes a free good will never mean that the product itself must become a free good. In the case in question, however, not even the capital *goods* need become free goods in order that the rate of interest may fall to zero. All that is required is that the value of the services which depend on the existence of a certain capital good be no higher than the cost of reproduction of a good that will render the same service or, what amounts to the same thing, than the value in their alternative current uses of the services of the factors of production required for this reproduction. There is no reason why, in order that this may come about, these services should also become free goods.

I do not, of course, contend that a fall of the rate of interest to zero is an event in the least likely to occur at any future time in which we are at all interested. But, like all questions of what is *probable*, this is altogether irrelevant for theoretical analysis. What is of importance are the conditions under which this would be possible. Now if a condition were reached in which no further lengthening of the investment periods of individual resources (either by lengthening the process or by increasing the durability of goods in which they are invested) would lead to a further increase of output, new savings could not help to

---

[35] [2], p. 284.

increase output. In the usual terminology the marginal productivity of capital would have fallen to zero because no more satisfaction would depend on a particular capital good ("stored up labor") than would depend on the quantity of labor and other products which are needed to replace it. So long as any of the factors required for this purpose remain scarce, the capital goods themselves and *a fortiori* the final consumers' goods made with their help will also remain scarce. And there can be no doubt that this point where further accumulation of capital would no longer increase the quantity of output obtainable from the factors used in its production, even if almost infinitely distant, would still be reached long before the point where no satisfaction whatever would be dependent on the existence of these factors.

It is not difficult to see how Professor Knight's habit of thinking not only of capital in the abstract but even of particular capital goods as permanent has led him to his peculiar conclusion. Permanent goods which can be produced—if there is such a thing, namely a good which is expected not only to last forever physically, but also to remain permanently useful stand in this respect in a somewhat exceptional position. The value of such a good expected to render permanently useful services would at a zero rate of interest necessarily be infinite so long as its services have any value at all, and goods of this kind would therefore be produced until the value of the services of one more unit would be zero. And until the services of these goods had become free, there would be a demand for capital for producing more and the rate of interest could not fall to zero. The person making a final investment of this kind, bringing the value of the services down to zero, would of course find that he had made a mistake and lost his investment; and the demand for capital for this purpose would stop when it became known that the investment of one further unit had this effect.

But even if the value of the permanent goods should have to fall to zero in order that the rate of interest may become zero also, this does, as shown above, by no means imply that the value of the nonpermanent goods should also have to fall to zero. On each good may depend no more utility than can be had from the current use of the factors required for its reproduction, but the value of such goods will still be equal to that utility.

In concluding this section it may be pointed out that there is, of course, a very important reason why in a changing world the rate of interest will never fall to zero, a reason which Professor Knight's assumption of the permanence of capital would exclude, namely, that in a world of imperfect foresight capital will never be maintained intact in any sense, and every change will always open possibilities for the profitable investment of new capital.

VI. Problems of Capital and "Perfect Foresight"

There remain a number of points of not inconsiderable importance which, however, if this article is not to grow to disproportionate size, can be touched upon but shortly. Perhaps the most interesting is the suggestion, which occurs here and there in Professor Knight's articles, that all his deductions about the nature of capital are based on the assumption of perfect foresight.[36] If this is to be taken quite seriously it would represent a main addition to the older Clarkian doctrine of the permanence of capital and to some extent also justify it. It would do so, however, at the expense of restricting its validity to a sphere in which problems of capital in the ordinary sense do not occur at all and certainly deprive it of all relevance to the problems of economic dynamics. But since Professor Knight's purpose is, *inter alia*, to

---

[36] Cf. particularly [2], pp. 264 (n. 2), 270, 273, and 277. In his latest articles ([7] and [8]) Professor Knight seems however inclined to concede that the period of production analysis has some limited application to static conditions most rigidly defined, and is inapplicable under dynamic conditions! Are we to understand that Professor Knight now wants to abandon all that part of his earlier criticism which was based on the most extreme static assumptions imaginable, i.e., on the assumption of perfect foresight?

demonstrate that my analysis of certain types of industrial fluctuations is based on a fallacy in the field of the theory of capital it can evidently not be his intention to base all his argument on this assumption. Hence it seems worthwhile to explore shortly the question of what problems of capital still exist under such an assumption.

If we assume that perfect foresight has existed from the beginning of all things, a question of how to use capital as a separate factor of production would not arise at all. All processes of production would have been definitely determined at the beginning and no further question would arise of how to use any of the instruments created in the course of the process which might be used for other purposes than those for which they were originally intended. If indeed there are natural nonpermanent resources in existence at the beginning, a "capital problem" might arise in connection with the original plan.[37] But once this original plan is made and so long as it is adhered to, no problem of maintenance, replacement or redistribution of capital, nor indeed any other economic problem, would occur.

Economic problems of any sort, and in particular the problem of how to use a given stock of capital goods most profitably, arise only when it is a question of adjusting the available means to any new situation. In real life, such unforeseen changes occur, of course, at every moment, and it is in the explanation of the reaction to these changes that the existing "capital" is required as a datum. But the concept of capital as a quantitatively determined

---

[37] It might be mentioned, incidentally, that this would not be a problem of the preservation of natural resources in the usual sense, i.e., of preservation of the particular resource, but only of its replacement by some produced means of production which will render services of equivalent value. This applies equally to the practical problem of the preservation of exhaustible natural resources where it is by no means necessarily most economical to extend their life as far as possible rather than to use their amortization fund for the creation of some new capital goods.

self-perpetuating fund does not help us here in any way. In fact, if the justification of this concept lies in the assumption of perfect foresight it becomes clearly inapplicable, since a "factor" which remains in any sense constant only if complete foresight is assumed cannot possibly represent a "datum" on which new decisions can be based. As has been shown, it would be erroneous to assume that this given "factor" is given as a definite quantity of value, or as any other determinate quantity which can be measured in terms of some common unit. But while the only exact way of stating the supply condition of this factor would be a complete enumeration and description of the individual items, it would be hasty to conclude that they have no common quality at all which entitles us to class them into one group. This common quality of being able to substitute to some extent one item for another is the possibility of providing a temporary income while we wait for the services of other factors invested for longer periods. But, as we have seen, no single item represents a definite quantity of income. How much income it will yield and when it will yield it depends on the use made of all other goods. In consequence, the relevant datum which corresponds to what is commonly called the supply of capital and which determines for what period current factors will be expediently invested is nothing but the alternatively available income streams which the existing capital goods can produce under the new conditions.

It would be difficult to believe that Professor Knight should for a moment have really thought that the concept of capital as a self-maintaining fund of determinate magnitude has any application outside a fictitious stationary state if he had not himself—at least at an earlier date—clearly recognized that the problems of capital fall largely outside the framework of static analysis.[38] In

---

[38] [4], p. 206: "The one important difference between price analysis in the case of interest and that of ordinary prices arises from the fact that saving and investment is a cumulative process. It is a phase of economic growth, outside the framework of the conventional 'static' system, unfortunately so called."

view of these utterances it would seem unlikely that he should now take pains to develop a concept which is valid only on the most rigidly "static" assumptions. The emphasis which he now places on the complete mobility of capital certainly conveys the impression that he wants to apply his concept to dynamic phenomena. It is at least difficult to see what other purpose this emphasis can serve, because certainly nobody has ever doubted that where all the future is correctly foreseen and always has been so no problem of mobility of capital will arise. And although he qualified his statements about the mobility of capital by the assumption of complete foresight,[39] this does not prevent him from disparaging the value of any reasoning based on the limitations of the mobility of capital under dynamic conditions. This attitude is not very far from the assertions sometimes found in the literature that apart from "frictions," invested capital ought to be regarded as completely mobile between different uses (presumably without any loss in value), and that "any theory that is based on partial immobility of invested capital is essentially a frictional one."[40] This clearly assumes the existence of a separate substance of capital apart from its manifestation in concrete capital goods, a "fund" of a mystical quantity which cannot be described or defined but which, if Professor Knight has it his way, is to have a central position in our analytical apparatus. It has the somewhat questionable advantage that there is no way of deciding whether any statement about this quantity is true or false.

---

[39] [2], p. 270.

[40] H. Neisser, "Monetary Expansion and the Structure of Production," *Social Research* 1, no. 4 (November 1934).

Investment That Raises the Demand for Capital

Investment That Raises the Demand for Capital

The purpose of this article is to state a proposition which underlies the modern "monetary overinvestment theories" of the trade cycle in a form in which, as far as I know, it has never before been expressed but which seems to make this particular proposition so obvious as to put its logical correctness beyond dispute. This, of course, does not necessarily mean that the theories which rely largely on this proposition provide an adequate account of all or any trade cycles. But it should do something to show the inadequacies of those current theories which completely disregard the effect in question. It should, moreover, clear up some of the confusion and misunderstandings which have made it so difficult to come to an agreement on the purely analytical points involved.

It will surprise nobody to find the source of this confusion in the ambiguity of the term "capital." In static analysis, the term capital refers equally to the aggregate value of all capital goods and to their "quantity," measured in terms of cost (or in some other way). But this is of little significance because in equilibrium these two magnitudes must necessarily coincide. In the

---

This article first appeared in *The Review of Economic Statistics* 19, no. 4 (November 1937): 174–77.

analysis of dynamic phenomena, however, this ambiguity becomes exceedingly dangerous. In particular, the static proposition that an increase in the quantity of capital will bring about a fall in its marginal productivity (which for the purposes of this article I shall call the rate of interest), when taken over into economic dynamics and applied to the quantity of capital goods, may become quite definitely erroneous.

The Relative Significance of the Amount of Investment and of the Form That It Takes

The assumption that an increase in the quantity of capital goods will necessarily decrease the return to be expected on further investment is generally treated as obvious. It is, therefore, desirable to state the actual relations between the two magnitudes in a form which may, perhaps, sound somewhat paradoxical. The main thesis of this article will be that the effect which the current production of capital goods will have on the future demand for investable funds will depend not so much on the quantity of capital goods produced, as on the kind of capital goods which are produced or on the particular forms which current investment takes, and that an increase in the current output of capital goods will frequently have the effect not of lowering but of raising the future demand for investable funds, and thereby the rate of interest.

Each separate step of the argument which leads to this conclusion is a familiar and obvious proposition. The first main point is that most investment is undertaken in the expectation that further investment, for which the equipment that formed the object of the first investment will be needed, will take place at a later date. This may be expressed by saying that current investment will be guided by the expectation that investment will continue at a certain rate for some time to come, or that the rate of interest will stay at a certain figure. The success of current investment will depend upon this expectation being fulfilled. Most individual acts of investment must be regarded, therefore, as mere links in a chain which has to be completed if its parts are to serve the function for which they were intended, even though the chain consists of separate and successive acts of different entrepreneurs. The manufacturer of any kind of machines who increases his plant can do so only in the expectation that the users of these machines will at some later time be willing to install additional machines, and that these machines may be wanted only if somebody else will later be willing to invest in their products, etc., etc.

The first investment of such a chain, therefore, will be undertaken only if it is expected that in each link of this chain, a certain rate of interest can be earned. But this does not mean that, once this investment has been made, the process of further investments will not be continued if conditions change in an unfavorable direction—if, for example, the rate of interest at which money can be borrowed rises. If the investments already made are irrevocably committed to the particular purpose, this provides a margin within which the total profits to be expected on the whole chain of successive investments may fall without affecting the profitability of the further investments still needed to complete the process. For if the fixed capital already created is specific to the particular purpose, it will, of course, be used even if the return covers little more than the cost of using it (but not interest and amortization); and since the owners of this fixed capital will find it in their interest to use it so long as they get only a little more than mere operating cost, nearly the whole amount which it was originally expected would be earned as interest and amortization becomes available, as it were, as a premium on investment in the later stages of the process. The amount by which entrepreneurs in these later stages need to pay less for the products of the earlier stages, because the equipment there is already in existence, thus becomes available for expenditure on the completion of the process. And the greater the amount of investment which has already been made compared with that which is still required to utilize the equipment already in existence, the greater will be the rate of interest which can advantageously be borne in raising capital for these investments completing the chain.

"Completing Investments" and the Rate of Interest

Obviously then, the demand for capital at any particular moment depends not so much on the productivity that the existing structure of real capital would have if completed—the long-term schedule of the productivity of investment—as on the proportion between that part of it which has already been completed and that part which has yet to be added to complete it. Only for a very small fraction of the total investments—the marginal investments which represent the beginning of new chains of investment—will the demand for funds promptly react to a change in the rate at which capital can be borrowed. For the rest, the demand for capital will be highly inelastic with respect to changes in the rate of interest.

The consequences of this can readily be shown by a schematic example. Assume that past investments have been guided by the expectation that a rate of interest of 4 percent would continue to rule for some time, but that in order to complete the investments which have been undertaken in this expectation a greater supply of loanable funds would be required than is actually forthcoming. Assume further that, if investments in the recent past had been guided by the expectation of a 5 percent rate of interest, the amount of further loans required to continue these investment processes would just exhaust the current supply. This does not mean that once investments have been undertaken in the expectation of a rate of 4 percent, a rise of the interest rate to 5 percent—that is, to the figure which, if correctly foreseen, would have represented an equilibrium rate—will now be sufficient to reduce demand for loans to the level of the supply. If a considerable part of the equipment to be used has already been produced, many investments, which it would never have been profitable to start if a rate of interest of 5 percent had been foreseen, will be well worthwhile continuing, even at a rate much higher than 5 percent. The loss will fall entirely on those entrepreneurs who in the past, in the expectation of the lower rate of interest, have already erected a new plant, etc. But the concessions in price, below their actual cost of production, which they will be compelled to make, will enable the other entrepreneurs, whom they supply with equipment, to go on with the installation of new machinery, which would not have been possible if developments had been foreseen correctly from the outset. The construction of a large hydroelectric plant that would have been profitable if the rate of interest had remained at 4 percent will prove unprofitable if the rate of interest rises. But, once it has been constructed and charges for electric power adjusted to get maximum profit over current expenditure, it will give rise to a further demand for capital for the installation of electric motors, etc., which will not be sensibly reduced even by a rate of interest much higher than 5 percent.

How far the rate of interest will have to rise to bring the demand for loans down to the available supplies will depend, as we have seen, on the proportion between that part of the complete investment processes which had been carried out before the unexpected rise in the rate of interest occurred, and that part of this total expenditure which has yet to be incurred. If, in a particular instance, interest at 4 percent on the capital already invested and amortization of that capital would have represented 30 percent of the expected price of the final commodity in the production of which it was to be used, then interest charges involved in utilizing the existing plant and its products would have to rise so as to absorb the whole of this 30 percent of the final price, before the demand for capital for this purpose would be effectively curtailed. If, of the remaining 70 percent of the expected total cost of the final product, 15 percent was allowed for further interest at 4 percent, interest rates would have to rise to approximately 12 percent before the profitability of the investments completing the process already begun would be reduced to zero.

Against this whole argumentation it might be objected that it completely ignores the effect of the rise in interest rates on current replacement of the capital in the "earlier stages" which has partly or entirely lost its value. It is certainly true that these items of equipment will not be replaced. But the implication that this will in any way relieve the demand for funds for investment is certainly erroneous. Insofar as those items in the normal course of affairs would already need replacement, these replacements would have been financed out of amortization currently earned. They would not have constituted a demand on the funds available for investments. But if—and this is more likely—they had not yet become ripe for replacement, the amortization earned would temporarily be available for investment elsewhere. The fact that no amortization or only a reduced quota will be earned will then mean a reduction of the supply of investable funds, that is, it will represent a factor which tends to raise rather than lower the rate of interest.

Causes of an Urgent Demand for Funds for Completing Investments

The causes which are likely to bring about such a situation remain to be considered. Under what conditions will the demand for the additional capital required to complete a given capital structure drive up the rate of interest to a figure very much higher than the rate which is compatible with the permanent maintenance of that structure?

In principle the answer is surely clear. Anything which will lead people to expect a lower rate of interest, or a larger supply of investable funds, than will actually exist when the time comes for their utilization, will in the way we have suggested force interest rates to rise much higher than would have been the case if people had not expected such a low rate. But, while it is true that an unexpected decrease in the rate of saving, or an unforeseen appearance of a new demand for capital—a new invention, for instance—may bring about such a situation, the most important cause practically of such false expectations probably is a temporary increase in the supply of such funds through credit expansion at a rate which cannot be maintained. In this case, the increased quantity of current investment will induce people to expect investment to continue at a similar rate for some time, and in consequence to invest now in a form which requires for its successful completion further investment at a similar rate.[1] It is not so much the quantity of current investment but the direction it takes—the type of capital goods being produced—which determines the amount of future investment required if the current investments are to be successfully incorporated in the structure of production. But it is the amount of investment made possible by the current supply of funds which determines expectations about the future rate of investment and thereby the form that the current investment will be given. We can now see the justification for the somewhat paradoxical form in which the main thesis of this article was originally stated. An increase in the rate of investment, or the quantity of capital goods, may have the effect of raising rather than lowering the rate of interest, if this increase has given rise to the expectation of a greater future supply of investable funds than is actually forthcoming.

If this proposition is correct, and if its assumptions are empirically justified, this means that much of the purely monetary analysis of the trade cycle now current is built on very insufficient foundations. If it is correct, the common assumption that the expected return on investment, or the "marginal efficiency of capital," can be treated as a simple decreasing function of the quantity of capital goods in existence, or of the current rate of investment, will have to be abandoned, and with it much of the

---

[1] For a somewhat fuller statement of these connections see my articles "Preiserwartungen, monetäre Störungen und Fehlinvestitionen," *NationalØkonomisk Tidsskrift* 73, no. 3 (1935) (also a French version in the *Revue des Sciences Economiques* [October 1935]), and "The Maintenance of Capital," *Economica* n.s. 2 (August 1935), particularly pp. 268 *et seq.*

argument based on the supposed tendency of the "marginal efficiency of capital" to fall more rapidly than the money rate of interest. If past investment is often found to make further investment more rather than less profitable, this would also mean that the rise of the rate of interest toward the end of a boom—which so many authors believe can be explained only by monetary factors affecting the supply of loanable funds—can be adequately explained by real factors affecting the demand. It shows, moreover, that a purely monetary analysis, which runs in terms of mere rates of investment without analyzing the concrete structure of these investments and the influence which monetary factors can have on this real structure of production, is bound to neglect some of the most significant elements in the picture. And, perhaps, it also explains why a careful analysis of the time structure of production (not in terms of an "average" period of production) is a necessary basis for a satisfactory analysis of the trade cycle.

Bibliography

Adams, A.B. *Profits, Progress and Prosperity.* New York: McGraw-Hill, 1927.

Aftalion, A. *Journal d'Economie Politique.* 1909.

——. *Les crises périodiques de surproduction.* Paris: Marcel Rivière, 1913.

Akerman, G. *Realkapital und Kapitalzins.* Part 1. Stockholm, 1923.

Altschul, E. "Konjunkturtheorie und Konjunkturstatistik." *Archiv für Sozialwissenschaft und Sozialpolitik* 55 (1926).

Amonn, A. "Cassel's System der Theoretischen Nationalökonomie." *Archiv für Sozialwissenschaften und Sozialpolitik* 51 (1924).

Anderson, B.M. *Value of Money.* New York: Macmillan, 1917.

Angell, J.W. *The Theory of International Prices: History, Criticism and Restatement.* Cambridge, Mass.: Harvard University Press, 1926.

Ashton, T.S. "Economic and Social Investigations in Manchester, 1833–1933." *A Centenary History of the Manchester Statistical Society.* London: P.S. King & Son, 1934.

Beckerath, H. v. *Kapital und Geldmarkt.* Jena: Gustav Fischer, 1916.

Behrens. W.G. *Das Geldschöpfungsproblem.* Jena: Gustav Fischer, 1928.

Bergmann, E. v. *Geschichte der nationalökonomischen Krisentheorien.* Stuttgart: Kohlhammer, 1895. Reprinted "Geschichte der Nationalökonomischen Krisentheorien." *Zeitschrift für Volkswirtschaft, Sozialpolitik und Verwaltung* 7 (1898).

Böhm-Bawerk, E. v. *Positive Theorie des Kapitalzinses.* 3rd ed. Jena: Gustav Fischer, 1921.

———. *Positive Theory of Captial.* New York: Macmillan, 1923.

Bortkiewicz, L. v. *Die Frage der Reform unserer Währung* 6 (1919).

Bouniatian, M. "Industrielle Schwankungen, Bankkredit und Warenpreise." *Archiv für Sozialwissenschaften und Sozialpolitik* 58 (1927).

———. *Studien zur Theorie und Geschichte der Wirtschaftskrisen.* Munich, 1908.

Bresciani-Turroni, C. *Le Vicende del Marco Tedesco.* Milano: Università Bocconi, 1931.

Budge, S. *Grundzüge der theoretischen Nationalökonomi.* Jena: Gustav Fischer, 1925.

Bullion Report. Octavo edition. London, 1810.

Bullion Report. Ed. Carman. 1894.

Cairnes, J.E. "Essays Towards a Solution of the Gold Question." *Essays in Political Economy, Theoretical and Applied.* London: Macmillan, 1873.

Cantillon, R. *Essai sur la nature du commerce en général.* Ed. Henry Higgs. London: Frank Cass, 1931.

Carell, E. *Sozialökonomische Theorie und Konjunkturproblem.* Munich and Leipzig: Duncker & Humblot, 1929.

Carison, S. "On the Notion of Equilibrium in Interest Theory." *Economic Studies* 1 (1935).

Carver, T.N. *Quarterly Journal of Economics* (1903–04).

Cassel, G. *Economic Journal* 38 (December 1929).

———. *Money and Foreign Exchange After 1914.* London: Constable, 1922.

———. *Theory of Social Economy.* New York: Harcourt, Brace, 1932.

Crick, W.F. "The Genesis of Bank Deposits." *Economica* 7, no. 20 (June 1927).

Currie, L. *The Supply and Control of Money in the United States.* Cambridge, Mass.: Harvard University Press, 1934.

Davenport, H.J. *The Economics of Enterprise.* New York: Macmillan, 1915.

Dernburg, B. *Schriften des Vereines für Sozialpolitik* 175.

Donner, O., and A. Hanau. "Untersuchung zur Frage der Marktzusammenhänge." *Vierteljahrshefte zur Konjunkturforschung.* 3rd year, no. 3 A. Institut für Konjunkturforschung, Berlin, 1928.

Ebenstein, A. *Friedrich Hayek: A Biography.* New York: Palgrave, 2001.

Edgeworth, F.Y. "Thoughts on Monetary Reform." *Economic Journal* (1895). Reprinted in "Questions Connected with Bimetallism." *Papers Relating to Political Economy.* London: Macmillan, 1925. Vol. 1.

Egner, E. *Zur Lehre vom Zwangsparen* (1928).

Ellis, H.S. "Die Bedeutung der Productionsperiode für die Krisentheorie." *Zeitschrift für Nationalökonomie* 4 (1935).

Eucken, W. *Schriften des Vereins für Sozialpolitik* 175 (1929).

Fanno, M. *Beiträge zur Geldtheorie.* Vienna: Springer, 1933.

———. *Le Banche e il Mercato Monetario.* Rome: Athenaeum, 1913.

Fetter, F. "Interest Theories and Price Movements." *American Economic Review* 17 (March 1927).

Fisher, I. *Appreciation and Interest.* Publications of the American Economic Association, 3rd series, 11, no. 4 (1896).

———. "The Business Cycle Largely a 'Dance of the Dollar'." *Journal of the American Statistical Association* (December 1923).

———. *Making of Index Numbers.* New York: Houghton Mifflin, 1922.

———. *Theory of Interest.* New York: Macmillan, 1930.

Foster, J.L. *An Essay on the Principles of Commercial Exchanges.* 1804.

Foster, W.T., and W. Catchings. "Better Jobs and More of Them: The Government's Part in Preventing Unemployment." Reprinted from the *Century Magazine* (July 1929).

———. *Business without a Buyer.* Publications of the Pollak Foundation for Economic Research, No. 10. Boston and New York, Houghton Mifflin, 1927; 2nd rev. ed. 1928.

———. *The Dilemma of Thrift.* Newton, Mass.: Pollak Foundation, 1926.

———. *Money*. Publications of the Pollak Foundation for Economic Research, No. 2. Boston and New York: Houghton Mifflin, 1923; 3rd ed. 1928.

———. *Pollak Prize Essays: Criticisms of "Profits."* Newton, Mass.: Pollak Foundation, 1927.

———. *Profits*. Publications of the Pollak Foundation for Economic Research, No. 8. Boston and New York: Houghton Mifflin, 1925.

———. *The Road to Plenty*. Publications of Pollak Foundation for Economic Research, No. 11. New York: Houghton Mifflin, 1928.

Friday, D. *Profit, Wages and Prices.* New York: Harcourt, Brace, 1921.

Fullarton, John. *On the Regulation of Currencies.* 2nd ed. London: John Murray, 1845.

Garrison, R.W. *Time and Money: The Macroeconomics of Capital Structure.* New York: Routledge, 2001.

Gilbert, J.C. "The Present Position of the Theory of International Trade." *The Review of Economic Studies* 3, no. 1 (October 1935).

Gregory, T.E. *The Gold Standard and Its Future.* 3rd ed. New York: E.P. Dutton, 1932.

———. "Introduction." Tooke and Newmarch, *History of Prices and of the State of the Circulation.* 4 vols. London: P.S. King, 1929.

Guyot, Yves. *La Science Économique.* English translation, *Principles of Social Economy.* London: Sonnenschein, 1884.

Haberler, G. *Der Sinn der Indexzahlen.* Tübingen: Mohr, 1927.

———. "Hahns Volkswirtschaftliche Theorie des Bankkredits." *Archiv für Sozialwissenschaften* 57 (1927).

Hahn, A. *Volkswirtschaftlichen Theorie des Bankkredits.* Tübingen: Mohr, 1920.

———. "Zur Frage des volkswirtschaftlichen Erkenntnisinhaltes der Bankbilanzziffern." *Vierteljahrshefte zur Konjunkturforschung* 1, no. 4 (1927).

———. "Zur Theorie des Geldmarktes." *Archiv für Sozialwissenschaften und Sozialpolitik* 51 (1924).

Halm, G. "Das Zinsproblem am Geld- und Kapitalmarkt." *Jahrbücher far Nationalökonomie und Statistik,* 3rd series 70, no. 125 (1926).

Hansen, A.H. *Business Cycle Theory: Its Development and Present Status.* Boston: Ginn, 1927.

———. *Cycles of Prosperity and Depression.* Madison: University of Wisconsin Press, 1921.

Hansen, A., and H. Tout. "Annual Survey of Business Cycle Theory: Investment and Saving in Business Cycle Theory." *Econometrica* 1, no. 2 (April 1933).

Hardy, C.O. *Risk and Risk Bearing.* Chicago: University of Chicago Press, 1923.

Harrod, R.F., ed. *International Economics.* Cambridge Economic Handbooks No. 8. London: Nisbet, 1933.

———. *The International Gold Problem.* Royal Institute of International Affairs. London: Oxford University Press, 1931.

Harvey, Sir Ernest. *Minutes of Evidence taken before the Committee on Finance and Industry.* London, 1931. Vol. 1.

Hasting, A.B. *Costs and Profits.* New York: Houghton, Mifflin, 1923.

Hawtrey, R.G. *Currency and Credit.* 3rd ed. New York: Longmans, Green, 1928.

———. "Money and Index Numbers." *Journal of the Royal Statistical Society* 93 (1930). Part 1.

———. *Monetary Reconstruction.* London: Longmans, Green, 1923; 2nd ed. London: Longmans, Green, 1926.

———. "The Monetary Theory of the Trade Cycle and its Statistical Test." *Quarterly Journal of Economics* 41, no. 3 (May 1927).

———. *Trade and Credit.* London: Longmans, 1928.

Hayek, F.A. "A Note on the Development of the Doctrine of 'Forced Saving'." *Quarterly Journal of Economics* (November 1932).

———, ed. *Beiträge zur Geldtheorie.* Vienna: Springer, 1933.

———. "Capital and Industrial Fluctuations." *Econometrica* 2 (April 1934).

———. *Choice in Currency: A Discussion with Friedrich von Hayek.* Washington, D.C.: American Enterprise Institute for Public Policy Research, 1975.

———. "Credit and the Trade Cycle." *Schriften des Vereins für Sozialpolitik* 175 (1929).

———. "Das intertemporale Gleichgewichtssystem der Preise und die Bewegungen des 'Geldwertes'." *Weltwirtschaftliches Archiv* 28 (1928).

———. "Das Schicksal der Goldwährung." *Der Deutsche Volkswirt* (1932).

———. *Denationalisation of Money—The Argument Refined: An Analysis of the Theory and Practice of Concurrent Currencies*, 2nd ed. London: Institute of Economic Affairs, 1978.

———. "Der Stand und die nächste Zukunft der Konjunkturforschung." *Festschrift für Arthur Spiethoff.* Munich: Duncker & Humblot, 1933.

———. "The Development of the Doctrine of Forced Saving." *Quarterly Journal of Economics* (November 1932).

———. "Die Währungspolitik der Vereinigten Staaten seit der Überwindung der Krise von 1920." *Zeitschrift für Volkswirtschaft und Sozialpolitik,* N.F. 5 (1925).

———. *Economica* 33 (August, 1931). Part 1.

———. *Economica* 35 (February, 1932). Part 2.

———. "Einige Bemerkungen über das Verhältnis der Geldtheorie zur Konjunkturtheorie." *Schriften des Vereins für Sozialpolitik* 173 (1928).

———. *Full Employment at Any Price.* London: Institute of Economic Affairs, 1975.

———. *Geldtheorie und Konjuncturtheorie.* Vienna: Holder-Pichler-Tempsky, 1929.

———, ed. *Gesammelte Abhandlungen.* Tübingen: Mohr, 1929.

———. *Hayek on Hayek: An Autobiographical Dialogue.* Ed. Stephen Kresge and Leif Wenar. Chicago: University of Chicago Press.

———. "Introduction" to Vol. 1 of the *Collected Works of Carl Menger.* Series of Reprints of Scarce Tracts in Economics. London: London School of Economics, 1934.

———, ed. "Introduction." Henry Thornton, *Paper Credit of Great Britain.* London: Allen & Unwin, 1939.

———. Investment that Raises the Demand for Capital. *The Review of Economic Statistics* 19, no. 4 (November 1937).

———. "Kapitalaufzehrung." *Weltwirtschaftliches Archiv* 36 (July 1932).

———. "The Maintenance of Capital." *Economica* n.s. 2 (August 1935).

———. *Monetary Nationalism and International Stability*. London: Longmans Green, 1937.

———. *Monetary Theory and the Trade Cycle*. London: Routledge, 1933; Jonathan Cape, 1933.

———. "Money and Capital: A Reply to Mr. Sraffa." *Economic Journal* (June 1932).

———. "The Mythology of Capital." *Quarterly Journal of Economics* 50 (February 1936).

———. "On the Relationship between Investment and Output." *Economic Journal* (June 1934).

———. "The 'Paradox' of Saving." Originally "Gibt es einen Widersinn des Sparens?" *Zeitschrift für Nationalökonomie* 1, no. 3 (1929). English translation by Nicholas Kaldor and Georg Tugendhat and published in *Economica* 32 (May 1931).

———. "Preiserwartungen, monetäre Störungen und Fehlinvestitionen." *NationalØkonomisk Tidsskrift* 73, no. 3 (1935). French version in *Revue des Sciences Economiques* (October 1935).

———. *Prices and Production*. London: Routledge and Sons, 1931; 2nd ed. London: Routledge and Kegan Paul, 1935.

———. "The Pure Theory of Money: A Rejoinder to Mr. Keynes." *Economica* (November 1931).

———. "Reflections on the Pure Theory of Money of Mr. J.M. Keynes." *Economica*, nos. 33–35 (1931–32).

———. "Rejoinder." *Economica* 34 (1931).

———. *The Road to Serfdom*. Chicago: University of Chicago Press, 1976.

———. *Studies in Philosophy, Politics and Economics*. New York: Simon and Schuster, 1969.

———. "Über den Einfluss monetärer Faktoren auf den Konjunkturzyklus." *Schriften des Vereins für Sozialpolitik* 173, no. 2 (1928).

———. "Über neutrales Geld." *Zeitschrift für Nationalökonomie* 4 (October 1933).

Heinze, G. *Static or Dynamic Interest Theory*. Leipzig: H. Beyer, 1928.

Hicks, J.R. "A Suggestion for the Simplification of the Theory of Money." *Economica* n.s. 2, no. 6 (February 1936).

Holtrop, M.W. *De Omloopssnelheid van het Geld.* Amsterdam: H.J. Paris, 1928.

Huerta de Soto, J. *Money, Bank Credit, and Economic Cycles.* Trans. Melinda A. Stroup. Auburn, Ala.: Ludwig von Mises Institute, 2006.

Hume, D. "Of Money." *Essays Moral, Political and Literary* (1742). Part 2.

Jevons, W.S. *A Serious Fall in the Value of Gold Ascertained and Its Social Effects Set Forth.* London: Edward Stanford, 1863.

———. *Investigations in Currency and Finance.* London: Macmillan, 1884.

———. *Theory of Political Economy.* 4th ed. London: Macmillan, 1911.

Joplin, T. *An Analysis and History of the Currency Question.* London: J. Ridgway, 1832.

———. *Outlines of a System of Political Economy.* London: Ridgway and Baldwin, 1823.

Joseph, P., and K. Bode. "Bemerkungen zur Kapitalund Zinstheorie." *Zeitschrift für Nationalökonomie* 4 (1935).

Jöhr, A. *Schriften des Vereins für Sozialpolitik* 175 (1929).

Juglar, C. *Des crises commerciales et leur retour périodique,* 2nd ed. Paris: Guillaumin, 1889.

———. *Du change et de la liberté d'émission.* Paris: Guillaumin, 1868.

Keynes, J.M. *A Treatise on Money.* 2 vols. London: Macmillan, 1930.

———. *Economica* (November 1931).

———. *Economic Journal* 41 (1931).

———. *Essays in Persuasion.* London: Macmillan, 1931.

———. "Rejoinder to Mr. D.H. Robertson." *Economic Journal* (December 1931).

King, Lord. *Thoughts on the Effects of the Bank Restriction.* London, 1803.

King, W.J. *Journal of the American Statistical Association* (March 1928). Supplement.

Knight, F. "Capitalist Production, Time and the Rate of Return." *Economic Essays in Honour of Gustav Cassel.* London: George Allen and Unwin, 1933.

———. "Capital Time, and the Interest Rate." *Economica* n.s. 1, no. 3 (August 1934).

———. "Comment." *Journal of Political Economy* (October 1935).

———. "Interest." *Encyclopaedia of Social Sciences* 8 (1932).

———. *On Quantitative Thinking in Economics.* Oxford: Clarendon Press, 1935.

———. "Professor Fisher's Interest Theory: A Case in Point." *Journal of Political Economy* 39, no. 2 (April 1931).

———. "Professor Hayek and the Theory of Investment." *Economic Journal* 45, no. 177 (March 1935).

———. "The Ricardian Theory of Production and Distribution." *The Canadian Journal of Economics and Political Science* 1, no. 1 (February 1935).

———. *Risk, Uncertainty and Profit.* New York: Houghton Mifflin, 1921.

———. "The Theory of Investment Once More: Mr. Boulding and the Austrians." *Quarterly Journal of Economics* 50 (1936).

Kock, K. "A Study of Interest Rates." *Stockholm Economic Studies* no. 1 (London: P.S. King, 1929).

Koopmans, J.G. "Zum Problem des 'Neutralen' Geldes." *Beiträge zur Geldtheorie.* Ed. F.A. Hayek. Vienna: Springer, 1933.

The Improvement of Commercial Relations between Nations: The Problem of Monetary Stabilization. Separate Memoranda from the Economists consulted by the Joint Committee of the Carnegie Endowment and the International Chamber of Commerce and Practical Conclusions of the Expert Committee appointed by the Joint Committee. Paris, 1936.

Lampe, A. *Zur Theorie des Sparprozesses und der Kreditschöpfung.* Jena: Gustav Fischer, 1926.

Landauer, C. *Planwirtschaft und Verkehrswirtschaft.* Leipzig: Duncker & Humblot, 1931.

Lawrence, J.S. "Borrowed Reserves and Bank Expansion." *Quarterly Journal of Economics* 42 (1928).

Lavington, F. *The English Capital Market.* London: Methuen, 1921.

Leaf, W. *Banking.* London: Williams & Norgate, 1926.

Lexis, W. *Verhandlungen der deutschen Silberkomission.* Berlin, 1894.

Lederer, E. "Konjunktur und Krisen." *Grundriss der Sozialökonomik* 4, no. 1 (1926).

———. "Zur Morphologie der Krisen." *Die Wirtschaftstheorie der Gegenwart.* Ed. H. Mayer. Vienna: Springer, 1928. Vol. 4.

Lowe, A. "Wie ist Konjunkturtheorie überhaupt möglich?" *Weltwirtschaftliches Archiv* 24 (1926).

Löwe, A. "Der gegenwärtige Stand der Konjunkturtheorie in Deutschland." *Die Wirtschaftswissenschaft nach dem Kriege, Festgabe für Lujo Brentano zum 80. Geburtstag.* Ed. M. Bonn and M. Palyi. Munich: Duncker & Humblot, 1925.

———. "Über den Einfluss monetärer Faktoren auf den Konjunkturzyklus." *Schriften des Vereins für Sozialpolitik* 173 (1928).

Lutz, F. *Das Grundproblem der Geldverfassung.* Stuttgart: Kohlhammer, 1936.

Machlup, F. *Börsenkredit, Industriekredit und Kapitalbildung.* Vienna: Springer, 1931.

———. "Professor Knight and the 'Period of Production'." *Journal of Political Economy* (October 1935).

Macleod, H.D. *Dictionary of Political Economy.* London: Octavo edition, 1863.

———. *Theory and Practice of Banking.* London: Longmans, Green, Reader and Dyer, 1855.

Maier, K.F. *Goldwanderungen.* Jena: Gustav Fischer, 1936.

Malthus, T.R. Unsigned review. *Edinburgh Review* 17, no. 34 (February 1811).

Marshall, A. *Industry and Trade.* London: Macmillan, 1919.

———. *Money, Credit, and Commerce.* London: Macmillan, 1926.

———. *Official Papers by Alfred Marshall.* London: Macmillan, 1926.

———. *Principles of Economics.* 1st ed. London: Macmillan, 1891.

Martin, P.W. *The Flaw in the Price System.* London: P.S. King, 1924.

———. *The Limited Market.* London: P.S. King, 1926.

———. *Unemployment and Purchasing Power.* London: P.S. King, 1929.

Mayer, H. "Produktion." *Handwörterbuch der Staatswissenschaften.* 4th ed. Jena: Gustav Fischer, 1925. Vol. 6.

———, ed. *Wirtschaftstheorie der Gegenwart.* Vienna: Springer, 1931. Vol. 2.

Miksch, L. *Gibt es eine allgemeine Uberproduktion?* Jena: Gustav Fischer, 1929.

Mill, J.S. *Essays on Some Unsettled Questions of Political Economy.* London: Parker, 1844.

———. *Principles of Political Economy.* Ed. William James Ashley. London: Longmans Green, 1848.

Mises, L. v. *Geldwertstabilisierung und Konjunkturpolitik.* Jena: Gustav Fischer, 1928.

———. *Theorie des Geldes und der Umlaufsmittel.* Munich: Duncker & Humblot, 1912; 2nd ed. Munich: Duncker & Humblot, 1924.

———. *The Theory of Money.* London: Jonathan Cape, 1934.

Mitchell, W.C. *Business Cycles: The Problem and Its Setting.* New York: National Bureau of Economic Research, 1927.

Mitchell, W.C., and J. Lescure. *Des Crises générales et périodiques de surproduction.* Paris: Domat, 1913.

———. "Krisenlehre." *Die Wirtschaftstheorie der Gegenwart.* Ed. H. Mayer. Vienna: Springer, 1931. Vol. 4.

Morgenstern, O. "Qualitative und Quantitative Konjunkturforschung." *Zeitschrift für die gesamte Staatswissenschaft* 84 (1928).

———. *Wirtschaftsprognose: Eine Untersuchung ikrer Voraussetzungen und Möglichkeiten.* Vienna: Springer, 1928.

Neisser, H. *Der Tauschwert des Geldes.* Jena: Gustav Fischer, 1928.

———. "Monetary Expansion and the Structure of Production." *Social Research* 1, no. 4 (November 1934).

———. "Theorie des wirtschaftlichen Gleichgewichtes." *Kölner sozialpolitische Vierteljahrschrift* 6 (1927).

Nurkse, R. "The Schematic Representation of the Structure of Production." *Review of Economic Studies* 2 (1935).

Paish, F.W. "Banking Policy and the Balance of International Payments." *Economica* n.s. 3, no. 2 (November 1936).

Palmer, J. Horsley. *Report on the Committee of Secrecy on the Bank of England Charter.* London, 1833.

Persons, W.M. "A Non-technical Explanation of the Index of General Business Conditions." *The Review of Economic Statistics* 2 (1920).

———. "Cyclical Fluctuations of the Ratio of Bank Loans to Deposits." *Review of Economic Statistics* (1924).

———. "Theories of Business Fluctuations." *Quarterly Journal of Economics* 41 (1926).

Phillips, C.A. *Bank Credit.* New York: Macmillan, 1920.

Pierson, N.G. *Gold Scarcity.* Trans. R. Reisch. *Zeitschrift für Volkswirtschaft, Sozialpolitik und Verwaltung* 4, no. 1 (Vienna, 1895).

———. "The Problem of Value in a Socialist Community." *Collectivist Economic Planning.* London: Routledge and Kegan Paul, 1935.

Pigou, A.C. *Industrial Fluctuations,* 2nd ed. London: Macmillan, 1929.

———. *Is Unemployment Inevitable?* London: Macmillan, 1925.

Polak, N.J. *Grundzüge der Finanzierung.* Berlin, 1926.

Price, B. *Chapters on Practical Political Economy.* London: Kegan Paul, 1878.

Raguet, C. *A Treatise on Currency and Banking.* London: Grigg & Elliot, 1839.

Reed, H.L. *Federal Reserve Policy 1921–1930.* New York: McGraw-Hill, 1930.

Riefler, W.W. *Money Rates and Markets in the United States.* New York and London: Harper and Brothers, 1930.

Reisch, R. "Die 'Deposit'-Legende in der Banktheorie." *Zeitschrift für Nationalökonomie* 1 (1930).

---. "Die Wirtschaftliche Bedeutung des Kredites im Lichte von Theorie und Praxis." *Mitteilungen des Verbandes Österreichischen Banken und Bankiers,* nos. 2–3 (1928).

Report of the Proceedings of the Meeting of Economists held at the Antwerp Chamber of Commerce on July the 11th, 12th, and 13th, 1935. Published by the Antwerp Chamber of Commerce.

Report of the Federal Reserve Board for 1923. Washington, D.C.: Government Printing Office, 1924.

Ricardo, D. *Economic Essays.* Ed. E.K.C. Gonner. London: G. Bell and Sons, 1923.

---. *The High Price of Bullion, a Proof of the Depreciation of Bank Notes.* 3rd ed. 1810; 4th ed. 1811.

---. *Letters of David Ricardo to Hutches Trower and Others.* Ed. J. Bonar and J. Hollander. Oxford: Clarendon Press, 1899.

---. *The Works of David Ricardo.* Ed. J.R. McCulloch. London: John Murray, 1846.

Robbins, L. *Economic Planning and International Order.* London: Macmillan, 1937.

---. *The Great Depression.* London: Macmillan, 1934.

Robertson, D.H. *Banking Policy and the Price Level.* London: P.S. King, 1926.

---. *Economica* 23 (June 1928).

---. *Industrial Fluctuations.* London: P.S. King, 1915.

---. *Money,* new revised edition. London: Macmillan, 1928.

---. "The Monetary Doctrines of Messrs. Foster and Catchings." *Quarterly Journal of Economics* 43 (May 1929).

Rodkey, R.G. *The Banking Process.* New York: Macmillan, 1928.

Röpke, W. "Kredit und Konjunktur." *Jahrbücher für Nationalökonomie und Statistik,* 3rd series, 69 (1926).

Rothbard, M.N. *Man, Economy, and State: A Treatise on Economic Principles.* 2nd ed. Auburn, Ala.: Ludwig von Mises Institute, 1993. 2 Vols.

Schlesinger, K. *Theorie der Geld und Kreditwirtschaft*. Munich and Leipzig: Duncker & Humblot, 1914.

Schumpeter, J. "Kapital." *Handwörterbuch der Staatswissenschaften*. 4th ed. (1923).

———. *Theorie der Wirtschaftlichen Entwicklung*. Munich: Duncker & Humblot, 1911; 2nd ed. 1926.

Seltzer, L.H. "The Mobility of Capital," *Quarterly Journal of Economics* 46 (1932).

Senior. N.W. *Biographical Sketches*. London: Longman, Green, 1863.

———. *Industrial Efficiency and Social Economy*. Ed. S.L. Levy. New York: Henry Holt, 1928.

Simons, H.C. "Rule versus Authority in Monetary Policy." *Journal of Political Economy* 44, no. 1 (February 1936).

Smith, Adam. *Wealth of Nations*. Ed. E. Cannan. London: Methuen, 1904.

Snyder, C. "Deposits Activity as a Measure of Business Activity." *Review of Economic Statistics* (1924). Reprinted in *Business Cycles and Business Measurements*. New York: Macmillan, 1927.

———. "The Influence of the Interest Rate on the Business Cycle." *American Economic Review* 15 (December 1925). Reprinted in *Business Cycles and Business Measurements*. New York: Macmillan, 1927.

Spiethoff. A. "Das Verhältnis von Kapital, Geld und Güterwelt." Schmoller's *Jahrbuch* 33 (1909).

———. "Der Kapitalmangel in seinem Verhältnis zur Güterwelt." Schmoller's *Jahrbuch* 33 (1909).

———. "Der Begriff des Kapital und Geldmarktes." Schmoller's *Jahrbuch* 44 (1920).

———. "Die äussere Ordnung des Kapital und Geldmarktes." Schmoller's *Jahrbuch* 33 (1909).

———. "Die Lehre vom Kapital." *Die Entwicklung der Deutschen Volkswirtschaft im 19. Jahrhundert* 1 (1908).

———. "Die Quantitätstheorie, insbesondere in ihrer Verwertbarkeit als Haussetheorie." *Festgaben für A. Wagner zur 70 Wiederkehr seines Geburtstages*. Leipzig: Hinrich, 1905.

———. "Krisen." *Handwörterbuch der Staatswissenschaften.* 4th ed. (1925). Vol. 6.

———. "Vorbemerkungen zu einer Theorie der Überproduktion." *Schmollers Jahrbuch* 26 (1902).

Stewart, D. *The Collected Works of Dugald Stewart.* Ed. Sir William Hamilton. London: Longman, Brown, Green, 1855.

Strigl, R. "Die Produktion unter dem Einfluss einer Kreditexpansion." *Schriften des Vereins für Sozialpolitik* 173, no. 2 (1928).

———. *Kapital und Produktion.* Vienna: Springer, 1934.

Stucken, R. *Theorie der Konjunkturschwankungen.* Jena: Gustav Fisher, 1926.

Taussig, F.W. "Capital, Interest and Diminishing Returns." *Quarterly Journal of Economics* 12 (May 1908).

———. *Principles of Economics,* 3rd ed. New York: Harper & Row, 1915.

———. *The Silver Situation in the United States.* New York: G.P. Putnam, 1893.

Thornton, H. *An Enquiry into the Nature and Effects of the Paper Credit of Great Britain.* London: J. Hatchard, 1802.

———. The debate in the House of Commons on the report of the Bullion Committee on the 7th and 14th May, 1811. London, 1811.

———. *Paper Credit of Great Britain.* 1802.

Timoshenko, V.P. "The Role of Agricultural Fluctuations in the Business Cycle." *Michigan Business Studies* 2, no. 9 (1930).

Tooke, T., and W. Newmarch. *A History of Prices and the State of the Circulation.* 4 vols. London: P.S. King, 1928.

———. *An Inquiry into the Currency Principle.* London: Smith, Elder, 1844.

———. *Considerations on the State of the Currency.* London: John Murray, 1826.

———. *History of Prices, and the State of Circulation, in 1838 and 1839.* London: Longman, Brown, Green, and Longmans, 1840.

———. *Letter to Lord Grenville on the Effects ascribed to the Resumption of Cash Payments.* London: Murray, 1829.

Torrens. R. *Letter to the Rt. Hon. Viscount Melbourne.* London, 1837.

Wagner, A. *Beiträge zur Lehre von den Banken.* Leipzig: Voss, 1857.

Walras, L. *Théorie Mathématique du Billet de Banque* (1879). Reprinted in *Études d'Économie Politique Appliqué.* Lausanne and Paris, 1898.

Watkins, M.W. "Commercial Banking and the Formation of Capital." *Journal of Political Economy,* 27 (1919).

Weber, A. *Depositenbanken und Spekulationsbanken.* Munich: Duncker & Humblot, 1922.

Whale, P.B. "The Working of the Pre-War Gold Standard." *Economica* 4, no. 13 (February 1937).

Whittlesey, C.R. *International Monetary Issues.* New York: McGraw-Hill, 1937.

Wicksell, K. *Geldzins und Güterpreise.* Jena: Gustav Fischer, 1898.

———. *Lectures on Political Economy.* New York: Macmillan, 1935.

———. Review of Gustav Cassel's textbook. Schmollers *Jahrbuch für Volkswirtschaft, Gesetzbebung und Verwaltung* 53 (1928).

———. *Vorlesungen über Nationalökonomie auf Grundlage des Marginalprinzipes.* Jena: Gustav Fischer 1922.

Wieser, F. v. "Der Geldwert und seine geschichtlichen Veränderungen." *Zeitschrift für Volkswirtschaft, Sozialpolitik und Verwaltung* 13 (1904).

———. *Gesammelte Abhandlungen.* Ed. F.A. Hayek. Tübingen: Mohr, 1929.

———. *Social Economics.* Trans. A. Ford Hinrichs. New York: Adelphi, 1927.

Williams, J.H. *The Quarterly Journal of Economics* 45, no. 4 (August 1931).

Wilson, J. *Capital, Currency and Banking.* London: The Economist, 1847; 2nd ed. London: D.M. Aird, 1859.

Working, H. "Bank Deposits as a Forecaster of the General Wholesale Price Level." *The Review of Economic Statistics* (1926).

———. "Prices and the Quantity of the Circulating Medium, 1890–1921." *The Quarterly Journal of Economics* 37 (1923).

Young, A.A. "An Analysis of Bank Statistics for the United States." Reprinted from *The Review of Economic Statistics* (October 1924; January; April 1925; and July 1927). Cambridge, Mass.: Harvard University Press, 1928.

Name Index

Adams, A.B., 146–47, 163, 169, 176n, 187n
  Profits, Progress and Prosperity, 146n26
Aftalion, A.
  Journal d'Economie Politique, 30n28
  Les crises périodiques de surproduction, 29n
Akerman, G.
  Realkapital und Kapitalzins, 229n41, 281
Altschul, E.
  "Konjunkturtheorie und Konjunkturstatistik," 11n
Amonn, Professor, 110
  "An Analysis of Bank Statistics for the United States," (Young), 127n
  An Analysis and History of the Currency Question (Joplin), 208–209nn16–18
Anderson, B.M.
  Value of Money, 216n35
Angell, J.W.
  The Theory of International Prices, 214n30
  Theory of International Prices: History, Criticism and Restatement, 56n51

Ashton, T.S.
  A Centenary History of the Manchester Statistical Society, 278n66
Bagehot, W.
  The Rationale of Central Banking, 406n
Bamberger, L., 179n59
Beckerath, H.v.
  Kapital und Geldmarkt, 123n
Behrens, W.G.
  Das Geldschöpfungsproblem, 61n, 301n82
Benham, F., 335
Bentham, J., 118n134
  Manual of Political Economy, 210–11
Bergmann, E.v.
  Geschichte der nationalökonomischen Krisentheorien, 69n, 279n69
Bickerdike, C.F., 145n24
Bode, K., 500n
Böhm-Bawerk, E.v., xvi, xviii, xix, xx, 66n70, 69, 109n, 156, 180, 214, 245n, 254, 280, 319n, 436–37, 489, 493, 501, 510–11
  Positive Theorie des Kapitalzinses, 254n55

Positive Theory, 171n
Positive Theory of Capital, 437n
Bonnet, V., 279
Bortkiewicz, L.v.
  Die Frage der Reform unserer Währung 6, 61n
Bouniatian, M.
  "Industrielle Schwankungen, Bankkredit und Warenpreise," 83n, 88n94
  Studien zur Theorie und Geschichte der Wirtschaftskrisen, 76n78
Bradford, F.A., 92n
Bresciani-Turroni, C.
  Le Vicende del Marco Tedesco, 280
Budge, S.
  Grundzüge der theoretischen Nationalökonomie, 38n33, 98n106, 102n113
Bullock, Professor, 16n12
Burchardt, F., 53n45, 56n48, 63–67, 66n70, 113n124

Cairnes, J.E.
  Essay on the Australian Gold Discoveries, 204
  Essays in Political Economy, Theoretical and Applied, 204n
  "Essays towards a Solution of the Gold Question," *Essays in Political Economy, Theoretical and Applied*, 204n
Cantillon, Richard
  Essai sur la nature du commerce en général, 197
  Essai sur le Commerce, 202–03
Carell, E.
  Sozialökonomische Theorie und Konjunkturproblem, 13n9, 46n42
Carison, S.
  "On the Notion of Equilibrium in Interest Theory," 491n3
Carver, T.N.
  Quarterly Journal of Economics (1903–04), 30n28
Cassel, G., xvi, xix, 18n13, 48, 70, 71, 110, 279, 285
  Money and Foreign Exchange After 1914, 54n
  On Quantitative Thinking in Economics, 513n
  "System der Theoretischen Nationalökonomie," 110n
  Theory of Social Economy, 27n24, 40n
Catchings, W., 48n, 134–87, 245, 479
  "Better Jobs and More of Them: The Government's Part in Preventing Unemployment," 151n37
  Business without a Buyer, 136n3, 145
  The Dilemma of Thrift, 136n4, 139, 141, 148n, 149n
  Money, 136n1, 138
  Pollak Prize Essays: Criticisms of "Profits," 137n, 146n27, 150n35
  Profits, 136n2, 140–44, 235n47
  Progress and Plenty: A Way out of the Dilemma of Thrift, 148–50
  The Road to Plenty, 147–50
Clark, J.B., 229, 236n48, 489, 506n25
Conolly, F.G., 397–98
  The Improvement of Commercial Relations between Nations: The Problem of Monetary Stabilization, 397–98nn28–29
Courcelle-Seneuil, J.G., 279
Crick, W.F.
  "The Genesis of Bank Deposits," 81n, 86n, 91n
Currie, L.
  The Supply and Control of Money in the United States, 410n37

Davenport, H.J.
  The Economics of Enterprise, 81n
Davidson, David, 60n
Dernburg, B., 87n91, 88
  Schriften des Vereins für Sozialpolitik 175, 89n
Donner, O., 126
  "Untersuchung zur Frage der Marktzusammenhänge," 123n
Dunbar, C.F., 81n

Name Index   549

Ebenstein, A.
   Friedrich Hayek: A Biography, xvii
Edgeworth, F. Y., 284n71
   "Questions connected with Bimetallism," *Papers Relating to Political Economy*, 179n60, 278
   "Thoughts on Monetary Reform," 179n60
Egner, E., 118n134
   Zur Lehre vom Zwangsparen, 113n124
Ellis, H.S.
   "Die Bedeutung der Productionsperiode für die Krisentheorie," 491n3
Eucken, W.
   Schriften des Vereins für Sozialpolitik, 38n34, 59n59

Fanno, M.
   Le Banche e il Mercato Monetario, 114n130, 216n35
Ferrara, F., 81n
Fetter, F.A., 111–12, 123n
Fisher, I., xvi, xix, 54n, 81n, 156n, 198–99, 207, 377n, 477
   Appreciation and Interest, 113n125
   "The Business Cycle Largely a 'Dance of the Dollar'," 128n143
   Making of Index Numbers, 135
   Theory of Interest, 478n
Foster, J.L.
   An Essay on the Principles of Commerical Exchanges, 207n12
Foster, W.T., xvi, xix, 48n, 134–87, 245, 479
   "Better Jobs and More of Them: The Government's Part in Preventing Unemployment," 151n37
   Business without a Buyer, 136n3, 145
   The Dilemma of Thrift, 136n4, 139, 141, 148n, 149
   Money, 136–39
   Pollak Prize Essays: Criticisms of "Profits," 137n, 146n27, 150n35
   Profits, 136n2, 140–44, 235n47

   Progress and Plenty: A Way out of the Dilemma of Thrift, 148–50
   The Road to Plenty, 147–50
Friday, D.
   Profit, Wages and Prices, 216n35
Fullarton, J.
   On the Regulation of Currencies, 292n

Garrison, Roger W.
   Time and Money: The Macroeconomics of Capital Structure, xvi
Giffen, R., 56, 214
Gilbart, J.W., 288
Gilbert, J.C.
   "The Present Position of the Theory of International Trade," 362n
Gregory, T.E., 341n
   The Gold Standard and Its Future, 394n
   "Introduction," *Tooke and Newmarch's History of Prices*, 81n, 207n10, 209n20, 288n
Guyot, Y.
   La Science Économique (Principles of Social Economy), 279n70

Haberler, G., 284n71
   Der Sinn der Indexahlen, 179n63
   "Hahns Volkswirtschaftliche Theorie des Bankkredits," 81n
   Sinn der Indexzahlen, 428
Hahn, A., 76, 81n, 87n91, 479
   Volkswirtschaftlichen Theorie des Bankkredits, 57n55
   "Zur Frage des volswirtschaftlichen Erkenntnisinhaltes der Bankbilanzziffern," 127n
   "Zur Theorie des Geldmarktes," 123n
Halm, G., 114, 123–24
   "Das Zinsproblem am Geld- und Kapitalmarkt," 110n, 113n128, 123n
Hanau, A., 126
   "Untersuchung zur Frage der Marktzusammenhänge," 123n

Hansen, A.H., xvi, 178, 305–10, 315, 317, 319, 321–29
  "Annual Survey of Business Cycle Theory: Investment and Saving in Business Cycle Theory," 305n85
  Business Cycle Theory: Its Development and Present Status, 24n19, 146n26, 178n
  Cycles of Prosperity and Depression, 216n35
Hardy, C.O.
  Risk and Risk Bearing, 31–32nn30-32
Harrod, R.F., xxi, 379–80, 395
  International Economics, 379–80nn16–18
  The International Gold Problem, 379n
Harvey, Ernest, 366n
Hastings, A.B.
  Costs and Profits, 135
Hawtrey, R.G., xvi, 81n, 202n, 409, 479
  Currency and Credit, 352n
  Monetary Reconstruction, 97n, 102n114, 419n
  "The Monetary Theory of the Trade Cycle and its Statistical Test," 74n
  "Money and Index Numbers," 200n, 202n, 284n71
  Trade and Credit, 90n96
Hayek, F.A.
  biographical information, xi–xiv
  "Capital and Industrial Fluctuations," 193n, 245n, 265n, 269n
  Choice in Currency: A Discussion with Friedrich von Hayek, xxiv
  Choice in Currency: A Way to Stop Inflation, xxiii
  The Constitution of Liberty, xi
  "Credit and the Trade Cycle," 77n
  "Das intertemporale Gleichgewichtssystem der Preise und die Bewegungen des Geldwertes," 4n, 13n10, 63n, 105n, 124n, 164n, 216n35, 220n, 279, 284n72, 287n

  "Das Schicksal der Goldwährung" Der Deutsche Volkswirt, 4n
  Denationalisation of Money—The Argument Refined: An Analysis of the Theory and Practice of Concurrent Currencies, xxiv
  "Der Stand und die nächste Zukunft der Konjunkturforschung," *Festschrift für Arthur Spiethoff*, 193n
  "The Development of the Doctrine of Forced Saving," 211n24
  "Die Währungspolitik der Vereinigten Staaten seit der Überwindung der Krise von 1920," 4n
  Die Währungspolitik der Verinigten Staaten, 96n
  "Einige Bemerkungen über das Verhältnis der Geldtheorie zur Konjunkturtheorie," 3n2
  Full Employment at Any Price, xxiv
  Geldtheorie und Konjuncturtheorie, 3n1, 454n11
  "Gibt es einen Widersinn des Sparens?," 133n
  Hayek on Hayek: An Autobiographical Dialogue, xxiii
  "Kapitalaufzehrung," 4n, 121n, 193n
  "The Maintenance of Capital," 501, 529n
  Monetary Theory and the Trade Cycle, 166n, 193n, 196n, 225n40
  "Money and Capital: A Reply to Mr. Sraffa," 193n
  "A Note on the Development of the Theory of Forced Saving," 118n134, 193n
  "On the Relationship between Investment and Output," 193n, 230n43, 495n15
  "The 'Paradox' of Saving," 4n, 48n, 118n133, 193n, 230n43, 235n47, 284n71, 480n

Name Index

"Preiserwartungen, monetäre Störungen und Fehlinvestitionen," 529n
Prices and Production, 4n, 46n41, 56n48, 65n68, 98n106, 105n, 111n122, 118n134, 121n, 427n, 463n17, 480n
"The Pure Theory of Money: A Rejoinder to Mr. Keynes," 193n
"Reflections on the Pure Theory of Money of Mr. J.M. Keynes," 4n
The Road to Serfdom, xi, xxiii
"Stand und Zukunftsaufgaben der Konjunkturforschung," 322n, 326n93
Studies in Philosophy, Politics and Economics, xxiv
"Über neutrales Geld," 193n
Heinze, G.
   Static or Dynamic Interest Theory, 109n
Helfferich, C., 179n59
Hicks, J.R.
   "A Suggestion for the Simplification of the Theory of Money," 407n36
Hobson, J.A., 133
Holtrop, M.W., 156n
Hoover, Herbert, 150–51
   100 percent plan of banking, 410–13
Huerta de Soto, Jesús
   Money, Bank Credit, and Economic Cycles, xvi
Hume, D., 203–04
   "Of Money," 203n

Jevons, W.S., 203, 489
   Serious Fall in the Value of Gold, 278, 279n67
   Theory of Political Economy, 228–29n41
Jöhr, A., 82n86, 87n91
Joplin, T., 208–09, 213
   An Analysis and History of the Currency Question, 208–09nn16–18

Outlines of a System of Political Economy, 208n16
Joseph, P., 500n
"Bemerkungen zur Kapital und Zinstheorie," 491n3
Juglar, C.
   Des crises commerciales et leur retour périodique, 78n
   Du change et de la liberté d'émission, 78n

Kaldor, N., 133n
Keynes, J.M., xii, xv, xvi–xviii, xxiii, 338
   bank rate theory, 456–68
   credit cycle, 478–85
   effects of savings and investment on circulation, 468–76
   entrepreneur's profits concept, 428–34
   the Gibson Paradox, 476–78
   process of the circulation of money, 440–54
   processes of investment, 434–40
   Essays in Persuasion, 479n
   A Treatise on Money, 39n37, 357n, 425n1, 456n
King, Lord
   Thoughts on the Effects of the Bank Restriction, 207n11
King, W.J., 284n71
Knight, F., xvi, xviii–xix, 236n48, 489–520
   "Capital Time, and the Interest Rate," 490n
   "Capitalist Production, Time and the Rate of Return" *Economic Essays in Honour of Gustav Cassel*, 489n
   "Interest," *Encyclopedia of Social Sciences* 8, 490n
   "Professor Fisher's Interest Theory: A Case in Point," 490n
   "Professor Hayek and the Theory of Investment," 490n
   "The Ricardian Theory of Production and Distribution," 490n
   Risk, Uncertainty and Profit, 216n35

"The Theory of Investment Once More: Mr. Boulding and the Austrians," 490n
Kock, K.
"A Study of Interest Rates," 123n

Lampe, A.
Zur Theorie des Sparprozesses und der Kreditschöpfung, 111n121, 116n
Landauer, C.
Planwirtschaft und Verkehrswirtschaft, 272n
Lauderdale, Lord, 133, 212
Lavington, R.
The English Capital Market, 407n36
Lawrence, J.S.
"Borrowed Reserves and Bank Expansion," 92n
Leaf, W., 81n
Banking, 87n91
Lederer, E.
Grundiss der Sozialökonmik, 68n72
"Konjunktur und Krisen," 27n23
"Zur Morphologie der Krisen," 27n23
Lescure, J., 48, 68
Des Crises générales et périodiques de surproduction, 27n25
"Krisenlehre," 27n25
Leven, M., 284n71
Lexis, W., 284n71
Verhandlungen der deutschen Silberkomission, 179n59
Lowe, A., 13n9, 18n14, 53n45, 63–67, 99, 101
Der Gegenwärtige Stand der Konjunkturforschung, 24n20
Der gegenwärtige Stand der Konjunkturforschung in Deutschland, 76n79
"Der gegenwärtige Stand der Konjunkturtheorie in Deutschland," 10n
"Über den Einfluss monetärer Faktoren auf den Konjunkturzyklus," 12n, 64nn65–66, 99

"Wie ist Konjunkturtheorie überhaupt möglich?," 9n, 46n42, 64n67, 67n
Lucas, R., ix
Lutz, F.
Das Grundproblem der Geldverfassung, 410n38

Machlup, F.
Börsenkredit, Industriekredit und Kapitalbildung, 289n
"Professor Knight and the 'Period of Production'," 490n
Macleod, H.D.
Dictionary of Political Economy, 81n
Theory and Practice of Banking, 56n50
Maier, K.F.
Goldwanderungen, 354n
Marshall, A., xvii, 180, 207, 214, 215n, 284n71
Industry and Trade, 240n50
Money, Credit, and Commerce, 57n52
Official Papers by Alfred Marshall, 56–57n52, 73n, 179n57
Principles of Economics, 255n56
Martin, P.W., 163, 169, 479
The Flaw in the Price System, 141n14
Unemployment and Purchasing Power, 141n14, 163
Marx, K., 279
Mayer, H.
"Producktion," 229n42
Menger, C., 61n, 204n, 302
Collected Works of Carl Menger, 204n
Miksch, L.
Gibt es eine allgemeine Uberproduktion?, 19n
Mill, J.S., 118n134, 210, 236n48
Essays on Some Unsettled Questions of Political Economy, 112n, 213
Principles of Political Economy, 210n23, 213, 299n
Théorie des Débouchés, 19n, 133

Name Index   553

Miller, A.C., 7
Mills, J., 278
Mises, L.v., xii, xvi, xix, xx, 21, 60–63, 61n,
    67–68, 70, 76–77, 81n, 114, 118n134,
    180, 204–05, 216–17, 284n71, 302
  *Geldwertstabilisierung und Konjunk-
    turpolitik*, 57n54, 62n63, 179n62,
    407n35
  *Theorie des Geldes und der Umlaufs-
    mittel*, 57n54, 68n73, 98n106,
    196n, 216n35, 253, 297n
  The Theory of Money, 196n
  "Verhandlungen des Vereins für
    Sozialpolitik in Zurich," 65n69
Mitchell, W.C., 48, 68, 145
  *Business Cycles: The Problem and Its
    Setting*, 24n18, 30n28, 225n39
  *Des Crises générales et périodiques de
    surproduction*, 27n25
  "Krisenlehre," 27n25
Morgenstern, O.
  "Qualitative and Quantitative Kon-
    junkturforschung," 41n, 103n116
  *Wirtschaftsprognose: Eine Unter-
    suchung ikrer Voraussetzungen und
    Möglichkeiten*, 15n

Nasse, E., 179n59
Neisser, H., 118n134, 123n
  Der Tauschwert des Geldes, 76n80,
    81n, 87n90, 88n92, 94n102
  "Monetary Expansion and the
    Structure of Production," 520n40
  "Theorie des wirtschaftlichen Gle-
    ichgewichtes," 146n26
Newmarch, W.
  History of Prices, 81n
  *History of Prices, and the State of
    Circulation, in 1838 and 1839*,
    81n, 207n10, 209n20, 288n
Nicholson, J. S., 56, 214
Novogilov, V.V., 145n24, 146, 153n40
Nurkse, R.
  "The Schematic Representation of
    the Structure of Production,"
    491n3

Olmsted, F.L., 145n24, 155n

Paish, F.W., xxii, 335, 355n
  "Banking Policy and the Balance of
    International Payments," 354n
Palmer, J. Horsley, 209–10, 288
  *Report on the Committee of Secrecy on
    the Bank of England*, 210n21
Pennington, J., 81n
Persons, W.M., 150
  "Cyclical Fluctuations of the Ratio
    of Bank Loans to Deposits," 127n
  "A Non-technical Explanation of
    the Index of General Business
    Conditions," 16n
  "Theories of Business Fluctua-
    tions," 24n17
Phillips, C.A., 92n
  Bank Credit, 81n, 82n85, 86n
Pierson, N.G., 284n71
  Collectivist Economic Planning,
    398n30
  Gold Scarcity, 179n58
  "The Problem of Value in a Social-
    ist Community," 398n30
Pigou, A.C., xvi, xviii, 284n71
  Industrial Fluctuations, 11n, 41n,
    103n115, 119n, 179n64, 285n73
  Is Unemployment Inevitable?,
    216n35
Polak, N.J.
  Grundzüge der Finanzierung, 230n44
Price, B.
  *Chapters on Practical Political Econ-
    omy*, 279n68

"Qualitative and Quantitative Konjunk-
    turforschung" (Morgenstern), 41n,
    103n116
Quarterly Journal of Economics, 24n17,
    30n28, 74n, 92n, 118n134, 140n13,
    193n, 211n24, 469n, 489n, 495n14
"Questions connected with Bimet-
    allism," *Papers Relating to Political
    Economy* (Edgeworth), 179n60

Raguet, C.
   A Treatise on Currency and Banking, 278n64
Reed, H.R.
   Federal Reserve Policy 1921-1930, 128n142
Reisch, R., 87n91, 179n58
   "Die 'Deposit'-Legende in der Banktheorie," 81n
   "Die Wirtschaftliche Bedeutung des Kredites im Lichte von Theorie und Praxis," 82n86, 88n93
Ricardo, D., 212, 215n, 375
   Economic Essays, 56n49, 207n13
   High Price of Bullion, 211n25
   "The High Price of Bullion," *Economic Essays*, 56n49
   Letters of David Ricard to Hutches Trower and Others, 375n
   "On Machinery" *Principles*, 278
   Principles, 278
   "Principles of Political Economy and Taxation" *The Works of David Ricardo*, 207n14
Riefler, W.W.
   Money Rates and Markets in the United States, 123n
Robbins, L., xii, xvii, xxii, 335
   Economic Planning and International Order, 345n, 382n, 401n
   The Great Depression, 400n
Robertson, D.H., 283, 284n71, 294, 468, 469, 471–72
   Banking Policy and the Price Level, 60n, 118n134, 216n35, 224
   Industrial Fluctuations, 29n, 30n29
   "The Monetary Doctrines of Messrs. Foster and Catching," 140n13, 146n26, 150n36
   Money, 119n, 179n65, 454n10
Rodkey, R.G.
   The Banking Process, 81n
   "The Role of Agricultural Fluctuations in The Business Cycle" (Timoshenko), 90n97

Röpke, W., 101, 113n124, 118n134
   Kredit und Konjunktur, 21n, 98n105, 101n110–12
Rothbard, Murray
   Man, Economy and State: A Treatise on Economic Principle, xvi

Say, J.B.
   Théorie des Débouchés, 19n, 51, 133
   "The Schematic Representation of the Structure of Production" (Nurkse), 491n3
Schlesinger, K., 87n91
   Theorie der Geld und Kreditwirtschaft, 73n
Schumpeter, J., xvi, 48, 118n134, 123n, 236n48
   "Kapital," 513n
   Theorie der wirtschaftlichen Entwicklung, 27n22, 28n, 87n90, 216n35
Secord, G.H., 335
Seltzer, L.H.
   "The Mobility of Capital," 313n88
Senior, N.W.
   Biographical Sketches, 210n22
   Industrial Efficiency and Social Economy, 210n22
   "Lord King," *Edinburgh Review*, 210n22
Sidgwick, H., 56, 214
Simons, H.C.
   "Rule versus Authority in Monetary Policy," 410n38, 411–12nn39–45
Smith, Adam, 235, 428
   Wealth of Nations, 154n, 235n46
Smith, V.G.
   The Rationale of Central Banking, 406n
Snyder, C.
   "Deposits Activity as a Measure of Business Activity," 127n
   "The Influence of the Interest Rate on the Business Cycle," 126n

Name Index

Souter, R.W., 145n24, 180
Spiethoff, A., xvi, 18n13, 40, 70, 71, 279
  "Das Verhältnis von Kapital, Geld und Güterwelt," 123n
  "Der Begriff des Kapital und Geldmarktes," 123n
  "Der Kapitalmangel in seinem Verhältnis zur Güterwelt," 123n
  "Die äussere Ordnung des Kapital und Geldmarktes," 123n
  "Die Lehre vom Kapital," 281
  "Die Quantitätstheorie, insbesondere in ihrer Verwertbarkeit als Haussetheorie," 53n44
  "Krisen," 38n35, 39n37, 44n
  "Vorbemerkungen zu einer Theorie der Überproduktion," 281
Sraffa, P., xviii
Stewart, D., 212–13
  The Collected Works of Dugald Stewart, 212n26
Strigl, R.
  "Die Produktion unter dem Einfluss einer Kreditexpansion," 98n106, 254n54
  Kapital und Produktion, 254n54
Stuart, G.M. Verrijin, 61n
Stucken, R.
  Theorie der Konjunkturschwankungen, 59–60n61

Taussig, F.W., 240n50, 284n71
  "Capital, Interest and Diminishing Returns," 495n14
  Principles of Economics, 216n35
  The Silver Situation in the United States, 179n61
  Wages and Capital, 437
Thornton, H., 80n, 118n134, 211n24, 214, 215n
  An Enquiry into the Nature and Effects of the Paper Credit of Great Britain, 56n48
  Paper Credit of Great Britain, 205–09

Timoshenko, V.P.
  "The Role of Agricultural Fluctuations in The Business Cycle," 90n97
Tooke, T., 214
  Considerations on the State of the Currency, 209n20
  History of Prices, 81n
  History of Prices, and the State of Circulation, in 1838 and 1839, 81n, 207n10, 209n20, 288n
  An Inquiry into the Currency Principle, 154n, 209n19, 235n46
  Letter to Lord Grenville on the Effects Ascribed to the Resumption of Cash Payments, 81n
Torrens, R., 213
  Letter to the Rt. Hon. Viscount Melbourne, 81n
Tougan-Baranovsky, M.v., 279
Tout, H., 305–10, 315, 317, 319, 321–29
  "Annual Survey of Business Cycle Theory: Investment and Saving in Business Cycle Theory," 305n85
Tugendhat, G., 133n
Turing, A., ix

Veblen, T., 133

Wagner, A.
  Beiträge zur Lehre von den Banken, 214n29
Walras, L., 302
  Etudes d'économie politique appliquée, 118n134, 214n31
  Théorie Mathématique du Billet de Banque, 214n31
Watkins, M.W.
  "Commercial Banking and the Formation of Capital," 216n35
Weber, A., 113–14
  Depositenbanken und Spekulationsbanken, 81n, 114n129
Whale, P.B.
  "The Working of the Pre-War Gold Standard," 354n
Wheatley, John, 375n

Whittlesey, C.R., xxi–xxii
International Monetary Issues, 341n, 414n47
Wicksell, K., xvi, 21, 57–60, 62, 67, 70, 76n81, 114, 118n134, 180, 214–17, 281, 301, 436, 454, 456–58, 468, 479
Geldzins and Güterpreise, 57n53, 57–58nn56–58, 59n60, 78n, 81n, 95n, 113n124, 113n127, 214n32, 216n34, 458
Lectures on Political Economy, 229n41
Vorlesungen, vol. 2, *Geld und Kredit*, 13n10, 113n126
Vorlesungen über Nationalökonomie auf Grundlage des Marginalprinzipes, 56n48, 57n53, 58n58, 458
Wieser, F.
Abhandlungen, 55n
"Der Geldwert und seine geschichtlichen Veränderungen," 55n
"Der Geldwert und seine Veränderungen," 303n
Gesammelte Abhandlungen, 303n
Social Economics, 255n57
Williams, J.H., 469n
Williams, T.H., 278
Wilson, J.
Capital, Currency and Banking, 278n65
Withers, H., 81–82
Working, H.
"Bank Deposits as a Forecaster of the General Wholesale Price Level," 127n
"Prices and the Quantity of the Circulating Medium, 1890–1921," 127n

Young, A.A., 145, 150
"An Analysis of Bank Statistics for the United States," 127n
Young, O.D., 145

Subject Index

acquisitive capital, 38–40
American Economic Review, 96–97n, 126n
American Federal Reserve System. *See* Federal Reserve System
Archiv für Sozialwissenschaften, 81n
Archiv für Sozialwissenschaften und Sozialpolitik, 83n, 110n, 123n
Austrian economics, xv–xvi

Bank Act of 1844, 342, 344, 412
Bank of England, 206
Bank of International Settlements, 414
Bank Restrictions, 205
banks
    central. *See* central banks
    Chicago Plan of Banking Reform, 410–13
    circulation of money and, 443, 449–51, 456–61, 465, 470–76
    commercial and credit creation, 79–89
    credit, 106–07, 127–30, 143, 291–92, 307, 326
    effects of on trade cycles. *See* monetary theories of the trade cycle
    Federal Reserve System and, 16, 17n

national monetary systems. *See* national monetary systems
prices and credit cycle, 253, 268–69, 274–75
barter system
    assumption of in non-monetary theory, 42–45
    compared to money economy, 21, 53, 55, 59
    savings and, 38
    supply and demand in, 135
Bullion Report, 206–07, 207n15, 213
business forecasts, 14–17, 40–42

The Canadian Journal of Economics and Political Science, 490n
capital
    acquisitive, 38–40
    circulating, 146, 163, 167–72, 277, 459–61
    concepts concerning period of investment, 489–20
    fixed. *See* fixed capital
    fluctuations, 305–29
    formation and consumption, 115–18
    international movements of. *See* international capital movements

investment and the demand for, 423–530
production of and increase in money, 210–20
rates of interest and, 112–13
capital equipment, 30–31, 466
See also fixed capital
capitalist economy, 33, 101, 155
capitalistic methods of production
consequences of, 253, 260, 267, 272, 283–84
credit and, 281
effects of consumption on, 272
extensions of, 162n–63, 170, 177
transitions in, 226–28, 237–52, 436, 481
Carnegie Endowment, 397n
cash reserves, 83–94, 97
catallactic theories, 61n
catallaxy, ix
central banks
credit and, 5, 291–92, 407–09, 417–20
depressions and, xx, 298
elastic currency, 286–88
exchange rates and gold reserves, 413–16
mixed currencies and, 359–60
monetary policy, 298, 459
national reserve systems and, 345–48
role of, 365–66
World Saving Day, 134
Century Magazine, 136n4, 148–50, 151n37
Chamber of Commerce, International, 397n
Chicago School of economics, xviii
circulating capital, 146, 163, 167–72, 277, 459–61
circulation of money
diagram, 441
velocity of. *See* velocity of circulation

coefficient of money transactions, 295–96, 308
consumption, production equation, 138, 142
consumption goods, 135, 137–42, 148–49, 153–69, 173–87
credit
assumption of in non-monetary theory, 42–47
bank, 106–07, 127–30, 143, 291–92, 307, 326
to consumers, 274–75
creation by commercial banks, 79–89
cycles of, 75, 253–81, 478–85
effects of increased demand, 90–96
expansion. *See* credit expansion
forms of, 290
supply of and non-monetary theories of trade cycle, 42–48
system, description of, 291–92
See also interest
credit expansion
causes of cyclical fluctuations and, 79, 89–96, 103
depressions and, 5–7, 274–75
forced savings and, 319
statistical analysis and, 17n
cumulative propogation of effects of demand, 30–31, 35
currencies
elastic, 283–99
independent, 367–83
international. *See* international currencies
international capital movements and, 386–91
mixed, 359–65
national. *See* national currencies
purely metallic, 341–44, 353–59
cyclical fluctuations. *See* monetary theories of the trade cycle

deflation, 5–6, 377–83
depressions
analysis of Keynes money theory and, 480–81, 484–85

Subject Index

central banks and, xx, 298
credit expansion, 6–7, 103, 274–75
currency systems and, 337
monetary policies and, 300
non-monetary theories of trade cycle and, 64, 111
savings in barter economy and, 38
scarcity of gold and, 197
shrinkage of production and, 306–09, 323, 327–29
underconsumption theories and, xix
diagrams
changes in stages of production, 228, 233, 239, 244, 246
circulation of money, 441
marginal productivity in stages, 262
disproportionality theories. *See* non-monetary theories of trade cycle
division of firms, 294–95

Econometric, 193n
economic forecasts, 14–17, 40–42
Economic Journal, 179n60, 193n, 285n73, 473n, 475n, 468, 490n
Economic Studies, 491n3
Economica , 81n, 133n, 193n, 283, 354n, 407n36, 455n, 462n, 490n, 529n
Edinburgh Review, 204n, 223
elastic currency, 283–299
elasticity of volume of money
credit money and, 406–07, 410
fluctuations in economy and, 101
rates of interest and, 458
theories of trade cycle and, 45–49, 58, 74
velocity of circulation, 296–97
See also credit
empirical studies and trade cycle theory, 9–17
endogenous theories of trade cycles, defined, 40
entrepreneur's profits concept, 428–34
equation of exchange, 199
equilibrium theory

definition, 19n15
non-monetary theories of trade cycle and, 26, 28, 44, 47
trade cycle theory and, 10–11, 13n9, 18–20, 55
equipment, capital, 30–-31, 466
exogenous theories of trade cycles, 75–77
factors of production
changes in, 152
definition, 226
prices of, 161
transference of, 168
ultimate, 154
Federal Budget Board, 151
Federal Reserve System, 7, 286, 346, 393, 413–17
Federal Unemployment Stabilization Board, 151
fixed capital
compared to circulating, 277–78, 459–61
investments in, 146, 163, 166–71
trade cycle theory, 29, 112, 120, 122
forced savings
capital goods and, 315–22
definition, 118–22, 210
effects on prices, 216–17
effects on production, 306, 309–10
inflation and, 319, 466, 479, 481
forecasts, economic, 14–17, 40–42
Foster and Catchings, underconsumption theory of
background, 134–37
criticism of, 145–47, 151–80
development of consequences, 147–51, 180–87
general principles, 137–45
Frazers Magazine, 204n

Gibson Paradox, 476–78
gold standard
central banks and, xx, xxi, 414
exchange system, 386
internationalism of, 342–44

mixed system, 351
national monetary systems and, 334–35, 337–38
problems of, 403–06
problems of monetary theory and, 299–300
return to, 197
See also international standard

Harvard Barometer, 16n
Harvard Economic Service, 126
Harvard Economic Society, 16n12
homogenous currency
    Chicago Plan of Banking Reform and, 411
    compared to national currencies, 348–50
    definition, 340–43
    international capital movements and, 388–91
    international flows of money and, 351, 353–59
    mixed currencies and, 361
    national reserve systems and, 391–93

independent national currencies, 376–83, 393–96
    National Reserve System and, 391–93
    international currencies
    Chicago Plan of Banking Reform, 411
    gold standard and, 334, 337–38, 393, 405
industrial fluctuations, 305–29
industrial output, causes of variation in, 223–26
inflation, , 381, 382
    central banks and, 79, 365–66
    changes in quantity of money and, 357, 377–83
    credit and, 97, 117–18, 269
    forced savings and, 121, 319, 466, 479, 481
    gold standard and, 404

as means to fight depression, 298, 308
nature of, 339–43
underconsumption theory of Foster and Catchings and, 150
war and post war, 183n, 197
See also international currencies; international standard
inflationism, 178–79
Institute for Business Cycle Research, xii
interest
    function of, 36–40, 514–18
    as regulator for development of goods, 45
    See also credit
interest, rate of
    bank liquidity and, 91–98, 103
    completing investments and, 526–30
    demand for goods and, 257–58, 264–67
    differences between rates, 122–29
    effects in non-monetary theories of trade cycle, 36–40
    effects on production, 57–67, 70
influence on prices, 210–21
international capital movements, 389–90, 395–96, 398–400
International Chamber of Commerce, 397n
international currency movements, 358, 362, 364
interest brake, 47, 96
intermediate products
    definition, 227
    schematic representation, 228, 233, 239, 244, 246
international capital movements, 388
    control of, 396–401
    definition and classification, 385–88
    homogenous international currency and, 388–91
international flows of money, 351–62, 364
    national reserve systems and, 348–50

Subject Index

nature of, 340–43
See also international monetary system
international monetary system
compared to monetary nationalism, 333
international standard
Chicago Plan of Banking Reform, 410–13
credit money and, 406–10
credit policy of central banks, 417–20
exchange rates and gold reserves, 413–17
gold standard, problems of, 403–06
See also gold standard
investment
demand for capital and, 423–530
effects on circulation, 468–76
non-monetary theories of trade cycle and, 29, 38–40
periods of, 489–520
processes of, 434–40
investments and, 164–68, 425, 447–448
natural compared to money, 77–78, 454, 457–59
quantity of money and, 205–10
role in trade cycle theory, 107–22

Journal of American Statistical Association, 128n143, 284n71
Journal of Political Economy, 216n35, 410n38, 490n
Journal of Royal Stastical Society, 200n

Keynes, J.M.
bank rate theory, 456–68
credit cycle, 478–85
effects of savings and investment on circulation, 468–76
entrepreneur's profits concept, 428–34
the Gibson Paradox, 476–78
process of the circulation of money, 440–54
processes of investment, 434–40

Lausanne School of economics, 19n, 302

marginal utility theory, 204–05
means of production
durable, 273
effect of changes on saving, 155–78, 181–87
investment function and, 500
original. *See* original means of production
rates of interest and, 266–67
media of exchange
definition, 286–87
See also money
merging of firms, 294–95
metallic currencies, 341–44, 353–59
See also homogenous currency
Michigan Business Studies, 90n97
mixed currencies
international flows of money and, 359–65
nature of, 342–48
monetary nationalism, xxi
causes of growth, 374–77
central banks, 365–66
compared to international monetary system, 351–59
currencies, 348–50, 367–74
definition, 339–40
mixed or reserve system, 343–48
See also national monetary systems
monetary systems
international standard. *See* international standard
national. *See* national monetary systems
monetary theories of the trade cycle
consequences of adjustments in volume of money, 95–103
credit creation of central banks, 90–94
effects of changes in equilibrium rate, 109–13
effects of changes in volume of money and, 63–71

elasticity of volume of money as characteristic, 74–78
fluctuations in price level and, 53–60
fluctuations in value of money and, 60–63
natural vs. actual rate of interest, 113–22
types of actual rates of interest, 122–30
money
  circulation diagram, 441
  effects of changes in volume, 105–30, 142–43, 308
  elastic currency concept, 283–99
  elasticity of volume. *See* elasticity of volume of money
  influences on prices, 197–221
  international flows of, 351–66
  neutral value of, 220–21, 301–04
  quantity and production of capital, 210–20
  quantity of and effects on production, 241–52
  quantity of and rates of interest, 205–17
  supply of and price disturbances, 265–69
  value of. *See* value of money
  value of compared to volume of, 60–63
  velocity of circulation. *See* velocity of circulation
  volume of. *See* volume of money
  See also currencies
money transactions, coefficient of, 295–96, 308

National Bureau of Economic Research, 156n
NationalØkonomisk Tidsskrift, 529n
national currencies
  as commodities, 341n
  compared to international monetary system, 333
  international capital movements and, 393–96
  rates of exchange, 348–50, 370–74
  See also national monetary systems
national monetary systems
  central bank policy, 365–66
  definition, 339–40
  general observations, 339–43
  independent national currencies, 348–50, 367–83
  international flows of money, 351–67
  interntional capital movements and, 385–401
  See also national currencies
National Reserve System, xxi, 343–48, 391–93
natural economy, 51
non-monetary theories of trade cycle
  credit supply and, 42–48
  production techniques and, 29–38
  psychological theories, 40–42
  savings and investment and, 38–40
  semi-monetary explanantions, 48–49
  types of, 23–29

original means of production
  capitalistic methods of production, 228–29, 231–32, 236–48
  definition, 226–27
  schematic representation, 227, 233, 239, 244, 246
output of consumers goods, schematic representation, 228, 233, 239, 244, 246

Peel's Act of 1844, 410–12
Phillips curve, ix
Political Discourses (Hume), 203
Pollak Foundation for Economic Research, 135, 136nn1–4
price cycles, 64
price mechanism
  non-monetary theories of trade cycle, 32–35
  working of and credit cycle, 253–81

price stabilizers, xix–xx, 4–7
producers' goods
    classes of, 255–56
    definition, 227
production
    definition, 226
    means of. *See* means of production
    schematic representation of changes in structure, 228, 233, 239, 244, 246
    schematic representation of marginal productivity in stages, 262
    stages of, 35–38, 154–60, 171–75, 178, 181–85
    techniques of and non-monetary theories of trade cycle, 29–38
production period, theories based on, 31–32
production-consumption equation, 138, 142
psychological theories of trade cycle, 29, 40–42
public works, 148–51, 300, 307–08
purchasing power
    artificial maintenance of, 484
    commercial, 97n
    compared to value of money, 61
    consumer, 118, 120, 133, 143, 147
    creation by commercial banks, 88
    of money, 428, 450–51, 454
    price level and, 60n
    producers', 182

quantitative vs. qualitative methods of investigation, 198–99

ratio of cash to deposits, 83–94, 97
"realistic" theories of trade cycles, 48
Report of the Proceedings of the Meeting of Economists, 395n
reserve ratio, 83–94, 97
reserves, cash, 83–94, 97
resources in production, 272–75
The Review of Economic Statistics, 17n12, 127n, 523n

Review of Economic Studies, 491n3

savings
    effects of changes in production, 237–41
    effects on circulation, 468–76
    forced. *See* forced savings
    monetary theories of the trade cycle and, 111
    non-monetary theories of trade cycle and, 29, 38–40
    underconsumption theory of Foster and Catchings and. *See* Foster and Catchings, underconsumption theory of
    voluntary, 306
Schriften des Vereins für Sozialpolitik, 3nn2–3, 38n34, 59n59, 77n, 87n91, 89n, 98n106
Social Research, 520n40
socialist economy, compared to capitalist economy, 33
stabilizers, price, xix–xx, 4–7
stages of production, 35–38, 154–60, 171–75, 178, 181–85
state actions, 300
"state" theory, 61n
statistical research and trade cycle theory, 9–17, 125–30
Stockholm Economic Studies, 123n
supply and demand
    in barter economy, 135
    disturbances of, 51
    economic equilibrium and, 46
    effect of credit supply, 47
    prices as equilibrating mechanism, 19, 33–34, 37, 43, 264
    real capital, 217

taxation, 300
techniques of production and non-monetary theories of trade cycle, 28–35
theories
    equilibrium. *See* equilibrium theory
Three Market Barometer, 126
trade cycle. *See* trade cycle theory

underconsumption. *See* underconsumption theories
time, length of and production, 29–31
trade barriers, 6
trade cycle theory
    exogenous compared to endogenous theories, 75–78
    monetary approaches. *See* monetary theories of the trade cycle
    non-monetary approaches. *See* non-monetary theories of trade cycle
    starting points for, 18–21
    statistical research and, 9–17, 125–30

underconsumption theories
    depression and, xix
    savings and, 315
    teachings of Foster and Catchings. *See* Foster and Catchings, underconsumption theory of
    trade cycle theory and, 18, 48

value of money
    influence on prices, 197–99, 202–05, 219–21
    monetary theories of the trade cycle, 52–56, 59–63, 67–70
velocity of circulation
    elasticity of currency and, 296–97
    production process and, 185, 195, 238
    savings and, 169, 174, 458, 470–71
    supply of and money and, 308
volume of money
    as basis for equilibrium theory, 55
    definition, 46n41
    monetary theories of the trade cycle, 54–55, 59–65, 74–75, 78–80, 106–07
    savings and, 142–44, 147–49, 165–66, 177–81, 185–86

Weltwirtschaftliches Archiv, 4n, 9n, 13n9, 46n42, 105n, 121n, 164n, 193n